Handbook of Technological Pedagogical Content Knowledge (TPACK) for Educators

The second edition of the *Handbook of Technological Pedagogical Content Knowledge (TPACK) for Educators* addresses the concept and implementation of technological pedagogical content knowledge—the knowledge and skills that teachers need in order to integrate technology meaningfully into instruction in specific content areas. Driven by the growing influence of TPACK on research and practice in both K–12 and higher education, the second edition updates current thinking about theory, research, and practice.

Offering a series of chapters by scholars in different content areas who apply the technological pedagogical content knowledge framework to their individual content areas, the volume is structured around three themes:

- Current thoughts on TPACK Theory
- Research on Technological Pedagogical Content Knowledge in Specific Subject Areas
- Integrating Technological Pedagogical Content Knowledge into Teacher Education and Professional Development

The *Handbook of Technological Pedagogical Content Knowledge (TPACK) for Educators* is simultaneously a mandate and a manifesto on the engagement of technology in classrooms.

Mary C. Herring is Professor of Instructional Technology at the University of Northern Iowa and former Chair of AACTE's Committee on Innovation and Technology.

Matthew J. Koehler is Professor of Educational Psychology and Educational Technology at Michigan State University.

Punya Mishra is Professor of Educational Technology and Director of the M.A. in Educational Technology program at Michigan State University.

Handbook of Technological Pedagogical Content Knowledge (TPACK) for Educators

Second Edition

Edited by
Mary C. Herring, Matthew J. Koehler,
Punya Mishra

Second edition published 2016
by Routledge
711 Third Avenue, New York, NY 10017

and by Routledge
2 Park Square, Milton Park, Abingdon, Oxon OX14 4RN

Routledge is an imprint of the Taylor & Francis Group, an informa business

© 2016 Taylor & Francis

The right of Mary C. Herring, Matthew J. Koehler, and Punya Mishra to be identified as the authors of the editorial material of this work, and of the authors for their individual chapters, has been asserted by them in accordance with sections 77 and 78 of the Copyright, Designs and Patents Act 1988.

All rights reserved. No part of this book may be reprinted or reproduced or utilised in any form or by any electronic, mechanical, or other means, now known or hereafter invented, including photocopying and recording, or in any information storage or retrieval system, without permission in writing from the publishers.

Trademark notice: Product or corporate names may be trademarks or registered trademarks, and are used only for identification and explanation without intent to infringe.

First edition published 2008 by Routledge

Library of Congress Cataloging-in-Publication Data
Names: Herring, Mary C., editor of compilation. | Mishra, Punya, editor of compilation. | Koehler, Matthew J., editor of compilation.
Title: Handbook of technological pedagogical content knowledge (TPACK) for educators / edited by Mary C. Herring, Punya Mishra, Matthew J. Koehler. Other titles: Handbook of TPACK for educators
Description: Second edition. | New York, NY : Routledge, 2016. | Includes bibliographical references and index.
Identifiers: LCCN 2015031115 | ISBN 9781138779389 (hardback) | ISBN 9781138779396 (pbk.) | ISBN 9781315771328 (ebook)
Subjects: LCSH: Pedagogical content knowledge—Handbooks, manuals, etc. | Educational technology—Study and teaching—United States—Handbooks, manuals, etc. | Teachers—Training of—United States—Handbooks, manuals, etc.
Classification: LCC LB1028.3 .H356 2016 | DDC 371.33071/1—dc23 LC record available at http://lccn.loc.gov/2015031115

ISBN: 978-1-138-77938-9 (hbk)
ISBN: 978-1-138-77939-6 (pbk)
ISBN: 978-1-315-77132-8 (ebk)

Typeset in Minion
by Apex CoVantage, LLC

Printed and bound in the United States of America by
Edwards Brothers Malloy on sustainably sourced paper

*For our children and grandchildren
Shelly, Bob, Ryan, Jordan, Tyler, Madison, and Brody
Isla and Coen
Soham and Shreya
You give us the impetus to continue the work of
improving the world of education.*

*"I think one of the greatest enemies in the use of technology,
however, is the idea that if you use the technology you have
to throw other things out of the window."*

John Eaton

Contents

Acknowledgments   x

1   Introduction to the Second Edition of the TPACK Handbook   1
Mary C. Herring, Matthew J. Koehler, Punya Mishra, Joshua M. Rosenberg, Jolene Teske

SECTION I
Theory   9

2   Theoretical Considerations of Technological Pedagogical Content Knowledge   11
Charoula Angeli, Nicos Valanides, Andri Christodoulou

3   Using Theoretical Perspectives in Developing an Understanding of TPACK   33
Joke Voogt, Petra Fisser, Jo Tondeur, Johan van Braak

4   Developing TPACK: Envisioning Technological Pedagogical Reasoning   53
Vicky Smart, Glenn Finger, Cheryl Sim

SECTION II
Research   63

5   Exploring the Use of Qualitative Methods to Examine TPACK   65
Leanna Archambault

6   A Review of the Quantitative Measures of Technological Pedagogical Content Knowledge (TPACK)   87
Ching Sing Chai, Joyce Hwee Ling Koh, Chin-Chung Tsai

7   Understanding Teachers' TPACK Through Observation   107
Denise A. Schmidt-Crawford, Shu-Ju Diana Tai, Wei Wang, Yi Jin

Contents

8 Support for Technology Integration: Implications From and For the TPACK Framework ... 119
Noortje Janssen, Ard W. Lazonder

9 Transforming Teachers' Knowledge for Teaching With Technologies: An Online Learning Trajectory Instructional Approach ... 131
Margaret L. Niess

10 Universal Design for Learning (UDL) Infused Technological Pedagogical Content Knowledge (TPACK) Model Prepares Efficacious 21st-Century Teachers ... 143
Beatrice Hope Benton-Borghi

SECTION III
Implications for Practice ... **167**

11 Developing and Assessing TPACK Among Pre-Service Teachers: A Synthesis of Research ... 169
Chrystalla Mouza

12 In-Service Teachers' TPACK Development: Trends, Models, and Trajectories ... 191
Judith B. Harris

13 TPACK Development in Higher Education ... 207
Mary C. Herring, Sohyun Meacham, Daniel Mourlam

14 Opportunities and Challenges of TPACK-Based Professional Development on a Global Scale ... 225
Mark Hofer, John K. Lee, David A. Slykhuis, James Ptaszynski

15 Understanding the Role of a School Principal in Setting the Context for Technology Integration: A TPACK Perspective ... 235
Vinesh Chandra

16 Making Meaningful Advances: TPACK for Designers of Learning Tools ... 247
Karin Forssell

17 Designing Professional Development to Support Teachers' TPACK in Elementary School Mathematics ... 259
Drew Polly, Chandra Hawley Orrill

18 TPACK-Based Professional Development Programs in In-Service Science Teacher Education ... 271
Evrim Baran, Sedef Canbazoglu-Bilici, Erdem Uygun

19 Music TPACK in Higher Education: Educating the Educators 285
   Jordan Mroziak, Judith Bowman

20 The Impact of Digital Storytelling on the Development of
   TPACK Among Student Teachers in Taiwan 297
   Amber Yayin Wang

About the Contributors 309
Chapter Acknowledgments 319
Index 321

Acknowledgments

"There is no real ending. It's just the place where you stop the story."
—Frank Herbert

The second edition of *TPACK* would not have been made possible without the help of many individuals and we (Mary, Matt, and Punya) have no doubt that we will miss mentioning and crediting one or more people who contributed to the development of this book. That said, we start at the beginning (and as *The Sound of Music* lyrics go, that's "a very good place to start").

We thank the editors of the first edition of the *TPACK* handbook. Led by Joel Cobert, they are, in alphabetical order: Kim Boyd, Kevin Clark, Sharon Guan, Judi Harris, Mario Kelly, and Ann Thompson. Without the first edition there would be no second!

This second edition would not have been possible without the unstinting help of Alex Masulis and Daniel Schwartz from Taylor & Francis. Alex was the epitome of patience as we academics went our own merry pace. He was gentle in his nudges, never giving up on us and always being an email or phone call away. Daniel provided daily support that was invaluable. Jennifer Bonnar was our patient and helpful project manager.

Special thanks must go to Josh Rosenberg and Jolene Teske for their outstanding support in the creation of this book. Though their names do not appear on the cover, this book would not have been possible without their hard work dealing with people, technology, and the challenges of both. They met all of these challenges with alacrity and good cheer.

Thanks also to all the authors featured in this handbook for sharing their knowledge and scholarship with us. This book is what it is because of their willingness to do the work and to take time to write and revise and revise again, often under tight deadlines.

Finally, thanks to the broader research and scholarly community who took the ideas as first laid out in Mishra & Koehler's 2006 article and probed and prodded, extended and revised, and debated, both in the flesh (in conferences and other meetings) and in words (online and in print). Together, this global community of scholars and researchers has created the energy and willingness to engage with the ideas, along with a commitment to teachers and teacher education, that has both given this book its urgency and a reason for its existence.

Introduction to the Second Edition of the TPACK Handbook

*Mary C. Herring, Matthew J. Koehler, Punya Mishra,
Joshua M. Rosenberg, Jolene Teske*

One of the earliest examples of educational technology appears in the writing of Quintilian (35–100 AD) over 2,000 years ago. Describing a possible innovation in teaching writing, he wrote:

> As soon as the child has begun to know the shapes of the various letters, it will be useful to have them cut out on a board, in as beautiful script as possible, so that the pen may be guided along the grooves. Thus mistakes such as occur with wax tablets will be impossible to make for the pen will be confined between the edges of the letters and will always be prevented from going astray.
>
> (cited in Illich, 1993, p. 9)

Even in this example from over 2,000 years ago, we can still identify themes that resonate in contemporary conceptualizations of educational technology. For instance, Quintilian expresses a theory of learning that focuses on the importance of practice and the role of technology in scaffolding learning. There is also an understanding that different technologies (such as wax tablets) may provide different affordances that make that tool more or less suited to the activity. Finally, there is a deep connection between the content to be taught (e.g., writing or penmanship) and the design of the tool (cut-out letters to guide learners). In some sense, the underlying ideas of TPACK—that technology, pedagogy, and content are intricately linked—have always been an important part of thinking about educational technology. Yet, the interplay between content, pedagogy, and technology has often been an implicit part of educational thinking.

Since the introduction of the TPACK framework (Koehler & Mishra, 2009; Mishra & Koehler, 2006), scholarship that explicitly explores these connections has flowered. Though issues of technology integration in teaching had long been in the forefront of much scholarship, the introduction of the TPACK framework has served to integrate many lines of research, while at the same time focusing research on the interplay of content, pedagogy, and technology. Of course, it can be argued that something like the TPACK framework was in the zeitgeist—as Mishra and Koehler (2006) have noted, there were myriad scholars who had been proposing something similar. So, in some sense, the attention given to the TPACK framework was a product of timing and, perhaps, luck.

Regardless, the impact of the TPACK framework has been considerable. The TPACK community has become a rich, vibrant, and international one, with scholars from around the globe studying theoretical issues and practical applications of the framework (Voogt, Fisser, Pareja Roblin, Tondeur, & van Braak, 2013). At the time of writing of this introduction, the Mishra and Koehler (2006) article introducing the framework has been cited over 3,000 times in scholarly publications (according to Google Scholar). At TPACK.org, there are over 6,000 registered users with shared interests that have compiled a bibliography of TPACK-related literature with over 600 articles (and steadily growing). A quick survey of the topics covered in this bibliography illustrates the breadth and depth of research using and conceptualizing the TPACK framework. That is, research spans multiple content areas including mathematics, science, social studies, music, history, physical education, and more. Also, the TPACK framework engages a broad spectrum of researchers and education professionals who are working to understand its theoretical and practical implications.

Many factors played a role in bringing TPACK into the consciousness of the broader educational technology community. This includes the publication of the first *Handbook of Technological Pedagogical Content Knowledge (TPCK) for Educators* in 2008. Under the aegis of the Innovation and Technology Committee of the American Association of Colleges of Teacher Education, the first handbook provided a space for a more detailed articulation of the TPACK framework itself, as in the two introductory chapters by Koehler and Mishra (2008) and Kelly (2008). Drawing from research from experts across the nascent community advancing TPACK scholarship, the first handbook also grounded TPACK in specific subject areas and in teacher education and professional development settings. Additionally, it focused on defining TPACK and integrating it into teacher education and professional development.

Yet, eight years have passed since the publication of the first edition of the *Handbook*. Driven by the growing influence of TPACK on research and practice in both K–12 and higher education, the time is right for a second edition that updates current thinking about theory, research, and practice. It is therefore fitting that we introduce this volume by first taking a moment to reflect back on the history of the TPACK concept, as well as why it has influenced both research and practice in the field of educational technology and teacher education.

The Challenges of Researching Educational Technology

Much of the educational technology research literature is conceptually fragmented and relies heavily on case studies (Ronau & Rakes, 2012). This is understandable given the rapid pace at which technology evolves, where every new tool provides new opportunities for use within education. It is not surprising that most frameworks that are used usually are appropriated from outside of the education and teacher education literature, such as from psychological or sociological theories of learning. As a result, the literature contains many studies spanning multiple frameworks and methodologies, making it unclear how they fit within each other, and there is significant definitional variation of how constructs and concepts are used and understood with little synthesis across studies and little programmatic research. Writing of this in another context, Potter (2008) describes this as the "honeybee" approach to research, describing it as follows:

> where scholars are busy bees whose attention is attracted by so many interesting topics (flowers in bloom). They flit from one topic to another as they make their way across the field of flowers. The positive aspect of this "honeybee" nature of the research is that many topics get explored. Also, the travels of the bees have an effect of cross-pollinating topics with ideas and methods from other topics. However, there is a limitation to this honeybee approach. While flowers benefit from the cross-pollination and can grow on their own, research topics need scholars to stay in one place and build a system of explanation on each topic to the extent that scholars spend time trying out lots of different topics, the field stays thin—that is, there are few places where scholars conduct programmatic research that builds depth.
>
> (Potter, 2008, p. 13)

Thus, the fragmented nature of the field of educational technology research, its ever expanding literature, and the lack of programmatic work all lead to the need for some approaches and frameworks that are "home-grown" (for want of a better word). Such home-grown constructs would include conceptualizations and demarcations of the domain that are emergent from the demands of the domain itself. It is not surprising that the two frameworks that have had significant impact in the recent past in the domain of teacher education and teacher professional development have been Shulman's construct of Pedagogical Content Knowledge and the TPACK framework (which, essentially, is an extension of Shulman's seminal work). Both frameworks emerge from *within* the discipline of teacher education and are not imported from a different domain such as psychology, sociology, or cognitive science. This is not to say that psychological, sociological, or cognitive principles and ideas do not have a role to play in developing our understanding of teacher knowledge, but rather that they are subsumed or integrated *within* a framework that respects the contours of the domain of practice that constitute teacher education, teacher professional development, and technology integration.

The Value of Frameworks

At some level, any framework provides two key functions (Maxwell, 2012). First, it acts as a *coat closet*—it provides a high-level "big picture" view for making sense of what you see. Particular pieces of data, or specific research studies, which otherwise may seem unconnected or irrelevant to one another can now be related to each other. The ability to find connections between studies is particularly important in the field of educational technology, where new technologies often lead to studies that appear to be new and specific to the affordances of particular tools and technologies. Second, a framework can act as a *spotlight*, illuminating what you see, drawing attention to particular events of phenomena, and shedding light on relationships that may otherwise have gone unnoticed or misunderstood.

In other words, the TPACK framework provides a visual or written product that "explains, either graphically or in narrative form, the main things to be studied—the key factors, concepts, or variables—and the presumed relationships among them" (Miles & Huberman, 1994, p. 18). A framework such as the TPACK framework provides a model or a map of why the world is the way it is (Strauss, 1995). It is a simplification of the world, but a simplification aimed at clarifying and explaining some aspect of how it works. It does so by telling an enlightening story or providing an explanation about some phenomenon, one that gives you new insights and broadens your understanding of that phenomenon.

In a similar vein, Mishra and Koehler (2006) identified and described three key functions that they hoped the TPACK framework would perform—*descriptive, inference* generation, and *application*. In short, theory allows us to *describe* a phenomenon based on theoretical constructs—it lets us see the world through a particular lens. The TPACK framework provides the structure needed to describe technology integration as the interplay between technology, pedagogy, and content. Frameworks also guide *inference* making, based on what we observe or the data we collect. Like a spotlight, the TPACK framework draws attention to particular events of phenomena and sheds light on relationships that leads to inferences. And finally, the TPACK framework can scaffold how findings can be *applied* to other contexts.

It is important to note, however, that all theories and frameworks are abstractions that focus attention on the big picture. Their weakness, however, is that in order to grasp that bigger picture, they often elide details. By being top-down constructs, frameworks can sometimes be mistaken for reality, rather than abstracted representation of reality. Thus, as empirical scholars, we need to understand the dual need—to develop theoretical constructs that allow for us to generalize across cases and yet be deeply grounded in the reality of the world. Elbow (1973, 2006) suggests that one way of keeping ourselves honest, as a discipline, is to play both the "believing game" and the "doubting game." In the case of the former, we accept the theory as it is and seek to apply it across contexts, using it to deepen our understanding of the phenomena under investigation. In the latter, we seek to challenge the theory, looking for its flaws and weaknesses, pushing and probing its hidden fault lines so as to keep it honest, as it were.

The research on TPACK over the past decade has seen both examples of these "games." There are scholars who have played the "doubting game" by questioning the framework and underlying theory about the nature, organization, independence, and interdependence of the underlying constructs and the important role of context. This has clearly led to the flowering of a strong line of theoretical work. Others have gone the other route, playing the "believing game," taking the framework as it stands and trying to apply the framework. This application can be seen both in research, as scholars seek to better measure TPACK and its effectiveness, and in practical application, as practitioners seek to guide the development of TPACK in pre- and in-service teachers.

The rest of the handbook can be seen as an expansion of a broader set of ideas. On one hand we have the theoreticians who are playing the doubting game, which forms some of the first section of this handbook. On the other hand are the researchers and practitioners who accept the framework as is and seek to conduct research or study its impact on practice. Thus, the next two sections of the handbook focus on Research and Practice.

Organization of This Handbook

The handbook is organized into three sections. In the first, theory—how TPACK is conceptualized across the authors' scholarship, as well as the work of others—is explored. Next, in the section on research, the authors describe studies of TPACK, focusing specifically on methodological and analytic approaches. Finally, on application, we investigate the challenges of applying TPACK theory and research to practice.

Section I: Theory

Section I provides an updated understanding of Technological Pedagogical Content Knowledge (TPACK). Authors provide a review of TPACK development as a construct, encourage purposeful advances in the development of teachers, and explore it conceptually through the lens of a 21st-century educator.

Angeli, Valanides, and Christodoulou provide a chronological review of TPACK as a valid construct and framework. While educational researchers have been and are working toward the same goal of integrating technological skills into classrooms, these authors offer that we must, as an international community, narrow the definition and determine one specific framework for future work. Of particular significance, according to the authors, is the issue of whether TPACK can be seen as being transformative or integrative in nature. Voogt, Fisser, Tondeur, and van Braak seek to develop a "theory of practice" to guide the development of teachers' TPACK. Drawing on the philosophy of technology, the theory of situated cognition, and a theory of teaching as design, the authors focus on the active and constructive role of the teacher, arguing for the need for approaches that are intentional and reflective, design-based, and collaborative. Smart, Finger, and Sim reframe Schulman's famed Nancy, the exceptional teacher of the latter 20th century, and introduce Carmelina, the exceptional teacher of the 21st century. By exploring the reasoning of both teachers, they investigate how pedagogical reasoning has changed since Shulman introduced the term. They explore the fit of a new term, "technological pedagogical reasoning," for describing teaching in the 21st century.

Section II: Research

The second section of this handbook focuses on research, providing both reviews of the literature and an array of studies aimed at furthering the understanding of TPACK in practice. Archambault offers a comprehensive review of qualitative measures and approaches that have been developed and used to study the development of TPACK in both pre-service and in-service populations. Chai et al., in contrast, offer a review of studies that employ quantitative measures of TPACK. Both Archambault and Chai and colleagues note that the complex nature of TPACK, the essential subjectivity that lies at the heart of the social sciences, demands the need for more research around content areas, teacher's thinking, and design processes.

The next set of chapters provides a sampling of current research around the TPACK framework. First is a case study by Schmidt-Crawford, Tai, Wang, and Jin, in which they observe exceptional educators and their use of TPACK. The next three articles focus on developing TPACK. Janssen and Lazonder report on a two-part study conducted to determine how teachers develop TPACK through providing specific support for them in the lesson-planning process. Niess describes the results of a study on the design and implementation of a learning trajectory focused on TPACK in an online course. Findings indicate that teachers develop TPACK most effectively when skills are taught and integrated in classes and opportunities for application are provided. Benton-Borghi ends the second section with a study combining TPACK with Universal Design for Learning (UDL). Combining these two approaches develops the teachers' skills in the integration of technology for all students in courses with and without diversity and disability.

Section III: Implications for Practice

The greatest value of the TPACK framework has been in its application to practice both in higher education and K–12 contexts. This is the focus of the third section. The chapters in this section are tightly tied to the context within which learning happens. This can be seen by a focus on a specific period (pre-service or in-service) or specific domains (science, mathematics, language arts, and foreign languages).

The first two chapters provide us with the broad contours of the literature on the development of TPACK among pre-service and in-service teachers. Mouza synthesizes prior research on the ways in which pre-service teachers' TPACK has been measured in the contexts in which they teach and describes the strategies teacher educators and researchers have explored to develop their TPACK. Harris provides an overview of the ways in which in-service teachers' TPACK has developed, specifically focusing on 12 distinct pathways from the literature.

Herring, Meacham, and Mourlam focus on TPACK development among higher education faculty and the importance of leadership structures across universities to support faculty using technology in a comprehensive and learner-centered way. Hofer, Lee, Slykhuis, and Ptaszynski describe their work on a TPACK-based faculty development initiative enacted and implemented through the Microsoft Technology Enriched Instruction Program.

The next two chapters demonstrate extensions of the TPACK framework and the development of TPACK in new domains. Chandra investigates how the school leadership affects the context of technology integration through a year-long case study of a high school principal, while Forssell explores how designers of learning tools and technologies can utilize TPACK in their work.

The last four chapters focus on specific domains for the application and development of TPACK, from music to math, science to language arts. Polly and Orrill focus on designing professional development among elementary school mathematics teachers, while Baran, Canbazoglu-Bilici, and Uygun explore continuous in-service professional development for science teachers. In contrast, Mroziak and Bowman investigate the development of music TPACK in higher education to demonstrate how technology is integrated into musical practice. Wang discusses the creation of digital stories by pre-service teachers as a way to develop the TPACK of teachers who teach English as a foreign language.

Conclusion

The growth and richness of TPACK research over the past decade makes it difficult if not impossible to capture it completely in this handbook. What we have attempted is to combine broader reviews of the literature and field with specific studies and research papers. This way, we believe, we could at least offer a sampling of the work that is currently underway.

The diversity of approaches in this handbook means that different readers may use the handbook in different ways. Those who are new to TPACK may focus on the first section (on theory). Researchers designing studies or looking to compare their work to related scholarship may consult the second section (on research). Finally, those looking to directly apply TPACK to their work as professional development providers, administrators, or teacher educators may find the third section (applications to practice) most helpful. We hope that, as a whole, this handbook provides the reader with a broad overview of TPACK with specific insights into the theory, research, and application of the framework across multiple contexts.

References

Elbow, P. (1973). *Writing without teachers*. New York: Oxford University Press.
Elbow, P. (2006). The believing game and how to make conflicting opinions more fruitful. In C. Weber (Ed.), *Bringing light into the darkness: A guide to teaching peace, empathy, and understanding* (pp. 16–25). Portsmouth, NH: Heinemann.
Illich, I. (1993). *A vineyard of the text: A commentary to Hugh's Didascalicon*. Chicago, IL: University of Chicago Press.
Kelly, M.A. (2008). Bridging digital and cultural divides: TPCK for equity of access to technology. In AACTE Committee on Innovation and Technology (Eds.), *Handbook of technological pedagogical content knowledge (TPCK) for educators* (pp. 30–60). New York: Routledge.
Koehler, M.J., & Mishra, P. (2008). Introducing TPCK. In AACTE Committee on Innovation and Technology (Eds.), *Handbook of technological pedagogical content knowledge (TPCK) for educators* (pp. 3–29). New York: Routledge.
Koehler, M.J., & Mishra, P. (2009). What is technological pedagogical content knowledge? *Contemporary Issues in Technology and Teacher Education (CITE)*, 9(1), 60–70.
Maxwell, J.A. (2012). *Qualitative research design: An interactive approach*. Thousand Oaks, CA: SAGE Publications.
Miles, M.B., & Huberman, A.M. (1994). *Qualitative data analysis*. Thousand Oaks, CA: SAGE Publications.

Mishra, P., & Koehler, M. J. (2006). Technological pedagogical content knowledge: A framework for teacher knowledge. *Teachers College Record, 108*, 1017–1054. doi:10.1111/j.1467-9620.2006.00684.x

Potter, W. J. (2008). *Arguing for a general framework for mass media scholarship.* Thousand Oaks, CA: SAGE Publications.

Ronau, R. N., & Rakes, C. R. (2012). Making the grade: Reporting educational technology and teacher knowledge research. In R. N. Ronau, C. R. Rakes, & M. L. Niess (Eds.), *Educational technology, teacher knowledge, and classroom impact: A research handbook on frameworks and approaches* (pp. 323–332). Hershey, PA: Information Science Reference.

Strauss, A. (1995). *Qualitative analysis for social scientists.* Cambridge, UK: Cambridge University Press.

Voogt, J., Fisser, P., Pareja Roblin, N., Tondeur, J., & van Braak, J. (2013). Technological pedagogical content knowledge–A review of the literature. *Journal of Computer Assisted Learning, 29*, 109–121.

Section I
Theory

2

Theoretical Considerations of Technological Pedagogical Content Knowledge

Charoula Angeli, Nicos Valanides, Andri Christodoulou

Introduction

In 2005, Technological Pedagogical Content Knowledge (TPCK or TPACK) was introduced to the educational research community as a framework for technology integration, as well as a body of knowledge of what teachers need to know to teach with technology (Angeli & Valanides, 2005; Koehler & Mishra, 2005; Niess, 2005). During the last decade, TPCK has received great attention from the research community, and, as a result, a considerable number of relevant articles appeared in the literature (Voogt, Fisser, Pareja Roblin, Tondeur, & van Braak, 2013).

It is imperative to mention that up until 2005, research on teacher technology integration was mainly atheoretical in nature. However, the gradual integration of technology in classroom practices created a need for the development of theoretical models to guide teachers' cognition about technology integration. Researchers argued that in order to promote teaching with technology, teachers needed to develop a specialized body of knowledge for dealing with the complex teaching and learning situations that occur during the integration of technology in their actual teaching practices (Bransford, Goin, Hasselbring, Kinzer, Sherwood, & Williams, 1986).

Accordingly, during the last ten years, TPCK researchers have been engaged in diligent and systematic research studies in order to provide a theory-based perspective on technology-enhanced teaching, moving away from trial-and-error instructional design decisions to more theory-informed decisions about technology integration. At the same time, TPCK research has provided the research community with a common language and a focus for productive discussions and joint knowledge construction regarding technology integration in teaching and learning.

While TPCK research is recognized as a significant contributor to the existing body of the educational literature, it is also regarded as a rather young research field that is still searching for a generally accepted and solid theoretical conceptualization. In accordance with this line of research, the authors herein provide an account about the current state of affairs regarding the theoretical development of TPCK as a construct and a framework. To this end, the authors engaged in a detailed review of the TPCK literature, and after a careful evaluation of the existing body of research, they discuss herein theoretical aspects of TPCK, as these relate to the following themes: (a) TPCK frameworks, (b) the integrative versus the transformative nature of TPCK as a body of knowledge, and (c) domain-general versus domain-specific TPCK. The authors discuss the findings, critique the existing body of research, and conclude with recommendations for a more productive and useful line of TPCK research in the future.

Based on the analysis of 28 articles that dealt explicitly with the theoretical aspects of TPCK, the authors conclude by addressing the following questions: (a) Do we need more TPCK frameworks? (b) Do we need more research validating the components of TPCK frameworks? (c) Is TPCK domain-generic or domain-specific? (d) Is TPCK integrative or transformative?

Method

First, the authors used Google Scholar as their primary search engine for locating primary research articles. The initial search used as its main search criterion the phrase "technological pedagogical content knowledge" as a topic and a title, from 2005 (the year that the term was first introduced) to 2014. The search yielded 1,475 publications. In an effort to report robust research results, the authors also used two other popular data sources for searching, namely, Thomson Reuters (ISI) Web of Knowledge—Social Science Citation Index (SSCI), as well as Scopus. The search key employed for Web of Knowledge was the phrase "technological pedagogical content knowledge" as a topic and a title, yielding 78 and 43 results, respectively. In Scopus, a general search on "technological pedagogical content knowledge" resulted in 182 publications. After eliminating duplicates, as well as papers that were not published in referred journals, 178 journal articles were left for detailed examination. All three authors carefully examined the abstract and the research purpose of each of the 178 articles, and agreed, after discussion, that only 28 of them dealt explicitly with the theoretical aspects of TPCK.

Subsequently, the three authors carefully read all 28 articles. For each article, a one-page summary was prepared and approved by all authors. Then, each of the authors separately conducted a constant comparative analysis between the 28 summaries in order to identify different aspects or themes regarding the theoretical conceptualization of TPCK. The purpose of this analysis was to organize the 28 summaries in different piles/categories. The constant comparative analysis method constitutes the core of qualitative analysis in the grounded theory approach developed by Glaser and Strauss (1967) and Strauss and Corbin (1990). The percentage of agreement in categorizing each summary in the same pile was 93% between the first and second author, 90% between the second and third author, and 89% between the first and third author. All discrepancies were easily resolved after joint discussion, and the outcome of this process was the categorization of the 28 summaries into three mutually exclusive piles/categories, as shown in Appendix A. The authors jointly decided how to label each category, based on the unique theoretical aspect about TPCK that was denoted in the summaries of each category. One category was labeled "TPCK frameworks," another category was labeled "The integrative versus the transformative nature of TPCK as a body of knowledge," and finally the last category was labeled "Domain-general vs. domain-specific TPCK."

Results

TPCK Frameworks

In the early 2000s, the educational community negatively appraised the lack of theory and conceptual frameworks to inform and guide research and teacher preparation in technology integration (Angeli & Valanides, 2005; Angeli, 2005; Koehler & Mishra, 2008; Margerum-Lays & Marx, 2003; Mishra & Koehler, 2006; Niess, 2005; Pierson, 2001). This compelled the enrichment of Pedagogical Content Knowledge (PCK), an existing construct that was first introduced by Shulman (1986), to account for the knowledge that teachers need to develop for successfully teaching with technology and becoming successful facilitators of technology-enhanced student learning. PCK is regarded as a construct that usefully blends the traditionally separated knowledge bases of content and pedagogy (Mishra & Koehler, 2006). Shulman's (1986, 1987) notion of PCK refers to a body of knowledge, which is highly context sensitive, cannot be conceptualized in isolation from teachers' classroom and teaching experiences, and is above and beyond a simple synthesis of knowledge of subject matter and pedagogy (Yeh, Hsu, Wu, Hwang, & Lin, 2014). For Shulman (1986), PCK "embodies the aspects of content most germane to its teachability" (p. 9) and refers to the transformation of content into forms that are pedagogically sound. In essence, the transformation of subject matter for teaching entails a dramatic shift in teachers' understanding "from being able to comprehend subject matter for themselves, to become able to elucidate subject matter in new ways, recognize and partition it, clothe it in activities and emotions, in metaphors and exercises, and in examples and demonstrations, so that it can be grasped by students" (Shulman, 1987, p. 13). Thus, PCK relates to the transformation of several types of knowledge and includes an understanding of what makes the learning of specific concepts easy or difficult (Shulman, 1986).

While Shulman (1986) alluded to media in his PCK framework, he did not explicitly refer to technology and its relationship to content, pedagogy, and learners. Thus, Shulman (1986) did not explain how teachers use technology's potential to transform content and pedagogy for learners. From this perspective, technology knowledge (TK) became another essential category of teachers' knowledge base, and its addition expanded PCK to TPCK, providing a powerful mechanism to study and understand teacher cognition about the educational affordances of technology in teaching and learning (Angeli & Valanides, 2005; Mishra & Koehler, 2006; Angeli & Valanides, 2009). In essence, TPCK researchers worked toward enhancing or extending Shulman's PCK to address the knowledge needed to teach with technology (Angeli & Valanides, 2005, 2009, 2013; Mishra & Koehler, 2006; Schmidt, Baran, Thompson, Mishra, Koehler, & Shin, 2009; Niess, 2005, 2011).

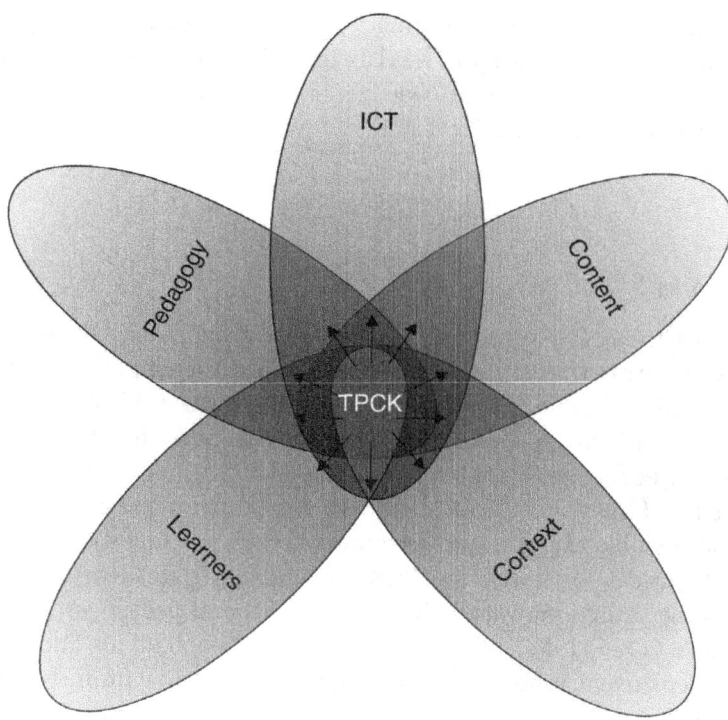

Figure 2.1 ICT-Related PCK (adapted from Angeli & Valanides, 2005)

In 2005, several seminal articles appeared concurrently (e.g., Angeli & Valanides, 2005; Koehler & Mishra, 2005; Niess, 2005) giving new directions toward the development of a unified theoretical and conceptual framework about technology integration. Niess (2005) proposed the term TPCK to refer to technology-enhanced PCK. Based on the work of Shulman (1987), as well as Grossman's (1989, 1990) work on the four central components of PCK, she amended Grossman's (1990) components with technology and provided a framework for describing teachers' TPCK. Around the same time, Angeli and Valanides (2005) used ICT-related PCK (see Figure 2.1), a framework that enhanced Shulman's (1986) and Cochran, DeRuiter, and King's (1993) work on PCK by adding knowledge about ICT (information and communication technologies), and proposed ICT-related PCK as a unique body of knowledge, defined in terms of the interaction of five different knowledge bases, namely, content knowledge, pedagogical knowledge, learner knowledge, ICT knowledge, and knowledge of context. Angeli and Valanides (2005) also proposed that TPCK, as a unique body of knowledge, is better understood in terms of competencies that teachers need to develop in order to be able to teach with ICT adequately. These competencies relate to knowing how to:

1. Identify topics to be taught with ICT in ways that signify the added value of ICT tools, such as topics that students cannot easily comprehend or that teachers face difficulties

teaching, or presenting, effectively in class. These topics may include abstract concepts (i.e., cells, molecules) that need to be visualized, phenomena from the physical and social sciences that need to be animated (i.e., water cycle, the law of supply and demand), complex systems (i.e., ecosystems, organizations) in which certain factors function systemically and need to be simulated or modeled, and topics that require multimodal transformations (i.e., textual, iconic, and auditory), such as phonics and language learning.
2. Identify appropriate representations for transforming the content to be taught into forms that are pedagogically powerful and difficult to support by traditional means. These include interactive representations, dynamic transformation of data, dynamic processing of data, multiple simultaneous representations of data, and multimodal representations of data.
3. Identify teaching tactics that are difficult or impossible to implement by other means, such as the application of ideas in contexts that are not experienced in real life. For example, exploration and discovery in virtual worlds, virtual visits (i.e., virtual museums), testing of hypotheses, simulations, complex decision-making, modeling, long distance communication and collaboration with experts, long distance communication and collaboration with peers, personalized learning, adaptive learning, and context-sensitive feedback.
4. Select tools with appropriate affordances to support 2 and 3 above.
5. Infuse computer activities with appropriate learner-centered strategies in the classroom. This includes any strategy that puts the learner at the center of the learning process to express a point of view, observe, explore, inquire, think, reflect, discover, and problem solve.

In 2006, the term TPCK became widely popular and was adopted, to a good extent by educational researchers, after Mishra and Koehler (2006) introduced their framework, building on Shulman's (1986, 1987) two knowledge bases—content and pedagogy—and adding a third knowledge base into the framework, namely, technology. As shown in Figure 2.2, the TPCK framework is most commonly represented using a Venn diagram with three overlapping circles, each depicting a distinct form of teacher knowledge.

As shown in Figure 2.2, Koehler and Mishra (2008) conceptualized the TPCK framework in terms of seven knowledge domains, namely, (a) content knowledge (CK), which is knowledge about the actual subject matter that is intended to be learned or taught, (b) pedagogical knowledge (PK), which is knowledge about the processes and practices or strategies about teaching and learning, (c) technological knowledge (TK) that constitutes knowledge about operating digital technologies, (d) pedagogical content knowledge (PCK)—the interaction of PK and CK, (e) technological content knowledge (TCK)—the interaction of TK and CK, (f) technological pedagogical knowledge (TPK)—the interaction of TK and PK, and (g) technological pedagogical content knowledge (TPACK)—the interaction of PCK, TCK, and TPK. PCK involves the knowledge of representing content knowledge and adopting pedagogical reasoning to make the specific content more accessible to the learners. TCK refers to the technological representation of content knowledge without any account to teaching (Cox & Graham, 2009). TPK refers to pedagogically sound ways of using technology with no reference toward any specific subject matter. Finally, TPCK is

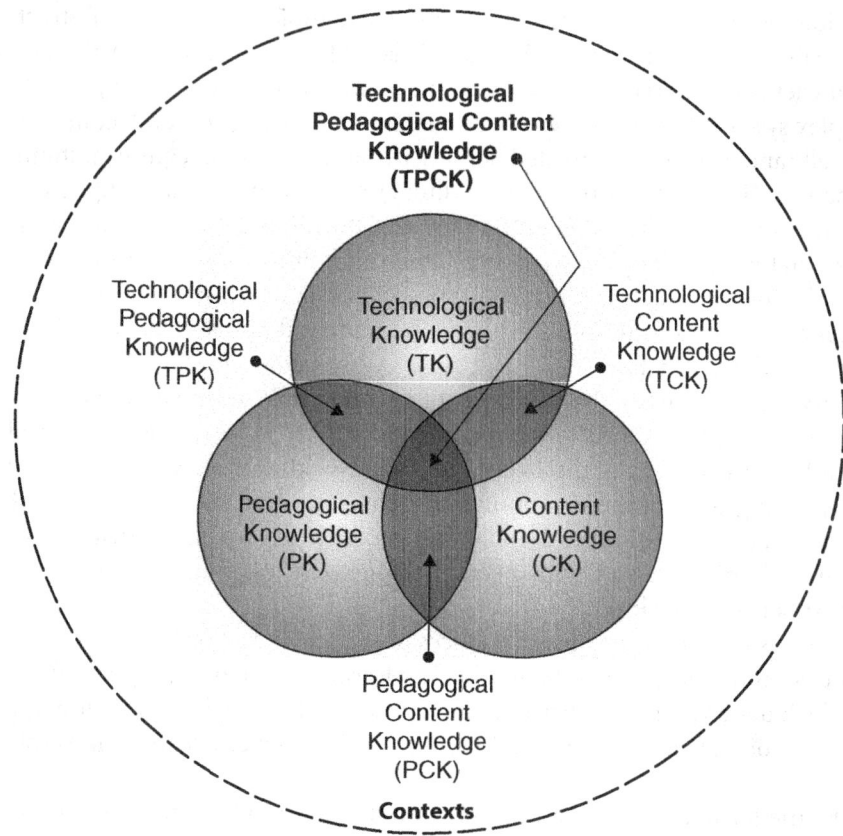

Figure 2.2 Technological Pedagogical Content Knowledge Framework (adapted from Koehler & Mishra, 2008)

regarded as the contextualized and situated synthesis of teacher knowledge about teaching specific content through the use of educational technologies that best embody and support it in ways that optimally engage students of diverse needs and preferences in learning (Chai, Chin, Koh, & Tan, 2013; Harris & Hofer, 2011; Lin, Tsai, Chai, & Lee, 2013; Mishra & Koehler, 2006; Koehler, Mishra, & Yahya, 2007). The TPCK framework posits implicitly that teachers' TPCK can be developed through the integration of PCK, TCK, and TPK.

In 2007, Mishra and Koehler's TPCK changed to TPACK, which was proposed as a term that could be more easily spoken and remembered (Thompson & Mishra, 2007). According to Thompson and Mishra (2007), TPACK captures the fact that these three knowledge domains should not be taken in isolation, but as an integrated whole, a Total PACKage, as it has been referred to in the literature. Even though the acronym TPACK has become ubiquitous and has been used considerably in the technology integration literature, it has not been adopted by everyone (Voogt et al., 2013). It is worth mentioning that while earlier work of Mishra and Koehler (2006) did not explicitly reflect the role of context in teachers' decisions regarding technology integration, their later work expanded the notion of TPCK into a situated form of knowledge, acknowledging that successful technology integration requires teachers' understanding of the complex relationships between content, pedagogy, technology, and knowledge of the surrounding educational context (including knowledge about the students, the school, the school social networks, parental concerns, the available infrastructure, etc.) (Koehler & Mishra, 2008).

After 2008, a number of other TPCK models appeared in the literature. Researchers, in their effort to address the wide range of complexities and intricacies of technology integration in education, invested efforts into devising more complicated TPCK models in order to account for the role of a number of other variables that are intrinsic in a specific educational context. Therefore, current TPCK research about the theoretical conceptualization of TPCK includes efforts that seek to enrich and deepen the initial theoretical models in order to best address the complexity of technology integration (e.g., Benton-Borghi, 2013; Porras-Hernández & Salinas-Amescua, 2013; Yeh et al., 2014; Lee & Tsai, 2010). The authors herein present three of these models, based on their own professional judgment about the merit of the models proposed.

Yeh et al. (2014) suggested TPACK-Practical (see Figure 2.3) in an effort to propose a model that is both knowledge- and experience-based, acknowledging the fact that teachers'

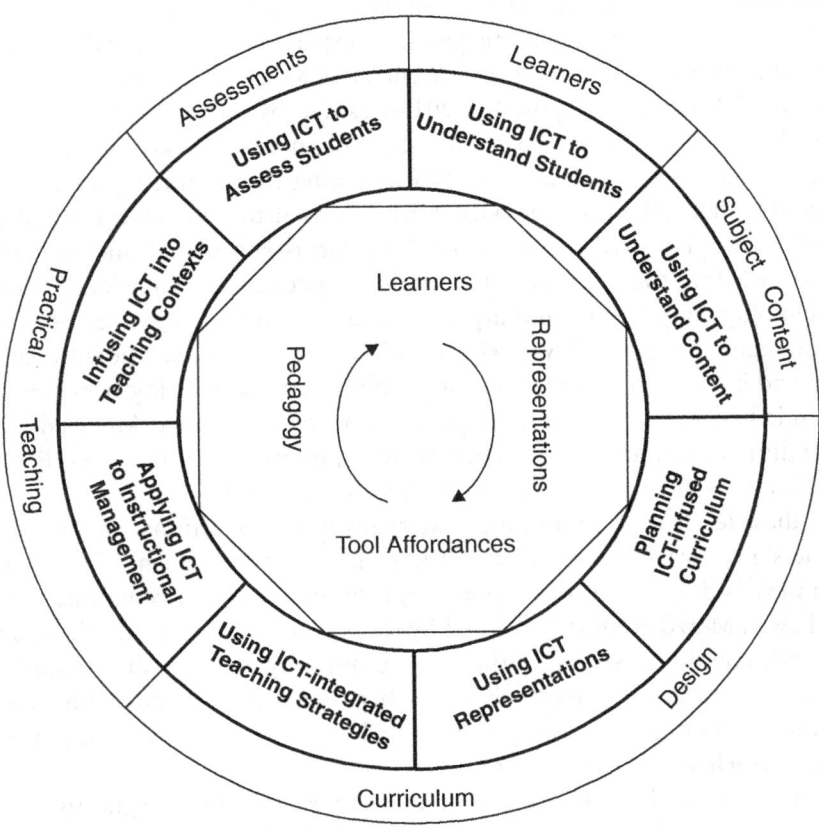

Figure 2.3 TPACK-Practical (adapted from Yeh et al., 2014)

teaching experience can be an indicator of teacher proficiency in TPACK (Jang & Tsai, 2012). Using the Delphi technique, Yeh et al. (2014) transformed and expanded the existing TPACK model by collecting and organizing experts' ideas to determine what kind of knowledge may represent experienced teachers' TPACK-Practical. In TPACK-Practical, TPACK is regarded as not only a coherently woven body of knowledge that teachers possess and apply when dealing with lesson design, but also as something that is more than that incorporating rounds of knowledge transformation. As shown in Figure 2.3, the research panel proposed a framework of TPACK-Practical, with eight knowledge dimensions (i.e., using ICT to understand content, using ICT to understand learners, planning ICT-infused curriculum, using ICT representations, using ICT-integrated teaching strategies, applying ICT to instructional management, infusing ICT into teaching contexts, and using ICT to assess students) in five pedagogical areas (i.e., subject matter, learners, curriculum design, assessments, and practical teaching), which teachers follow during instructional decision planning about the uses of technology in their teaching practices. Yeh et al. (2014) validated their model and, although ICT was found substantially important to teachers' and learners' understanding of content knowledge, the findings revealed that a better development of ICT applications in teaching management would not only enhance teachers' management of student learning progress, but would also contribute to increased use of technology in their teaching. The findings of the study are of course restricted, due to the different disciplinary backgrounds of the research panel, and thus it is highly probable that the participation of experts from different disciplines and different teaching contexts will result in a different TPACK-Practical framework.

Another model that was proposed in 2013 was that by Porras-Hernández and Salinas-Amescua (2013), which sought to strengthen and enrich the existing ICT-related PCK framework (Angeli & Valanides, 2005) by integrating the complexity of context knowledge more systematically in order to establish a consensus and achieve a better comprehension of teacher knowledge (see Figure 2.4). Porras-Hernández and Salinas-Amescua (2013) acknowledged that current TPCK models regard context knowledge as equally pivotal in technology integration, and argued that despite this, context has been referred to in a rather vague and general way with multiple meanings (i.e., student characteristics, classroom and institutional conditions for learning, situated teaching activities, and teachers' epistemic beliefs). Therefore, they proposed to regard context knowledge along two important dimensions, namely (a) scope (macro-, mezzo-, and micro-level context) and (b) actor (students' and teachers' inner and external context).

Each of these levels includes not only externally given conditions that affect and designate teachers' practice, but also objects of knowledge that the teacher learns to construe. Macro context is defined by social, political, technological, and economic conditions at the global level. Mezzo context is defined by the social, cultural, political, organizational, and economic conditions settled in the local community and the educational institution. Finally, micro context is the level where teachers enjoy greater independence and deals with in-class conditions for learning (e.g., available resources, norms and policies, beliefs, expectations, teachers' and students' goals).

In addition, Porras-Hernández and Salinas-Amescua (2013) argue that in order to comprehend how teachers incorporate technologies in their practices, it is important to

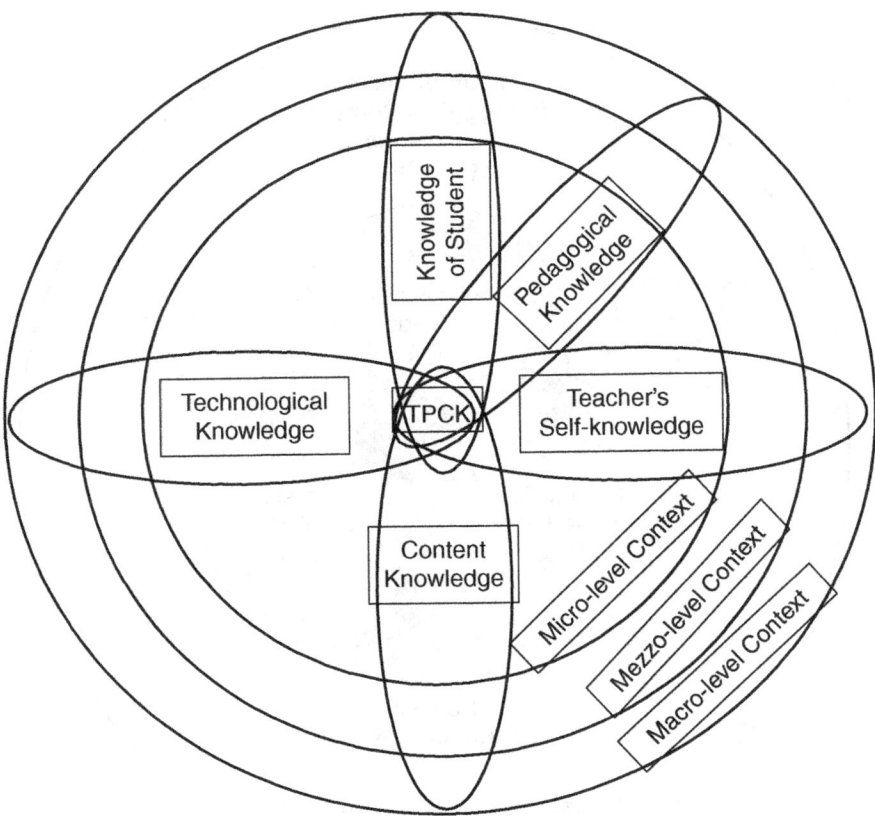

Figure 2.4 Representation of the ICT-PCK Framework Integrating the Complexity of Different Context-Level Variables (adapted from Porras-Hernández & Salinas-Amescua, 2013)

consider teachers' and students' (actors') unique characteristics, as they are brought in the context as separate objects of knowledge with internal (e.g., students' needs, preferences, prior knowledge, teachers' self-efficacy, pedagogical beliefs, subject or school culture) and external contexts (e.g., ethnicity, culture, community, and socioeconomic background).

Last, but not least, Benton-Borghi (2013) worked toward infusing into the existing TPACK framework notions from the Universal Design Learning (UDL) framework in order to satisfy the needs of all learners, including those with special education needs (see Figure 2.5 and also the chapter by Benton-Borghi in this volume). Rose and Meyer (2000, 2002) designated UDL as a set of principles for curriculum development that provides equal opportunities for every individual to learn through the affordances of technology. The increased inclusion of students with disabilities in general education along with the needs that arise in order to satisfy the special needs of these students align well with education's shift toward a digital format, since digital technologies are considered as necessary means for alleviating impediments to learning (Edyburn, 2005; Rose & Meyer, 2002).

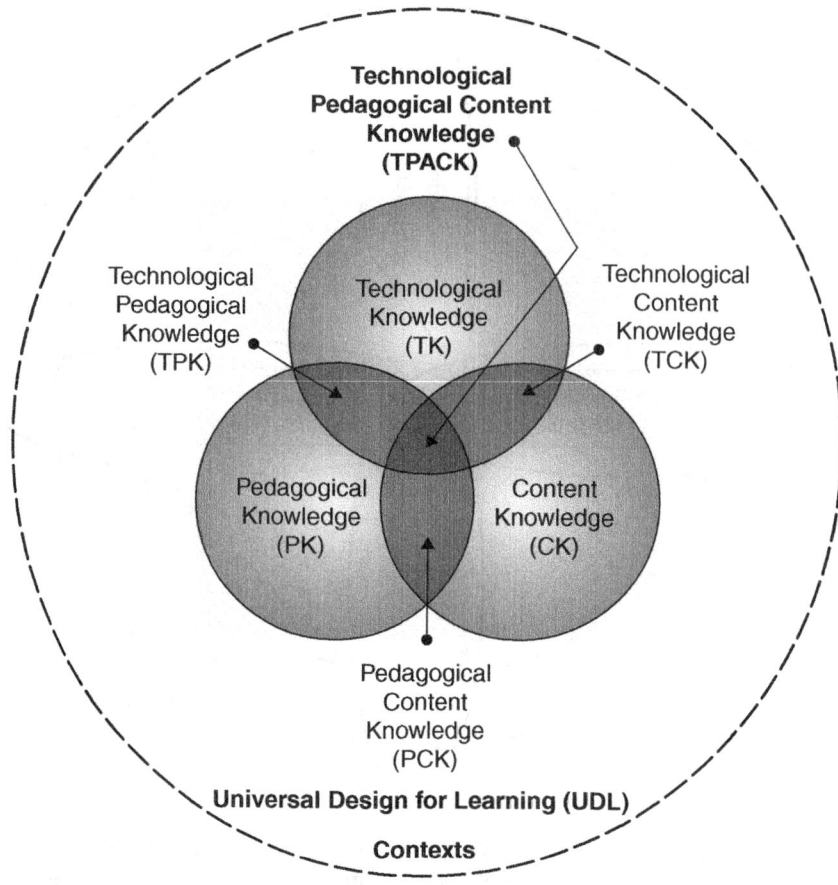

Figure 2.5 Universal Design for All-TPACK Model (adapted from Benton-Borghi, 2013)

The multimodal affordances that technologies provide through access, scaffolding, remediation, acceleration, and differentiation can reinforce equity and inclusivity, considering diversity and exceptionality among students. Hence, for general education teachers to integrate technology to teach the full spectrum of learners, especially learners with disabilities or at-risk learners, there must be a theoretically sound and coherent conceptual framework to aid the development of such teacher knowledge. Therefore, Benton-Borghi (2013) proposed that a blended model of UDL infused TPACK would enhance the collaboration between general and special education and would increase teacher efficacy to teach diverse and exceptional students. The TPACK model infused with UDL principles lies in the intersection of TPK, TCK, and PCK infused with UDL for empowering teachers to design technology-mediated instruction for all students. According to Benton-Borghi (2013), the synthesis of these two frameworks has the potential to assist all teachers to develop a more coherent understanding of the interactions among all of the components of TPACK infused with UDL principles. Anything less than this effort, according to

Benton-Borghi (2013), will continue to perpetuate the separation of general and special education, with general education teachers unable or not eager to take responsibility to teach all students in their classrooms.

The Integrative Versus Transformative Nature of TPCK Knowledge

From 2009 onward, there has been an interesting discussion in the literature about the nature of the TPCK knowledge. In essence, two different epistemological stances about TPCK dominated the discourse, namely, the integrative view and the transformative view. Earlier, Gess-Newsome (2002) had already acknowledged a continuum of positions among the researchers on the nature of PCK, identifying the integrative perspective at the one end of the continuum and the transformative perspective at the other end of the continuum. The same unresolved issue seems to undermine the nature of TPCK. The question of interest here is whether TPCK is a distinct, or unique, body of knowledge developed by the contributions of several other bodies of knowledge (i.e., the transformative view) or whether it is an integration of separate bodies of knowledge and their interplaying connections that take place spontaneously during teaching (i.e., the integrative view). Although both views regard TPCK as an extension of Shulman's (1986, 1987) notion of PCK, they are based on different epistemological stances regarding the nature of TPCK (Angeli & Valanides, 2009, 2013). Obviously, if the epistemological aspect of TPCK remains vague and unsettled, then a high degree of perplexity about the theoretical conceptualization of the construct, and, consequently, its development and assessment, will exist among the TPCK researchers and the educational research community at large. In addition, the usability of the TPCK research and its applicability in teacher development settings, as well as real classrooms, will not be undertaken with high degrees of confidence and real value to the teachers' profession.

Analytically, the integrative view is reflected in the TPACK framework proposed by Koehler and Mishra (2008) (see Figure 2.2), and it conceptualizes TPCK as an integrative body of knowledge, defined by its subcomponents as these are formed in consequence of the intersections between pedagogy and content (PCK), technology and content (TCK), and technology and pedagogy (TPK). According to the integrative view, these subcomponents are integrated "on the spot" during teaching, allowing teachers to make decisions about the educational uses of technology in their respective classrooms.

The transformative view of TPCK is projected in Angeli and Valanides' (2005) ICT-related PCK framework (see Figure 2.1). Here, TPCK is conceptualized as a unique and distinct body of knowledge that goes beyond simple integration, or accumulation, of the constituent knowledge bases, toward transformation of these contributing knowledge bases into something new and unique (Angeli & Valanides, 2009). Substantial empirical evidence, originating from iterative investigations about the educational uses of computer technology, revealed that growth in the related constructs of TPCK without particular instruction, targeting exclusively the development of TPCK, did not automatically result in TPCK growth (Angeli & Valanides, 2005; Angeli, 2005; Valanides & Angeli, 2006, 2008a, 2008b). Interestingly, only when TPCK training was directed explicitly toward the development of a united construct, rather than striving for the development of separate bodies of knowledge, pre-service and in-service teachers were able to demonstrate adequate skills and knowledge for designing technology-enhanced learning activities. Therefore, after a series of empirical investigations, Valanides and Angeli (2006, 2008a, 2008b) arrived clearly at the conclusion that knowledge and growth in each contributing knowledge base alone does not automatically result in TPCK growth.

TPCK as Domain-General or Domain-Specific Knowledge

A challenging theoretical question that deserves more systematic and robust research investigation is whether TPCK constitutes domain-general knowledge or domain-specific knowledge. In more practical terms, does a teacher who teaches language arts need to develop a different TPCK body of knowledge than a teacher who teaches math or science to competently teach with educational technologies? According to Chai et al. (2013), an appropriate level of contextualization is necessary due to the existence of different content domains, tools, and pedagogical strategies. Voogt et al. (2013), in their review of the literature, found that subject-specific TPACK studies are largely restricted to the areas of science (e.g., Jimoyiannis, 2010; Guzey & Roehrig, 2009; Lin et al., 2013), mathematics (e.g., Niess, 2005), and social studies (e.g., Doering & Veletsianos, 2008), whereas in the areas of language arts and humanities they are not that common (e.g., Chai et al., 2013).

Within the context of social studies, Doering and Veletsianos (2008), Doering, Scharber, Miller, and Veletsianos (2009), and Doering, Veletsianos, Scharber, and Miller (2009), after examining student experiences with geospatial technologies in K–12 classrooms, concluded that the integration of geospatial technologies would not be successful unless teachers develop a specialized body of knowledge that they called Geographical Technological Pedagogical Content Knowledge (G-TPCK). Their conclusions have implications for pre-service and in-service teacher education programs, urging teacher educators to consider the development of teachers' TPCK within the specificities of the subject matter of geography.

Regarding the subject matter of mathematics, Niess (2005, 2011) emphasized the development of mathematical TPCK in mathematics teacher preparation programs, acknowledging the impact of technology on the learning of mathematics. Niess (2011) developed the Mathematics Teacher TPACK Development Model, while she also framed the model by proposing TPACK standards and descriptors for mathematics teachers. Additionally, within the field of mathematics, Guerrero (2010) recommended four components of mathematical TPACK, namely, conceptions and use, technology-based mathematics instruction, technology-based classroom management, and depth and breadth of mathematics content. The proposed components were accompanied by examples of particular uses of technology in mathematics education.

In the area of computer science, Ioannou and Angeli (2013) and Angeli (2013) examined whether TPCK as proposed by Angeli and Valanides (2005, 2009) was an adequate framework to guide the professional development of secondary education computer science teachers in learning how to design technology-enhanced activities with various educational technologies. Ioannou and Angeli (2013) found that encouraging computer science teachers to think about technology integration as a transformation process forced them to reflect deeply about their content domain, considering students' intrinsic difficulties in understanding abstract computer science concepts and how the use of technology could alleviate these learning difficulties. Ioannou and Angeli (2013) concluded that the existing TPCK framework (Angeli & Valanides, 2009) was effective in guiding the integration of educational technologies in computer science education, but also inferred that more studies addressing different topics from the secondary education computer science curriculum are needed before any final conclusions can be reached.

Lastly, within the context of science education, Jimoyiannis (2010) proposed the Technological Pedagogical Science Knowledge (TPASK) framework, aiming to help science teachers to design and integrate TPASK-based learning activities in their instruction, in order to amplify students' learning in science. The TPASK framework demonstrates ways to improve science teacher education through appropriate uses of technology. According to Jimoyiannis (2010), "TPASK represents what science teachers need to know about ICT in science education" (p. 1264). He also assumed an integrative model to conceptualizing TPASK through a number of constitutional components, such as pedagogical science knowledge—PSK, technological science knowledge—TSK, and technological pedagogical knowledge—TPK.

Discussion of Results

Undoubtedly, research on TPCK has proliferated during the last decade, and a substantial body of research has become available for consideration and reflection. As Graham (2011) also stated, the TPCK framework has become ubiquitous in the educational research community, with a major group of researchers embracing it with significant initial excitement, as evidenced by the rapid growth of publications in the recent years. While on the theoretical side there are certainly some aspects that remain unresolved, it is with certainty that the authors herein conclude that the TPCK researchers have greatly contributed with their work to the fields of teacher education and educational technology.

Based on the results presented herein, the authors reflect, pose, and provide answers to the following questions, as these naturally emerged from the issues raised and presented in this chapter: (a) Do we need more TPCK frameworks? (b) Do we need more research validating the components of TPCK frameworks? (c) Is TPCK domain-generic or domain-specific? (d) Is TPCK integrative or transformative?

Do We Need More TPCK Frameworks?

It is the authors' informed conclusion that there are already enough TPCK frameworks, or variations of them, in the literature, and that no more research efforts and resources should be invested toward this direction. Of course, one could argue that the multiplicity of contexts, the continual rise of new technologies, and the reality of different content domains, practices, and subject matters fully justify the undertaking of new research efforts devoted toward the development of new TPCK frameworks. However, the same argument can also be used to discourage the research community from further pursuing this line of research; that is to say, if different contents, practices, contexts, and technologies require a new or their own theory, then what will the value be of having multiple theories with little generalizability across the educational terrain? Research toward this direction will only lead to professional isolation and lack of constructive dialogue and collaboration among the educational researchers. It is, therefore, the authors' conviction that TPCK can be represented using a generic conceptual model, but that this model will necessarily act in contextualized ways, due to the different specificities of the underlying situation. Therefore, future research efforts should aim not toward proposing new TPCK models, but toward identifying and defining the boundaries of the generalizability of the one and unified TPCK framework. In proposing one unified generic TPCK framework, the research community can greatly benefit from the organization of an international summit focusing explicitly on clarifying the theoretical conceptualization of TPCK, both as a body of knowledge and a framework. A group of expert TPCK researchers, from different disciplines and contexts across the world, need to come together to devise a definition and a model for TPCK. After a decade of research in the area, the authors herein believe that the community has now reached a level of maturity and readiness for successfully undertaking such an endeavor.

Do We Need More Research Validating the Components of TPCK Frameworks?

What it is already known is that in an effort to amplify the theoretical value of the TPACK framework, for example, a number of studies were conducted to empirically validate the construct validity of its core components and subcomponents (Archambault & Crippen, 2009; Chai, Koh, & Tsai, 2010; Lee & Tsai, 2010; Archambault & Barnett, 2010; Burgoyne, 2010; Schmidt et al., 2009). Most of these studies unveiled several weaknesses of the current state of the TPACK framework, with some researchers questioning its validity (Angeli & Valanides, 2009; Graham, 2011; Archambault & Crippen, 2009; Shinas, Yilmaz-Ozden, Mouza, Karchmer-Klein, & Glutting, 2013). Earlier criticisms were expressed by Angeli and Valanides (2009), stating that "TPCK's degree of precision needs to be put under scrutiny" (p. 157). Later, similar concerns were repeated by Graham (2011) and Yeh et al. (2014), who criticized the current nature of the TPACK framework by arguing that it is deprived of a constant theoretical foundation and stable construct validity. Hence, the major challenge of the model is to precisely establish all TPACK constructs and clarify the boundaries between and amongst them, in order to give credence to it. In conclusion, empirical findings from studies, which endeavored to identify and measure instances of TPACK's subcomponents, have been rather discouraging, because it has been proven extremely difficult to define and distinguish them from related components (e.g., Chai, Koh, Tsai, & Tan, 2011; Harris & Hofer, 2011). In order to show the magnitude of the difficulty in defining precisely the constructs of the TPACK framework, the authors allude to the findings of Cox (2008), who reported a great variance among definitions found in the TPACK research literature for TPACK constructs. Particularly, Cox (2008) identified 13 distinct definitions for TCK, 10 definitions for TPK, and 89 different definitions for the central construct of TPCK. It is emphasized that these discrepancies found among the different definitions, reported in published research studies, are not of minor importance and pose a threat to the overall validity of the TPACK framework and TPCK research in general.

For these reasons, the authors propose that instead of investing so much time and effort toward proving the validity of the structural components of TPCK frameworks—an issue that appears to be indeterminate due to the uncertainty that arises as a result of fragmenting a whole body of knowledge into smaller domains (e.g., TPK, TCK, etc.)—time, money, and effort should be invested toward identifying the contribution of each knowledge domain (i.e., content knowledge, pedagogical knowledge, learner knowledge, context knowledge, and technology knowledge) to the development of TPCK as a whole body of knowledge. This line of research will be of utmost importance not only in terms of moving TPCK research one step forward, but also in terms of designing and organizing teacher education curricula and teacher professional development programs.

Is TPCK Domain-Generic or Domain-Specific?

The authors hypothesize that some aspects of TPCK are domain-generic and others domain-specific. This hypothesis is justified and consolidated by the fact that logically an appropriate level of contextualization is necessary due to the existence of different subject matters, their tools, and specific pedagogies. Therefore, from a methodological point of view, the authors encourage TPCK researchers to engage in rich empirical and qualitative investigations of how TPCK manifests itself in real practice within the context of different content domains, so that the generality and specificity issue of TPCK can be better explored. For example, it would be very informative and valuable to consider the specificity of TPCK within domains, where affect plays an important role in teaching and learning, such as, for example, the fine arts (i.e., music, drama, and dance), an area of research that has not yet been systematically pursued.

Is TPCK Integrative or Transformative?

Systematic research efforts need to be undertaken to clarify whether TPCK as a body of knowledge is integrative or transformative. To the best of our knowledge, we are not familiar with any other empirical studies that were undertaken to examine this issue, other than the ones that were carried out by us (e.g., Valanides & Angeli, 2008a, 2008b). Our research evidence strongly indicates that TPCK is transformative, but of course more research is needed to confirm this finding. We would like though, for the purposes of this chapter, to argue hypothetically here and assume for the sake of the argument that TPCK is integrative. That means that courses in general pedagogy, technological skills, and content would suffice in terms of adequately preparing teachers to teach with technology in their classrooms. Research evidence during the last 20 years, however, has showed exactly the opposite. Succinctly, the research evidence shows that in spite of the numerous efforts researchers and educators have undertaken over the years in preparing teachers to teach with technology, teachers still lack the skills and knowledge needed to enable them to teach adequately with technology (Niess, 2005; Chai et al., 2010). The failure to adequately prepare teachers to teach with technology has been attributed to various factors (NCEE,

2007; Mouza, 2009; Ottenbreit-Leftwich, Glazewski, Newby, & Ertmer, 2010), but one contributing factor the authors would like to mention here is directly related to the way teacher education courses are taught in teacher education departments and/or teacher professional development programs. Specifically, the teaching of methods courses and content courses is usually carried out in complete isolation from the teaching of technology courses, promoting, unfortunately, the development of a body of teacher knowledge that is highly fragmented. As a result, students and teachers fail to develop robust understandings of the interactions among technology, subject matter, and pedagogy. These research findings strengthen the view that TPCK cannot be a body of teacher knowledge that emerges spontaneously on the spot, but a body of knowledge that is unique and needs to be explicitly taught.

Therefore, based on the existing research evidence on technology integration, the authors conclude that TPCK cannot be an integrative body of knowledge, as research evidence points to the contrary. Therefore, the authors continue to support the view that TPCK is a unique body of knowledge that goes beyond mere integration or accumulation of the constituent knowledge bases, toward transformation of these contributing knowledge bases into something new. This means that growth in the individual contributing knowledge bases, without specific instruction targeting exclusively the development of TPCK, will not result in TPCK growth (Angeli & Valanides, 2009).

Concluding Remarks

The purpose of the chapter was to discuss the theoretical conceptualization of TPCK, both as a body of knowledge and a framework. The authors provided a chronological account of the theoretical advancement of TPCK, during the period from 2005 to 2014, and presented theoretical aspects of TPCK related to the following themes: (a) TPCK frameworks, (b) the integrative versus the transformative nature of TPCK as a body of knowledge, and (c) domain-general vs. domain-specific TPCK. After reflecting on and discussing the results, the authors conclude that future work on better understanding the theoretical conceptualization of TPCK, both as a framework and a body of knowledge, can benefit from the following: (a) Future research efforts should strive toward identifying and defining the boundaries of the generalizability of the one and unified TPCK framework, as this will be developed by an international group of TPCK experts. (b) Future research efforts should not invest time and effort toward proving the validity of the structural components of TPCK frameworks, but time, money, and effort should be invested toward identifying the contribution of each component, i.e., content knowledge, pedagogical knowledge, learner knowledge, context knowledge, and technology knowledge, to the development of TPCK as a body of knowledge. (c) Research efforts should be devoted to rich empirical and qualitative investigations of how TPCK manifests itself in real practice within the context of different content domains, so that the generality and specificity issue of TPCK can be better explored. (d) Systematic research efforts should be undertaken to examine the extent to which TPCK, as a body of knowledge, is integrative or transformative.

References

Angeli, C. (2005). Transforming a teacher education method course through technology: Effects on pre-service teachers' technology competency. *Computers & Education, 45*(4), 383–398.

Angeli, C. (2013). Teaching spreadsheets: A TPCK perspective. In D. Kadijevich, C. Angeli, & C. Schulte (Eds.), *Improving computer science education* (pp. 132–145). New York: Routledge.

Angeli, C., & Valanides, N. (2005). Pre-service teachers as ICT designers: An instructional design model based on an expanded view of pedagogical content knowledge. *Journal of Computer-Assisted Learning, 21*(4), 292–302.

Angeli, C., & Valanides, N. (2009). Epistemological and methodological issues for the conceptualization, development, and assessment of ICT-TPCK: Advances in technological pedagogical content knowledge (TPCK). *Computers & Education, 52*(1), 154–168.

Angeli, C., & Valanides, N. (2013). Technology mapping: An approach for developing technological pedagogical content knowledge. *Journal of Educational Computing Research, 48*(2), 199–221.

Archambault, L. M., & Barnett, J. H. (2010). Revisiting technological pedagogical content knowledge: Exploring the TPACK framework. *Computers & Education, 55*(4), 1656–1662.

Archambault, L. M., & Crippen, K. (2009). Examining TPACK among K–12 online distance educators in the United States. *Contemporary Issues in Technology and Teacher Education, 9*(1), 71–88.

Benton-Borghi, B.-H. (2013). A universally designed for learning (UDL) infused technological pedagogical content knowledge (TPACK) practitioners' model essential for teacher preparation in the 21st century. *Journal of Educational Computing Research, 48*(2), 245–265.

Bransford, D. J., Goin, I. L., Hasselbring, S. T., Kinzer, K. C., Sherwood, D. R., & Williams, M. S. (1986). Learning with technology: Theoretical and empirical perspectives. *Peabody Journal of Education, 64*(1), 5–26.

Burgoyne, N. (2010). *Investigating the reliability and construct validity of a measure of preservice teachers' self-efficacy for TPACK*. Unpublished master thesis. Provo, UT: Brigham Young University.

Chai, C. S., Chin, C. K., Koh, J. H. L., & Tan, C. L. (2013). Exploring Singaporean Chinese language teachers' technological pedagogical content knowledge and its relationship to the teachers' pedagogical beliefs. *The Asia-Pacific Education Researcher, 22*(4), 657–666.

Chai, C. S., Koh, J. H. L., & Tsai, C.-C. (2010). A review of technological, pedagogical, and content knowledge. *Education Technology & Society, 13*(4), 63–73.

Chai, C. S., Koh, J. H. L., Tsai, C.-C., & Tan, L. L. W. (2011). Modeling primary school pre-service teachers' technological pedagogical content knowledge (TPACK) for meaningful learning with information and communication technology (ICT). *Computers & Education, 57*(1), 1184–1193.

Cochran K. F., DeRuiter J. A., & King, R. A. (1993). Pedagogical content knowing: An integrative model for teacher preparation. *Journal of Teacher Education, 44*, 263–272.

Cox, S. (2008). *A conceptual analysis of technological pedagogical content knowledge*. Published dissertation. Provo, UT: Brigham Young University.

Cox, S., & Graham, C. R. (2009) Diagramming TPACK in practice: Using an elaborated model of the TPACK framework to analyze and depict teacher knowledge. *TechTrends, 53*(5), 61–69.

Doering, A., Scharber, C., Miller, C., & Veletsianos, G. (2009). Geothentic: Designing and assessing with technological pedagogical content knowledge. In G. L. Bull & L. Bell (Eds.), *Contemporary issues in technology and teacher education*, Vol. 9(3) (pp. 316–336). AACE.

Doering, A., & Veletsianos, G. (2008). An investigation of the use of real-time, authentic geospatial data in the K–12 classroom. *Journal of Geography, 106*(6), 217–225.

Doering, A., Veletsianos, G., Scharber, C., & Miller, C. (2009). Using the technological, pedagogical, and content knowledge framework to design online learning environments and professional development. *Journal of Educational Computing Research, 41*(3), 319–346.

Edyburn, D. L. (2005). Technology-enhanced performance. *Special Education Technology Practice, 7*(2), 16–25.

Gess-Newsome, J. (2002). Pedagogical content knowledge: An introduction and orientation. In J. Gess-Newsome & N. Lederman (Eds.), *PCK and science education* (pp. 3–17). New York: Kluwer Academic Publishers.

Glaser, B. G., & Strauss, A. L. (1967). *The discovery of grounded theory: Strategies for qualitative research.* Chicago: Aldine.

Graham, C. R. (2011). Theoretical considerations for understanding technological pedagogical content knowledge (TPACK). *Computers & Education, 57*(3), 1953–1960.

Grossman, P. L. (1989). A study in contrast: Sources of pedagogical content knowledge for secondary English. *Journal of Teacher Education, 40*(5), 24–31.

Grossman, P. L. (1990). *The making of a teacher: Teacher knowledge and teacher education.* New York: Teachers College Press.

Guerrero, S. (2010). Technological pedagogical content knowledge in the mathematics classroom. *Journal of Digital Learning in Teacher Education, 26*(4), 132–139.

Guzey, S. S., & Roehrig, G. H. (2009). Teaching science with technology: Case studies of science teachers' development of technology, pedagogy, and content knowledge. *Contemporary Issues in Technology and Teacher Education, 9*(1), 25–45.

Harris, J. B., & Hofer, M. J. (2011). Technological pedagogical content knowledge in action: A descriptive study of secondary teachers' curriculum-based, technology-related instructional planning. *Journal of Research on Technology in Education, 43*(3), 211–229.

Ioannou, I., & Angeli, C. (2013). Teaching computer science in secondary education: A Technological Pedagogical Content Knowledge perspective. In *Proceedings of WiPSCE '13, Aarhus, Denmark.* ACM 978-1-4503-2455-7/11/13.

Jang, S.-J., & Tsai, M.-F. (2012). Exploring the TPACK of Taiwanese elementary mathematics and science teachers with respect to use of interactive whiteboards. *Computers & Education, 59*(2), 327–338.

Jimoyiannis, A. (2010). Designing and implementing an integrated technological pedagogical science knowledge framework for science teachers professional development. *Computers & Education, 55*, 1259–1269.

Koehler, M. J., & Mishra, P. (2005). What happens when teachers design educational technology? The development of technological pedagogical content knowledge. *Journal of Educational Computing Research, 32*(2), 131–152.

Koehler, M. J., & Mishra, P. (2008). Introducing TPCK. In AACTE Committee on Innovation and Technology (Eds.), *Handbook of technological pedagogical content knowledge (TPCK) for educators* (pp. 3–29). New York: Routledge.

Koehler, M. J., Mishra, P., & Yahya, K. (2007). Tracing the development of teacher knowledge in a design seminar: Integrating content, pedagogy, and technology. *Computers & Education, 49*(3), 740–762.

Lee, M.-H., & Tsai, C.-C. (2010). Exploring teachers' perceived self-efficacy and technological pedagogical content knowledge with respect to educational use of the World Wide Web. *Instructional Science, 38*(1), 1–21.

Lin, T.C., Tsai, C.-C., Chai, C.S., & Lee, M.H. (2013). Identifying science teachers' perceptions of technological pedagogical content knowledge (TPACK). *Journal of Science Education and Technology, 22,* 325–336.

Margerum-Lays, J., & Marx, R.W. (2003). Teacher knowledge of educational technology: A case study of student/mentor teacher pairs. In Y. Zhao (Ed.), *What should teachers know about technology? Perspectives and practices* (pp. 123–159). Greenwich, CO: Information Age Publishing.

Mishra, P., & Koehler, M.J. (2006). Technological pedagogical content knowledge: A new framework for teacher knowledge. *Teachers College Record, 108*(6), 1017–1054.

Mouza, C. (2009). Does research-based professional development make a difference? A longitudinal investigation of teacher learning in technology integration. *Teachers College Record, 111*(5), 1195–1241.

NCEE (National Center for Educational Evaluation and Regional Assistance). (2007). *Effectiveness of reading and mathematics software programs: Findings from the first student cohort.* Washington, DC: US Department of Education, Institute for Education Sciences.

Niess, M.L. (2005). Preparing teachers to teach science and mathematics with technology: Developing a technology pedagogical content knowledge. *Teaching and Teacher Education, 21,* 509–523.

Niess, M.L. (2011). Investigating TPACK: Knowledge growth in teaching with technology. *Journal of Educational Computing Research, 44*(3), 299–317.

Ottenbreit-Leftwich, A., Glazewski, K., Newby, T., & Ertmer, P. (2010). Teacher value beliefs associated with using technology: Addressing professional and student needs. *Computers & Education, 55,* 1321–1335.

Pierson, M.E. (2001). Technology integration practice as a function of pedagogical expertise. *Journal of Research on Computing in Education, 33*(4), 413–429.

Porras-Hernández, L.H., & Salinas-Amescua, B. (2013). Strengthening TPACK: A broader notion of context and the use of teacher's narratives to reveal knowledge construction. *Journal of Educational Computing Research, 48*(2), 223–244.

Rose, D.H., & Meyer, A. (2000). Universal design for learning. *Journal of Special Education Technology, 15*(1), 67–70.

Rose, D.H., & Meyer, A. (2002). *Teaching every student in the digital age: Universal design for learning.* Alexandria, VA: ASCD.

Schmidt, D.A., Baran, E., Thompson, A.D., Mishra, P., Koehler, M.J., & Shin, T.S. (2009). Technological pedagogical content knowledge (TPACK): The development and validation of an assessment instrument for preservice teachers. *Journal of Research on Technology in Education, 42*(2), 123–149.

Shinas, V.H., Yilmaz-Ozden, S., Mouza, C., Karchmer-Klein, R., & Glutting, J.J. (2013). Examining domains of technological pedagogical content knowledge using factor analysis. *Journal of Research on Technology in Education, 45*(4), 339–360.

Shulman, L.S. (1986). Those who understand: Knowledge growth in teaching. *Educational Researcher, 15*(2), 4–14.

Shulman, L.S. (1987). Knowledge and teaching: Foundations of the new reform. *Harvard Educational Review, 57*(1), 1–22.

Strauss, A.L., & Corbin, J. (1990). *Basics of qualitative research: Grounded theory procedures and techniques.* Newbury Park, CA: SAGE Publications.

Thompson, A., & Mishra, P. (2007). Breaking news: TPCK becomes TPACK! *Journal of Computing in Teacher Education, 24*(2), 38–64.

Valanides, N., & Angeli, C. (2006). Preparing pre-service elementary teachers to teach science through computer models. *Contemporary Issues in Technology and Teacher Education—Science, 6*(1), 87–98.

Valanides, N., & Angeli, C. (2008a). Learning and teaching about scientific models with a computer modeling tool. *Computers in Human Behavior, 24*(2), 220–233.

Valanides, N., & Angeli, C. (2008b). Professional development for computer-enhanced learning: A case study with science teachers. *Research in Science and Technological Education, 26*(1), 3–12.

Voogt J., Fisser, P., Pareja Roblin, N., Tondeur, J., & van Braak, J. (2013). Technological pedagogical content knowledge: A review of the literature. *Journal of Computer Assisted Learning, 29*, 109–121.

Yeh, Y.-F., Hsu, Y.-S., Wu, H.-K., Hwang, F.-K., & Lin, T.-C. (2014). Developing and validating technological pedagogical content knowledge—Practical (TPACK-Practical) through the Delphi survey technique. *British Journal of Educational Technology, 45*(4), 707–722.

Appendix A

Year	Author(s)	TPCK Frameworks	Integrative vs. Transformative Conceptions of TPCK	Domain-General vs. Domain-Specific TPCK
2005	Niess, M. L.	X		
2005	Angeli, C.	X		
2005	Angeli, C., & Valanides, N.	X		
2005	Koehler, M. J., & Mishra, P.	X		
2006	Valanides, N., & Angeli, C.		X	
2006	Mishra, P., & Koehler, M. J.	X		
2007	Thompson, A., & Mishra, P.	X		
2008	Koehler, M. J., & Mishra, P.	X		
2008	Doering, A., & Veletsianos, G.			X
2008a	Valanides, N., & Angeli, C.		X	
2008b	Valanides, N., & Angeli, C.		X	
2009	Angeli, C., & Valanides, N.	X		
2009	Schmidt, D. A., Baran, E., Thompson, A. D., Mishra, P., Koehler, M. J., & Shin, T. S.	X		
2009	Doering, A., Scharber, C., Miller, C., & Veletsianos, G.			X
2009	Doering, A., Veletsianos, G., Scharber, C., & Miller, C.			X
2009	Guzey, S. S., & Roehrig, G. H.			X
2010	Jimoyiannis, A.			X

(Continued)

Year	Author(s)	TPCK Frameworks	Integrative vs. Transformative Conceptions of TPCK	Domain-General vs. Domain-Specific TPCK
2010	Guerrero, S.			X
2010	Lee, M.-H., & Tsai, C.-C.	X		
2010	Chai, C. S., Koh, J. H. L., & Tsai, C. C.			X
2011	Niess, M. L.			X
2013	Angeli, C., & Valanides, N.		X	
2013	Ioannou, I., & Angeli, C.			X
2013	Benton-Borghi, B.-H.	X		
2013	Porras-Hernández, L. H., & Salinas-Amescua, B.	X		
2013	Chai, C. S., Koh, J. H. L., & Tsai, C. C.			X
2013	Lin, T. C., Tsai, C. C., Chai, C. S., & Lee, M. H.			X
2014	Yeh, Y.-F., Hsu, Y.-S., Wu, H.-K., Hwang, F.-K., & Lin, T.-C.	X		

3

Using Theoretical Perspectives in Developing an Understanding of TPACK

Joke Voogt, Petra Fisser, Jo Tondeur, Johan van Braak

Introduction

In 2005, Koehler and Mishra (2005) introduced the term Technological Pedagogical Content Knowledge (TPCK, currently referred to as TPACK) as a conceptual framework to describe the knowledge base for teachers to effectively teach with technology. Since then TPACK has been embraced by many scholars and practitioners. Although TPACK appears to be an intuitive concept that easily resonates with practitioners, many scholars have suggested that it is far more complex. An extensive review of the literature on TPACK (Voogt, Fisser, Pareja Roblin, Tondeur, & van Braak, 2013a) showed that the widespread use of the TPACK framework has led to different interpretations of the framework and questioned some of the underpinnings of TPACK. These differences in interpretations concern (1) the way technology is conceptualized, resulting in different approaches for measuring a teacher's TPACK and (2) how TPACK relates to current understandings of teacher knowledge, in particular questioning how TPACK as a form of teacher knowledge interacts with teacher beliefs. Moreover, though there seems to be agreement that TPACK can best be developed through 'learning by design' (Koehler & Mishra, 2008), we know little about what makes 'learning technology by design' successful in developing TPACK and under which conditions.

The purpose of this chapter is to advance our understanding of TPACK and how TPACK can be developed using three complementary theoretical perspectives. First, to understand technological knowledge we use insights from the philosophy of technology about the relationship between technology, humans and the world (Ihde, 1993; Verbeek, 2005). Second, we use insights from the theory of situated cognition (Greeno et al., 1998) to develop a rich understanding of TPACK as a form of teacher knowledge. Third, we follow Laurillard (2012) by positioning teaching as a design science. In this way, we give room to understanding teachers' learning of TPACK by design. The common denominator of the three theoretical perspectives elaborated upon in this chapter is the active and constructive role of the teacher. The theory of technological mediation argues that teachers and technology coshape educational practice. The theory of situated cognition postulates that teachers actively construct their TPACK through formal knowledge and experiences in practice. By positioning teaching as a design science, we put the teacher in the role of designer of technology-enhanced learning. Based on the considerations this chapter offers, we finish the chapter with suggestions for future research and scholarship.

Mediation of Technology and Technological Knowledge

Technology is based on the Greek word *technè*, which means 'craft' or 'art' and the Greek word *logos*, meaning word or discourse. It refers to *concrete artifacts*, designed and produced by humans and the *use* of these artifacts by humans. In addition, technology also concerns the knowledge necessary to generate new technological solutions and refers to the knowledge about the technology design process and its applications in practice (Berting, 1992). All three meanings of technology are relevant for the role technology may play in education. The first two meanings of technology (technology as concrete artifacts and how we use them) will be addressed in this section, while the latter meaning of technology is relevant when discussing learning technology by design, which will be dealt with later in this chapter when we develop the third perspective, teaching as a design science.

Mediation of Technology

Technology is often seen as an extension of the human body (e.g. the microscope) or the human mind (e.g. the World Wide Web, artificial intelligence). While in such an instrumental perspective technologies are perceived as (neutral) means to an end, recent studies on the relationship between technology and people are based on a post-phenomenological approach and grounded in an understanding that technology and humans constitute each other (Ihde, 1993; Verbeek, 2005, 2011). This theory emerges from the assumption that things matter, emphasizing the material dimensions in the technology–human relationship. The theory of technological mediation assumes an active role of both, technology and people, in shaping their relationship. In this approach humans do not solely define if and how a specific technology is being used, but the technology itself helps to shape action as well. This notion is in line with social agency theory that also postulates that persons form relations with technology (Gell, 1998). It implies that people do not surrender themselves to the technology (Heidegger, 1977, in Kiran & Verbeek, 2010), but take responsibility for the way they are affected by the technology. It is through this active relationship that one can trust oneself to the technology (Kiran & Verbeek, 2010).

From the perspective of the theory of technological mediation, it is not enough to study only the intentions of technology users, but we also need to understand the intentions of technology itself. The term 'affordance', coined by the perceptual psychologist Gibson (1979), is often used in this respect. Affordance refers to what the physical environment in terms of properties offers to the organism (Gibson, 1979, in Goldstein, 1981). These properties are present in the physical environment, whether perceived or not by the organism, and often have to be learned (Goldstein, 1981). In the frame of technology, affordances refer to the properties of the technology and their meaning for its users. And just as we need to understand the properties of the physical environment, we need to understand the properties of technology as well.

Recognizing the relationship between technology and its users helps to understand the affordances of specific technologies. Ihde (1993) distinguishes between different types of relationships between users and technology. The *embodiment* relation is captured in technologies that can be considered an extension of the human body. A microscope is a good example, because it acts as an extension of the eye, helping us see the world at a much more detailed level. The *hermeneutic* relation refers to technologies that offer representations of the world that need interpretation before they are meaningful to us. A world globe or a simulation provides a different representation of the world—which allows us to perceive or understand aspects of a phenomenon that may not be immediately obvious. In the *alterity* relation, technologies relate to people as the 'quasi-other'. Automated learning systems, such as simple drill-and-practice software and digital games, 'communicate' with people and provide feedback on their actions. Finally, technologies can be in the background of people's lives, the *background* relation. We don't notice these technologies, unless they don't work as expected. For instance, in the Western world we cannot think of classrooms without the availability of the blackboard, tables and chairs. Wi-Fi, on the other hand, is not commonplace everywhere.

The mediation of technology affects how the world is present for us and how we experience the world. Technology is therefore never neutral. Through mediation of technology our experience of the world is transformed: Some aspects are revealed while other aspects are concealed (Ihde, 1993). For instance, a microscope reveals the details of the cell, but conceals the organism as a whole. Thus, the design of the technology determines how we experience reality. To understand the world through different representations—a core aspect of teaching and learning—we help students interpreting representations of the world as offered, for instance, by the globe or by simulations. In automated learning systems, the kind of interaction is determined by the design of the system, which does not allow for the spontaneous interaction between teachers and students or students and students available in face-to-face settings. Thus, the ways specific technologies represent reality provide limitations but also offer new possibilities to understand the world that could not be realized otherwise. For instance, a simulation provides us with the possibility to study and understand the effect of climate change on glaciers in a nutshell, while this process takes years in reality.

The relationship between technology and its affordances is not straightforward, because whether and how the affordances of a specific technology are being used depends on the actions of the user (Kiran & Verbeek, 2010; Webb & Cox, 2004). The design of a specific technology may invite users to specific action. Digital storybooks, for instance, invite students to 'read' the story. Drill-and-practice software designed to train simple math skills invite students to practice math. These examples seem to imply that technologies prescribe their use, which seems somewhat contrary to the idea that technology and humans constitute each other. However, many technologies can be used beyond the intentions of the designers. Virtual reality games were never designed as a means to relieve pain, though they are being used as such (Wiederhold & Wiederhold, 2007). On the other hand, the game play in digital games is designed to invite the user to continue playing, but consequently this may unintentionally lead to addiction. Most technologies are not developed for education per se and hence when applied in educational practice will be used beyond the initial intentions of the designers of a specific technology. Koehler and Mishra (2008) refer to this as the need to repurpose technology for educational use. Yet, when a technology stabilizes in its use in a specific context it may direct how people experience and interpret the world (Ihde, 1993). The use of the blackboard, for instance, can be considered stable and largely shapes our understanding of teaching and learning. The resemblance of the interactive whiteboard to the conventional blackboard has led to a fast uptake of this new technology, but also to a use that is often very similar to the use of the blackboard. Because of this, initially the affordances of the interactive whiteboard (Higgins, Beauchamp, & Miller, 2007) remained hidden. Finally, whether and how a technology is being used also depends on whether the technology is easily accessible and available for its users (Borgmann, 2006).

Technological Knowledge

The theory of technological mediation assumes that both teachers and technology take an active role in shaping the learning environment. The affordances of a technology need to be recognized and considered useful by teachers. In addition, teachers may use technology in ways different from its original design, allowing for undesirable, but also for creative, uses of a technology. We argue that teachers need a deep understanding of the affordances of specific technologies (cf. Brown, 2009) to help their students learn a specific topic or skill with the help of technology. We refer to this as Technological Knowledge. From this perspective, Technological Knowledge does not only refer to the instrumental skills needed to operate the technology (e.g. being able to use the technology, sometimes including simple troubleshooting), but also implies knowledge of the affordances of technologies to achieve personal and professional goals (cf. Jamieson-Proctor, Finger, & Albion, 2010). This view implies that there is no use in measuring Technological Knowledge when technology is operationalized as a general concept. What we need are instruments that aim to measure knowledge of the affordances of exemplary technologies relevant for education on the one hand while ignoring the details of all possible available applications for realizing this goal on the other hand (see, for example, Christensen et al., 2015). For instance, we want to determine whether teachers are able to use the affordances of technology for formative feedback with clickers in a whole classroom setting, but we do not necessarily want to know if they are aware of all the possible online applications that can be used in such a situation.

TPACK as a Form of Teacher Knowledge

Knowledge of the affordances of specific technologies (Technological Knowledge) is not enough to teach with technology. Teachers need to use their technological knowledge in concert with content knowledge and pedagogical knowledge. The integration of these three knowledge domains is known as Technological Pedagogical Content Knowledge (TPACK). In this section, we will develop a broad and in-depth understanding of TPACK by discussing TPACK from the perspective of current understandings of teacher knowledge.

When preparing their lessons, teachers decide if and how they make use of specific technologies. They often have several options to choose from. For instance, to help students understand the effect of climate change on glaciers, a teacher can decide to tell students to read a text about glaciers in their textbook, tell students to use a simulation to explore the relationship between the amount of snowfall and the temperature on the behavior of glaciers or present to them a video clip showing the same process and ask questions afterwards. In these three options, the learning goal is mediated by different technologies. When considering these different options, the teacher uses his or her knowledge of the affordances (technological knowledge) of the three technologies (the textbook, the simulation and the video clip). However, the teacher's decision is not only based on technological knowledge, but in relation with his or her knowledge of content and pedagogy (TPACK). In addition, the teacher has an in-depth understanding of the context, such as the kind of students in class, the accessibility of the different technologies, the amount of time available and other curriculum requirements. Besides, the teacher has beliefs about good teaching and the use of technology for teaching and learning. We refer to these considerations as *professional reasoning*, which concerns not only the preparation, but also the enactment of teaching practice (Brown, 2009; Voogt et al., 2013b; Webb & Cox, 2004). Knowledge, beliefs and interpretations of practice are often intertwined in teachers' reasoning and thinking about their professional work (Brown, 2009) as well as affected by experience and feedback (Webb & Cox, 2004). Greeno et al. (1998), when introducing the theory of situated cognition, argued that we can only understand individual teaching behavior in the context of larger social systems, including the environment. Thus, we need to understand how a teacher's professional reasoning is affected by its social dimensions. Explication of the professional reasoning of teachers provides insights into teachers' knowledge and beliefs. We will elaborate on teacher knowledge in the next section.

Teacher Knowledge

Verloop, Van Driel and Meijer (2001) defined teacher knowledge as "the whole of knowledge and insights that underlie teachers' actions in practice" (p. 446). It is a multidimensional concept (e.g. Calderhead, 1996, Verloop et al., 2001) that not only consists of formal theoretical knowledge derived from scientific research as acquired during pre-service education and continuous professional development, but also of the knowledge gained through day-to-day experiences in the field (Calderhead, 1996). This latter type of knowledge is often referred to as a teacher's practical knowledge (Van Driel, Verloop, & De Vos, 1998) or "wisdom of practice" (Shulman, 1986). From the perspective of situated cognition, a teacher's practical knowledge develops through the interactions with social subsystems (students, peer teachers, parents, technology, etc.).

While a teacher's formal knowledge is explicit public knowledge, based on accepted theory from scientific research, the accumulation of experiences from practice is often implicit, or 'tacit' knowledge (Eraut, 1994). We consider TPACK, similar to Pedagogical Content Knowledge (Shulman, 1986, 1987) and in line with the theory of situated cognition, as a form of teacher knowledge. Following Verloop et al. (2001), TPACK then can be defined as 'the whole of knowledge and insights that underlie teachers' actions *with technology* in practice'. Technology, as argued above, is an active agent in shaping educational practice. Therefore, the interaction between teachers and technology matters. Because of the interaction between formal and practical knowledge, teacher knowledge is highly personal (Conelly & Clandinin, 1985) and intertwined with the practicality of teaching (Boschman, McKenney, & Voogt, 2014; Doyle & Ponder, 1978).

TPACK as Personal Knowledge

As elaborated upon in the previous section, a teacher's TPACK is formed by explicit, formal knowledge and practical experiences. Pajares (1992), in his landmark study about teacher beliefs, found that beliefs play a critical role in teachers' actions. TPACK is therefore highly personal and impacted by a teacher's psychological attributes and beliefs.

Several scholars studied the relationship between teachers' use of technology in practice and beliefs about pedagogy and/or technology. Ertmer, Ottenbreit-Leftwich, Sadik, Sendurur, and Sendurur (2012) studied the relationship between beliefs about technology and practices of award-winning teachers, selected for their student-centered practices. They found that the teachers were able to enact practices that were aligned with their beliefs about technology, but they did not make explicit how these findings refer to a teacher's knowledge and insights that underlie teachers' actions *with technology* in practice, or their TPACK. Several studies (e.g. Niederhauser & Stoddart; 2001; Tondeur, Hermans, van Braak, & Valcke, 2008; Voogt, 2010) studied the relation between elementary teachers' use of technology and their pedagogical beliefs. These studies found that teachers who used open-ended software were more likely to have learner-centered pedagogical beliefs, and teachers who used only skill-based software were more likely to hold teacher-directed pedagogical beliefs. However, it should be noted that these studies also reported that the majority of teachers show practices representing a mix of student-centered and teacher-directed beliefs, which indicates a much more subtle relationship between a teacher's practice and their beliefs. While these studies provide insights in the complex relationship between beliefs and practice, they do not reveal how knowledge and insights (TPACK) interfere with practice and beliefs. Further research in understanding the interaction between knowledge, beliefs and practice is warranted to develop a better understanding of TPACK as personal knowledge.

TPACK and the Practicality of Teaching

The theory of situated cognition emphasizes the need to focus on understanding the behavior of social systems in order to understand the behavior of individuals in the system

(Greeno et al., 1998). This has led to an understanding that a teacher's TPACK is always embedded in the (social) context. For this reason, Koehler and Mishra (2008) added context to the conceptualization of TPACK. A teacher's TPACK is therefore situated and to a large extent determined by the practicality of educational practice with the demands, opportunities and constraints of the social system (Janssen, Westbroek, Doyle, & Van Driel, 2013). The practicality of educational practice is determined by its ecology, the environment that fundamentally shapes educational practice (cf. Krug & Arntzen, 2010; Trinidad, Newhouse, & Clarkson, 2004). These ecologies vary. The ecology of a face-to-face learning setting in a classroom with 20–25 children differs from the ecology of an online course where teachers and students have never met in person. Within their ecology, teachers develop an understanding of the probabilities of what might happen in the learning situation they create and develop heuristics for action. Such heuristics help teachers "to achieve the simplification and smoothness necessary to meet the design, interpretation, and performance demands of getting their work done efficiently" (Janssen et al., 2013, p. 9). Studying how different ecologies shape the context (their constraints and opportunities) of teaching with technology is important in understanding how a teacher uses TPACK in practice. Baran, Correia and Thompson (2013) studied how teachers had to change their teaching heuristics when the ecology changed from face-to-face teaching to an online teaching setting. In the transition process, the teachers used their experiences and views on teaching developed in face-to-face settings, in particular their understanding on how students learn. However, they had to make many practical changes when designing and enacting the online course, in particular by providing detailed structure, organizing teacher presence, providing feedback and building student–teacher relationships. While constituting a learning environment with the technology, they had to develop a new professional identity. Koh, Chai and Tay (2014) studied how the ecology of elementary school teachers in Singapore impacted the planning of technology-rich lessons in terms of intrapersonal, interpersonal, cultural/institutional and physical/technical components. They analyzed the discussion in teams of elementary school teachers while planning lessons and found that discussions about practical concerns hampered the teachers to talk about the pedagogical use of technology. Similarly, Boschman, McKenney and Voogt (2014) analyzed design talk during the collaborative design of a technology-enhanced module for early literacy. They found that discussions on practical concerns (e.g. how to organize classroom activities) outweighed deliberations about existing priorities (knowledge, skills, beliefs) and external priorities (requirements set by others). Existing priorities were found to be narrow in scope and important only at the start of the design process. These studies suggest that the practicality of teaching (Doyle & Ponder, 1978) impacts and even dominates how teachers use their TPACK in educational practice.

TPACK and Pre-Service Teachers

Teachers engage in a dynamic process of knowledge construction, which is fueled by the use of formal knowledge and further developed by experiences gained in day-to-day practice (Verloop et al., 2001). Teacher knowledge thus is dynamic and changes over time (Webb &

Cox, 2004). How this process of knowledge construction develops in individual teachers is highly personal, since it is intertwined with teachers' beliefs and affected by the ecologies that shape educational practice.

While formal learning during initial teacher education provides a teacher with a basic understanding of TPACK, TPACK develops at a more in-depth level during teaching in practice. So and Kim (2009) studied the relationship between TPACK and practice in a study with pre-service teachers. They found that with pre-service teachers, a teacher's knowledge and skills (which they referred to as espoused-TPACK) are not necessarily related to using this knowledge and skills in practice (referred to as in-use-TPACK). So and Kim provided two explanations for this finding, suggesting that it was caused by both a mismatch between knowledge, beliefs and practice and pre-service teachers' lack of repertoire for teaching with technology. While we already elaborated upon the first explanation earlier in this chapter (see 'TPACK as Personal Knowledge') we will elaborate on So and Kim's second explanation in this section. Niess (2005) studied how student teachers that followed a technology-enhanced mathematics and science curriculum developed their TPACK. Niess's study confirmed the limited TPACK of beginning teachers and the importance of classroom experience in developing TPACK. Her study showed that student teachers had to expand their understanding of the interactions between their knowledge of technology and their knowledge of subject matter. They had to learn to focus on students' understanding when involved in technology-enhanced learning activity instead of their own teaching. It implied that they had to adapt their view about a science and mathematics curriculum that is infused with technology. Niess showed that this was a highly personal experience for each student teacher in her study. Tondeur, Pareja Roblin, van Braak, Voogt and Prestridge (under review) studied how the use of technology of beginning elementary school teachers is impacted by the way they were prepared for technology use in their teacher education program. This study showed that beginning teachers value the use of technology for teaching and use a wide range of technology applications. However, they mainly use technology to structure their own teaching (teacher-directed), then to facilitate their students' learning (student-centered). The concrete experiences the beginning teachers had gained during student internships were found critical in their use of technology as beginning teachers. In particular, feedback and encouragement from their mentors during their internship practice helped them to gain confidence in teaching with technology and developed their TPACK.

Attention for teaching with technology in pre-service education is important to develop an understanding of TPACK. These studies also underpin the importance of integrating TPACK in subject matter method courses (cf. Hofer & Owings-Swan, 2005; Jimoyiannis, 2010). When subject matter is taken as starting point for designing technology-enhanced teaching and learning, the alignment with pedagogy and technology becomes easier and more appealing to many teachers (e.g. Jimoyiannis, 2010). However, we should also realize that in pre-service teacher education, student teachers develop just a basic understanding of TPACK. A deeper, more profound understanding is only developed through actual experience in educational practice.

The Knowledge Base of Teaching With Technology

We started this chapter by positioning TPACK as a conceptual framework for describing the knowledge base teachers need to teach effectively with technology. We argued that it is important to understand how a teacher's use of technology is not only affected by understanding the affordances of technology (technological knowledge) in concert with knowledge of content and pedagogy, but also by beliefs and by the social and material dimensions of teaching with technology. Our conceptualization of TPACK, as a form of teacher knowledge, provided us with an understanding that TPACK is a highly personal form of dynamic and situated knowledge. In this section, we discuss what this understanding implies for positioning TPACK as a framework for describing the knowledge base of teaching with technology.

To develop insights into an individual teacher's knowledge and beliefs about teaching with technology, we postulated that it is necessary to explicate a teacher's professional reasoning (Webb & Cox, 2004). Several studies attempted to unravel teachers' professional reasoning for using technology while designing and enacting technology in practice. Voogt et al. (2013b) used the concept of professional reasoning in a study aimed at eliciting teachers' use of technology in classroom practice. In total, 157 teachers provided a video clip to demonstrate their use of technology in a specific lesson. The teachers' professional reasoning was elicited by asking them to explain the reasons and nature of using technology for this purpose; their specific choice of pedagogy, technology and content; how this lesson would be different when technology would not have been used; and finally how they determine if lesson objectives are met. Teachers' reflections were analyzed using eight categories of teachers' practical knowledge: the subject/domain, students characteristics (either individual or in general), learning processes and conceptualization, educational goals, the curriculum, instructional techniques, interaction (either student–teacher interaction or student–student interaction) and class management (e.g. time management or dealing with disturbances). The findings of this study revealed three major reasons teachers had for using technology: technology helped them to reach their educational goals, technology facilitated learning processes and technology motivated students to learn. However, the researchers also found that teachers used general language to reason about the use of technology and were not able to explain in detail why they used this specific technology in this specific setting.

Other studies aimed at eliciting individual teachers' TPACK in use by analyzing the design conversations of teachers who collaboratively design technology-enhanced learning environments (Boschman, McKenney, & Voogt, 2014, 2015; Koh et al., 2014; Koehler, Mishra, & Yahya, 2007). Koehler et al. (2007) studied how student teachers and faculty collaboratively designed an online course. They analyzed the design conversations based on the seven knowledge domains that are distinguished in TPACK and found that the design conversations started with discussion about the separate domains (Content Knowledge, Pedagogical Knowledge and Technological Knowledge) but emerged over time in discussions about the overlapping domains (Pedagogical Content Knowledge, Technological Content Knowledge and Technological Pedagogical Knowledge), finalizing in integrating all seven knowledge domains in Technological Pedagogical Content Knowledge. Koh et al. (2014) studied how contextual factors impacted the design of technology-enhanced lessons by analyzing the design conversations of elementary school teachers. They found that practical concerns, and not so much a teacher's TPACK, dominated the discussion. Similar findings were found in the studies of Boschman et al. (2014, 2015). They analyzed design conversations of kindergarten teachers developing technology-enhanced material for early literacy and found that discussions on the practical problems that needed to be solved highly interacted with TPACK. Individual teacher's knowledge and beliefs about teaching with technology is based in the complexities of a teacher's practice. A teacher's professional reasoning about practice helps to reveal the knowledge and beliefs underlying that practice.

To be able to develop a knowledge base of teaching with technology, we need to capture the shared components of an individual teacher's TPACK. Following Verloop et al. (2001) we defined TPACK as 'the whole of knowledge and insights that underlie teachers' actions *with technology* in practice'. In line with this definition, the knowledge base of teaching with technology can be defined as 'all profession-related insights *about teaching with technology* that are potentially relevant to the teacher's activities' (adapted from Verloop et al., 2001, p. 443). While TPACK provides the framework for the knowledge base of teaching with technology, the specific content of the knowledge base depends on whether it is possible to explicate *the shared components* of teachers' formal and practical knowledge. The content of such a knowledge base can only be developed in close collaboration with teachers (cf. Van Driel & Berry, 2012).

Several studies attempted to provide input for such a knowledge base. Harris and Hofer (2009, 2011) developed taxonomies of learning activities (pedagogy) for specific subject matter domains and related those to possible uses of technology to support the instructional planning of teachers. Learning activities can be used as a planning tool for developing and describing plans for technology-enhanced learning. Harris and Hofer (2011) used their approach with practicing teachers. Angeli and Valanides (2009, 2013) started from the perspective of technology and used technology mapping to provide pre-service teachers with a strategy to make use of the affordances of technology within an authentic design task. Technology mapping provides teachers with strategies to align their knowledge about teaching and learning of subject matter in a specific context with the affordances and constraints of digital tools to develop technological solutions for pedagogical problems.

A different approach aimed at capturing the shared understanding of what is worthwhile to teach about technology in teacher education is a study about using technology in fostering early literacy in kindergarten undertaken in the Netherlands (Belo, McKenney, & Voogt, 2013; McKenney & Voogt, under review). In this study, the components of the knowledge base of teaching early literacy with technology in kindergarten is determined though a structured conversation between researchers and practitioners (teachers and teacher educators) in an effort to bring together explicit knowledge from research with experiences from practice. Based on a review of scientific studies on technology use in early literacy, a Delphi study was conducted in which researchers and practitioners discussed the relevance of findings from research for the teacher education curriculum. The study resulted in a description of the knowledge base of teaching with technology in early literacy in kindergarten (McKenney & Voogt, under review), which is now being discussed with teacher education institutions. These three examples use accumulated knowledge about the affordances of technology in relation to pedagogy and content with the aim of developing a knowledge base of teaching with technology for specific subject matter content. Such a knowledge base can support (student) teachers when they have to design and enact technology in their practice.

Teachers' individual knowledge and beliefs about teaching with technology determine to a large extent how technology is being used in practice. A shared knowledge base about teaching with technology may help teachers to challenge and expand their individual knowledge and beliefs. In particular, such a shared knowledge base can be used in pre- and in-service teacher education programs.

Teaching as a Design Science

We argued, based on the theory of technological mediation, that teachers and technology actively shape technology-rich environments for learning, featuring the material dimensions of the teacher–technology relationship. The theory of situated cognition helped us to understand TPACK development as a dynamic process of knowledge construction embedded in a teacher's social environment. These perspectives imply that teachers have a role as designer of technology-enhanced learning, which leads to the third perspective discussed in this chapter: the potential of design to learn and develop TPACK. The view of teachers as designers of (technology-enhanced) learning is not new. It fits with understanding teaching as a design science (e.g. Koehler et al. 2007; Laurillard, 2012). This leads us to the third meaning of technology as distinguished by Berting (1992), technology as the knowledge and practice of the technology design process.

While we do not expect teachers to design new technologies, we definitely see teachers as designers of technology-enhanced learning environments. For several reasons we consider the designer role important for teachers. First, engagement in design, preferably through collaborative design in teams, offers ample opportunities for teacher learning about TPACK (Voogt et al., 2015). Second, involvement in design fosters teachers' creativity, in particular when repurposing technology for helping students learn. Third, active involvement in the design of technology-enhanced learning environments helps teachers to develop ownership (Cviko, McKenney, & Voogt, 2014) of and to trust themselves with the technology (Kiran & Verbeek, 2010).

Learning TPACK Through Collaborative Design

Through engaging teachers in design, they actively shape technology-enhanced environments for learning. Several studies showed that collaborative design in teams of teachers offers ample opportunities for (student) teacher learning about TPACK (e.g. Agyei & Voogt, 2014; Polly, Mims, Shepherd, & Inan, 2010; Voogt et al., 2011). Teacher involvement in collaborative design typically results in teachers developing the concrete artifacts that constitute an environment for technology-enhanced learning. Grounded in the theory of situated cognition (Greeno et al., 1998) and cultural historical activity theory (Engeström, 1987; Miettinen, 2013), Voogt et al. (2015) identified three key features fostering learning in collaborative design processes: situatedness of the activity, teacher agency and the cyclical nature of learning and change as key features of learning in collaborative design processes.

Situatedness of the activity refers to designing technology-enhanced learning environments for use in their own or their fellow teachers' teaching. Teachers engaged in collaborative design solve relevant and challenging problems of teaching subject matter together with their peers. Cviko, McKenney and Voogt (2014), in a study about roles of teachers in the design of technology-enhanced learning for teaching early literacy, showed that teachers taking up the designer role developed feelings of ownership of the technology-enhanced learning activities, because of their engagement in the design process. In addition, these teachers also implemented the activities they had designed at a level that complied more with the affordances of the technology compared to teachers who implemented a set of activities developed by others.

Teacher agency refers to the relationship teachers develop with technology when engaged in the design of technology-enhanced environments for learning. Agency develops through the active and responsible role teachers take in design. Literature on teacher professional development (Fishman et al., 2013; Garet, Porter, Desimone, Birman, & Yoon, 2001) suggests that such active involvement, in particular when teachers are engaged for a certain period of time, is vital for their learning. Huizinga, Handelzalts, Nieveen, and Voogt (2015) showed that teachers who were actively involved in a two-year design project in the context of foreign language teaching took responsibility for introducing the designed artifacts to their peers who were supposed to use them. Being involved in the process of acquainting others with the materials, the teachers involved in the design of the materials developed their understanding of the essentials of their new materials further. In a large-scale project in Quebec aiming to develop a network of remote schools, teachers' collaborative design process resulted in exemplary evidence for student capacity to be involved in inquiry learning. Teachers used this evidence to convince other teachers to apply inquiry learning (Laferrière et al., 2008).

The *cyclical nature of learning and change* refers to design and learning as an iterative process. It is through reflections on the iterations of the design that teachers learn, in particular when these iterations include classroom try-outs (Voogt et al., 2011). The study of Kafyulilo, Fisser and Voogt (2014) showed that teachers involved in the design of technology-enhanced science lessons developed their TPACK through reflections on the enactment of the designed technology-enhanced lessons. They realized the importance of understanding students' learning problems while designing and improved their lessons based on students' feedback. In the Remote Network School project in Quebec, researchers and teachers collaboratively discussed formative evaluation results in order to improve the designed artifacts (Laferrière et al., 2008). These studies show that collaborative design of technology-enhanced learning is a cyclical process that coincides with the cyclical nature of learning. Active involvement in such process provides many opportunities for teachers to develop their TPACK. However, teachers often need support when collaboratively designing in teams, because teachers' experience with design diverges. While all teachers are involved in the (re-) design of artifacts, such as lesson plans, for use in their own context, most teachers have only limited experience with designing artifacts that go beyond simple lessons and have to be used by others. Teachers' design experiences beyond the context of their own teaching vary highly across contexts and artifacts (Goodyear & Markauskaite, 2009). In addition, pre-service teacher education programs hardly pay attention to design beyond lesson planning (McKenney, Kali, Markauskaite, & Voogt, 2015). Hence, there is a need to better understand the knowledge teachers need to design technology-enhanced learning.

Understanding Design: Teacher Design Knowledge

Similar to teacher knowledge, the kind of knowledge needed for design consists of explicit and implicit or tacit knowledge, usually alluded to answering "know what", "know why", "know how" and "know when/where/who" questions (Lundwall & Johnson 1994) for a specific context. In a recent study, McKenney et al. (2015) distinguish among three strands of studies, each providing different strategies and considerations related to these "know x" questions and resulting in profound insights in the kind of knowledge teachers need during the design of technology-enhanced learning environments. The strands are referred to as technical, phenomenological and realist.

The *technical strand* assumes that design is a systematic, rational and iterative process for solving (educational) problems. The approach stems from design models developed in the frame of educational design (e.g. Jonassen, 1990; McKenney & Reeves, 2012) and provides designers with powerful design heuristics. Research shows that teachers, when involved in the design of artifacts (be it simple lessons, series of lessons, or whole programs), often do not follow a systematic approach and need guidance (e.g. Hoogveld, Paas, & Jochems, 2005; Huizinga, Handelzalts, Nieveen, & Voogt, 2014). Examples of such guidance can be found in the taxonomies of learning activities (Harris & Hofer, 2009, 2011) and technology mapping (Angeli & Valanides, 2009, 2013) that were described earlier in this chapter (see 'The Knowledge Base of Teaching With Technology').

Contrary to the systematic strand, the *phenomenological* strand assumes that the design process is intuitive, based on the connoisseurship of the designers, and consequently allows for flexibility and creativity in the design process (Schön, 1983). Schön argues that the intuitive knowledge of designers is developed through 'reflection-in-action,' implying that designers reflect on and interpret their experiences gained in practice to guide their design. This strand very much aligns with the practical knowledge teachers' bring to the design process. The study of Koehler et al. (2007) is an example. In this study, faculty and student teachers use the distributed expertise available in the team to design an online course. Through the conversations in the team, TPACK is developed. The phenomenological strand also sees design as a form of art and challenges teachers to play with their knowledge during the design of technology-enhanced learning environments in order to develop creative pedagogical solutions. Koehler et al. (2011, p. 154) refer to this as deep-play, which "is creative, seeking to construct new ways of seeing the world, and new approaches to using technology, in order to develop creative pedagogical solutions."

The *realist* strand has a slightly different nature, because this strand does not hold assumptions about the ideal design process, as in the other two strands, but studies teachers' actual design practice. Design is considered a problem-solving approach for finding optimal solutions for ill-structured problems. This strands is interested in what teachers' as designers actually do, why they do it and how they do it and is particularly interested in the way teachers cope with the problems they face during design. The studies of Boschman et al. (2014, 2015) and Koh et al. (2014) referred to earlier in this chapter (see 'TPACK and the Practicality of Teaching') are examples of this approach.

These three strands provide insight into important elements of teacher design knowledge: knowledge of powerful design heuristics (technical strand), situated experience and creativity (phenomenological strand) and the need to have a realistic understanding of the design process (realist strand).

Conclusions and Recommendations for the Future

In this chapter, we discussed three complementary theoretical perspectives important for understanding teachers' learning about and using of technology in their teaching. We related these perspectives to TPACK. All three theoretical perspectives require teachers to actively engage in constructing their knowledge for teaching with technology. While we used the theory of situated cognition to discuss the social dimensions related to teaching with technology, we employed the theory of technological mediation to feature the material dimensions of the teacher–technology relationship. We see value in both approaches. After all, we believe that both social and material dimensions are at stake when teachers design and enact technology environments for learning, even more when they do so collaboratively. Although we fully agree that both dimensions matter and need each other, we also believe that there is a lacuna in the research about the active role material artifacts play in education (Lawn & Grosvernor, 2005; Tondeur, Van den Driessche, De Bruyne, McKenney, & Zandvliet, 2015). We argue that to understand technology use in education, we need to develop knowledge about the teacher–technology relationship. That is, we need to know how teachers (individually and collaboratively) give meaning to and use technologies, in teaching and learning, what their motives and expectations are, which routines they develop and how technologies direct their utilization. From this perspective, we advocate research aimed at disentangling teachers' professional reasoning with the aim to understand the complex relationships between specific technologies, teachers' TPACK and their beliefs about teaching and learning with technology. Having said this, we contend that research on TPACK should focus on understanding how teachers use their TPACK in what they do with technology in practice, why they do it and how they do it. This implies that we need to study what teachers see as the affordances of specific technologies, what they aim to realize with these technologies in the teaching learning process and what outcomes they expect for their students and/or their teaching. We contend that such research would result in a knowledge base of teaching with technology. We adhere to Van Driel and Berry (2012), who argue that teachers need to be involved in this process. We therefore believe that not only researchers should study the teacher–technology relationship, but that teachers themselves need to be engaged in exploring this relationship as well. They can do so while collaboratively and creatively designing technology-enhanced environments for learning for a specific purpose, guided by powerful design heuristics and a realistic view of the design process.

References

Agyei, D., & Voogt, J. (2014). Pre-service mathematics teachers' learning and teaching of activity-based lessons supported with spreadsheets. *Technology, Pedagogy and Education*. doi:10.1080/1475939X.2014.928648

Angeli, C., & Valanides, N. (2009). Epistemological and methodological issues for the conceptualization, development, and assessment of ICT-TPCK: Advances in technological pedagogical content knowledge (TPCK). *Computers & Education, 52*, 154–168.

Angeli, C., & Valanides, N. (2013). Technology mapping: An approach for developing technological pedagogical content knowledge. *Journal of Educational Computing Research, 48*(2), 199–221.

Baran, E., Correia, A-P., & Thompson, A.D. (2013). Tracing successful online teaching: Voices of exemplary online teachers. *Teacher College Record, 115*, 1–41.

Belo, N., McKenney, S., & Voogt, J. (2013). *Towards a knowledge base for using ICT to foster early literacy development: A review study*. Paper presented at EARLI, München, August 27–31, 2013.

Berting, J. (1992). *De technologische factor: Een sociaal-wetenschappelijke analyse*. De Lier: Academisch Boekencentrum.

Borgmann, A. (2006). Technology as a cultural force: For Alena and Griffin. *The Canadian Journal of Sociology, 31*(3), 351–360.

Boschman, F., McKenney, S., & Voogt, J. (2014). Understanding decision making in teachers' curriculum design approaches. *Educational Technology Research and Development, 62*, 393–416.

Boschman, F., McKenney, S., & Voogt, J. (2015). Exploring teachers' use of TPACK in design talk: The collaborative design of technology-rich early literacy activities. *Computers & Education, 82*, 250–262.

Brown, M. (2009). The teacher-tool relationship: Theorizing the design and use of curriculum materials. In J.T. Remillard, B. Herbel-Eisenman, & G. Lloyd (Eds.), *Mathematics teachers at work: Connecting curriculum materials and classroom instruction* (pp. 17–36). New York: Routledge.

Calderhead, J. (1996). Teachers: Beliefs and knowledge. In D. Berliner & R. Calfee (Eds.). *Handbook of educational psychology* (pp. 709–725). New York: MacMillan.

Christensen, R., Knezek, G., Alexander, C., Owens, D., Overall, T., & Mayes, G. (2015). Measuring 21st century skills in teacher educators. Paper presented at the Society for Information Technology in Teacher Education Conference, March 2–6, 2015, Las Vegas.

Conelly, F.M., & Clandinin, D.J. (1985). Personal practical knowledge and the modes of knowing: Relevance for teaching and learning. In E. Eisner (Ed.), *Learning and teaching the ways of knowing* (pp. 174–198). Chicago: University of Chicago Press.

Cviko, A., McKenney, S., & Voogt, J. (2014). Teacher roles in designing technology-rich learning activities for early literacy: A cross-case analysis. *Computers & Education, 72*, 68–79.

Doyle, W., & Ponder, G.A. (1978). The practicality ethic in teacher decision-making. *Interchange, 8*(3), 1–12.

Engeström, Y. (1987) *Learning by expanding: An activity-theoretical approach to developmental research*. Helsinki, Finland: Orienta-Konsultit.

Eraut, M. (1994). *Developing professional practice and competence*. London: Falmer Press.

Ertmer, P. A., Ottenbreit-Leftwich, A. T., Sadik, O., Sendurur, E., & Sendurur, P. (2012). Teacher beliefs and technology intergation practices: A critical relationship. *Computers & Education, 59*, 423–435.

Fishman, B., Konstantopoulos, S., Kubitskey, B. W., Vath, R., Park, G., Johnson, H., & Edelson, D. C. (2013). Comparing the impact of online and face-to-face professional development in the context of curriculum implementation. *Journal of Teacher Education, 64*(5), 426–438.

Garet, M. S., Porter, A. C., Desimone, L., Birman, B. F., & Yoon, K. S. (2001) What makes professional development effective? Results from a national sample of teachers. *American Educational Research Journal, 38*, 915–945.

Gell, A. (1998). *Art and agency. An anthropological theory.* Oxford: Oxford University Press.

Gibson, J. J. (1979). *The ecological approach to visual perception.* Boston: Houghton Miffin.

Goldstein, E. B. (1981). The ecology of J. J. Gibson's perception. *Leonardo, 14*(3), 191–195.

Goodyear, P., & Markauskaite, L. (2009). Teachers' design knowledge, epistemic fluency and reflections on students' experiences. Paper presented at the Higher Education Research and Development Society of Australasia (HERDSA) Conference, Darwin, Australia.

Greeno, J. G., & Middle School Mathematics Through Applications Project Group. (1998). The situativity of knowing, learning, and research. *American Psychologist, 53*(1), 5–26.

Harris, J., & Hofer, M. (2009). Instructional planning activity types as vehicles for curriculum-based TPACK development. In C. D. Maddux (Ed.), *Research highlights in technology and teacher education 2009* (pp. 99–108). Chesapeake, VA: Society for Information Technology in Teacher Education (SITE).

Harris, J. B., & Hofer, M. J. (2011). Technological pedagogical content knowledge in action: A descriptive study of secondary teacher' curriculum-based technology-related instructional planning. *Journal of Research on Technology in Education, 43*(3), 211–229.

Higgins, S., Beauchamp, G., & Miller, D. (2007). Reviewing the literature on interactive whiteboards. *Learning, Media and Technology, 32*(3), 213–225.

Hofer, M., & Owings-Swan, K. (2005). Digital moviemaking—The harmonization of technology, pedagogy and content. *International Journal of Technology in Teaching and Learning, 1*(2), 102–110.

Hoogveld, A. W. M., Paas, F., & Jochems, W. M. G. (2005). Training higher education teachers for instructional design of competency-based education: Product-oriented versus process-oriented worked examples. *Teaching and Teacher Education, 21*(3), 287–297. doi:10.1016/j.tate.2005.01.002

Huizinga, T., Handelzalts, A., Nieveen, N., & Voogt, J. (2014). Teacher involvement in curriculum design: Need for support to enhance teachers' design expertise. *Journal of Curriculum Studies, 46*(1), 33–57.

Huizinga, T., Handelzalts, A., Nieveen, N., & Voogt, J. (2015). Fostering teachers' design expertise in teacher design teams: Conducive design and support activities. *The Curriculum Journal, 26*(1), 137–163.

Ihde, D. (1993). *Philosophy of technology. An introduction.* New York: Paragon House.

Jamieson-Proctor, R., Finger, G., & Albion, P. (2010). Auditing the TK and TPACK confidence of pre-service teachers: Are they ready for the profession? *Australian Educational Computing, 25*(1), 8–17.

Janssen, F., Westbroek, H., Doyle, W., & Van Driel, J. H. (2013). How to make innovations practical. *Teacher College Record, 115*, 1–42.

Jimoyiannis, A. (2010). Designing and implementing an integrated technological pedagogical science knowledge framework for science teachers professional development. *Computers & Education, 55*(3), 1259–1269.

Jonassen, D. H. (1990). Thinking technology: Toward a constructivist view of instructional design. *Educational Technology, 30*(9), 32–34.

Kafyulilo, A., Fisser, P., & Voogt, J. (2014). Teacher design in teams as a professional development arrangement for developing technology integration knowledge and skills of science teachers in Tanzania. *Education and Information Technologies.* doi:10.1007/s10639-014-9321-0

Kiran, A. H., & Verbeek, P. P. (2010). Trusting ourselves to technology. *Knowledge, Technology & Policy, 23,* 409–427.

Koehler, M., & Mishra, P. (2008). Introducing TPCK. In AACTE Committee on Innovation and Technology (Eds.), *Handbook of technological pedagogical content knowledge (TPCK) for educators* (pp. 3–29). New York: Routledge.

Koehler, M., Mishra, P., & Yahya, K. (2007). Tracing the development of teacher knowledge in a design seminar: Integrating content, pedagogy and technology. *Computers & Education, 49*(3), 740–762. doi:10.1016/j.compedu.2005.11.012

Koehler, M. J., & Mishra, P. (2005). What happens when teachers design educational technology? The development of technological pedagogical content knowledge. *Journal of Educational Computing Research, 32*(2), 131–152.

Koehler, M. J., Mishra, P., Bouck, E. C., DeSchryver, M., Kereluik, K., Shin, T. S., & Wolf, L. G. (2011). Deep-play: Developing TPACK for 21st century teachers. *International Journal of Learning Technology, 6*(2), 146–163.

Koh, J. H. L., Chai, C. S., & Tay, L. Y. (2014). TPACK-in-action: Unpacking the contextual influences of teachers' construction of technological pedagogical content knowledge (TPACK). *Computers & Education, 78,* 20–29.

Krug, D., & Arntzen, J. (2010). Ecologies of learning: Efficacious learning and ICT pedagogical and technological adaptability. In S. Mukerji & P. Tripathi (Eds.), *Cases on interactive technology environments and transnational collaboration: Concerns and perspectives* (pp. 74–93). Hershey, PA: IGI Global.

Laferrière, T., Allaire, S., Breuleux, A., Hamel, C., Turcotte, S., Gaudreault-Perron, J., Inchauspé, P., & Beaudoin, J. (2008). *L'école éloignée en réseau: L'apprentissage des élèves.* Rapport de recherche, phase III, CEFRIO, Québec. http://www.eer.qc.ca/doc/2009/EER_rapport-synthese_phase-3.pdf

Laurillard, D. (2012). *Teaching as a design science: Building pedagogical patterns for learning and technology.* London: Routledge.

Lawn, M., & Grosvenor, I. (2005). *Materialities of schooling.* Providence, RI: Symposium Books.

Lundwall, B., & Johnson, B. (1994). The learning economy. *Journal of Industry Studies, 1*(2), 23–42.

McKenney, S., Kali, Y., Markauskaite, L., & Voogt, J. (2015). Teacher design knowledge for technology enhanced learning: An ecological framework for investigating assets and needs. *Instructional Science, 43,* 181–202.

McKenney, S., & Reeves, T. C. (2012). *Conducting educational design research.* London: Routledge.

McKenney, S., & Voogt, J. (under review). Expert views on TPACK for early literacy: Priorities for teacher education.

Miettinen, R. (2013). *Innovation, human capabilities, and democracy: Towards an enabling welfare state.* Oxford: Oxford University Press.

Niederhauser, D. S., & Stoddart, T. (2001). Teachers' instructional perspectives and use of educational software. *Teaching and Teacher Education, 17,* 15–31.

Niess, M. L. (2005) Preparing teachers to teach science and mathematics with technology: Developing a technology pedagogical content knowledge. *Teaching and Teacher Education, 21,* 509–523.

Pajares, M. F. (1992). Teachers' beliefs and educational research: Cleaning up a messy construct. *Review of Educational Research, 62*(3), 307–332.

Polly, D., Mims, C., Shepherd, C. E., & Inan, F. (2010). Evidence of impact: Transforming teacher education with preparing tomorrow's teachers to teach with technology (PT3) grants. *Teaching and Teacher Education, 26*, 863–870.

Schön, D. A. (1983). *The reflective practitioner: How professionals think in action*. New York: Basic Books.

Shulman, L. S. (1986). Those who understand: Knowledge growth in teaching. *Educational Researcher, 15*, 4–14.

Shulman, L. S. (1987). Knowledge and teaching: Foundations of the new reform. *Harvard Educational Review, 57*, 1–22.

So, H. J., & Kim, B. (2009). Learning about problem based learning: Student teachers integrating technology, pedagogy and content knowledge. *Australasian Journal of Educational Technology, 25*, 101–116.

Tondeur, J., Hermans, R., van Braak, J., & Valcke, M. (2008). Exploring the link between teachers' educational belief profiles and different types of computer use in the classroom. *Computers in Human Behavior, 24*, 2541–2553.

Tondeur, J., Pareja Roblin, N., van Braak, J., Voogt, J., & Prestridge, S. (under review). Preparing beginning teachers for technology integration in education: Ready for take-off?

Tondeur, J., Van den Driessche, M., De Bruyne, E., McKenney, S., & Zandvliet, D. (2015). The physical placement of classroom technology and its influences on educational practices. *Cambridge Journal of Education*. doi:10.1080/0305764X.2014.998624

Trinidad, S., Newhouse, P., & Clarkson, B. (2004). A framework for leading school change in using ICT. In S. Trinidad & J. Pearson (Eds.), *Using ICT in education: Effective leadership, change and models of best practice*. Singapore: Pearson Education Asia.

Verbeek, P. P. (2005). *What things do. Philosophical reflections on technology, agency, and design*. University Park, PA: Pennsylvania State University Press.

Verbeek, P. P. (2011). *Moralizing technology: Understanding and designing the morality of things*. Chicago: University of Chicago Press.

Van Driel, J. H., & Berry, A. (2012). Teacher professional development focusing on pedagogical content knowledge. *Educational Researcher, 41*, 26–28.

Van Driel, J. H., Verloop, N., & De Vos, W. (1998). Developing science teachers' pedagogical content knowledge. *Journal of Research in Science Teaching, 35*, 673–695.

Verloop, N., Van Driel, J. H., & Meijer, P. C. (2001) Teacher knowledge and the knowledge base of teaching. *International Journal of Educational Research, 35*, 441–461.

Voogt, J. (2010). Teacher factors associated with innovative curriculum goals and pedagogical practices: Differences between extensive and non-extensive ICT-using science teachers. *Journal of Computer Assisted Learning, 26*(6), 453–464.

Voogt, J., Fisser, P., Pareja Roblin, N., Tondeur, J., & van Braak, J. (2013a). Technological pedagogical content knowledge (TPACK)—A review of the literature. *Journal of Computer Assisted Learning, 29*(2), 109–121.

Voogt, J., Laferrière, T., Breuleux, A., Itow, R., Hickey, D., & McKenney, S. (2015). Collaborative design as a form of professional development. *Instructional Science, 43*, 259–282.

Voogt, J., van Braak, J., Heitink, M., Verplanken, L., Fisser, P., & Walraven, A. (2013b). *Didactische ICT-bekwaamheid van docenten* [Teachers' pedagogical ICT competencies]. Enschede: Universiteit Twente. http://www.kennisnet.nl/uploads/tx_kncontentelements/Kennisnet_verslag_definitief_11022014_didactische_ict_bekwaamheid.pdf

Voogt, J., Westbroek, H., Handelzalts, A., Walraven, A., McKenney, S., Pieters, J., & De Vries, B. (2011). Teacher learning in collaborative curriculum design. *Teaching and Teacher Education, 27*, 1235–1244.

Webb, M., & Cox, M. (2004). A review of pedagogy related to information and communication technology. *Technology, Pedagogy and Education, 13*(2), 235–286.

Wiederhold, M.D., & Wiederhold, B.K. (2007). Virtual reality and interactive simulation for pain distraction. *Pain Medicine, 8*(S3), S182–S188.

4

Developing TPACK
Envisioning Technological Pedagogical Reasoning

Vicky Smart, Glenn Finger, Cheryl Sim

Introduction

In this chapter, we explore and propose that teachers undertake technological pedagogical reasoning, which can assist in deepening an understanding of how we can represent the knowledge base of teaching. Technological Pedagogical Content Knowledge, introduced in the publication of the *Handbook of Technological Pedagogical Content Knowledge (TPCK) for Educators* (AACTE Committee on Innovation and Technology, 2008), understood Shulman's (1987) conceptualisation of pedagogical content knowledge (PCK) and his articulation of pedagogical reasoning and action, whereby teaching is emphasised as "comprehension and reasoning, as transformation and reflection" (p. 13). Almost three decades later, there continues to be research, opinion, debates, development of standards and reviews of teacher education, which attempt to identify and understand the knowledge base for teachers.

This chapter redirects our attention to Shulman's earlier, significant caution that we must continue to be aware that "the currently incomplete and trivial definitions of teaching held by the policy community comprise a far greater danger to good education than does a more serious attempt to formulate the knowledge base" (Shulman, 1987, p. 20). Drawing upon Shulman's portrayal of Nancy's representation of pedagogical excellence, we present Carmelina, whose pedagogical excellence takes place in a different and contemporary world than that of Nancy. This provides the platform on which a new knowledge base for teachers might be considered, as the descriptions of Nancy and Carmelina offer very different views of teaching reflecting technological changes. In developing their knowledge bases, this chapter suggests that technology has also had an impact on their pedagogical reasoning. To understand their pedagogical reasoning, we will attempt to answer the question: Is this pedagogical reasoning with technology or technological pedagogical reasoning?

Vicky Smart, Glenn Finger, Cheryl Sim

Prologue: A New Portrait of Expertise

In 1987, Lee Shulman authored an article titled 'Knowledge and Teaching: Foundations of the New Reform' that was published in the *Harvard Educational Review*. Shulman took this opportunity to envision his view of teachers' professional knowledge. Shulman's work was groundbreaking, as it was part of the movement away from looking at the behavioural aspects of teaching to developing a cognitive view in which the teacher is thinker, problem solver and planner. Shulman began his seminal article with the portrayal of an expert teacher named Nancy, an anonymous experienced teacher who was part of the Knowledge Growth in a Profession project at Stanford University. A researcher's view (Gudmundsdottir, 1988) of Nancy's teaching is captured in the first four pages of Shulman's 1987 article. Teaching and, in particular, teaching with technology has changed substantially since Nancy was first described. What might Nancy's teaching look like today?

Using *restorying* (Creswell, 2012) to provide a descriptive view of teaching practice, we begin this chapter with a revised version of Nancy, whom we call Carmelina (not her real name). Carmelina agreed to participate in the doctoral research project and in retelling Carmelina's story, we capture the hypothetical life of a teacher in 2014. Carmelina is described as being a model of pedagogical excellence evident through her restory of practical pedagogical wisdom and we can see how her teaching has been influenced by the use of technology.

> Carmelina checked her email on her laptop before getting ready for school. The previous night she had loaded her presentation and added review questions on *The Adventures of Huckleberry Finn* in her virtual classroom in the school learning management system (LMS). She added a few links to websites that contained video of the Mississippi River, which she was going to use in her lesson after questions the previous day. Overnight she had received three emails from her students with questions and suggested answers for the app she challenged them to find.
>
> She quickly responded with an announcement (in the LMS) to all students of a suggestion for an app they should download before their lesson. She advised them of the task sheet and of what they would be expected to do that day. She enabled the assignment task, already set up, so that all students could see the task sheet.
>
> On her way to school, she answered a phone call from her teacher assistant asking about the task sheet and how it can be modified for the student she supported. When she arrived at school, she found an email from the school administration advising her that there was a new student enrolled in her class. She logged into the student management system to access the student's details to update her class spreadsheet. Carmelina added the student into the LMS and sent them the welcome email.
>
> Carmelina entered the classroom to teach her first session of the day. She opened her laptop and marked the attendance, while students opened their own computing devices to access the virtual classroom in the LMS. She asked them to open their eBook to continue the conversation from their last lesson. Although there were a few students

away, she knew there were two groups of students in her class: those that had already watched the presentation and completed the review questions and those that had not. For the students that had finished, she asked them to review the app they found and prepare a demonstration to show the class. She asked one of the students to show the LMS to the new student and asked the new student to record the presentation using their smart phone, so they could remember key information when they try to log into the LMS later. For the second group, she asked them to listen to the prerecorded audio attached to her presentation with their own headsets and complete the review questions in their blog.

Carmelina asked all students to stop what they are doing and watch the electronic whiteboard. She showed the students a video of the Mississippi River, the setting for the novel. She explained how she rode on a paddle steamer in New Orleans. Next, she demonstrated an app using her tablet that had been electronically connected to the whiteboard. She asked the students to finish their review questions. She explained that the quiz would be available in five minutes and that all students needed to complete the quiz by 6 pm that evening. The quiz automatically opened at the time she set in the LMS.

As the students completed the quiz, they obtained immediate feedback with their results. The students were familiar with Carmelina's quizzes and used the grade book to check and compare their answers.

Carmelina handed out a paper copy of the assignment task and briefly explained the task to all the students. She was trying something new and had created a discussion board within the LMS for the assignment task. She advised the students to post any questions and said that she would regularly check the discussion board.

Later that day, Carmelina received an email from one of her student's parents requesting information about how their child was progressing. Carmelina quickly checked the LMS grading information, the student's access statistics and the student database for notes about the parents. She learned that their children's quiz results had been low and they hadn't been accessing the LMS outside of school hours. She replied to the parents with a summary of what she learned and asked the parents if there was anything she could do to help.

After dinner, Carmelina decided to check that her students had completed the quiz. She saw that all, except for two, had completed the quiz, and she sent those two a personalised email to remind them to complete the quiz before their lesson. She sent another email congratulating all of the other students with a summary of the class results. She adjusted the quiz closing time to 10 o'clock the next morning to allow the two students a little extra time and posted an announcement in the LMS to explain what the students would be doing for their next lesson. She checked if there were any questions on the discussion board and responded to three.

She turned off her laptop and tablet and prepared for bed.

Nancy taught in a classroom with probably a blackboard and chalk. Carmelina's teaching landscape was very different, with an electronic whiteboard, laptop and projector.

She had not *decided* to integrate technology, but, rather, it had become part of everyday life in her school. Carmelina worked in a classroom with an abundance of technology with students that had their own computing devices—tablets or laptops. This restory has been written to reflect a modern classroom as it is today. We believe Carmelina is a contemporary teacher who uses technology effectively for teaching and learning.

The description of Nancy is confined to the classroom and told by the researcher through her observations. Nancy's approach to teaching reading with the description in the narrative showing a teacher-directed approach.

> She was like a symphony conductor, posing questions, probing for alternative views, drawing out the shy while temping the boisterous. Not much happened in the classroom that did not pass through Nancy, whose pacing and ordering, structuring and expanding, controlled the rhythm of classroom life.
>
> (Gundmundsdottir as quoted by Shulman, 1987, p. 2)

Carmelina too was like a symphony conductor, posing questions and controlling the rhythm of her classroom, but she used technology to engage her students and extend her teaching beyond the walls of the classroom; she was not only physically their teacher but virtually as well. We agree with Mishra and Koehler (2006) in that

> what has changed since the 1980s is that technologies have come to the forefront of educational discourse primarily because of the availability of a range of new, primarily digital, technologies and requirements for learning how to apply them to teaching... these technologies have changed the nature of the classroom or have the potential to do so.
>
> (p. 1023)

A view of teaching today shows that Carmelina begins and ends at home from early morning to late in the evening. Technology has

- Extended the classroom far beyond the physical walls. With the use of the LMS, Carmelina had the ability to continue teaching outside of the classroom and to make her teaching richer inside the classroom.
- Made communicating with students, peers, parents and administration easier and quicker, allowing for more connections.
- Allowed access to more information about students and parents to effectively communicate more quickly and with more reliability.
- Made the processes of teaching easier and wider with access to more information and tools outside the boundaries of the school.
- Made teaching more visible to others, because it allowed for recording teaching moments that were accessible through the LMS.
- Changed the dynamics of the classroom, and with effective use could assist in managing behaviour and classroom routines.

Technology is a necessary part of Carmelina's teaching practices and it extends her teaching to enable learning to occur anywhere at any time. Learning becomes more fluid, depending on student need rather than at a scheduled time and place as in a classroom.

The New Technologically Enhanced Knowledge Base for Teachers

Looking closely at evidence from Nancy and Carmelina's restories and how that maps to the knowledge base described in Shulman's (1987) article, we can see the influence of technology. In the text that follows, we explain how each teacher exemplified each of the six knowledge bases.

Content Knowledge

Both teachers use Mark Twain's book as their content for this English unit. Nancy used the traditional paper-based novel. Carmelina used an eBook, and the eBook reader application allows the students to add comments and important snippets of information to aid in their learning. The eBook also contains some images and video to complement the story. Both teachers have very different approaches to their pedagogy. Nancy's pedagogy was limited to the classroom and was teacher directed with group discussion. Nancy, the same teacher who was named Linda in research completed by Grace Grant (1991), explained that "Linda use[d] tasks requiring memory or routine, such as note taking during discussion. Students are accountable both for listening attentively and for recording ideas from the discussion" (p. 403). Carmelina used the LMS to extend her pedagogy beyond the walls of the classroom. She used online quizzes with instant feedback to evaluate student knowledge and a discussion board in the LMS to answer questions. She included a traditional group work activity and asked students to peer support others.

Pedagogical Knowledge

Nancy's pedagogical strategies are elaborated in the restory, but without the researcher's observation, would remain private to Nancy and invisible to others. Shulman suggested this "individual and collective amnesia" was a frustration for teaching where its best creations were lost (Shulman, 1987, p. 11). Technology had enabled Carmelina to share her pedagogical thoughts with others, making it visible and providing a history. Important messages for students could be captured in video or as audio presentations. Students could revisit the messages at any time to help in their understanding of the content. Teaching for Carmelina was no longer a one-off and isolated activity where reliance was placed on students learning in the time and space of the classroom. Student activity was not restricted to within the classroom, but was a continuous learning experience anytime and anywhere.

Pedagogical Content Knowledge

Nancy had devised a general theoretical framework for the teaching of reading that she used to reinforce when teaching literacy. She believed that she used a model to help students improve their literacy skills, one which she had developed over years of teaching literacy, highlighting her strong pedagogical content knowledge. Carmelina also showed her pedagogical content knowledge but by using technology. Carmelina used the LMS to engage students and to deliver content in a format that students could relate to, as video, audio, quizzes, discussion boards and announcements. Carmelina knew that she had captured her pedagogical content knowledge within the LMS to share with students, parents, teaching peers and teacher assistants. With the content updated each year, she could have aspects that she turned on or off depending on the interest and academic levels of the students. Her technological pedagogical content knowledge (or TPACK) (Koehler & Mishra, 2005) enabled her to know what to use to engage students and when to allow them to decide on their own technology. She also knew when not to use technology.

Knowledge of Learners, Contexts and Educational Ends

Both Nancy and Carmelina showed knowledge of their learners and their educational contexts. Nancy's knowledge of learners was restricted to within the classroom and the content they were learning. Carmelina, on the other hand, showed a greater knowledge of learner characteristics by using technology. Nancy's goal was to improve her students' literacy to prepare them for university-level examinations, an education goal still pertinent today. Carmelina's goal was also to improve her students' literacy levels, but a parallel goal was to engage students through the use of technology. She changed their learning landscape from inside the classroom to virtual classrooms. One important difference was Carmelina's engagement with parents through technology to allow them to be part of the learning experience through the LMS or via email.

How Has Technology Impacted the Knowledge Base?

In 2014, it would be rare for a teacher to use a book or textbook as the only source of content when teaching. In Carmelina's case, she accessed the Internet to explore more details about the novel, author and story location. To do this she needed knowledge of technology to use her laptop, an Internet browser, simple search strategies and application of a critical eye to find the most appropriate materials. She needed to know how best to use her technology to share these resources with her students, how to use a laptop and projector and the software to play a video in the classroom. She needed to know how to use an LMS for her virtual classroom including, for example, how to add/edit content, enable/disable content and use announcements to communicate important messages with students. She needed to know how to use email with simple tasks of sending and receiving messages and how to record audio on a PowerPoint presentation. Each decision displayed the complexities of using technology in teaching, with these few examples highlighting the multifaceted technology knowledge she already possessed. Could this mean that technology knowledge is an additional knowledge that should be added to the knowledge base? We propose that technology knowledge should be added as the eighth domain. Technology knowledge represents the knowing how to use technology for teaching and learning. We caution that our understanding of the knowledge base is not *fixed* and *final*—there is still much to be learned about teacher's professional knowledge.

Our next question is, How do teachers use and develop their knowledge base? Fortuitously, Shulman provided an answer in terms of pedagogical reasoning. Shulman suggested:

> sound reasoning requires both a process of thinking about what they are doing and an adequate base of facts, principles and experience from which to reason. Teachers must learn to use their knowledge base to provide the grounds for choice and actions.
>
> (Shulman, 1987, p. 13)

Shulman explained that pedagogical reasoning essentially

> involves the exchange of ideas. The idea is grasped, probed and comprehended by a teacher, who then must turn it about in his or her mind, seeing many sides of it. Then the idea is shaped or tailored until it can in turn be grasped by students.
>
> (Shulman, 1987, p. 13)

We will now look at how these teachers pedagogically reason and the differences between the two to understand the impact of technology. Nancy's story is limited to what Shulman shared with us in his article, while we have the advantage of knowing Carmelina better through the video-stimulated interview, the think-aloud interview and her digital portfolio.

The Processes of Pedagogical Reasoning

Both teachers began with the same objective of teaching literacy to their students; the key differentiation was that Carmelina used digital technologies to enhance her instruction. In addition, while they both followed the same processes for transformation, their outcomes would look very different. We could expect that they both produced a unit plan, but the presentation and availability of the tools they used differed because of technology. Nancy would possibly have a paper-based plan, which might have been printed from a computer but more likely constructed by hand. Her teaching materials were possibly stored in a folder and she would add to the folder, as she had built her understanding from teaching the topic. Only Nancy knew the format and layout of her folder and how she used it.

In contrast, Carmelina would also produce a unit plan that would be available to her, her students, their parents and her peers through the virtual classroom. It was school policy for her to store all planning and assessment in the school LMS. Carmelina's work was available digitally anywhere and anytime she needed it, and she didn't need a paper-based folder for each unit. Carmelina also kept a backup copy of everything stored in the LMS on her laptop because she knew that technology could fail or be unavailable.

Nancy's transformation processes were in her head as Nancy had internalised her work over her many years of teaching this unit. Over 25 years of teaching, Nancy would have developed an excellent understanding of the reasons why and how best to deliver her content. She had developed a deep understanding from the texts she used, but her greatest strength was how she would teach her students, or her pedagogical content knowledge (PCK). Unlike Nancy, where all of her knowledge was internalised, Carmelina was building her content and pedagogical content knowledge in the virtual classroom and therefore externalising her PCK. She had determined the best way to communicate her content in a format to engage the students. It was quicker and much easier to access and her students could return to the material whenever they needed. The invisible acts of teaching had been captured in the LMS in order for students to be able to review and replay her teaching to improve their learning in time for assessment.

Nancy used a range of pedagogical approaches that were classroom based with a blend of teacher- or student-led activities. Carmelina used a blend of classroom and technological pedagogical approaches for planning and instruction that were not possible for Nancy. The concept of the ideal classroom that holds all information relevant for teaching this unit, along with video, audio and maybe even messages from the author, could not be realized without the affordances of technology. Now students can virtually visit the locations, hear commentary, connect with other students and continue the discussion outside the four walls of the classroom. Learning has been extended to allow students to further explore the materials to develop their own understanding and appreciation of Tom Sawyer. The virtual classroom can become the repository of many varied materials and links to the Web to construct interesting learning experiences and help the teacher explain with the best examples. The materials can be updated each year to suit a new cohort of students. It can complement the teacher's voice in providing visualizations that can help when telling an important story.

Both Nancy and Carmelina used in-class and post-class evaluation to check for student understanding. Nancy would use a paper-based system of assessment submission with feedback given on individual papers. Carmelina's assessment included quizzes, which were automatically marked and with students given immediate feedback. For Carmelina, all student assessment was submitted through the LMS where students were given feedback and their results using the grading tools. All assessment and feedback was stored in the LMS for review and could be revisited anytime by the teacher or the student.

For Nancy, reflections and new comprehensions are very internal, private processes which were not shared in her story, although Nancy or the other teachers involved in the Knowledge Growth in a Profession project showed evidence of reflection and new comprehensions for them to appear in the Model of Pedagogical Reasoning and Action (Shulman, 1987). Carmelina had captured her reflection and new comprehensions in the LMS by constantly turn things on and off, adding or deleting for the future. In preparing her digital portfolio she had provided insights into her reflection and new comprehensions for three units of teaching (Smart, Sim, & Finger, 2013a, 2013b). This leads to asking how technology has influenced Carmelina's pedagogical reasoning.

Conclusion

Carmelina's work incorporated a significant amount of technology that has impacted her knowledge base and pedagogical reasoning. All domains of her knowledge base were influenced or enabled with the use of technology, and many could not be developed without the use of technology. This leads us to suggest that there should be another domain to include technology knowledge for teaching. We suggest that she developed that knowledge through pedagogical reasoning with technology. Now the question is, Is this pedagogical reasoning with technology or technological pedagogical reasoning?

For Carmelina, all parts of her pedagogical reasoning involved technology. She needed technology to comprehend what she needed to teach. She needed technology to transform the content to teach to her students. Remember her students used their own technology for learning and so she needed to use technology to engage her students in using their technology for learning. She used technology to manage their behaviour and communicate what she wanted them to learn. She used technology to make learning interesting and to capture their work in order for her to make grading decisions. She used technology in the classroom and used her virtual classroom to enable learning anywhere and anytime. Finally, she used technology to externalize and record her teaching to allow her or her students to return to it at any time. Technology has significantly changed the way that Carmelina pedagogically reasoned, which is very different to how Nancy would have pedagogically reasoned. Technologies have created a very different view of these teachers' knowledge and their pedagogical reasoning.

The dominant discourse of teaching with technology has focused on teachers' TPACK and with limited references to Shulman's knowledge base and pedagogical reasoning. TPACK has become a popular framework for describing teachers' knowledge for integrating technology where TPACK plays a significant part in the *whole* knowledge base for teaching. In addition, TPACK is developed when teachers pedagogically reason with technology. We are suggesting just as Shulman suggested that the processes of pedagogical reasoning develops PCK and now, with the introduction of technology, teachers technologically pedagogically reason to develop their TPACK.

Is this change significant enough to justify adding 'technology' to pedagogical reasoning to form a new construct similar to how technology was added to pedagogical content knowledge to create TPACK? We think so. Technology has significantly changed how two experienced teachers reason, and this change justifies the creation of the new term 'technological pedagogical reasoning'. The story does not end here, as the authors continue researching to understand this new construct.

References

AACTE Committee on Innovation and Technology (2008). *Handbook of technological pedagogical content knowledge (TPCK) for educators*. New York: Routledge.

Creswell, J.W. (2012). *Qualitative inquiry and research design: Choosing among five approaches*. Los Angeles: SAGE Publications.

Grant, G.E. (1991). Ways of constructing classroom meaning: Two stories about knowing and seeing. *Journal of Curriculum Studies, 23*(5), 397–408.

Gudmundsdottir, S. (1988). *Knowledge use among experienced teachers: Four case studies of high school teaching.* Doctoral dissertation. Stanford University.

Koehler, M., & Mishra, P. (2005). What happens when teachers design educational technology? The development of technological pedagogical content knowledge. *Educational Computing Research, 32*(2), 131–152.

Mishra, P., & Koehler, M. (2006). Technological pedagogical content knowledge: A framework for integrating technology in teachers' knowledge. *Teachers College Record, 108*(6), 1017–1054.

Shulman, L.S. (1987). Knowledge and teaching: Foundations of the new reform. *Harvard Educational Review, 57*(1), 1–21.

Smart, V., Sim, C., & Finger, G. (2013a). Exploring teachers technological pedagogical reasoning through digital portfolios. International Society for Technology in Education (ISTE), San Antonio, Texas, United States.

Smart, V., Sim, C., & Finger, G. (2013b). A view into teacher's digital pedagogical portfolios showing evidence of their technological pedagogical reasoning. Society for Information Technology & Teacher Education International Conference 2013, New Orleans, Louisiana, United States.

Section II
Research

5

Exploring the Use of Qualitative Methods to Examine TPACK

Leanna Archambault

Since its articulation in 2005, the Technological Pedagogical Content Knowledge (TPACK) framework has transformed Shulman's notion of pedagogical content knowledge and brought the framework into the 21st century. At its core, it conveys an understanding of the complex relationships among students, teachers, content, technologies, practices, and tools. According to Koehler and Mishra (2005), "We view technology as a knowledge system that comes with its own biases, and affordances that make some technologies more applicable in some situations than others" (p. 132). Until the conceptualization of TPACK (Mishra & Koehler, 2006), a comprehensive conceptual framework was lacking in the field of educational technology. The development and application of TPACK has become extremely popular among researchers and practitioners alike (Cox & Graham, 2009).

Prior to delving further into the qualitative methods used to examine TPACK, it is helpful to examine the roots of the framework. TPACK was built on Shulman's (1986) Pedagogical Content Knowledge (PCK) framework, driven by the need for a more coherent theoretical framework specific to what teachers should know and be able to do. The PCK framework raised important questions such as, "What are the domains and categories of content knowledge in the minds of teachers?" and "How are content knowledge and general pedagogical knowledge related?" (p. 9). To convey the relationship between the organization of knowledge of a particular subject matter and knowledge of how to teach various content, Shulman developed the idea of Pedagogical Content Knowledge. PCK goes beyond content or subject matter knowledge, encapsulating knowledge on how to teach that particular content, including, "the most useful forms of representation of those ideas, the most powerful analogies, illustrations, examples, explanations, and demonstrations—in a word, the ways of representing and formulating the subject that make it comprehensible to others" (p. 9). The TPACK framework takes PCK a step further and combines the relationships between and among content knowledge (subject matter that is to be taught), technological knowledge (computers, the Internet, digital video, etc.), and pedagogical knowledge (practices, processes, strategies, procedures, and methods of teaching and learning). Koehler and Mishra (2005) define TPACK as the connections and interactions between these three types of knowledge.

Numerous scholars have developed related curriculum, texts, professional development modules, and advancements to the framework. Among these lines of research are multiple methods of measurement (Angeli & Valanides, 2009; Harris, Mishra, & Koehler, 2009; Niess, 2008; Schmidt et al., 2009). Since its inception, scholars and researchers have worked to find suitable methods and methodologies for measuring the framework. The purpose of this chapter is to focus on the qualitative measures that have been used to effectively assess TPACK.

Qualitative Methods

Qualitative approaches are invaluable in social science research, specifically when examining education within the context of individual classrooms (Creswell, 2014). Researching a complex framework such as TPACK requires an extensive set of research techniques and tools, particularly when examining its application to the K–12 classroom and implementation within teacher preparation programs. It is helpful to review the key components of qualitative research that distinguish qualitative approaches from quantitative ones. First, qualitative research takes place in a natural setting to see how participants behave and act in an authentic context. In addition to the context playing a major role, the researcher also is a key figure, personally conducting the research through direct observation, conducting interviews, or analyzing artifacts/rubrics/observation protocols. Often, a combination of these data sources are used, rather than relying on a single instrument developed by an external source (Creswell, 2014). Finally, instead of holding an a priori hypothesis and collecting data to test it using a deductive process, qualitative methods often employ both inductive and deductive analyses to build themes from data sources, and then reflexively go back and forth between the data and the emerging themes to develop a rich understanding of the phenomena.

Qualitative methods also rely on the flexibility of emergent design in which the plan for data collection may shift if needed. This is because the goal is to develop a holistic account of the complex issue being studied. It may involve gathering additional data to encapsulate the many factors of a problem (Creswell, 2014; Marshall & Rossman, 2011). According to Glesne (2011):

> Learning to do qualitative research is like learning to paint. Study the masters, learn techniques and methods, practice them faithfully, and then revise and adapt them to your own persuasions when you know enough to describe the work of those who have influenced you and the ways in which your modifications create new possibilities.
>
> (p. 3)

Applying these approaches, researchers have successfully employed and adapted existing qualitative methods to effectively measure TPACK in a variety of contexts.

Methodology

Reviewing relevant literature with respect to TPACK requires a systematic approach. To conduct the current review, ASU's LibraryOne search, a division of ProQuest, was used. This service provides a Google-like search that allows researchers to use a single search interface to access library content. In addition to LibraryOne, a search of the Association for the Advancement of Computers in Education (AACE)'s digital library, EdITLib, was conducted to gather relevant proceedings from the Society for Information Technology and Teacher Education (SITE) conference. Search terms included the following: "qualitative measures/methods technological pedagogical content knowledge," "qualitative research technological pedagogical content knowledge" and "technological pedagogical content knowledge assessment." This resulted in a total of 74 peer-reviewed articles. The number was further refined by excluding articles that were predominately quantitative in nature or that primarily implemented mixed methods. In addition, articles were limited to those that focused on TPACK among pre- or in-service teachers and/or those who prepared teachers (i.e., faculty members). The remaining literature was reviewed to ensure that each study included an in-depth qualitative analysis of TPACK within a given context, together with enough specific detail within the methodology section.

To organize the results, the current chapter used Koehler, Shin, and Mishra (2012)'s classification of four major categories of qualitative measure used to assess TPACK as a starting point, including observations, performance assessments, open-ended questionnaires, and interviews. However, after examining the existent qualitative literature, these categories were collapsed into three broad classifications: performance assessments, interviews, and observation tools. The identified categories of qualitative measures together with the resulting literature are described in Table 5.1. The current chapter includes a discussion of the studies identified in the table, followed by an exploration of what has been learned about TPACK from a qualitative research perspective.

Performance-Based Assessments

Performance assessments of TPACK use qualitative methods to examine participants' levels through the evaluation of real-world, authentic, high-level tasks (Koehler et al., 2012). These include creating lesson plans, design tasks, and learning activities (Hofer & Harris, 2011; Harris, Grandgenett, & Hofer, 2010), as well as design problems using case-based analyses (Brantley-Dias, Kinuthia, Shoffner, de Castro, & Rigole, 2007; Kinuthia, Brantley-Dias, & Clarke, 2010; Mouza & Karchmer-Klein, 2013). As Harris et al. (2010) reflect:

> Since teachers' knowledge is typically reflected through actions, statements, and artifacts, rather than being directly observable, instruments and techniques that assist the assessment of teachers' TPACK should provide ways for assessors to discern the dimensions and extent of teachers' TPACK in systematic, reliable, and valid ways.
> (p. 3834)

Table 5.1 Qualitative Literature Focused on Technological Pedagogical Content Knowledge

Qualitative Method Used	Description/Measure/ Instrument	Studies
Performance Assessments	Lesson plan evaluation tools, e.g., Technology Integration Assessment Rubric	Harris & Hofer, 2009; Harris, Grandgenett, & Hofer, 2010, 2012; Hofer & Grandgenett, 2012
	Evaluation of design tasks or learning activities	Graham, Borup, & Smith, 2012; Harris & Hofer, 2011; Harris, Hofer, Blanchard, Grandgenett, Schmidt, van Olphen, & Young, 2010; Harris, Mishra, & Koehler, 2009; Hofer & Harris, 2010; Koehler, Mishra and Yahya, 2007
	Case-based scenarios and case analysis	Brantley-Dias, Kinuthia, Shoffner, de Castro, & Rigole, 2007; Kinuthia, Brantley-Dias, & Clarke, 2010; Groth, Spickler, Bergner, & Bardzell, 2009; Mouza & Karchmer-Klein, 2013; Tai & Crawford, 2014
Interview Measures	Used as part of other qualitative methods to triangulate findings or validate instruments	Harris, Grandgenett, & Hofer, 2012; Jaipal & Figg, 2010; Mishra, Peruski, & Koehler, 2007; Ozgün-Koca, 2009; Williams, Foulger, & Wetzel, 2010
Observation Tools	Technology Integration Observation Instrument	Hofer, Grandgenett, Harris, & Swan, 2011; Harris et al., 2010

Performance assessments are geared toward helping to provide a consistent and accurate method of examining teacher knowledge and have been one of the most prevalent ways researchers have sought to qualitatively measure TPACK.

Technology Integration Assessment Rubric

Teachers' planning, instructional actions, interactions with students, and reflections can be examined to determine the nature and extent of their TPACK. In order to do so in a systematic manner, Harris et al. (2010) adapted the Technology Integration Assessment Instrument (TIAI) developed by Britten and Cassady (2005) to create the TPACK-based Technology Integration Assessment Rubric. Initially, the TIAI included seven dimensions for assessing the level of technology integration for a specific lesson plan: planning for technology use, content standards, technology standards, differentiation, use of technology for learning, use of technology for teaching, and assessment.

Rather than separating technology, pedagogy, and content as constructs, Harris et al. (2010) revised the TIAI to include technological pedagogical (TPK), technological content (TCK), and technological pedagogical content knowledge (TPACK). To establish content validity, six researchers were tasked with providing feedback regarding the revised instrument. Fifteen teachers experienced with technology integration met to use the rubric to assess numerous lesson plans to determine face validity. Based on the input and suggested revisions from both groups, researchers made improvements to the rubric. Reliability was established through having separate ratings sessions from two locations. Revisions were made to the rubric in between trials, and the trials were repeated in each location one month later. Researchers calculated an Intraclass Correlation Coefficient (ICC), the percent agreement computations to measure each rater's individual row score, as well as the rubric's total scores, and Cronbach's Alpha measure. Based on these measures, Harris et al. (2010) conclude, "The rubric's reliability calculations, along with its validity evaluations, suggests that we can confidently offer it for use by other researchers and educators" (p. 3838).

The rubric was then used to measure the development of TPACK among eight pre-service teachers from four major content areas (English, mathematics, social studies, and science) in a longitudinal study designed to examine TPACK throughout a three-semester master's in education initial licensure program (Hofer & Grandgenett, 2012). The authors used multiple data sources throughout various points of the program, including a TPACK survey with items geared toward measuring each construct (Schmidt et al., 2009), a lesson snapshot and reflection assignment, two lesson plans that included a self-reflection component, and interview data from students who implemented their planned lessons during their student teaching.

Working in pairs, researchers used the instrument to evaluate students' lesson plans in terms of TPK, TCK, and TPACK. They also coded the lesson snapshot together with its reflection, the reflections within the lesson plans, and the interview transcript data. The coding generated tabulations of TPACK constructs that could be evaluated statistically, using means, standard deviations, and paired t-tests to check for statistical significance (Hofer & Grandgenett, 2012). Interestingly, the researchers noted that it was easier to code the reflection statements as opposed to the lesson plans, because the reflections were more detailed and offered a more robust rationale for the decisions regarding instruction, and student thinking was more transparent within the written reflections. This may be a consideration when using the rubric to evaluate lesson plans to measure TPACK and its components.

Across the data sources, the TPK code was significantly higher than TCK or TPACK. Researchers note that this may be a function of the reflection prompts that asked students to detail an example of the successful use of educational technology in their subject area and to consider when the use of technology in teaching is appropriate or not (Hofer & Grandgenett, 2012). According to the authors, "To more closely investigate participants' relative emphasis or reliance on TPK, the prompts could perhaps be more directed to more clearly elicit their thinking" (Hofer & Grandgenett, 2012, p. 101). The study also found that while the quantitative measure of TPACK (Schmidt et al., 2009) displayed an increase, or growth, over time, the qualitative measures, including the TIAI, showed a dip during the spring semester in which student teaching took place. However, the authors note that all lessons showed adequate TPACK, with an overall mean of 2.91 out of 4.0, with a target score of 3.0 in each area of the instrument.

Overall, the study conducted by Hofer and Grandgenett (2012) demonstrated that their rubric could be used as an important component of a triangulated look at TPACK development over the course of a teacher education program through analyzing a survey instrument, lesson plans, and reflections/interviews. According to Hofer and Grandgenett (2012), "Within the context of this study, it appears that the methodology was useful for looking at TPACK development, and that there is the potential to further scale this approach across more students and a program of longer duration" (p. 101). Of note is that there was "remarkable consistency" among data sources, including those that were self-report as well as more "objective" measures such as lesson plans and reflections.

Learning Activities

Another qualitative mechanism for evaluating levels of TPACK is through examining the planning of instruction through the lens of activity types (Hofer & Harris, 2009). Hofer and Harris (2009) outline the five basic instructional decision actions made by teachers when planning a particular lesson or learning event:

- Choosing learning goals
- Making practical pedagogical decisions about the nature of the learning experience
- Selecting and sequencing appropriate activity types to combine to form the learning experience
- Selecting formative and summative assessment strategies that will reveal what and how well students are learning
- Selecting tools and resources that will best help students to benefit from the learning experience being planned

Learning activity types serve as a mechanism of planning and are used to create and detail how a planned lesson is designed to meet state and national standards. As Hofer and Harris (2009) explained:

> Each activity type captures what is most essential about the structure of a particular kind of learning action as it relates to what students do when engaged in that particular learning-related activity (e.g., "group discussion;" "role play;" "fieldtrip"). Activity types are combined to create lesson plans, projects and units.
>
> (p. 101)

What is useful about activity types is that the uses of specific educational technology tools are not made until critical learning outcomes and content activities have been determined. This ensures that selecting the technologies best serves the learning goals of the activity rather than taking on a "technocentric" focus and are simply being implemented for the sake of technology. The first step is for teachers to become skilled in developing and integrating technology-enriched learning activity types in a specific content area. Then, they work toward selecting various learning activities types to combine and to build their TPACK in the process. Harris, Mishra, and Koehler (2009) see significant potential in this approach because it is content-driven by the structure of the activity within each disciplinary discourse, thus moving away from the risk of becoming "technocentric."

Classifying and describing these activity types among the various content areas to create taxonomies has taken a significant amount of time and effort and is in large part due to the work completed by Hofer and Harris (2009). According to the researchers, just within social studies, there are 44 learning activity types that have been categorized into either student knowledge building or student knowledge expression. Within the 17 knowledge-building activity types, there is a spectrum from more general kinds of activities, such as reading and discussing text, to activities that are more content-related, such as sequencing events or creating a timeline. The 27 student knowledge expression tasks break into either convergent types that have students demonstrate their knowledge in similar ways or divergent types that encourage students to display their individualized understandings of the content (Harris & Hofer, 2011). In addition to social studies, taxonomies also exist for K–6 literacy, mathematics, music, physical education, science, secondary English/language arts, social studies, visual arts, and world languages (Harris et al., 2010). These taxonomies contain sample activity types together with possible matched technology tools to support learning. Useful resources are made accessible via the Learning Activity Type Wiki, available at http://activitytypes.wm.edu (Harris & Hofer, 2011).

Although taxonomies provide an excellent foundation for beginning to integrate technology into lessons in a meaningful way, through combining activity types into more intricate lessons and groups of lessons, or units, the affordances of organizing the learning activities can be realized. The goal in identifying, classifying, and sharing these activities is to provide teachers and teacher educators with a wide range of curriculum-based learning activities, together with the possible ways that various technology tools can be used to support each learning activity (Harris et al., 2009). Once identified, teachers can more readily select among the learning activities to tailor their instruction to meet the learning needs of students, along with the possible constraints, such as access to technology resources, that need to be considered in order to successfully implement the use of technology to support curriculum-based content (Harris et al., 2009). Through teachers' careful selections among activity types and the creative ways in which they combine activities, researchers are able to examine their unit plans, along with additional data sources such as reflections on their planning and interview data, to examine TPACK among practicing teachers (Harris & Hofer, 2011).

Using this approach, Harris and Hofer (2011) interviewed seven veteran social studies teachers from six states who were participating in TPACK-based professional development over the course of five months. They documented the teachers' TPACK at the beginning and at the conclusion of the experience, focusing on how/why teachers combined content, pedagogy, and technology to create their units. Using an interpretivist qualitative methodology (Corbin & Strauss, 2008), the researchers examined the data to develop common data units, codes, definitions, and interpretations, using the underlying lesson idea for the unit of analysis. Harris and Hofer analyzed teachers' units, along with their pre- and post-written reflections for evidence of PCK, TCK, TPK, and TPACK and changes of these constructs and created data summaries for each area, noting individual descriptions of planning processes.

Among the findings, participating teachers considered the nature of the content and then paired learning activities based on this assessment as opposed to students' learning needs. While little evidence of TCK was found, teachers expressed that content was the driving force in the selection of resources/materials to be used. Rather than seeing technology as a means to fundamentally change the instructional approach, teachers saw it as an extension of the lesson/unit. In terms of TPK, planning decisions were distributed between how pedagogy and technology interacted. When it came to TPACK, participating teachers considered the content they needed to convey, their views and beliefs about how best to relate this content to their students in an engaging manner, and then how various technological tools could be used to support the learning process. In this study, "fit" was also a major theme, and the authors posited that "fit" was how the teachers conceptualized and operationalized TPACK (Harris & Hofer, 2011). This notion of "fit" is an important aspect to identifying and measuring TPACK, as it represents an effective consideration of the curriculum, pedagogical strategies, and digital or nondigital technologies (Hofer & Grandgenett, 2012). As a result of the professional development conducted as part of the study, teachers reported being more aware of the many varied options for "technology-enhanced" learning activities and planned to use a wider range of learning activities supported by technology in their future teaching (Harris & Hofer, 2011). The authors note that, "The results of this study suggest that a content-based, activity-types approach to technically inclusive instructional planning is compatible with existing approaches to teaching" (Harris & Hofer, 2011, p. 226).

The learning activity types approach helps teachers integrate technology in a way that is content-driven, is focused on student needs, and leverages the affordances of the technology to support the curriculum (Harris et al., 2010). This is important because it helps move teachers from only considering pedagogical content knowledge to contemplating how the affordances of digital and nondigital technologies could support student learning through curriculum-based content (Harris et al., 2009). It is also practical in the sense that teachers center their planning around curriculum goals first, and then consider possible learning activities. By utilizing this planning approach, researchers can classify lesson/unit artifacts created by teachers, together with gathering teacher reflections on the process and, finally, interviewing teachers regarding the rationale behind their instructional selections. Analyzing these data using qualitative methods can present a more holistic depiction of TPACK levels and their changes over time and/or as part of a specific intervention.

Design Tasks

Along with analyzing lesson/unit artifacts among teachers, the application of this approach can be applied to designers at the university level as well. Koehler, Mishra, and Yahya (2007) focused on the conversations of what they deemed "design talk" to examine the type of dialogue that takes place in design teams as they work to address the challenges of integrating

TPACK using authentic design problems, or the *learning technology by design* process. The attempt of this study was to better understand the process and mechanisms by which TPACK evolved. Through the development of an online course, the researchers gathered field notes of two different groups as they engaged in design discussions, together with emails sent between group members, notes/artifacts created by the groups, and ongoing check-in surveys as a means of measuring progress. A content analysis of the field notes served as the primary analysis. Researchers created a TPACK-based protocol for coding the field notes from selected weeks within the beginning, middle, and end of the course. Using each of the TPACK domains as codes, they conducted a systematic quantitative analysis of the occurrence of T, P, C, TP, TPC, and TPACK. The researchers found that both groups progressed from considering technology, pedagogy, and content as separate, independent areas to a more integrated view. The qualitative analysis allowed for visualization of how the design talk evolved over time to include "the development of deeper understandings of the complex web of relationships between content, pedagogy and technology and the contexts within which they function" (p. 758).

Design tasks have also been used with pre-service teachers to examine evidence of their TPACK in instructional planning and decision-making. Graham, Borup, and Smith (2012) provided 133 pre-service teachers with a specific content-related, grade-level objective and then had them design a corresponding learning activity that implemented the use of digital technology. Students were then asked why they chose to use the technology in the way they described. The advantage of this approach was that it offered pre-service teachers several opportunities to practice instructional decision-making and to examine how they planned to use technology to support their teaching.

To analyze the design tasks of pre-service teachers, the researchers used open coding based on students' rationales and evidence of TPACK. Through a recursive process of meeting, comparing codes, and identifying themes, the researchers attained thematic saturation to develop a codebook. Researchers then selected 200 of the nearly 800 design tasks at random, distributed over the pre- and post-assessments along with the four content areas. These tasks were examined for evidence of six major coding areas: one for technological knowledge—TK.tg (technology general); two for technological pedagogical knowledge—TPK.sg (knowledge of general instructional strategies) and TPK.lg (knowledge of general learner characteristics); and three for TPACK as a whole—TPACK.sc (content-specific instructional strategies), TPACK.lc (knowledge of learner content understanding), and TPACK.rt (knowledge of transforming content representations for teaching) (see Graham et al., 2012, Appendix I, Table A). Researchers were able to reach 100% inter-rater reliability through meeting to resolve discrepancies (Graham et al., 2012). From this study, 48% of codes were attributed to technological pedagogical knowledge, 42% were related to TPACK, and 10% related to technical knowledge.

The design task study conducted by Graham et al. (2012) represents two important contributions to a qualitative approach to research. First, although the definitions provided for each component of TPACK continue to be elaborated and refined, often enough detail for distinguishing between and among TK, TPK, and TPACK within coding schemes is lacking. According to the authors, "These boundaries highlight the evolution of the educational technology field and the growing importance of content-specific applications of technology... The current research provides insight for researchers attempting to make such distinctions" (Graham et al., 2012, p. 542). A second addition is the articulation of various themes pertaining to the rationale/reasoning of instructional decision making as students' decisions relate to TPACK. Unfortunately, content-specific strategies (TPACK.sc) were the least identified. The researchers posit that this may be a function of sequencing of the content-focused methods courses within the teacher education program (Graham et al., 2012).

Through design task analysis using TPACK as a lens, Graham et al. (2012) were able to qualitatively assess how pre-service teachers went about making instructional decisions and how they planned to integrate technology as a part of their future teaching. This type of analysis can help to determine teacher education program needs, particularly when it comes to educational technology. Examining TPACK among instructional design tasks can help programs recognize what is working well as well as what needs to be improved. Graham et al. (2012) suggest that, "The findings include implications not only for *what* should be emphasized in technology integration courses but also for *when* technology integration should be taught and *who* should be teaching it" [emphasis in original] (p. 544).

Case-Based Approaches

A similar approach to using design tasks, lesson plans, and lesson type activities to measure a TPACK is the use of a case study, particularly during the process of preparing pre-service teachers. According to Kinuthia et al. (2010), "Case-based learning creates a student-driven learning environment in which a case serves as the focal point for a particular learning objective." (p. 648). Implementing a case study approach involves having students analyze a provided case through reading or viewing (in the case of a video-based case), answering reflective questions, discussing the nuances of the case in small groups, generating a report of their findings relative to the case, and finally, writing an individual reflection (Brantley-Dias et al., 2007).

The case-based method was used to examine pedagogical technology integration content knowledge (PTICK), a construct closely related to TPACK but that also includes reflective and community knowledge. Discussing the qualitative assessment of PTICK is included in this chapter because of its close connection to TPACK, together with the unique approach presented through using a case-based learning strategy to foster the development of pedagogical content knowledge for technology integration (Kinuthia et al., 2010). For further discussion of the nuances of PTICK, see Brantley-Dias et al. (2007).

Using a content analysis approach (Merriam, 1998), Brantley-Dias et al. (2007) classified concepts from 14 English education and 19 science education students enrolled in a 45-credit intensive alternative teacher licensure program. Data sources consisted of students' initial responses, case reflections, and reports generated from cases provided generated as part of their educational technology course, using content-focused cases provided in *Educational Technology in Action: Problem-based Exercises for Technology Integration*

(Roblyer, 2004). The researchers developed a common coding mechanism, discussed analysis, and established inter-rater reliability. Once codes were established, themes and patterns were identified within and across cases. Examining multiple data sources offered a more holistic depiction and provided corroborating evidence to be able to triangulate the findings (Creswell, 1998).

Through their case study analysis, Brantley-Dias et al. (2007) found that pre-service teachers seemed to show the greatest growth increasing their PCK, their reflective knowledge and technology integration conceptual knowledge, or what could be considered TCK. Gains pertaining to self-efficacy and skills related to technical procedural knowledge were also evident. In addition, participants demonstrated growth in their understanding that ongoing professional development to stay current in procedural knowledge of integrating new technologies would be a requisite skill. Pre-service teachers also showed development in their technology integration conceptual knowledge, through responses focused on instructional strategies, planning, assessment, management, and student grouping specific to the implementation of technology in the classroom. The case analysis approach proved useful, not only with measuring what the authors identify as PTICK, but also as a reflective component for preparing future teachers. Through the case study process and by employing the use of a problem-centered approach, future teachers were able to consider content-specific teaching contexts that addressed pedagogical considerations together with the real-world challenges of integrating technology in a classroom setting.

In a similar study, Kinuthia et al. (2010) examined eight pre-service math teachers who had undergraduate degrees in mathematics or a mathematics-related area and who were seeking licensure as part of an alternative licensure program. Within their educational technology course, the instructors used the same text (Roblyer, 2004), which provided case-based scenarios. These cases included detailed depictions of secondary teachers who were dealing with various technology integration dilemmas. Pre-service teachers worked through the case-based scenarios by completing accompanying questions at the end of the description, a joint report based on small group discussions, and individual reflections. In addition to using these data sources, researchers also conducted a one-hour focus group interview at the end of the program designed to elicit responses regarding the efficacy of their coursework in helping them to integrate technology in their teaching.

Kinuthia et al. (2010) used content analysis (Merriam, 1998) to code relevant concepts and ideas within the artifacts created by the pre-service teachers. Three major themes were identified from the data: (1) cases as a tool to develop teacher identity as a technology integrator, (2) cases as a tool for assimilation and accommodation, and (3) cases as a tool for creating communities of practice. Overall, pre-service teachers showed growth in their pedagogical and reflective knowledge together with an awareness of the connection between the case analyses and their own learning experiences. As with the study by Brantley-Dias et al. (2007), the results from Kinuthia et al. (2010) provide a beginning for understanding the use of a case-based learning in the development of PTICK/TPACK as part of a teacher preparation program.

A different case study approach to examining teaching practice through the lens of TPACK is described by Groth, Spickler, Bergner, and Bardzell (2009). Using qualitative data, including teachers' written lesson plans, transcripts/videos of implemented lessons, reviews of lessons by faculty members, and recordings/transcripts of reflections about the implemented lessons, the researchers provide an example of a lesson study of TPACK, or LS-TPACK. Using this method, teachers first work together to construct a lesson that uses technology, which is subsequently reviewed by a supervising university faculty member. After teachers have integrated the feedback and revised the lesson, they then video record the delivery of the lesson in the actual classroom. Finally, teachers and faculty review the video together and reflect/debrief on the outcome. The LS-TPACK process produces a volume of qualitative data that is then used to create a case-study database (Yin, 2003). According to the researchers, one of the advantages with this approach is that it ties assessment of practice together with professional development, since teachers review possible changes in their practice during the assessment process. However, it is noted that measuring individual teacher knowledge is not feasible. Rather, the LS-TPACK method helps to identify the reasoning of groups of teachers, thus making it useful, particularly in schools that implement communities of practice (CoP) models (Lave & Wenger, 1991) to create such lesson study groups. Groth et al. (2009) see the LS-TPACK case study model as an excellent mechanism for gathering evidence to examine teaching practice and the development of TPACK among lesson study group members.

Case Development

Mouza and Karchmer-Klein (2013) use case development to apply TPACK to designing, enacting, and reflecting on the use of technology in the classroom. The researchers implemented case development through a four-stage case development process in which 58 pre-service teachers (1) took a technology inventory based on their field placement setting, (2) chose a lesson plan developed as part of their educational technology course that integrated the use of technology, (3) taught the selected lesson in their field placement, and finally (4) wrote a detailed case report including a case narrative along with analysis and reflection concerning the process. Researchers then evaluated the case reports together with their accompanying lesson plans, which allowed them to see how pre-service teachers conceptualize the interplay among technology, pedagogy, and content and the development of their TPACK during the process.

Mouza and Karchmer-Klein (2013) used the Technology Integration Assessment Rubric (Harris et al., 2010) to rate each lesson according to the rubric categories on a scale from 1 to 4. They also coded each case and lesson for evidence of TPACK, achieving 100% inter-rater reliability after meeting to resolve discrepancies. Mouza and Karchmer-Klein (2013) found that the pre-service teachers identified the interplay between content, pedagogy, and technology, or "fit" that TPACK represents as evidenced by the mean of 3.16 out of 4.0 on the Technology Integration Assessment Rubric. In addition, participants recognized content-based activities and the technology tools that could support learning. However, some future teachers expressed a disconnect between what was identified in their lesson plans and the implementation of the lesson in the classroom. While a lesson plan may have had a high rating on the Technology Integration Assessment Rubric, the case report could have shown disparities in their understanding and enactment of TPACK in their teaching (Mouza & Karchmer-Klein, 2013). This led the researchers to conclude that TPACK needs to be considered in relation to actual teaching rather than on solely a theoretical basis. They argue that lesson plans must be assessed in conjunction with their implementation in order to get an accurate portrayal of pre-service teachers' TPACK. Because TPACK is heavily impacted by the understanding of pedagogy with relationship to content and technology, case development proved to be an excellent mechanism for pre-service teachers to gain applied experience through planning technology-infused lessons, enacting these lessons, and then analyzing and reflecting on the process (Mouza & Karchmer-Klein, 2013).

Another case-based approach to measuring TPACK among four elementary (K–6) classroom teachers was used by Tai and Crawford (2014). The authors used a qualitative case study to analyze classroom observations and teacher interviews using a TPACK observation protocol and interview guide created for the study. Using grounded theory (Strauss & Corbin, 1998), the researchers started with open coding to identify codes and subsequent themes, based on the seven domains within the TPACK framework. They created a codebook that contained a definition for each code as well as examples and keywords from the data set. After each teacher observation and interview, the researchers revisited the codebook to analyze each new data source, adding new codes and themes as necessary. Tai and Crawford (2014) reported that the codebook contained 39 main codes (60 counting all subcodes) that represent the seven domains within the TPACK framework. This work continues to develop with the goal of developing an observation instrument that can be used to document observable TPACK behaviors used in K–12 classrooms. According to the researchers, "The value of designing such an instrument will help validate, with observed behaviors, how teachers are actually applying TPACK and how that knowledge is then used to facilitate classroom instruction and impact student learning" (p. 2655). Moving beyond self-report measures, the use of a case-study approach that implements observations together with interview responses assists scholars with the triangulation of data sources to gather evidence of teachers' TPACK and the impact that such knowledge has on classroom practice.

Analyzing real-world, authentic tasks is a valuable mechanism for evaluating TPACK. As discussed, these performance assessments include developing lesson plans, designing tasks, creating learning activities, and analyzing design problems using case-based approaches. Performance-based assessments allow researchers to probe the rationale behind teachers' thought processes. Teachers' decision-making is often reflected throughout their planning and is evident through artifacts along with justifications for instructional decisions. Performance assessments offer valid measures of investigating TPACK and exploring teacher knowledge, which may not be directly observable during live lessons. In addition, the analysis of artifacts goes further than self-report alone. As such, performance assessments are an important component to qualitatively examining TPACK among future and current educators.

Interview Measures

Interviews are another major important component of qualitative studies designed to measure TPACK. Interviews are comprised of a set of verbal questions posed by the interviewer and responded to by the participant (Koehler et al., 2012). In general, responses are archived through video recording, audio recording, and/or journaling and then transcribed for analysis. Typically, researchers use open coding to identify themes and patterns among the responses, and this analysis is used as a way to triangulate findings together with other data sources (Creswell, 2014). For example, Kinuthia et al. (2010) used focus group interviews as part of their case study approach to examining TPACK among pre-service teachers. Additional studies, such as Ozgün-Koca (2009), used the same questions in a semi-structured group interview as from an open-ended writing prompt asking 27 pre-service mathematics teachers about their beliefs on the use of graphing calculators in mathematics instruction. The TPACK framework was then used to code the ways in which pre-service teachers discussed their thoughts specific to the use of graphing calculators in mathematics instruction. Using both written responses together with in-person interview data presented an advantage:

> Although writings guaranteed that the pre-service teachers had sufficient private time to respond without pressure, interviews were added to provide an environment where group communication and interaction could be observed. Document analysis is strengthened when augmented with interviews. Thus, the two forms of data collection with different encounter levels provided rich sources of data for this study.
> (Ozgün-Koca, 2009, p. 213)

Ozgün-Koca found that when it came to exploring student learning and their approach to instruction in relationship to the TPACK framework, pre-service teachers viewed graphing calculators as effective visualization and transformational tools for teaching mathematical concepts.

Another example of using interviews to triangulate data for the purposes of measuring TPACK is found in a study by Jaipal and Figg (2010). Using interviews in conjunction with questionnaires and observations, the researchers interviewed four pre-service teachers. These data were used to debrief overall teaching experiences with technology during the participant's practicum and functioned as a triangulation mechanism for data gathered as part of the study. To analyze the gathered data, Jaipal and Figg (2010) used a cross-case analysis to examine field notes, observations, and transcriptions of video- and audio-recorded interviews to identify TK, TPK, and TCK. The researchers used these findings to help define and specify aspects of each of these constructs. TK was broken into general skill level with a specific tool, general comfort with the tool specific to the instructional goal, and awareness/attitude toward the continued need for professional development. TPK was made up of planning choices including activity choices, sequencing, and differentiation. In addition, a part of TPK was implementation involving preparation, classroom management, and modeling to and for students. Finally, TCK was comprised of matching tools to subject matter content and matching tools to subject matter teaching models (Jaipal & Figg, 2010). This enhanced definition of TK, TCK, and TPK help define the framework as a whole and have implications for teacher preparation programs. As the authors note:

> As shown by the findings, TPK involves many characteristics that should be addressed in teacher education courses prior to the practice teaching. Even though pre-service teachers may be very skilled in computer use (TK) and have a broad knowledge of the technology appropriate for their subject matter content (TCK), there is still a pedagogical component that is unique to technology-enhanced lessons (TPK).
>
> (Jaipal & Figg, 2010, p. 433)

In addition to using interview measures to examine the practices of pre-service teachers, other researchers have used this approach to study a constructivist-based professional development model. Williams, Foulger, and Wetzel (2010) conducted interviews of teacher education faculty members who had participated in a series of workshops to redesign and teach a unit that infused an innovative use of technology. The interview questions were deigned to map to each of the domains of the TPACK framework, and the data was analyzed through a grounded theory approach, using open coding (Strauss & Corbin, 1998) as well as constant comparison to examine if the response mapped to the intended TPACK domain. The researchers then compared responses across faculty members to determine additional subcategories and themes. In terms of TPACK, Williams et al. (2010) found that faculty who knew the content well and resigned their unit to enhance their course were those who were skilled at collaborative pedagogy to begin with, but indicated limited technology content knowledge. Through the introduction of Web 2.0 tools within the professional development model, faculty indicated the ability to effectively introduce social networking tools into their courses to build on the interconnected elements of technology, pedagogy, and content.

Along these lines, other studies have used interviews as the primary data source to explore how faculty integrate new understandings of technology with current practices of pedagogy and content while designing and teaching a new online course (Mishra, Peruski, & Koehler, 2007). Data consisted of three interviews: during the design process, midway while teaching the course, and finally, at the completion of the course. Additional data sources included observations of the design teams' work and of the faculty during the process together with artifacts consisting of various iterations of the development of the online course. The artifacts and observations were used to confirm or refute the interview data. Researchers reported reviewing the transcribed interviews multiple times and creating a cross-case chart that was organized using understandings of PC, TP, TC, and TPACK as constructs. Among the findings, Mishra et al. (2007) found that these constructs were not mutually exclusive; however, there was a clear pattern of emerging TPACK. They concluded that while faculty began with robust PCK, the requirement for them to use technological tools required them to rethink the content, pedagogy, and technology and, in particular, the relationships between all three domains. The authors conclude that TPACK was a useful framework for studying teachers' integration of technology, content, and pedagogical knowledge as it developed over time.

Interviews have also been utilized to test the validity of development TPACK performance assessments as well as observation tools. Harris, Grandgenett, and Hofer (2012) used interviews of 12 teachers who were experienced in using technology to test the validity and reliability of their lesson plan instrument. This was done in large part because of the annotated nature of the teachers' lesson plans, making it difficult to assess TPACK due to a lack of data. For each interview, trained coders who were experienced technology users themselves used the Technology Integration Assessment Rubric to evaluate the levels of TPACK within the interview responses. Harris, Grandgenett, and Hofer (2012) indicate that through the coding of the interviews, the scoring teachers reinforced the ability of the rubric to adequately assess the level of technology integration that was discerned from the lesson plans, offering suggestions for improvement that were implemented. Using the rankings of the teachers, researchers were able to then generate inter-rater reliability, internal consistency, and test–retest reliability to conclude that the Technology Integration Assessment Rubric has strong reliability.

Interviews conducted as part of qualitative studies measuring TPACK offer an excellent mechanism for triangulating data or to validate an instrument, particularly when examining design tasks and lesson plans to explore teachers' thought processes and rationales behind their instructional decisions (Hofer et al., 2011). Together with performance-based assessments and interview measures, observation tools are another key component, particularly when it comes to documenting "TPACK in action." The following section describes key validated observation tools used to measure TPACK.

Observation Tools

In response to the inherent challenges of using self-report instruments to measure teacher knowledge, researchers have also worked to develop validated and reliable rubrics designed to be used in classroom observation to help assess the extent to which TPACK is evident in teaching. Observation is an extremely useful method for documenting what is occurring in the classroom setting. To measure TPACK in practice, Hofer, Grandgenett, Harris, and Swan (2011) adapted their TPACK-based Technology Integration Assessment Rubric based on its previous success to develop the Technology Integration Observation Instrument (Harris et al., 2010). Both TPACK instruments are made freely available via Creative Commons license at http://activitytypes.wm.edu/Assessments/assessmentsindex.html.

The observation rubric is geared toward both live instruction as well as video-recorded lessons. In the user guide, the developers note that the instrument was created to assess the level of technology integration in an observed lesson. However, it cautions that the rubric is best used in conjunction with other data sources of teaching effectiveness, because the instrument is specifically designed to measure curriculum-based technology integration (User Guide: Technology Integration Observation Instrument, 2011). Seven TPACK researchers evaluated the rubric to establish construct and face validity. Hofer et al. (2011) established a reliable instrument to evaluate TPACK within classroom teaching: "Our testing results suggest that this is a valid and reliable instrument to use to assess enacted TPACK in observed lessons taught by either pre-service or in-service teachers" (p. 43).

Although a video recording of a lesson only captures content in the specific frame and the recording cannot document a number of variables, such as school/classroom climate, there are advantages to using the Technology Integration Observation Instrument to analyze video-recorded lessons. These include offering a shared data source for viewers, the ability to concentrate on the analysis of key aspects of the observation, the ability to view a lesson as many times as needed by multiple researchers, and helping to standardized the process of observation (Brunvand, 2010). With these affordances in mind, Hofer et al. (2011) note that the data garnered from the Technology Integration Observation Instrument are more rich and complex using video than the data generated from a static written lesson plan. As a result, scoring could either be more or less consistent. While video recording may provide greater detail and a more accurate picture of actual technology integration, there is a larger time commitment to viewing, reviewing, and scoring a video-recorded lesson, which could negatively impact the instrument's reliability. Those who used both the Technology Integration Observation Instrument and the Technology Integration Assessment Rubric reported the richness of data available from observed teaching as opposed to what can be gleaned from a written lesson plan. As a result, Hofer et al. (2011) recommend using multiple data types and sources to help build a more robust understanding of a teacher's "TPACK in action."

Observation tools have long been used to garner insights into teacher practice. Through the use of validated instruments, observation protocols have been implemented to explore TPACK within live lessons as well as within video recordings of lessons. As discussed, each observation format has various positive aspects as well as drawbacks. The use of observation tools represents researchers' efforts to explore TPACK beyond solely self-report measures. Used in conjunction with performance assessments, observation protocols can yield in-depth and detailed insights into teachers' TPACK, particularly when examining classroom application.

Learning About TPACK From a Qualitative Perspective

A variety of insights can be gleaned from examining the current research on evaluating TPACK using qualitative measures. First and foremost, TPACK has proved to be a useful lens for researchers in examining the development of pre-service and in-service teachers when it comes to the meaningful use of technology to transform practice (Harris et al., 2010; Hofer & Harris, 2010; Koehler & Mishra, 2009). It has provided the ability for teacher education programs to analyze their approach to technology integration (Graham et al., 2012) as well as to provide pre-service teachers an excellent means through which they can reflect on their planning and practice (Groth et al., 2009; Mouza & Karchmer-Klein, 2013). However, the framework remains a work in progress, as researchers attempt to further refine, clarify, and apply each of the constructs to better understand the complexities of effective teaching (Graham, Borup, & Smith, 2012).

What is also clear from the qualitative literature is that multiple measures and data sources are needed in order to get a better understanding of TPACK, as well as how the framework affects actual practice, or "TPACK in action" (Hofer et al., 2011). The qualitative research in this area shows that targeted interventions, such as professional development and teacher education programs specifically addressing technology, pedagogy, and content, can and do have a positive impact on teachers and their practice. It is important to note that the inherent nature of qualitative research is heavily bound contextually. This, coupled with the difficulty of measuring a construct that is still being defined and interpreted, makes generalizing about the framework difficult and complex from a qualitative perspective.

From the large quantity of research that has been generated since the articulation of TPACK, one of the major challenges has been to define and operationalize the components of the framework (Archambault & Crippen, 2009; Brantley-Dias & Ertmer, 2013; Graham, 2011). Qualitative research in this area has revealed issues with making distinctions between and among the constructs of TPK, TCK, and overall TPACK (Brantley-Dias et al., 2007; Hofer & Grandgenett, 2012). In certain cases, TPK was found higher than TCK or TPACK (Graham et al., 2012; Hofer & Grandgenett, 2012). In other studies, little evidence of TCK was found, even though participants indicated that the content was the impetus for selecting various resources as part of their lesson (Harris & Hofer, 2011). As a result, the idea of finding "fit" was developed within qualitative research to represent how teachers effectively considered content, pedagogical strategies, and digital or non-digital technologies (Harris & Hofer, 2011; Hofer & Grandgenett, 2012). Being able to better distinguish the constructs of the framework, including "fit," is an essential component necessary when attempting to measure and explore the application of TPACK in practice. This is important as the field works to move the framework toward having additional value beyond a theoretical sense.

Once clear definitions are in place, researchers also need to describe applied coding schemes pertaining to the framework. While the definitions provided for each component of TPACK continue to be honed and further described, many studies do not provide enough detail for distinguishing between and among the overlapping areas of the TPACK framework. Graham et al. (2012) mention this issue specifically and seek to address it by carefully articulating their coding mechanism to help other researchers make such distinctions, particularly when it comes to identifying TPACK within the context of various content areas. Jaipal and Figg (2010) also break down components of the framework into specific areas and in doing so, help to further clarify TK, TCK, and TPK that comprise TPACK as a whole. The methodology of qualitative research, including specific coding schemes, together with the development of instruments and rubrics designed to measure TPACK, needs to be detailed such that future researchers can apply them in a systematic manner and build on existing work in this area to move the framework forward.

Another major component is the creation and validation of instruments that can be used in a variety of instructional settings. For example, in constructing an instrument or rubric, such as the Technology Integration Assessment Rubric (Harris et al., 2010), key criticisms involve the use of non-descriptive terms such as "strongly," "partially," and "marginally," which are hard to apply consistently. Another debate surrounds the issue of using a general rubric to measure TCK without reference to using technology to teach a given content area

(Brantley-Dias & Ertmer, 2013). What is needed is the development of validated qualitative instruments within the major content areas that can help teacher educators foster the effective use of technology specific to each discipline.

Along these lines, evaluating artifacts with enough detail to get a sense of what is intended and the reasoning behind such intention using the TPACK framework is also challenging. This is a problem when conducting artifact analysis, such as evaluating lesson plans for aspects of TPACK. Hofer and Grandgenett (2012) note that the scoring of reflection statements was easier than lesson plans because the reflections contained more detailed information including a rationale for instructional decisions, allowing a glimpse at pre-service teachers' thought processes. Harris et al. (2010) also recognize the difficulty with utilizing the Technology Integration Assessment Rubric without detailed lessons: "For this instrument to be maximally useful, the planning documents being evaluated need to be written in enough detail so that scorers can make well-informed choices in each of the rubric's four dimensions" (Harris et al., 2010, p. 3838). In order to apply validated instruments or to code using a consistent, coherent system to measure TPACK and its related constructs, researchers must ensure that there is enough specificity in gathered artifacts including lesson plans, design tasks, case studies, reflections, and the like.

In addition to the difficulty of defining and measuring TPACK across multiple contexts and gathering artifacts with enough detail, another area for further consideration is using the framework to both describe the knowledge of in-service and pre-service teachers along with then being able to evaluate the enactment of that knowledge in practice. Mouza and Karchmer-Klein (2013) highlight this dilemma, arguing that to effectively assess TPACK among pre-service teachers, artifacts such as lesson plans need to be evaluated together with their implemented versions. This is because well-developed lesson plans could provide certain indicated levels, while the ability to translate the knowledge into action may signify others. The potential disconnect between what teachers know and what they are able to do could be indicative of the articulation problems within the framework, specifically when it comes to qualitative approaches to measure TPACK among pre- and in-service teachers. However, this can be mitigated through the use of multiple data sources to triangulate findings, and further clarification should be included as part of the focus of future research.

Conclusion

Since its inception, TPACK has presented a comprehensive conceptual framework that has unified the field of educational technology and has been able to refocus the emphasis on content as a major component of effective technology integration (Mishra & Koehler, 2006). The development and application of TPACK has gained traction among researchers and practitioners alike and has experienced tremendous growth in a relatively short period of time (Cox & Graham, 2009). Along with this growth, qualitative measures have also increased, consisting predominantly of performance assessments of various kinds, interviews, and observation protocols to evaluate TPACK among current and future teachers. There are many important recommendations for teacher education programs and professional development programs that emerge from this literature. What is significant is the contextual nature of qualitative research and the opportunity and need for additional research to further the use of the framework in a variety of settings, particularly within specific content areas. Qualitative methods and reflective practices will be essential in seeking to develop teachers who understand and can use the affordances of technology to transform content to build student understanding.

References

Angeli, C., & Valanides, N. (2009). Epistemological and methodological issues for the conceptualization, development, and assessment of ICT-TPCK: Advances in technological pedagogical content knowledge (TPCK). *Computers & Education, 52*(1), 154–168.

Archambault, L. M., & Crippen, K. J. (2009). Examining TPACK among K–12 online distance educators in the United States. *Contemporary Issues in Technology and Teacher Education, 9*(1). Retrieved from http://www.citejournal.org/vol9/iss1/general/article2.cfm

Brantley-Dias, L., & Ertmer, P. A. (2013). Goldilocks and TPACK: Is the construct 'just right?' *Journal of Research on Technology in Education, 46*(2), 103–128.

Brantley-Dias, L., Kinuthia, W., Shoffner, M. B., de Castro, C., & Rigole, N. J. (2007). Developing pedagogical technology integration content knowledge in pre-service teachers: A case study approach. *Journal of Computing in Teacher Education, 23*(4), 143–150.

Britten, J. S., & Cassady, J. C. (2005). The technology integration assessment instrument: Understanding planned use of technology by classroom teachers. *Computers in the Schools, 22*(3), 49–61.

Brunvand, S. (2010). Best practices for producing video content for teacher education. *Contemporary Issues in Technology and Teacher Education, 10*(2), 247–256.

Corbin, J., & Strauss, A. (2008). *Basics of qualitative research: Techniques to developing grounded theory* (3rd ed.). Los Angeles, CA: SAGE Publications.

Cox, S., & Graham, C. R. (2009). Diagramming TPACK in practice: Using an elaborated model of the TPACK framework to analyze and depict teacher knowledge. *TechTrends: Linking Research & Practice to Improve Learning, 53*(5), 60–69.

Creswell, J. (1998). *Qualitative inquiry and research design: Choosing among five traditions.* Thousand Oaks, CA: SAGE Publications.

Creswell, J. (2014). *Research design: Qualitative, quantitative, and mixed methods approaches* (4th ed.). Thousand Oaks, CA: SAGE Publications.

Glesne, C. (2011). *Becoming qualitative researchers: An introduction.* Boston: Pearson.

Graham, C. R. (2011). Theoretical considerations for understanding technological pedagogical content knowledge (TPACK). *Computers & Education, 57*(3), 1953–1960.

Graham, C. R., Borup, J., & Smith, N. B. (2012). Using TPACK as a framework to understand teacher candidates' technology integration decisions. *Journal of Computer Assisted Learning, 28*(6), 530–546.

Groth, R., Spickler, D., Bergner, J., & Bardzell, M. (2009). A qualitative approach to assessing technological pedagogical content knowledge. *Contemporary Issues in Technology and Teacher Education, 9*(4). Retrieved from http://www.citejournal.org/vol9/iss4/mathematics/article1.cfm

Harris, J., & Hofer, M. (2009). Instructional planning activity types as vehicles for curriculum-based TPACK development. In C. D. Maddux (Ed.), *Research highlights in technology and teacher education 2009* (pp. 99–108). Chesapeake, VA: Society for Information Technology in Teacher Education (SITE).

Harris, J.B., Grandgenett, N.F., & Hofer, M.J. (2012). Testing an instrument using structured interviews to assess experienced teachers' TPACK. In C.D. Maddux, D. Gibson, & R. Rose (Eds.), *Research highlights in technology and teacher education* (pp. 15–22). Chesapeake, VA: Society for Information Technology & Teacher Education (SITE).

Harris, J.B., & Hofer, M.J. (2011). Technological pedagogical content knowledge (TPACK) in action: A descriptive study of secondary teachers' curriculum-based, technology-related instructional planning. *Journal of Research on Technology in Education, 43*(3), 211–229.

Harris, J.B., Hofer, M.J., Blanchard, M.R., Grandgenett, N.F., Schmidt, D.A., van Olphen, M., & Young, C.A. (2010). "Grounded" technology integration: Instructional planning using curriculum-based activity type taxonomies. *Journal of Technology and Teacher Education, 18*(4), 573–605.

Harris, J.B., Mishra, P., & Koehler, M.J. (2009). Teachers' technological pedagogical content knowledge and learning activity types: Curriculum-based technology integration reframed. *Journal of Research on Technology in Education, 41*(4), 393–416.

Hofer, M., & Grandgenett, N. (2012). TPACK development in teacher education: A longitudinal study of preservice teachers in a secondary M.A.Ed. program. *Journal of Research on Technology in Education, 45*(1), 83–106.

Hofer, M., Grandgenett, N., Harris, J., & Swan, K. (2011). Testing a TPACK-based technology integration observation instrument. In M. Koehler & P. Mishra (Eds.), *Proceedings of Society for Information Technology & Teacher Education International Conference 2011* (pp. 4352–4359). Chesapeake, VA: AACE.

Hofer, M., & Harris, J. (2010). Differentiating TPACK development: Using learning activity types with in-service and pre-service teachers. In C.D. Maddux, D. Gibson, & B. Dodge (Eds.). *Research highlights in technology and teacher education* (pp. 295–302). Chesapeake, VA: Society for Information Technology and Teacher Education.

Hofer, M., & Harris, J. (2011). Learning activity types wiki. Retrieved from http://activitytypes.wmwikis.net

Jaipal, K., & Figg, C. (2010). Unpacking the "Total PACKage": Emergent TPACK characteristics from a study of pre-service teachers teaching with technology. *Journal of Technology and Teacher Education, 18*(3), 415–441.

Kinuthia, W., Brantley-Dias, L., & Clarke, P.A.J. (2010). Development of pedagogical technology integration content knowledge in preparing mathematics pre-service teachers: The role of instructional case analyses and reflection. *Journal of Technology and Teacher Education, 18*(4), 645–669.

Koehler, M., & Mishra, P. (2005). What happens when teachers design educational technology? The development of technological pedagogical content knowledge. *Educational Computing Research, 32*(2), 131–152.

Koehler, M., & Mishra, P. (2009). What is technological pedagogical content knowledge? *Contemporary Issues in Technology and Teacher Education, 9*(1), 60–70.

Koehler, M.J., Mishra, P., & Yahya, K. (2007). Tracing the development of teacher knowledge in a design seminar: Integrating content, pedagogy, & technology. *Computers & Education, 49*(3), 740–762.

Koehler, M.J., Shin, T.S., & Mishra, P. (2012). How do we measure TPACK? Let me count the ways. In R.N. Ronau, C.R. Rakes, & M.L. Niess (Eds.), *Educational technology, teacher knowledge, and classroom impact: A research handbook on frameworks and approaches* (pp. 16–31). Hershey, PA: IGI Global.

Lave, J., & Wenger, E. (1991). *Situated learning: Legitimate peripheral participation.* New York: Cambridge University Press.

Marshall, C., & Rossman, G. B. (2011). *Designing qualitative research* (5th ed.). Thousand Oaks, CA: SAGE Publications.

Merriam, S. B. (1998). *Qualitative research and case study applications in education*. San Francisco: Jossey-Bass.

Mishra, P., & Koehler, M. J. (2006). Technological pedagogical content knowledge: A new framework for teacher knowledge. *Teachers College Record, 108*(6), 1017–1054.

Mishra, P., Peruski, L., & Koehler, M. (2007). Developing technological pedagogical content knowledge (TPCK) through teaching online. In R. Carlsen et al. (Eds.), *Proceedings of Society for Information Technology & Teacher Education International Conference 2007* (pp. 2208–2213). Chesapeake, VA: Association for the Advancement of Computing in Education (AACE).

Mouza, C., & Karchmer-Klein, R. (2013). Promoting and assessing pre-service teachers' technological pedagogical content knowledge (TPACK) in the context of case development. *Journal of Educational Computing Research, 48*(2), 127–152.

Niess, M. L. (2008). Guiding pre-service teachers in developing TPCK. In AACTE Committee on Innovation and Technology (Ed.), *Handbook of technological pedagogical content knowledge (TPCK) for educators* (pp. 223–250). New York: Routledge.

Ozgün-Koca, S. A. (2009). The views of pre-service teachers about the strengths and limitations of the use of graphing calculators in mathematics instruction. *Journal of Technology and Teacher Education, 17*(2), 203–227.

Roblyer, M. (2004). *Educational technology in action: Problem-based exercises for technology integration*. Upper Saddle River, NJ: Pearson/Merrill Prentice Hall.

Schmidt, D. A., Baran, E., Thompson, A. D., Koehler, M. J., Mishra, P., & Shin, T. (2009). Technological pedagogical content knowledge (TPACK): The development and validation of an assessment instrument for pre-service teachers. *Journal of Research on Technology in Education, 42*(2), 123–149.

Shulman, L. (1986). Paradigms and research programs in the study of teaching: A contemporary perspective. In M. C. Wittrock (Ed.), *Handbook of research on teaching* (3rd ed., pp. 3–36). New York: MacMillan.

Strauss, A., & Corbin, J. (1998). *Basics of qualitative research: Techniques and procedures for developing grounded theory*. Thousand Oaks, CA: SAGE Publications.

Tai, S.J.D., & Crawford, D. (2014). Conducting classroom observations to understand TPACK: Moving beyond self-reported data. In M. Searson & M. Ochoa (Eds.), *Proceedings of Society for Information Technology & Teacher Education International Conference 2014* (pp. 2661–2664). Chesapeake, VA: Association for the Advancement of Computing in Education (AACE).

User Guide: Technology Integration Observation Instrument (2011). Retrieved from Learning Activity Types Wiki at http://activitytypes.wmwikis.net/Assessments

Williams, M. K., Foulger, T., & Wetzel, K. (2010). Aspiring to reach 21st century ideals: Teacher educators' experiences in developing their TPACK. In D. Gibson & B. Dodge (Eds.), *Proceedings of Society for Information Technology & Teacher Education International Conference 2010* (pp. 3960–3967). Chesapeake, VA: Association for the Advancement of Computing in Education (AACE).

Yin, R. K. (2003). *Case study research: Design and methods* (3rd ed.). Thousand Oaks, CA: SAGE Publications.

6

A Review of the Quantitative Measures of Technological Pedagogical Content Knowledge (TPACK)

Ching Sing Chai, Joyce Hwee Ling Koh, Chin-Chung Tsai

Introduction

Quantitative measurements can be used to support the construct validation of theoretical frameworks in education, to examine the relationships among theoretical constructs, and to assess intervention outcomes, as well as to understand the specific perceptions and efficacies of teachers and students.

Since the publication of the first few TPACK journal articles (see Angeli & Valanides, 2005; Mishra & Koehler, 2006), quantitative measures of TPACK have developed rapidly. Many researchers have attempted to verify, modify, and refine the TPACK framework, as well as to expand its applicability for enhancing pedagogical practices. In this review, the authors aim to consolidate the important contributions of quantitative-oriented journal articles of TPACK and examine emerging trends such as rubric development. Gaps in the current research as well as possible future directions for developing the quantitative measures of TPACK are discussed.

Method

Identifying Journal Articles

The focus of this review was restricted to peer-reviewed journal articles using quantitative measures of TPACK. A total of 22 papers that used quantitative measures of TPACK were identified from two recent reviews of TPACK (Chai, Koh, & Tsai, 2013b; Voogt, Fisser, Pareja Roblin, Tondeur, & van Braak, 2013). In addition to these 22 papers, the authors searched the Scopus database, Education Research Complete, and ERIC for other refereed journal articles that were published between 2011 and 2014 and that were not included in the two previous reviews. This review is therefore limited to what the authors could identify within the stated databases. The keywords used for searching for the articles were "technological pedagogical content knowledge" and "TPACK OR TPCK." All identified articles were reviewed, and articles reporting quantitative results were retained. For studies that employed mixed methods, only the quantitative portion was retained for analysis. In total, 45 journal articles were identified for this review.

Coding Scheme Employed

A coding scheme consisting of three main categories was adapted from Chai et al.'s (2013b) review. These were (a) basic data: authors, year of publication, journal, localities of study; (b) research methods: research approaches (quantitative or mixed method), research design (design-based research, case study, intervention, survey study, instrument validation, etc.), research questions, participants, instrument used, variables investigated (including demographic variables), data collected, method of analysis; and (c) content analyses: research context (pre-service, in-service, others such as students' perceptions of teachers' TPACK), technology, pedagogy, and content area. A research assistant first coded the articles based on the above. The researchers subsequently reviewed the coding. As the coding was based objectively on what was reported in the articles, there were few disputes, and those that did arise were resolved by the researchers. The researchers subsequently categorized and summarized the studies to date, with specific foci on what has been achieved and what needs more attention due to the gaps in the current studies or for TPACK development.

Cox and Graham's (2009) work on delimiting the TPACK factors, especially with regard to the boundaries of the overlapping TPACK factors, was adopted when the survey items were assessed for face validity. Currently, TCK seems to be the most unclear construct, and this chapter adopts the position that it is technologically represented content knowledge without pedagogical consideration.

Findings

The findings for the review are organized into three major sections. The first section examines surveys that have been created and validated to date, as well as how they have been used to explore interrelationships among the TPACK factors and other factors, such as teachers' beliefs and demographic variables, and as a means of evaluating course outcomes. The second section reviews measurements of teachers' TPACK performance through the analysis of products or artifacts, as well as comprehension tests. The third section discusses the possibilities of measuring design processes for creating TPACK among teachers and educators.

TPACK Survey Studies

Surveys have been the most preponderant quantitative measure used for researching TPACK during the past decade. The surveys can be classified as general TPACK surveys or specialized surveys for specific technologies, pedagogies, or content areas, as presented in the next few sections. The TPACK surveys reported below are generally reliable as their Cronbach alpha reliabilities are all above 0.7.

General TPACK Surveys

Koehler and Mishra (2005) were reportedly the first two researchers to use a survey instrument to measure their master students' TPACK development as they learned to design online learning activities. These authors attempted to address participants' perceptions of the learning environment, the evolution of their thinking, and the increasing development of their TPACK throughout the design process. The survey consisted of 33 items scored on a seven-point Likert scale with two open-ended questions. The scores of the items from the 4th and 13th weeks of the semester were compared using paired-sample t-tests adjusted with a sequential Holm procedure. The authors concluded that the participants enjoyed the learning environment more, learned more theory and practical skills, and gained deeper understanding of online teaching. Not all of the TPACK items used in their study could be clearly distinguished using the seven TPACK constructs. For example, TPACK item 1 was "I am learning a lot of practical technology skills that I can use" and item 2 was "I am thinking more critically about technology than before" (p. 147). The first item is about TK while the second cannot be clearly categorized within any of the seven TPACK constructs. Nonetheless, this study exemplified how surveys could be used to examine teachers' TPACK development.

Schmidt, Baran, Thompson, Mishra, Koehler, and Shin (2009) were the first to create a TPACK survey with items constructed to measure pre-service teachers' self-reported perceptions or self-efficacies for the seven factors of TPACK. Their survey initially comprised 75 items and was scored on a five-point Likert scale ranging from strongly disagree (1) to strongly agree (5). Content validity of the survey was reviewed by three experts in TPACK, and the survey was thereafter administered to 124 American pre-service elementary and early childhood teachers. An exploratory factor analysis (EFA) was conducted for each of the seven TPACK factors, possibly because the sample size precluded the execution of a full EFA. Nonetheless, the process was able to provide "evidence of the internal structure of the seven dimensions" (Cavanagh & Koehler, 2013, p. 140). The EFAs resulted in the deletion of 28 items to derive a final list of 47 items for this TPACK survey.

One issue that surfaced from this study was the operationalization of content-related constructs such as pedagogical content knowledge (PCK) and technological content knowledge (TCK). Technically, Schmidt et al.'s (2009) study examined four kinds of content knowledge (CK), with three items each for mathematics, social studies, science, and literacy. However, the content areas were not examined separately for the constructs of PCK and TCK, as each of these factors had four items considering the different subject areas concurrently. For example, a PCK item was phrased as "I know how to select effective teaching approaches to guide student thinking and learning in literacy/science/mathematics/social studies." Despite this, Schmidt et al.'s work laid an important foundation for the subsequent development of additional TPACK survey instruments.

Koh, Chai, and Tsai (2010) adapted Schmidt et al.'s (2009) survey by changing and expanding the content-related factors (i.e., CK, PCK, TCK, TPACK) for Singapore pre-service teachers. Two sets of CK items were incorporated into the survey to capture the teachers' two main curriculum subjects. The survey also included two additional items for each set of CK items: "I can think about the subject matter like an expert who specializes in my curriculum subject" and "I have various ways and strategies of developing my understanding of my curriculum subject" to further assess the teachers' perceived efficacy for the content areas. To potentially increase the sensitivity of the instrument, the rating scale was changed to a seven-point Likert scale. The 29 items of this instrument were reviewed by five experts in information and communications technologies (ICT) for education. Factor analyses with both EFA and confirmatory factor analysis (CFA) were conducted on a randomly split sample of 1,185 elementary and middle school pre-service teachers, and five factors were identified: TK, CK, PK with PCK, TPK, and TCK with TPACK, and an additional factor formed by two TPK items focusing on teachers' thinking about the use of technology. The study indicates that when the factors were analyzed together, construct validity for all seven factors may be problematic.

A further study based on the adapted Schmidt et al.'s (2009) survey was conducted among Singapore pre-service teachers. Chai, Koh, and Tsai (2010) adapted four factors (TK, CK, PK, TPACK) from Schmidt et al.'s (2009) instrument and collected precourse (N = 439) and post-course (N = 365) data from the pre-service teachers trained to teach middle school students. EFA and CFA identified the four factors. In addition, CK, PK, and TK were all predictors of TPACK in the regression analyses conducted with both the pre-test and post-test, which revealed that the pre-service secondary teachers' self-efficacy for the four measured factors improved significantly with good effect sizes. The study seems to indicate that when the intermediate factors were excluded, a clear factor structure could be identified. However, this is akin to treating TPACK as integrative, and it ignores the contribution of the overlapping constructs.

More recently, Kaya and Dag (2013) translated Schmidt et al.'s (2009) survey into Turkish, and surveyed 352 primary school pre-service teachers. They reported that 10 factors from the EFA (i.e., four CK factors plus the other six factors) were identified. In addition, they performed CFA on the 10-factor model, and the fit indices generated supported a good model fit.

Another attempt to create and validate a general TPACK survey was reported by Sahin (2011), in which the author used item pool, analyses of validity and reliability, discriminant validity, and test–retest reliability as part of the validation process. Sahin conducted EFA using results obtained from 348 pre-service teachers. The reported Pearson's correlations between some factors are quite high (PK with PCK, 0.8; TCK with TPK, 0.79; and TCK with TPCK, 0.79). Items of TCK include "I have knowledge in using technologies helping to reach course objectives easily in my lesson plan," and "I have knowledge in preparing a lesson plan requiring use of instructional technologies" (p. 105), which seem more like TPK than TCK. Sahin also assessed the discriminant validities of the factors by correlating TPACK factors with different aspects of pre-service teachers' learning outcomes. For example, students' grades from a computing course were correlated with TK, scores for a content-based course were correlated with CK, while teachers' grade point average was correlated with TPACK. Significant correlations ranging from 0.17 to 0.34 among students' grades and the TPACK factors provided some evidence that TPACK survey scores can be useful measures of the various aspects of teachers' knowledge.

The general TPACK surveys may not allow researchers to draw more specific implications for teacher professional development. For example, Schmidt et al.'s (2009) PCK items were phrased as "I know how to select effective teaching approaches to guide student thinking and learning in literacy/mathematics/social studies/science," with one item per subject. This may not be enough to assess PCK for each subject, and a similar argument could be made for the TCK and TPACK items. Developing surveys for specific technology, pedagogy, and content is necessary for further theory building.

TPACK Surveys for Specific Technology

Going beyond the general measures of TPACK, there were two surveys designed to measure teachers' TPACK efficacy with respect to the specific technologies of online teaching and Web-based learning, respectively (Archambault & Barnett, 2010; Lee & Tsai, 2010). Archambault and Barnett (2010) designed a survey with 24 items to assess the seven TPACK factors, and subjected the items for expert review and two rounds of think-aloud piloting before administering the survey to online teachers of virtual schools in the United States. In all, 596 teachers responded to the survey. An EFA with Varimax rotation yielded three factors instead of the seven factors hypothesized. These were TK, a combined factor of PK, CK, and PCK, and another combined factor of TCK, TPK, and TPACK. These authors concluded that the seven theorized TPACK factors might not exist in practice.

Lee and Tsai (2010), on the other hand, constructed a 30-item survey based on 6 factors for Web-based learning (Web-general, Web-communicative, Web-PK, Web-CK, Web-PCK, and attitude towards Web-based instruction) that were scored with a 6-point Likert scale. These authors obtained five out of the six hypothesized factors with an EFA (N = 558) where the factors of Web-PK and Web-PCK were loaded together. The five-factor structure was confirmed with confirmatory factor analysis. Lee and Tsai's (2010) findings were similar to Archambault and Barnett's (2010) in that the technology-related PK and technology-related PCK loaded as one. Both studies indicated some difficulties with creating survey items that could be clearly distinguished for the seven TPACK factors. It could reflect that, in practice, teachers may not consciously consider the overlapping areas of knowledge as being separate, even though they are theoretically distinctive (see Cox & Graham, 2009).

These two studies indicate that there may be a need to create more context-specific TPACK surveys. Recently, Hsu, Liang, Chai, and Tsai (2013) ventured into developing a survey for game-based TPACK. The three factors they selected were game knowledge (GK), game pedagogical knowledge (GPK), and game pedagogical content knowledge (GPCK), corresponding to TK, TPK, and TPACK for digital games. EFA identified the three factors with 78% of variance explained. The Taiwanese preschool teachers' (N = 352) game-based TPACK was investigated with other variables, such as learning opportunities for games, attitude toward game-based learning, and experiences with playing digital games. The latter variables were found to predict the teachers' GK, GPK, and GPCK.

Another technology that has attracted some attention among researchers is digital video. Krauskopf, Zahn, and Hesse (2012) and Blonder, Jonatan, Bar Dov, Benny, Rap, and Sakhnini (2013) investigated TPACK for the use of teaching videos through mixed methods. Krauskopf et al. (2012) measured 60 pre-service teachers' PK by adapting 22 items from a test on declarative pedagogical knowledge, captured the pre-service teachers' mental models of YouTube through open-ended questions, and asked the pre-service teachers to state ideal and intended use of YouTube. The test results and the coded responses contributed to the mediation analysis, which provided evidence that the pre-service teachers' intended and ideal use of YouTube are mediated by their PK and their mental models of YouTube functions. Blonder et al.'s (2013) research focuses on equipping 16 high school chemistry teachers with the knowledge of editing videos with Windows Movie Maker. The teachers rated themselves on 11 video editing skills before and after the course, and the Wilcoxon Signed Rank test revealed that they acquired better video editing skills and were able to articulate various content-specific uses of videos (for example the submicro domain) in the classroom.

The interactive whiteboard (IWB) has also been a technology that has attracted a number of articles focusing on TPACK (Jang & Tsai, 2012; Koh & Divaharan, 2013). In particular, Jang and Tsai (2012) developed an IWB-TPACK questionnaire that was initially constructed with eight factors (the seven TPACK factors plus a context factor about students' prior knowledge, misconceptions, and assessing these matters). The 40-item questionnaire was reduced to a 30-item questionnaire with only four factors after the factor analysis. Although they were able to identify CK and TK as distinctive factors, the items from PK, PCK, and the context factor were combined as the PCK (context) factor. Items from TCK, TPK, and TPCK were relabeled as TPCK (context). Based on this questionnaire, teachers who used IWBs scored themselves higher for all four factors than those who did not.

TPACK Surveys for Specific Pedagogy

An example of a pedagogy-specific TPACK survey development is highlighted in the work of Chai and colleagues (Chai, Koh, & Tsai, 2011a; Chai, Koh, Tsai, & Tan, 2011b), where a TPACK for Meaningful Learning survey was progressively formulated and revised towards meaningful learning with an ICT framework (Howland, Jonassen, & Marra, 2012). Meaningful Learning is an ICT-based framework that emphasizes authentic learning in a cooperative social setting, directed by students' active and constructive efforts to make sense of what they are learning. Initial work for this TPACK survey was started by Chai, Koh, Tsai, and Tan (2011b), who refined the PK items used in Koh et al. (2010) to reflect the pedagogical emphases of the constructivist-oriented meaningful learning framework. The TK factor was expanded with items associated with Web 2.0 technologies. Using EFA and CFA, five factors (TK, PK, CK, TPK, and TPACK) were identified. Structural Equation Modeling (SEM) showed that the factors were significant predictors of TPACK for the pre-test. These relationships were similar to those in the post-test, except that PK did not predict TPACK directly but through TPK. The SEM provides some empirical support for Mishra and

Koehler's (2006) postulation that teachers' TPACK could be dependent on both elementary forms of knowledge (TK, PK, and CK), as well as its intermediary constructs (TPK).

Several refinements were subsequently made to Chai et al.'s (2011b) instrument to improve the distinctions between constructs. The phrase "Without using technology, I . . ." was added to the PCK items. Second, the TPK items were revised to correspond to the meaningful learning framework. Finally, additional items for TCK that were related to content-specific software for researching and advancing the content knowledge were included to better distinguish TCK from TPK (see Chai, Koh, & Tsai, 2011a).

These refinements enable Chai, Koh, and Tsai (2011a) to identify the seven postulated TPACK factors through both EFA and CFA. An eighth factor, however, emerged because the CK items split into two factors according to the teachers' first and second curriculum subjects. This shows that a TPACK survey may need to be created for specific CK, which could be a problem for many elementary school teachers, as they are usually trained to teach multiple subjects. Another weakness of this research is the use of the same sample (N = 214) of pre-service teachers for both the EFA and CFA.

A slightly improved version of the above instrument (focusing on one main teaching subject with an additional TCK item) was implemented with practicing Singaporean teachers (N = 455) to generate a path model (Koh, Chai, & Tsai, 2013). The CFA identified the seven TPACK factors with acceptable fit, thereby extending the validity of this TPACK survey to practicing teachers. The authors further tested 12 hypotheses to determine the direct effects of TK, PK, and CK on TPACK, their effects on the intermediate factors of TPK, PCK, and TCK, and also the effects of the intermediate factors on TPACK. The SEM confirmed all the hypothesized paths except for two—where both CK and PCK had no significant direct effects on TPACK. These results provide partial support for Mishra and Koehler's (2006) conception that TK, PK, and CK had both direct effects on TPACK and indirect effects through the intermediate factors of TPK and TCK. Nevertheless, the insignificant effects of CK and PCK on TPACK may indicate that when practicing teachers decide not to use technology, their instructional planning would culminate in constructing PCK where technology-related knowledge sources are not activated. Whether such demarcations between PCK and TPACK are present during teachers' instructional planning is an area that should be further examined through qualitative research.

A further enhancement to the TPACK for Meaningful Learning survey was reported in Chai, Ng, Lee, Hong, and Koh (2013c), as the TPACK items were revised to describe meaningful learning pedagogies, which is a change from the general technology integration items adapted from Schmidt et al. (2009). For example, two sample items for TPACK are:

- I can formulate in-depth discussion topics about the content knowledge and facilitate students' online collaboration with appropriate tools (e.g., Google Sites, Discussion Forums).
- I can structure activities to help students to construct different representations of the content knowledge using appropriate ICT tools (e.g., Webspiration, Mindmaps, and Wikis).

A total of 550 Asian pre-service teachers from Singapore, Taiwan, Hong Kong, and China participated in the survey. The 36-item survey was presented in English and Chinese bilingual mode to fit the language background of the participants. The construct validity of this 36-item survey was established through CFA with adequate model fit after the removal of six items. In comparison to Koh et al.'s (2013) SEM, the Asian pre-service teacher's model seemed to be less connected than that of the Singaporean practicing teachers. In particular, direct effects of TK, CK, and PK on TPACK were not significant for the Asian pre-service teachers, while PCK was found to be a significant predictor of TPACK.

The series of developmental steps undertaken by TPACK researchers reveals the need to iteratively test instruments and how the effort of measuring TPACK can be affected by a switch in focus from technology to pedagogy and the challenges involved in measuring TPACK for diverse teacher populations. Nonetheless, such efforts advance understanding of the interrelationship between the TPACK factors.

The TPACK for Meaningful Learning survey was applied to another group of Singaporean practicing teachers (N = 354). The EFA and CFA both supported the construct validity. The study investigated the influences of demographic variables (age, gender, teaching experience, and teaching level) on TPACK. Gender differences were reported for TK, TCK, and TPACK, with the male teachers rating themselves higher than their female counterparts. Stepwise regression analysis revealed that teaching level and teaching experience have significant influence on the development of TPACK, but not age and gender. The authors conjectured that the more experienced teachers seemed less confident with the constructivist-oriented TPACK, perhaps because they may be more well-versed in preparing students for examination, and that primary school teachers may be less confident than secondary teachers in TPACK, as they have more subjects to teach. More studies on the influence of demographic influences seem necessary.

This review has only been able to identify TPACK surveys for one specific pedagogical focus, Meaningful Learning. There may be a need for researchers to create other surveys that correspond to other pedagogical approaches, such as inquiry-based learning in science.

TPACK Surveys for Specific Content

Content-specific quantitative measures of TPACK have also emerged in the TPACK literature, largely in the area of science. For example, Graham, Burgoyne, Cantrell, Smith, St. Clair, and Harris (2009) constructed a four-factor TPACK survey specifically for science. Only the technology-related factors of TK, TPK, TCK, and TPACK were chosen, and related items were constructed around scientific principles, topics, phenomena, and data collection. While the face validity of this survey seems good, the small sample (N = 16) precluded further statistical analyses.

Bilici, Yamak, Kavak, and Guzey (2013) constructed another TPACK survey specifically for science. The authors conducted an EFA and CFA with two samples of pre-service science teachers (N = 420, N = 388). Of the 84 items, 52 with factor loadings of 0.3 and above were retained, and 8 factors, including the 7 TPACK factors, were identified. The additional factor labeled as CxK refers to contextual knowledge of students' socioeconomic background, home environment, and the school environment. An example of one item for CxK is "I consider students' home environment in my teaching" (p. 49). However, the correlations between TCK, PCK, TPK, and TPACK are high, ranging between 0.78 and 0.9, which may indicate that one or more factors are redundant.

Jang and Tsai (2013) adapted from their earlier work (Jang & Tsai, 2012) a TPACK survey for Taiwanese secondary science teachers that included CK, TK, and two other factors known as PCK in context and TPACK in context. They argue that PCK and TPACK in context refer to the teachers' specific knowledge of their teaching context, which includes an understanding of students and the school technological environment. The survey was validated through principal component analysis, which some researchers may argue is less desirable. Further analyses of variances indicate that experienced science teachers rated themselves stronger in CK and PCK in context, while the less experienced teachers rated themselves higher in TK and TPACK in context. In addition, male teachers tended to rate themselves higher in TK than females. This study indicates that the notion of context is receiving attention in the emerging research.

Another development in the formulation of content-specific TPACK surveys is the adaptation of Chai et al.'s (2011a) survey for different content areas. An example is replacing the CK items of Chai et al.'s (2011a) survey with items for science knowledge. For example, in Lin, Tsai, Chai, and Lee's (2013) study of Singapore science teachers' TPACK, the first CK item is "I have sufficient knowledge of science," while the first TCK item is "I can use software that is created specifically for science (e.g., data loggers for science)" (p. 331). Using CFA, the authors derived an acceptable model fit, and the 12 hypotheses of basic knowledge predicting the overlapping areas of knowledge were all supported by the SEM. Another example is in Chai, Chin, Koh, and Tan's (2013a) study which adapted Chai et al.'s (2011a) survey for the teaching of Chinese language. All content-related items were recrafted specifically for the Chinese language. For example, one of the TCK items is "I am able to use software designed specifically for Chinese language (e.g., electronic dictionary, corpus, educational websites for Chinese language)." The authors also included two additional constructs that measured teachers' beliefs regarding traditional teacher-centric pedagogies and constructivist-oriented student-centric beliefs. CFA confirmed that the nine-factor model (seven TPACK factors with two belief factors) was acceptable. These studies illustrate that one way of developing content-specific TPACK surveys could be to build upon validated general TPACK surveys. As more technologies become available for the representation of CK, for example the emergence of Google Earth for the teaching of geography or Google Sketch-up for design and technology, it seems likely that more content-specific surveys will be created.

Moving Beyond the Seven Factors of TPACK

Many of the survey studies reviewed thus far have extended beyond survey validation to examine the relationships between TPACK and factors such as demographics, beliefs, and contextual knowledge, as well as students' perceptions of teachers' TPACK. In terms of demographics, there were mixed results. Koh et al. (2010) found that male pre-service teachers reported stronger ratings for TK, CK, and knowledge of teaching with technology. Pre-service teachers educated for elementary and middle schools also differed in their perceptions of CK, with the middle school pre-service teachers reporting higher scores. The finding that male teachers were more confident in the technology-related aspects of TPACK also emerged in Jang and Tsai's (2013) TPACK survey for science. Furthermore, Lee and Tsai's (2010) Web-TPACK survey found that age and teaching experience were negatively correlated to all the Web-related factors (e.g., Web-general, Web-PK, Web-CK, and Web-PCK). On the other hand, Koh, Chai, and Tsai (2014) found that teachers' age and gender were not related to their TPACK for Meaningful Learning. Like Jang and Tsai (2013), Koh et al. (2014) found experienced teachers to be more confident regarding factors related to CK and PCK.

Interestingly, both Jang and Tsai (2013) and Lee and Tsai (2010) found that the less experienced teachers were more confident regarding factors related to TK and TPACK. Findings from cluster analyses of Singapore pre-service and in-service teachers using the TPACK for Meaningful Learning survey also reported differences between younger and older pre-service teachers, with the younger teachers reporting higher confidence in all TPACK factors (Koh & Chai, 2014). On the other hand, the two clusters derived for in-service teachers did not differ in terms of their CK, PCK, age, or years of service at the beginning of their ICT training, as they only differed in their perceptions of PK, TCK, TPK, and TPACK. The study also reported differences in training effects for the different clusters of the pre-service and in-service teachers from the post-training analyses. These results suggest the need to pay attention to the different TPACK profiles of teachers as they enter ICT training. Those who were more confident initially appeared more able to grasp the connections between technology, pedagogy, and content as they expressed even higher confidence in TPACK after ICT training. For those who began ICT training with lower confidence in the various areas of TPACK, it appeared that they were still developing an appreciation for intermediate forms of knowledge such as TPK and TCK during the training.

Another important area is related to teachers' beliefs. Chai et al.'s (2013a) study of Chinese language teachers' TPACK and their pedagogical beliefs showed that TPACK is different from teachers' beliefs, and that teachers' constructivist-oriented beliefs are significantly correlated to their constructivist-oriented TPACK, albeit weakly. Lee and Tsai (2010) found that teachers with higher self-efficacy for TPACK also reported more positive attitudes towards Web-based instruction. On the other hand, teachers' perceptions of or beliefs about learning are also associated with their TPACK. Kramarski and Michalsky (2009, 2010) investigated pre-service teachers' TPACK development in conjunction with self-regulation in learning, and their study indicated that support for self-regulated learning may be necessary for enhancing TPACK. In a similar vein, Horzum (2013) investigated the four technology-related factors of TPACK using Schmidt et al.'s (2009) survey, together with teachers' perceptions of deep learning approaches, surface learning approaches, and a mixture of deep and surface learning approaches. It was found that pre-service teachers with deep and mixed approaches to learning were able to make significant improvements in their TPACK perceptions when their pre- and post-course ratings were compared.

Variables associated with the learning environment have been investigated along with TPACK factors. Koh, Woo, and Lim (2013) created a survey for evaluating technology integration courses by integrating TPACK items with teachers' perceptions of their course experiences. When the survey was implemented with a cohort of 869 pre-service teachers, regression analyses found that the teachers' perceptions of experiences with respect to the delivery, content, and environment during a technology integration course are predictors of their TPK, TCK, and TPACK.

Researchers have also looked into teachers' understanding of TPACK from the perspective of the students. Shih and Chuang (2013) developed and validated a survey that assessed college students' perceptions of their professors' knowledge of using technology in teaching. The four-factor survey is comprised of items for CK (9 items), TK (11 items), TPACK (24 items), and teachers' knowledge of students' understanding (6 items). The TPACK items were formulated based on Angeli and Valanides' (2009) notion of transformative TPACK. CFA was performed and the indices of the root mean square error of approximation (RMSEA) and the standardized root mean square residual (SRMR) established adequate model fit with one item excluded. Item fitness was established with the Rasch model. The study results show that the instrument is valid and reliable. This survey could serve as a means to understand technology-enhanced learning experiences from students' perspectives.

Summary of TPACK Survey Studies

Overall, it seems that researchers are largely able to identify all seven factors of TPACK with different levels of specificity for technology, pedagogy, and content areas. Content, substantive, structural, and generalizability evidence has accumulated throughout the past decade of work (see Cavanagh & Koehler, 2013). The criticisms of the lack of construct validation for the seven TPACK factors (e.g., Brantley-Dias & Ertmer, 2013) could be addressed when these recent developments of TPACK surveys are considered. In addition, demographic variables such as gender, age, and teaching experience are related to teachers' TPACK. Other associated variables include teachers' beliefs, self-regulated learning, their learning approaches, and the learning environment.

Given that TPACK can be considered as a form of knowledge creation, it may be fruitful to study TPACK with other scales associated with knowledge creation or creative thinking. Whether or not teachers accept the role of knowledge creator could also be important to investigate. As TPACK is researched more and more with other associated variables, surveying the seven factors may result in very long survey, which could cause survey fatigue. One possible future direction would be to focus only on selected factors. The TPACK factor (i.e., the final integrated factor) and PCK factor are arguably the more important factors.

Measuring Teachers' Lesson Design Competencies

While TPACK survey studies have used quantitative measures to assess teachers' perceptions of TPACK, a second kind of quantitative measure attempts to assess the quality of teachers' design for technology-integrated lessons. Angeli and Valanides (2005) first developed a rating scale to measure pre-service teachers' technology-integrated lesson plans for ICT-related PCK development. These authors embarked upon three cycles of design-based research to develop and improve their model for enhancing pre-service teachers' competencies in lesson design, which is known as technology mapping (TM). Technology mapping is a process whereby the teachers identify topics and content knowledge that learners have problems with, transform the content with appropriate technological affordances, and engage learners with pedagogically productive and computer-based activities (Angeli & Valanides, 2009, 2013). The scoring of pre-service teachers' TPACK performance of the design tasks is based on (1) the selection and description of appropriate topics for which traditional means of representation can be enhanced, (2) the identification of technological representations to transform CK, (3) the identification of teaching strategies, (4) the selection and design of computer-based learning activities, and (5) the identification of integration activities. The scoring of the dimensions progresses from either 0 or 1 (Angeli & Valanides, 2005), to 1–5 (Angeli & Valanides, 2009), and up to 20 (Angeli & Valanides, 2013). Inter-rater analysis was employed to prevent biased ratings. Through the scoring of pre-service teachers' performance, they were able to document the pre-service teachers' development of TPACK throughout their technology integration course.

Kramarski and Michalsky (2009, 2010), as mentioned earlier, saw the importance of supporting pre-service teachers' self-regulation as they engaged in the development of their TPACK. These authors tested teachers' TPACK development with and without metacognitive self-questioning supports throughout the different stages of the lesson design process (e.g., during planning, action and performance, and evaluation). Other than measuring the pre-service teachers' design ability with scoring rubrics partially adopted from Angeli and Valanides (2009), they also designed TPACK comprehension tests for the pre-service teachers using case studies of technology integration. The pre-service teachers answered ten open-ended questions at five levels (comprehension, application, analysis, synthesis, evaluation) with two questions at each level. The answers were scored with the range of zero to three, with zero indicating a failure to respond and three indicating a high level of comprehension. The authors recommended that such comprehension tests provide an objective means of assessing teachers' TPACK.

Graham, Borup, and Smith (2012) also developed tests for primary school pre-service teachers (N = 133) that required them to design an instructional activity using technology and to articulate its rationale. They developed six categories of rationale through content analysis of the teachers' responses, including one category of TK that is about the benefits of using technology in general; two categories of TPK related to technology being used to support specific pedagogical activities or learner characteristics; and three categories of TPACK that are related to subject-specific instructional activities, learner's understanding of the subject matter, and transforming content for better teaching. The pre- and post-tests revealed that after going through the course, the pre-service teachers articulated significantly more rationales associated with the TPK and TPACK categories. The findings indicate that the pre-service teachers were developing TPK and TPACK. This result is consistent with the general outcome of the TPACK survey studies (see Chai et al., 2010, 2011b). While there were more rationales articulated in the overlapping areas of TPACK, whether or not they are logical or sound and whether they have resulted in better quality lesson design, was not analyzed in the study.

Koh (2013) published a scoring rubric to assess teachers' design of lesson activities based on the meaningful learning framework (Howland et al., 2012). She scored 217 lesson activities that Singaporean pre-service teachers created for Chinese language learning. The analyses revealed that the pre-service teachers were creating active learning, but they were lacking in the design of authentic problems and creating constructive and collaborative learning activities. These results were similar to the findings of So and Kim (2009).

This section illustrates several ways in which teachers' TPACK can be measured through evaluation of their performance when they are engaged in design activities. One obvious limitation of the studies reviewed above is that they are confined to pre-service teacher education. Practicing teachers may perform differently in the tests developed by Graham et al. (2012) or Kramarski and Michalsky (2009, 2010), but these have yet to be studied.

Measuring the Processes of TPACK Construction

The third category of quantitative TPACK measures was observed in studies that measured the effectiveness of the processes through which teachers construct TPACK by unpacking either their reflection or design talk through content analysis. Whether or not content analysis should be regarded as qualitative or quantitative can be a matter of argument. For the sake of comprehensiveness, four content analysis studies to date are reviewed here. Koehler, Mishra, and Yahya (2007) were the first researchers to begin quantifying the process of TPACK construction. They collected detailed notes of two design teams' group discussion, supplemented by e-mails, self-progress surveys, and other artifacts. The design episodes were coded with content analysis related to the seven factors of TPACK plus three additional codes of miscellaneous, social, and group dynamics. The same coder coded and recoded the data at different intervals with 90% overall agreement. The fifteen weeks of discussion were separated into three stages (five weeks each), and chi-square analysis revealed that one group's talk differed significantly, while that of the other group did not. Both groups, however, recorded low percentages of talk around content and technology, and generally low percentages of discussion regarding content, technology, and pedagogy. Nevertheless, talk related to the latter kind increased throughout the 15 weeks. Studies by Koh and Divaharan (2011, 2013) examined pre-service teachers' written reflections throughout a module in which they explored the pedagogical uses of interactive whiteboards and found similar results. Using content analysis, teachers' reflections were coded and counted according to the seven TPACK categories. The authors found that TK and TPK were more predominant at the beginning of the module, whereas the proportion of reflections attributable to TPACK had increased by the end of the module. These studies indicate that integrated sources of TPACK could emerge through teacher involvement in design work.

Another study, by Koh, Chai, and Tay (2014), found that besides TPACK factors, contextual factors such as school policies and logistics, school technological infrastructure, teachers' beliefs and teachers' perceptions of interpersonal factors, such as collaboration among peers, influenced how teachers applied their TPACK when designing technology-integrated lessons. Using content analysis, the authors coded the design discussions of three groups of elementary school teachers across a semester. Chi-square analysis indicated that groups with a larger-than-expected number of discussion units associated with school policies and logistics had lower-than-expected frequency of discussion units associated with TPACK. Groups with higher occurrences of TPACK tended to be facilitated by experienced educational technologists. Therefore, even though TPACK may emerge through design, the facilitation of design activities may be another important issue to consider in terms of teachers' TPACK development.

Discussion and Future Directions

The preceding section reviewed research using three kinds of quantitative measures of TPACK: surveys, lesson design measurement rubrics, and quantitative content analysis of teachers' design processes. In this section, the overall development of each kind of quantitative measure of TPACK and possible future directions are discussed.

TPACK Surveys

TPACK survey studies form the bulk of the quantitative measures employed in the TPACK studies. Overall, the collective effort of the TPACK research community has advanced TPACK survey development to the point that several choices of instrumentation to assess TPACK in a general way may be available. As TPACK researchers examine TPACK development from the different contexts of content, technology, and pedagogy, deeper understanding and more skillfully crafted survey items are likely to emerge. In fact, if researchers study each factor more closely, they will find that there may be several different ways to represent the knowledge for each factor, and that one can draw upon several validated instruments to adapt the survey to fit their contexts. For example, Chai, Koh, Ho, and Tsai (2012) formulated a distinct factor of cyber wellness to assess pre-service teachers' awareness of issues pertaining to cyber safety. This factor was identified as distinct from TPK but, in essence, it may be regarded as part of TPK as it is associated with the pedagogical knowledge that teachers need when using Web-based technology. Similarly, if classroom management in ICT-based classrooms is a concern, it is not difficult to formulate its related items as part of TPK. In other words, TPK should and can be further factorized.

As TPACK is positioned as a situated form of knowledge that is complex in nature (Mishra & Koehler, 2006), an obvious future direction for TPACK surveys is definitely the creation of surveys for specific contexts of technology, pedagogy, and content. Building on the foundation of the pool of items available to date for different TPACK factors, more items can be developed with a higher degree of specificity. For example, one could imagine designing a TPACK survey specifically for problem-based learning supported by simulation and discussion forums for the medical sciences. One could also create specific TPACK surveys for mobile learning or the flipped classroom. Survey instruments with a high degree of specificity would allow educators to better assess the state of TPACK. Another area of development could be surveys of school leaders' understanding of TPACK. It is obvious that school leaders' understanding may influence their decisions and consequent design of school policies and department directions.

A problem often encountered in TPACK survey research is the merging of factors during statistical analyses for construct validation. A third area of future research could be to consolidate the strategies for the effective design of items for each TPACK category. For example, when researchers are crafting the items to represent the various factors, they should strategically choose items that are not near the boundaries of the overlapping constructs (see Cox & Graham, 2009). Graham et al. (2009) stated that when they were formulating their survey, the TPK items were constructed in a general manner that could be suitable for all content areas, whereas the TPACK items were crafted specifically for science education. At this juncture, it should also be noted that more quantitative studies have been conducted by Asian than by Western researchers. TPACK surveys validated in the East need to be validated in the West to check for cultural differences. Comparative studies could be another interesting area of future research.

In terms of the categories of teachers surveyed, it was found that more studies have been conducted with pre-service and practicing teachers from elementary to secondary education, with some studies emerging for teachers in the early childhood setting (Liang, Chai, Koh, Yang, & Tsai, 2013). However, instructors in higher education settings have rarely been surveyed about their TPACK. Rienties, Brouwer, and Lygo-Baker (2013) reported some positive effects of an online development course with data collected through the TPACK framework from teachers in higher education. A closer examination of their survey reveals that the sample items may be difficult to interpret. For example, the sample item provided for the TPACK factor is "designing teaching in which students use ICT requires changes in how we teach and what we teach" (p. 127). It appears that the clarity of the item may need improvement. Given that university teachers may be the most crucial people in shaping students' notions of learning with technology for their respective disciplines, this is an obvious gap for future research.

In a similar vein, students' notions of learning with and without technology are at least partially shaped by the teachers' PCK and TPACK. Surveys and hierarchical linear models could be constructed to understand how current students see the role of technology in their learning, and how this is influenced by their teachers' use of technology. This could be an important area of research to convince educators of the usefulness of the TPACK framework.

In sum, quantitative measures of TPACK have attracted much attention from researchers working on technology integration. Successful validation of some of these quantitative instruments have allowed researchers to assess the profile teachers' TPACK, build structural equation models to study the interrelationship between the TPACK constructs, test the effectiveness of pre-service and in-service teachers' professional development programs, and to study the interrelationships between TPACK and other educational variables such as demographic variables or teachers' self-regulation during design. The research to date has greatly enriched our understanding of teachers' TPACK, but more work can still be done to increase the types of survey.

Assessment of Lesson Planning with TPACK

This is a developing area of TPACK quantitative measures. The value of such studies lies in the formulation of tests and rubrics that can be used to assess and guide teachers' development of lesson plans for technology integration. The assessments can be used to facilitate the planning of professional development from pre-service to in-service stages by mapping out clear TPACK development trajectories. One way of improving the depth of such measures may be to consider how concurrent tests of comprehension and lesson design evaluation can be used to better assess and guide teacher performance. This is because being able to understand and articulate the rationale for making instructional decisions may or may not indicate a teacher's competency to design strong technology-integrated lessons. Even though the authors believe that these two aspects should be highly correlated, further analysis of their relationships should be undertaken.

A second area of future development could be to generate more varied categories of design rationale through more qualitative studies. Where a body of rationales can be developed and validated for different kinds of technologies, content, and pedagogies, these can act as dependent variables of the teachers' design performance, guiding teachers to consider their design intents more deeply. Finally, these tests and rubrics of TPACK could also be adapted to form lesson observation rubrics to measure teachers' actual performance when they are conducting technology-integrated lessons. How the various factors of TPACK are manifested in the classroom and how the factors shape the effectiveness of the lesson are relationships that could be better understood with these quantitative measures to improve teaching practice.

Content Analysis of TPACK During Lesson Design

Collaborative design talk has been identified as a means of constructing TPACK (Koehler et al., 2007). As the quality of the collaborative design processes is pivotal to the constructed TPACK, researchers should explore ways of measuring design talk processes. However, the categories for coding design talk and the methods for assessing the design talk are not very well defined (Razzouk & Shute, 2012). Besides the "coding and counting" approach used in quantitative content analysis, having participants rate the qualities of the design talks they experienced could be another way of assessing their perceptions of the process. However, this should perhaps be triangulated with experts' assessment. Content analysis could show where the foci of the talks are, but the rubrics for assessing the quality may need to be developed based on the grounded approach. Researchers may need to compare multiple transcripts of design talks for TPACK creation and articulate the criteria for scoring the talks. Another method to consider would be the creation of linkographs, whereby indices are computed by examining the forward and backward links between design ideas explicated during design talk (Goldschmidt, 1995). There is much potential in developing these quantitative measures within educational contexts. By doing so, it would provide the critical data needed for finding ways to enhance design talk and, correspondingly, design capacities among teachers.

Cross Validation of Measurements

It is natural to ask whether self-reported TPACK perceptions, the processes evaluated, and the performance scored by experts with reference to selected rubrics agree. Cavanagh and

Koehler (2013) pointed out that such work contributes to providing external evidence to enhance the validity of the research. In this regard, Kopcha, Ottenbreit-Leftwich, Jung, and Baser (2014) attempted to measure 27 pre-service teachers' TPACK self-efficacy with Schmidt et al.'s (2009) survey and also to evaluate the teachers' lesson planning documents with the rubrics created by Harris, Grandgenett, and Hofer (2010, as cited by Kopcha et al., 2014; not included in this review as it is a conference proceeding). The scores for TCK, TPK, and TPACK generated by the two different measurements were compared. The case study reveals difficulties in identifying the discriminant validity of the two measures and that the convergent validity of the TPACK construct was insignificant. In other words, the pre-service teachers may perceive themselves as efficacious in designing ICT integrated lessons, but their lesson planning performance as assessed by experts may not agree with their self-assessment. Kopcha et al. (2014) cautioned that their case study may not be generalizable and that both measures may need further improvement. Nonetheless, the study draws attention to the need to provide triangulated findings to improve the rigors of quantitative TPACK research. The different ways of measuring TPACK may also need further alignment in terms of what they are measuring before one could draw conclusions regarding convergent and discriminant validity between different methods of measurement. More research is definitely needed in this area.

Conclusion—Towards an Integrated Approach

With the current development of validated surveys, scoring rubrics, and quantitative content analyses of the processes, it seems natural to ask which might be a better measure of TPACK. TPACK is a complex and situated form of knowledge created through design. Teachers draw upon TPACK to design lessons, and the implementation of lessons provides important enacted feedback for reflection on and improvement of their TPACK. Throughout this process, their perceptions and beliefs could intervene in the kinds of design decisions that they make. The three areas of measures are needed to understand teachers' thinking and design processes as well as the quality of the lessons designed. A comprehensive picture of teachers' TPACK would require multiple assessments from both quantitative and qualitative perspectives, using both approaches at the general TPACK level as well as those for specific technologies, content, and pedagogies. The development of an integrated and robust system of quantitative TPACK measurements is an important trajectory to support good teaching practices. It is a critical area needing much development and research.

References

Angeli, C., & Valanides, N. (2005). Preservice elementary teachers as information and communication technology designers: An instructional systems design model based on an expanded view of pedagogical content knowledge. *Journal of Computer Assisted Learning, 21*(4), 292–302.

Angeli, C., & Valanides, N. (2009). Epistemological and methodological issues for the conceptualization, development, and assessment of ICT-TPCK: Advances in technological pedagogical content knowledge (TPCK). *Computers & Education, 52*(1), 154–168.

Angeli, C., & Valanides, N. (2013). Technology mapping: An approach for developing technological pedagogical content knowledge. *Journal of Educational Computing Research, 48*(2), 199–221.

Archambault, L.M., & Barnett, J.H. (2010). Revisiting technological pedagogical content knowledge: Exploring the TPACK framework. *Computers & Education, 55*(4), 1656–1662.

Bilici, S.C., Yamak, H., Kavak, N., & Guzey, S.S. (2013). Technological pedagogical content knowledge self-efficacy scale (TPACK-SeS) for preservice science teachers: Construction, validation, and reliability. *Eurasian Journal of Educational Research, 52*, 37–60.

Blonder, R., Jonatan, M., Bar Dov, Z., Benny, N., Rap, S., & Sakhnini, S. (2013). Can You Tube it? Providing chemistry teachers with technological tools and enhancing their self-efficacy beliefs. *Chemistry Education Research and Practice, 14*(3), 269–285.

Brantley-Dias, L., & Ertmer, P.A. (2013). Goldilocks and TPACK: Is the construct 'just right?' *Journal of Research on Technology in Education, 46*(2), 103–128.

Cavanagh, R.F., & Koehler, M.J. (2013). A turn toward specifying validity criteria in the measurement of technological pedagogical content knowledge (TPACK). *Journal of Research on Technology in Education, 46*(2), 129–148.

Chai, C.S., Chin, C.K., Koh, J.H.L., & Tan, C.L. (2013a). Exploring Singaporean Chinese language teachers' technological pedagogical content knowledge and its relationship to the teachers' pedagogical beliefs. *The Asia-Pacific Education Researcher, 22*(4), 657–666.

Chai, C.S., Koh, J.H.L., Ho, H.N.J., & Tsai, C.C. (2012). Examining preservice teachers' perceived knowledge of TPACK and cyberwellness through structural equation modeling. *Australasian Journal of Educational Technology, 28*(6), 1000–1019.

Chai, C.S., Koh, J.H.L., & Tsai, C.C. (2010). Facilitating preservice teachers' development of technological, pedagogical, and content knowledge (TPACK). *Educational Technology & Society, 13*(4), 63–73.

Chai, C.S., Koh, J.H.L., & Tsai, C.C. (2011a). Exploring the factor structure of the constructs of technological, pedagogical, content knowledge (TPACK). *The Asia-Pacific Education Researcher, 20*(3), 607–615.

Chai, C.S., Koh, J.H.L., & Tsai, C.C. (2013b). A review of technological pedagogical content knowledge. *Educational Technology & Society, 16*(2), 31–51.

Chai, C.S., Koh, J.H.L., Tsai, C.C., & Tan, L.L.W. (2011b). Modeling primary school preservice teachers' technological pedagogical content knowledge (TPACK) for meaningful learning with information and communication technology (ICT). *Computers & Education, 57*(1), 1184–1193.

Chai, C.S., Ng, E.M.W., Lee, W.H., Hong, H.Y., & Koh, J.H.L. (2013c). Validating and modeling technological pedagogical content knowledge (TPCK) framework among Asian preservice teachers. *Australasia Journal of Educational Technology, 29*(1), 41–53.

Cox, S., & Graham, C.R. (2009). Diagramming TPACK in practice: Using an elaborated model of the TPACK framework to analyze and depict teacher knowledge. *TechTrends: Linking Research & Practice to Improve Learning, 53*(5), 60–69.

Goldschmidt, G. (1995). The designer as a team of one. *Design Studies, 16*(2), 189–209.

Graham, C.R., Borup, J., & Smith, N.B. (2012). Using TPACK as a framework to understand teacher candidates' technology integration decisions. *Journal of Computer Assisted Learning, 28*(6), 530–546.

Graham, R., Burgoyne, N., Cantrell, P., Smith, L., St. Clair, L., & Harris, R. (2009). Measuring the TPACK confidence of inservice science teachers. *TechTrends: Linking Research & Practice to Improve Learning, 53*(5), 70–79.

Horzum, M.B. (2013). An investigation of the technological pedagogical content knowledge of preservice teachers. *Technology, Pedagogy and Education, 22*(3), 303–317.

Howland, J. L., Jonassen, D. H., & Marra, R. M. (2012). *Meaningful learning with technology*. Upper Saddle River, NJ: Pearson.

Hsu, C. Y., Liang, J. C., Chai, C. S., & Tsai, C. C. (2013). Exploring preschool teachers' technological pedagogical content knowledge of educational games. *Journal of Educational Computing Research, 49*(4), 461–479.

Jang, S. J., & Tsai, M. F. (2012). Exploring the TPACK of Taiwanese elementary mathematics and science teachers with respect to use of interactive whiteboards. *Computers & Education, 59*(2), 327–338.

Jang, S. J., & Tsai, M. F. (2013). Exploring the TPACK of Taiwanese secondary school science teachers using a new contextualized TPACK model. *Australasian Journal of Educational Technology, 29*(4), 566–580.

Kaya, S., & Dag, F. (2013). Turkish adaptation of technological pedagogical content knowledge survey for elementary teachers. *Educational Sciences: Theory and Practice, 13*(1), 302–306.

Koehler, M. J., & Mishra, P. (2005). What happens when teachers design educational technology? The development of technological pedagogical content knowledge. *Journal of Educational Computing Research, 32*(2), 131–152.

Koehler, M. J., Mishra, P., & Yahya, K. (2007). Tracing the development of teacher knowledge in a design seminar: Integrating content, pedagogy and technology. *Computers & Education, 49*(3), 740–762.

Koh, J. H. L. (2013). A rubric for assessing teachers' lesson activities with respect to TPACK for meaningful learning with ICT. *Australasian Journal of Educational Technology, 29*(6), 887–900.

Koh, J. H. L., & Chai, C. S. (2014). Teacher clusters and their perceptions of technological pedagogical content knowledge (TPACK) development through ICT lesson design. *Computers & Education, 70*, 222–232.

Koh, J. H. L., Chai, C. S., & Tay, L. Y. (2014). TPACK-in-action: Unpacking the contextual influences of teachers' construction of technological pedagogical content knowledge (TPACK). *Computers & Education, 78*, 1–10.

Koh, J. H. L., Chai, C. S., & Tsai, C. C. (2010). Examining the technological pedagogical content knowledge of Singapore preservice teachers with a large-scale survey. *Journal of Computer Assisted Learning, 26*(6), 563–573.

Koh, J. H. L., Chai, C. S., & Tsai, C. C. (2013). Examining practicing teachers' perceptions of technological pedagogical content knowledge (TPACK) pathways: A structural equation modeling approach. *Instructional Science, 41*(4), 793–809.

Koh, J. H. L., Chai, C. S., & Tsai, C. C. (2014). Demographic factors, TPACK constructs, and teachers' perceptions of constructivist-oriented TPACK. *Educational Technology & Society, 17*(1), 185–196.

Koh, J. H. L., & Divaharan, S. (2011). Developing preservice teachers' technology integration expertise through the TPACK-developing instructional model. *Journal of Educational Computing Research, 44*(1), 35–58.

Koh, J. H. L., & Divaharan, S. (2013). Towards a TPACK-fostering ICT instructional process for teachers: Lessons from the implementation of interactive whiteboard instruction. *Australasian Journal of Educational Technology, 29*(2), 233–247.

Koh, J. H. L., Woo, H. L., & Lim, W. Y. (2013). Understanding the relationship between Singapore preservice teachers' ICT course experiences and technological pedagogical content knowledge (TPACK) through ICT course evaluation. *Educational Assessment, Evaluation and Accountability, 25*(4), 321–339.

Kopcha, T. J., Ottenbreit-Leftwich, A., Jung, J., & Baser, D. (2014). Examining the TPACK framework through the convergent and discriminant validity of two measures. *Computers & Education, 78*, 87–96.

Kramarski, B., & Michalsky, T. (2009). Three metacognitive approaches to training preservice teachers in different learning phases of technological pedagogical content knowledge. *Educational Research and Evaluation, 15*(5), 465–485.

Kramarski, B., & Michalsky, T. (2010). Preparing preservice teachers for self-regulated learning in the context of technological pedagogical content knowledge. *Learning and Instruction, 20*(5), 434–447.

Krauskopf, K., Zahn, C., & Hesse, F.W. (2012). Leveraging the affordances of YouTube: The role of pedagogical knowledge and mental models of technology functions for lesson planning with technology. *Computers & Education, 58*(4), 1194–1206.

Lee, M.H., & Tsai, C.C. (2010). Exploring teachers' perceived self-efficacy and technological pedagogical content knowledge with respect to educational use of the World Wide Web. *Instructional Science, 38*(1), 1–21.

Liang, J.C., Chai, C.S., Koh, J.H.L., Yang, C.J., & Tsai, C.C. (2013). Surveying inservice preschool teachers' technological pedagogical content knowledge. *Australasian Journal of Educational Technology, 29*(4), 581–594.

Lin, T.C., Tsai, C.C., Chai, C.S., & Lee, M.H. (2013). Identifying science teachers' perceptions of technological pedagogical and content knowledge (TPACK). *Journal of Science Education and Technology, 22*(3), 325–336.

Mishra, P., & Koehler, M. (2006). Technological pedagogical content knowledge: A framework for teacher knowledge. *The Teachers College Record, 108*(6), 1017–1054.

Razzouk, R., & Shute, V. (2012). What is design thinking and why is it important? *Review of Educational Research, 82*(3), 330–348.

Rienties, B., Brouwer, N., & Lygo-Baker, S. (2013). The effects of online professional development on higher education teachers' beliefs and intentions towards learning facilitation and technology. *Teaching and Teacher Education, 29*, 122–131.

Sahin, I. (2011). Development of survey of technological pedagogical and content knowledge (TPACK). *Turkish Online Journal of Educational Technology, 10*(1), 97–105.

Schmidt, D.A., Baran, E., Thompson, A.D., Mishra, P., Koehler, M.J., & Shin, T.S. (2009). Technological pedagogical content knowledge (TPACK) the development and validation of an assessment instrument for preservice teachers. *Journal of Research on Technology in Education, 42*(2), 123–149.

Shih, C.L., & Chuang, H.H. (2013). The development and validation of an instrument for assessing college students' perceptions of faculty knowledge in technology-supported class environments. *Computers & Education, 63*, 109–118.

So, H.J., & Kim, B. (2009). Learning about problem based learning: Student teachers integrating technology, pedagogy and content knowledge. *Australasian Journal of Educational Technology, 25*(1), 101–116.

Voogt, J., Fisser, P., Pareja Roblin, R.N., Tondeur, J., & van Braak, J. (2013). Technological pedagogical content knowledge—A review of the literature. *Journal of Computer Assisted Learning, 29*(2), 109–121.

7

Understanding Teachers' TPACK Through Observation

Denise A. Schmidt-Crawford, Shu-Ju Diana Tai, Wei Wang, Yi Jin

Introduction

This chapter examines how a case study approach can be used to understand teachers' technological pedagogical content knowledge (TPACK). Classroom observations and follow-up interviews were used to document the TPACK knowledge and competency of exemplary teachers who are using technology as an integral part of their teaching practices. A qualitative case study approach, guided by the Data Analysis Spiral (Creswell, 2013), was used. Each participant was observed twice teaching in a classroom, and interviews were conducted with teachers after each classroom observation. A coding system and comparative analysis were used to identify themes from the observation and interview data collected to describe teachers' TPACK. Ultimately, the goal of this research is to better understand how to assess the nature of teachers' TPACK using triangulated measures within the context of K–8 classrooms. This chapter begins with a brief review of various research methods that have been used to assess teachers' development of TPACK.

Literature Review

The TPACK framework, proposed by Mishra and Koehler (2006), functions as a conceptual lens that helps researchers examine how teachers are using technology in teaching. While first generation TPACK research mainly focused on defining and conceptualizing the seven constructs of TPACK, recent studies have shifted their focus to using the framework to comprehend teachers' knowledge of integrating technology, hence TPACK, to facilitate and enhance their teaching and if such knowledge develops through technology interventions. Building on the history of using survey methodology to examine teachers' knowledge with regards to technology integration, researchers designed survey instruments to assess teachers' TPACK. Several questionnaires were designed to examine the development of TPACK (e.g., Archambault & Crippen, 2009; Chai, Koh, & Tsai, 2010; Koehler & Mishra,

2005; Sahin, 2011; Schmidt et al., 2009). For example, Archambault and Crippen (2009) constructed a 24-item questionnaire and surveyed 596 K–12 online teachers who rated their PK, CK, and PCK knowledge at the highest level, but were not as confident in the knowledge domains related to technology. Schmidt et al. (2009) developed a questionnaire targeted on elementary pre-service teachers who will be teaching multiple subject areas. That instrument contains 47 items using a 5-point Likert scale and 3 open-ended questions with the goal of measuring the development of pre-service teachers' self-perceived TPACK. Within a pre- and post-survey design, Schmidt et al. (2009) found that after completing an introductory instructional technology course, statistically significant gains were found in all seven knowledge domains among pre-service teachers, with the largest growth in the areas of TK, TCK, and TPACK. Although each of these instruments were designed and implemented for different participants and in different contexts, all have contributed to informing the field about the development of teachers' knowledge in TPACK using self-reported measures.

Studies are now being designed that use other data sources to examine teachers' TPACK development (Koehler, Shin, & Mishra, 2012). These include approaches and tools such as performance assessment rubrics (e.g., Angeli & Valanides, 2009; Harris, Grandgenett, & Hofer, 2010), open-ended questionnaires (e.g., Robertshaw & Gillam, 2010; So & Kim, 2009), teacher interviews (e.g., Harris, Grandgenett, & Hofer, 2012; Mishra, Peruski, & Koehler, 2007; Ozgün-Koca, Meagher, & Edwards, 2009; Williams, Foulger, & Wetzel, 2010), and observations (Agyei & Voogt, 2011; Hofer, Grandgenett, Harris, & Swan, 2011; Koehler, Mishra, & Yahya, 2007). Harris and colleagues emphasize that "self-report data should therefore be triangulated with external assessments of teachers' TPACK" (Harris et al., 2010, p. 324). Thus, research efforts focused on using multiple data sources are needed to advance our understanding of teachers' TPACK.

Despite the abundance of studies that focus on investigating teachers' development of TPACK, the majority of results published come from self-reported data. While self-report data can shed important light on this topic, there is still a chance that potential errors can occur while participants attempt to recall their experiences (Kilickaya, 2009), and that such data do not provide compelling evidence or capture actual technology integration practices in classrooms (Marquez Chisholm & Padgett, 2004). Thus, it is timely and critical that research around this important topic begin to utilize systematic and empirical methods in order to measure TPACK (the intersection of TK, PK, and CK). This study seeks to understand teachers' TPACK by conducting both classroom observations and interviews. As past researchers have noted, direct observation in classrooms yields abundant information about the nature of effective teaching (Good & Brophy, 2000), while others add that the successful integration of technology in relationship to effective teaching is dependent on how well teachers plan instruction (Harris & Hofer, 2009). The next logical step is to observe how a teacher applies TPACK while executing a lesson (Kereluik, Casperson, & Akcaoglu, 2010), and afterwards talk with the teacher to unpack the actual planning and execution of that lesson.

The purpose of this study was to observe exemplary technology-using teachers in classrooms to examine their TPACK. Two research questions guided the investigation: (1) How frequently do exemplary technology-using teachers exhibit the seven domains in the TPACK framework (TK, PK, CK, PCK, TCK, TPK, and TPACK)? and (2) What TPACK characteristics were identified for each TPACK domain respectively? The next section describes the research methodology used for this study.

Methodology

This study follows a descriptive holistic single case study approach (Yin, 2003) to examine the phenomenon of exemplary technology-using teachers' TPACK using two different data sources: observation to identify teachers' TPACK through the execution of lessons and interview to unpack teachers' planning and rationale.

Participants

Study participants were four K–8 classroom teachers teaching in three different school districts. Administrators and technology coordinators from school districts in close proximity to our institution were contacted to nominate K–8 teachers who they considered "exemplary, technology-using educators." This group was asked to nominate teachers who were viewed by others and themselves as their district's classroom leaders in respect to using technology in innovative and effective ways in classrooms. Proximity to each participant (within 60 miles) was important to the study design because of the multiple classroom observations that were required for each participant. Nine teachers were nominated and four agreed to participate in the study. Table 7.1 provides further description of participants.

Research Procedures

After receiving consent, two classroom observations were scheduled with each participant, with a follow-up interview conducted right after the observations. The interview addressed

Table 7.1 Description of Teacher Participants

Name (Pseudonym)	Degree(s)	Years Taught	Grade Levels Taught	Access to Technology
Alice	BS & MEd	39	2	25 station computer lab
Brian	BS & MS	15	5, 8	25 station computer lab & classroom set iPads
Candice	BA & MEd	13	3, 4	Laptop cart
Daniel	BS	1	5	1:1 iPad program

questions that emerged from the classroom observations and allowed teachers the opportunity to elaborate on their actions and thoughts. Two researchers were present for each observation and an observation protocol was used to guide the observations. Researchers documented what was observed in classrooms and wrote down questions that came up while observing the teachers. During the interviews, the participants were asked a list of predetermined questions (about background and teaching experiences) along with questions that emerged during the observations. Data collected from the observations and interviews were then sorted into units of meaning (UoMs) for coding and analysis based on Mohan's (2007) concept of a social practice (known as an "activity").

Data Sources

A descriptive case study approach (Yin, 2003) was used to examine what teachers' TPACK characteristics looked like while teaching in classrooms. Data were collected using two data sources: observations and interviews. To ensure systematic measures between the observation and interview data, two instruments were developed for the data collection. An observation protocol guided by the TPACK framework and an interview guide were used.

TPACK Observation Protocol

The TPACK observation protocol was developed, piloted among multiple observers (i.e., the authors), and modified to advocate systematic observational measures in the data collection process (Borg & Gall, 1996; Borrego & Cook Hirai, 2004). This protocol was created based on four of the seven knowledge domains within the TPACK framework: Content, Pedagogy, Technology, and TPACK (Mishra & Koehler, 2006). Three to five prompting questions were provided for each domain to guide and focus the observers during each observation. A brief lesson plan/description was collected from each teacher prior to the observation to situate the observers in that particular class. Observers also wrote down questions on the form that came up while observing the teacher. These questions were then asked for clarifying purposes during follow-up interviews (Duff, 2008; Gillham, 2008; Niess, 2011). All observers used this protocol to record two observations for each participant.

Interview Guide

The interview guide was created to collect participants' background information and to ask a set of questions that required teachers to examine and reflect on their teaching. The researchers used prompts from the interview guide, such as, "Why did you see the need to use technology in this lesson?," "What do you think went well? What did not?" and "What changes would you make if you were to teach the lesson again?" to help facilitate the participants' reflection process after each observation. All interviews were recorded, transcribed, and sorted into UoMs for coding and analysis.

Data Analysis

Data analysis was guided by the Data Analysis Spiral (Creswell, 2013). The intention of the study was to identify observable TPACK teacher characteristics in order to begin defining what TPACK "looks like" in the four classrooms where teachers were observed. The study followed Creswell's (2013) notion of a zigzag process where data are collected and analyzed by going "out to the field to gather information, into the office to analyze the data, back to the field to gather more information, into the office, and so forth" (p. 86). While coding and analyzing the observation and interview data collected from the four participants, the Data Analysis Spiral was used then to guide the analysis process "in analytic circles rather than using a fixed linear approach" (Creswell, 2013, p. 142).

Data collected from each participant were organized into a "data set," which included four digital files—two observations and two interviews. Mohan's (2007) concept of a social practice (known as an "activity") was used to organize the observation and interview data into smaller units, units of meaning (UoMs), for coding and data analysis. The open coding process began by analyzing one participant's entire "data set."

Following this zigzag process of data collection and analysis, each participant's data set was sorted into UoMs and then distributed to two researchers (i.e., two authors) for coding. Two researchers coded each data set separately using a codebook that included codes identified and developed to date. The goal was for each researcher to align each UoM in the data set with an existing code or to create a new code as needed. After completing the coding separately, the coding results from the two researchers were compared and recorded. The two researchers then met to discuss the coding results with the goal to reach an agreement on codes assigned to all the UoMs as well as on any new codes created. The agreement between the two researchers reached 97% after the discussion. The 3% of UoMs that the two coders could not reach an agreement were sent to a third researcher for blind coding. At that point, the three researchers met to discuss and reach agreement on placing the final code for the UoM. This procedure was repeated for coding each participant's data set. After all four data sets were coded, the occurrences of teachers' TPACK knowledge were counted based on the seven knowledge domains in the TPACK framework to illustrate the teachers' demonstrated TPACK knowledge in their teaching.

In sum, a recursive data analysis process using the Data Analysis Spiral (Creswell, 2013) was applied while coding all four participants' data sets. Although the researchers coded each participant's data set separately, using clearly defined UoMs, they always returned to the previous analysis and results to review and revise existing codes and themes. New codes were created when necessary and all codes were recorded in a codebook. After the coding was completed, the occurrences of each TPACK domain in all participants' classrooms were counted and calculated into a percentage to present the frequency in which these four technology-using teachers exhibited TPACK in their classroom.

Findings

Based on the analysis of the observation and interview data, these four technology-using teachers were found to exhibit all seven TPACK knowledge domains in their teaching with the highest percentage recorded as TPACK. Second, 11 themes and 53 TPACK characteristics (i.e., codes) were identified as a result of observing these four teachers while teaching in classrooms (see Table 7.2). These 53 TPACK-related characteristics (i.e., codes) that were identified across all 7 knowledge domains and 11 themes emerged from the 53 TPACK characteristics. Findings indicate that using classroom observations and follow-up interviews with teachers can lend new insight while trying to understand teachers' TPACK.

Teachers' Frequency of Exhibiting TPACK

Based on the collective coding analysis of the observation and interview data, it was found that the TPACK knowledge domains that participants exhibited and talked about most frequently were TPACK (34%), PCK (24%), and TPK (12%) (see Figure 7.1). Participants exhibited and discussed TK (10%), TCK (9%), and PK (9%) as well. However, the domain of CK (2%) was observed and talked about less frequently by the participants.

Examining the two data sources (i.e., observations and interviews) separately, participants were *observed* to exhibit PCK, TPACK, and PK most frequently, 30%, 23%, and 16%, respectively. However, the interview data revealed that participants most frequently *shared* reflective thoughts and insights that aligned with TPACK (43%), PCK (18%), and TPK (13%). Thus, these four technology-using teachers exhibited TPACK both in their actions (teaching) and in their knowledge (telling/reflecting). These teachers also frequently exhibited and shared their PCK, which illustrates that teachers still have a keen ability to apply the pedagogical skills necessary to teach content (Shulman, 1986). Although teachers were observed applying PK (16%) in classrooms, this domain was rarely mentioned during the interviews (3%). Teachers' TPK was observed (11%) and described during interviews (13%), illustrating that these technology-using teachers were developing some expertise in this domain and were enacting that knowledge while teaching.

One finding worth noting was that teachers' TCK (9%) was observed in classrooms and was mentioned (9%) by teachers in follow-up interviews. Harris and Hofer (2011) have argued that TCK definitions are inconsistent across research studies. Previous research

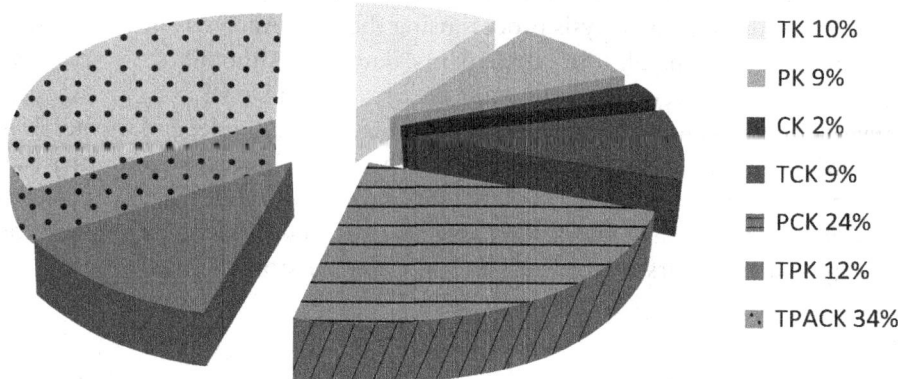

Figure 7.1 Frequency of TPACK-Related Codes

Table 7.2 TPACK Themes and Characteristics Identified

Themes (Occurrence in TPACK Domains)	Definition of Themes	TPACK Domains (# of Characteristics Identified)						
		TK (10)	PK (3)	CK (3)	TCK (4)	PCK (11)	TPK (9)	TPACK (13)
Use (6)	Teacher demonstrates the ability to use technology and/or pedagogy for content teaching.	✓			✓	✓	✓	✓
Match Affordance (5)	Teacher selects technology and/or pedagogy to match the teaching/learning objectives.	✓			✓	✓	✓	✓
Prepare (5)	Teacher demonstrates the ability to use technology and/or pedagogy to prepare for content teaching.	✓			✓	✓	✓	✓
Collaborate (4)	Teacher collaborates with others to use technology and/or pedagogy for content teaching.	✓	✓					✓
Engage (4)	Teacher uses technology and/or pedagogy to engage students in content learning.	✓				✓	✓	✓
Learner Centered (4)	Teacher uses technology and/or pedagogy to create student-centered environment for content learning.		✓			✓	✓	✓
Reflect (4)	Teacher reflects on his/her use of technology and/or pedagogy for content teaching.	✓				✓	✓	✓
Troubleshoot (3)	Teacher demonstrates the ability to troubleshoot.	✓			✓		✓	
Connect (3)	Teacher uses technology and/or pedagogy to connect students' learning to others.					✓	✓	✓
Assess (2)	Teacher uses technology and/or pedagogy to assess student learning.					✓		✓
Transfer (1)	Teacher demonstrates the ability to help students transfer technology knowledge from one context to another.	✓						
Others	Teacher demonstrates the ability to integrate technology and/or pedagogy into content teaching, e.g., teacher exhibits CK, coordinate technology, and scaffold content learning.	✓ ✓		✓ ✓ ✓		✓ ✓	✓	✓ ✓ ✓ ✓

findings indicated that TCK was typically the domain having the lowest mean on survey responses when examining teacher knowledge (Graham, Cox, & Velasquez, 2009; Richardson, 2009), while others reported limited evidence or emphasis of teachers applying TCK in classrooms (Harris & Hofer, 2011; Swan & Hofer, 2011). For the purpose of this study, TCK was defined as the "knowledge of how technology can create new representations for specific content. It suggests that teachers understand that, by using a specific technology, they can change the way learners practice and understand concepts in a specific content area" (Schmidt et al., 2009). Several UoMs were coded within the TCK domain in this study. For example, Candice prepared a wiki so that students could use and add information during their social studies unit of study about the regions of the United States. This UoM was coded as "TCK_Prepare" by both researchers during the data analysis. Candice created a new representation (i.e., wiki) for the specific content being taught (i.e., regions of the United States). This finding implies that teachers can be observed using TCK, which contradicts findings from previous studies (Graham, Cox, & Velasquez, 2009; Lux, 2010; Niess, Lee, Sadri, & Suharwoto, 2006).

TPACK Characteristics Identified

After data analysis and interpretation, it was clear that particular TPACK characteristics were both observed and described by these four technology-using teachers. Again, Table 7.2 presents the 53 TPACK-related characteristics (i.e., codes) that were identified across all 7 knowledge domains. Subsequently, 11 themes emerged from those 53 TPACK characteristics.

These 11 themes were identified after closely examining the 53 TPACK-related characteristics that represented the common ground of how these four teachers exhibited and talked about their TPACK in classrooms. "Use" was a theme identified in six of the seven TPACK knowledge domains. Participants demonstrated not only the "Use" of technology or pedagogy for teaching (Use_TK, Use_PK) but also the "Use" of technology and/or pedagogy with content knowledge (Use_TCK, Use_PCK, Use_TPK, and Use_TPACK) in mind. The next most frequent themes observed were "Prepare" and "Match Affordance." Both were observed in five of the seven TPACK domains. Every participant was observed using technology and/or pedagogy as he/she prepared to teach content. For instance, Daniel prepared a template in Pages (a word processor) to introduce his students to the concept of persuasion. This UoM was coded "Prepare_TPACK" by each coder during the data analysis.

Although the "Prepare" theme could be explicitly observed in classrooms, the "Match Affordance" theme needed to be verified through the follow-up interviews with participants. For example, Daniel was observed incorporating the *Subtext* app (space for teachers and students to have digital book discussions) into a lesson while teaching persuasive writing. Students read a persuasive piece that Daniel uploaded to *Subtext*, and then were asked to identify the key persuasive elements in the text by highlighting sentences on their iPads. Based on observation notes, both researchers documented two themes, "Prepare" and "Match Affordance," during this teaching episode. However, the "Match Affordance" theme was further verified during the follow-up interview where Daniel stated, "I used it [*Subtext*] mainly because it gives English resources on getting non-fiction. . . . It also has the feature of highlighting. I can see all of the kids' highlights. I can see their comments."

Likewise, the themes of "Reflect" and "Transfer" could not be easily identified by using observation data only. Several times participants demonstrated their ability to "Reflect" during the follow-up interviews when they had the opportunity to elaborate further on what they were teaching and why. Participants would frequently make connections between the lesson just observed to previous lessons they had already taught. Brian was asked how his mock trial case lesson was different from before, and he then elaborated at length on the changes that were made this time around. This illustrates how Brian reflects upon his teaching practices and takes the necessary steps to improve upon them from year to year.

When aligning these themes to the seven TPACK knowledge domains, it was found that TPACK, PCK, and TK were identified with 13, 11, and 10 characteristics respectively. The TPK domain had nine different characteristics, and PK and CK had the fewest characteristics identified with three each. Although it was difficult to observe CK in isolation of pedagogy and technology, there was still evidence that participants exhibited knowledge of the content that he/she was teaching, made interdisciplinary connections, and provided accurate responses to students' content-related questions. These findings illustrate that teachers incorporated not only the three foundational TPACK knowledge domains (TK, PK, and CK) in isolation in their teaching, but rather the characteristics within the integrated domains of PCK, TCK, and TPK and, most importantly, TPACK.

Discussion and Conclusion

The purpose of this study was to observe K–8 technology-using teachers in classrooms, with the goal of identifying specific TPACK characteristics that were exhibited by the teachers while teaching. In sum, the teachers exhibited and/or discussed 53 TPACK-related characteristics (TPACK-13, PCK-11, TK-10, TPK-9, TCK-4, PK-3, and CK-3), which then aligned with 11 specific themes. Findings from these teachers' observations help to provide a deeper understanding of TPACK in terms of bridging the gap between research and practice. These results provide an initial response to the question, "What does TPACK look like in classrooms?" Moreover, findings also suggest that characteristics do exist for each of the seven TPACK domains and these characteristics can be observed in practice. Specific themes, such as "Reflect" and "Transfer," do need further investigation while talking with teachers. Thus, this study illustrates the value of using multiple data sources while examining teachers' TPACK.

As mentioned, surveys are commonly used to investigate the development of pre-service and/or in-service teachers' self-perceived knowledge of TPACK (e.g., Archambault & Crippen, 2009; Koehler & Mishra, 2005; Schmidt et al., 2009). Using multiple data sources, such as those used for this study, holds promise and value in terms of confirming findings from self-reported investigations. Future research should aim to build upon self-report results by aligning key TPACK characteristics, like those identified in this study, with items present on existing surveys. As a result, survey items may need revising or additional items added in order to strengthen the reliability and validity of existing instruments and their ability to measure each TPACK domain. This study also is a first step in the process of developing a robust classroom observation tool that lists observable characteristics and/or codes that align with all seven TPACK domains. Such an instrument would be extremely useful in assisting teachers, school administrators, and/or teacher educators with identifying specific TPACK domains that need attention when preparing teachers to integrate technology.

In sum, a case study approach was used to better understand teachers' TPACK by observing exemplary teachers who were using technology as an integral part of their teaching practices. All participants were observed applying their knowledge of each TPACK domain while teaching, which then led to the identification of specific characteristics that were aligned to the seven domains. These findings offer a possible next step in developing a more systematic approach for assessing teachers' TPACK. Triangulating data from multiple sources appears promising as researchers continue to refine and improve the existing research approaches being used to measure TPACK.

References

Agyei, D., & Voogt, J. (2011). Determining teachers' TPACK through observations and self-report data. In M. Koehler & P. Mishra (Eds.), *Proceedings of Society for Information Technology & Teacher Education International Conference 2011* (pp. 2314–2319). Chesapeake, VA: Association for the Advancement of Computing in Education (AACE).

Angeli, C., & Valanides, N. (2009). Epistemological and methodological issues for the conceptualization, development, and assessment of ICT-TPCK: Advances in technological pedagogical content knowledge (TPCK). *Computers & Education, 52*(1), 154–168.

Archambault, L., & Crippen, K. (2009). Examining TPACK among K–12 online distance educators in the United States. *Contemporary Issues in Technology and Teacher Education, 9*(1), 71–88.

Borg, W. R., & Gall, M. D. (1996). *Educational research: An introduction.* White Plains, NY: Longman Publishers.

Borrego, I., & Cook Hirai, D. (2004). Does self-reflection/observation impact teacher effectiveness? In R. Ferdig et al. (Eds.), *Proceedings of Society for Information Technology & Teacher Education International Conference 2004* (pp. 3217–3222). Chesapeake, VA: Association for the Advancement of Computing in Education (AACE).

Chai, C. S., Koh, J.H.L., & Tsai, C. C. (2010). Facilitating preservice teachers' development of technological, pedagogical, and content knowledge (TPACK). *Educational Technology & Society, 13*(4), 63–73.

Creswell, J. W. (2013). *Research design: Qualitative, quantitative, and mixed methods approaches.* Thousand Oaks, CA: SAGE Publications.

Duff, P. (2008). *Case study research in applied linguistics.* New York: Taylor & Francis.

Gillham, B. (2008). *Developing a questionnaire* (2nd ed.). London, UK: Continuum International Publishing Group Ltd.

Good, T., & Brophy, J. (2000). *Looking in classrooms* (8th ed.). New York: Longman.

Graham, C., Cox, S., & Velasquez, A. (2009). Teaching and measuring TPACK development in two preservice teacher preparation programs. In I. Gibson et al. (Eds.), *Proceedings of Society for Information Technology & Teacher Education International Conference 2009* (pp. 4081–4086). Chesapeake, VA: Association for the Advancement of Computing in Education (AACE).

Harris, J. B., Grandgenett, N., & Hofer, M. (2010). Testing a TPACK-based technology integration assessment rubric. In D. Gibson & B. Dodge (Eds.), *Proceedings of Society for Information Technology & Teacher Education International Conference 2010* (pp. 3833–3840). Chesapeake, VA: Association for the Advancement of Computing in Education (AACE).

Harris, J. B., Grandgenett, N., & Hofer, M. (2012). Using structured interviews to assess experienced teachers' TPACK. In P. Resta (Ed.), *Proceedings of Society for Information Technology & Teacher Education International Conference 2012* (pp. 4696–4703). Chesapeake, VA: Association for the Advancement of Computing in Education (AACE).

Harris, J. B., & Hofer, M. J. (2009). Technological pedagogical content knowledge (TPACK) in action: A descriptive study of secondary teachers' curriculum-based, technology-related instructional planning. Paper presented at the annual meeting of the American Educational Research Association (AERA), San Diego, CA.

Harris, J. B., & Hofer, M. J. (2011). Technological pedagogical content knowledge (TPACK) in action: A descriptive study of secondary teachers' curriculum-based, technology-related instructional planning. *Journal of Research on Technology in Education, 43*(3), 211–229.

Hofer, M., Grandgenett, N., Harris, J., & Swan, K. (2011). Testing a TPACK-based technology integration observation instrument. In M. Koehler & P. Mishra (Eds.), *Proceedings of Society for Information Technology & Teacher Education International Conference 2011* (pp. 4352–4359). Chesapeake, VA: Association for the Advancement of Computing in Education (AACE).

Kereluik, K., Casperson, G., & Akcaoglu, M. (2010). Coding pre-service teacher lesson plans for TPACK. In D. Gibson & B. Dodge (Eds.), *Proceedings of Society for Information Technology & Teacher Education International Conference 2010* (pp. 3889–3891). Chesapeake, VA: Association for the Advancement of Computing in Education (AACE).

Kilickaya, F. (2009). The effect of a computer-assisted language learning course on pre-service English teachers' practice teaching. *Educational Studies, 35*(4), 437–448.

Koehler, M. J., & Mishra, P. (2005). What happens when teachers design educational technology? The development of technological pedagogical content knowledge. *Journal of Educational Computing Research, 32*(2), 131–152.

Koehler, M. J., Mishra, P., & Yahya, K. (2007). Tracing the development of teacher knowledge in a design seminar: Integrating content, pedagogy and technology. *Computers & Education, 49*(3), 740–762.

Koehler, M. J., Shin, T. S., & Mishra, P. (2012). How do we measure TPACK? Let me count the ways. In R. N. Ronau, C. R. Rakes, & M. L. Niess (Eds.), *Educational technology, teacher knowledge, and classroom impact: A research handbook on frameworks and approaches* (pp. 16–31). Hershey, PA: IGI Global.

Lux, N. J. (2010). Assessing technological pedagogical content knowledge. Doctoral dissertation. Retrieved from ProQuest Dissertations and Theses database. UMI No. 763640461

Marquez Chisholm, I., & Padgett, H. (2004). Observations of faculty integration of technology into teacher preparation. In R. Ferdig et al. (Eds.), *Proceedings of Society for Information Technology & Teacher Education International Conference 2004* (pp. 3498–3504). Chesapeake, VA: Association for the Advancement of Computing in Education (AACE).

Mishra, P., & Koehler, M. J. (2006). Technological pedagogical content knowledge: A framework for teacher knowledge. *Teachers College Record, 108*(6), 1017–1054.

Mishra, P., Peruski, L., & Koehler, M. (2007). Developing technological pedagogical content knowledge (TPCK) through teaching online. In R. Carlsen et al. (Eds.), *Proceedings of Society for Information Technology & Teacher Education International Conference 2007* (pp. 2208–2213). Chesapeake, VA: Association for the Advancement of Computing in Education (AACE).

Mohan, B. (2007). Knowledge structures in social practices. In J. Cummins & C. Davison (Eds.), *International Handbook of English Language Teaching* (pp. 303–315). Boston, MA: Springer US.

Niess, M. L. (2011). Investigating TPACK: Knowledge growth in teaching with technology. *Journal of Educational Computing Research, 44*(3), 299–317.

Niess, M. L., Lee, K., Sadri, P., & Suharwoto, G. (2006). Guiding inservice mathematics teachers in developing a technology pedagogical knowledge (TPCK). In annual meeting of the American Educational Research Association, San Francisco, CA.

Ozgün-Koca, S. A., Meagher, M., & Edwards, M. T. (2009). Pre-service teachers' emerging TPACK in a technology-rich methods class. *The Mathematics Educator, 19*(2), 10–20.

Richardson, K. W. (2009). Looking at/looking through: Teachers planning for curriculum-based learning with technology. Doctoral dissertation. Retrieved from ProQuest Dissertations and Theses database. UMI No. 3371354

Robertshaw, M. B., & Gillam, R. B. (2010). Examining the validity of the TPACK framework from the ground up: Viewing technology integration through teachers' eyes. In D. Gibson & B. Dodge (Eds.), *Proceedings of Society for Information Technology & Teacher Education International Conference 2010* (pp. 3926–3931). Chesapeake, VA: Association for the Advancement of Computing in Education (AACE).

Sahin, I. (2011). Development of survey of technological pedagogical and content knowledge (TPACK). *Turkish Online Journal of Educational Technology-TOJET, 10*(1), 97–105.

Schmidt, D. A., Baran, E., Thompson, A. D., Mishra, P., Koehler, M. J., & Shin, T. S. (2009). Technological pedagogical content knowledge (TPACK): The development and validation of an assessment instrument for preservice teachers. *Journal of Research on Technology in Education, 42*(2), 123–149.

Shulman L. S. (1986) Those who understand: Knowledge growth in teaching. *Educational Researcher, 15*, 4–14.

So, H. J., & Kim, B. (2009). Learning about problem based learning: Student teachers integrating technology, pedagogy and content knowledge. *Australasian Journal of Educational Technology, 25*(1), 101–116.

Swan, K., & Hofer, M. (2011). In search of technological pedagogical content knowledge: Teachers' initial foray into podcasting in economics. *Journal of Research on Technology in Education, 44*(1), 75–98.

Williams, M. K., Foulger, T., & Wetzel, K. (2010). Aspiring to reach 21st century ideals: Teacher educators' experiences in developing their TPACK. In D. Gibson & B. Dodge (Eds.), *Proceedings of Society for Information Technology & Teacher Education International Conference 2010* (pp. 3960–3967). Chesapeake, VA: Association for the Advancement of Computing in Education (AACE).

Yin, R. K. (2003). *Case study research: Design and methods* (3rd ed.). Thousand Oaks, CA: SAGE Publications.

8

Support for Technology Integration

Implications From and For the TPACK Framework

Noortje Janssen, Ard W. Lazonder

Introduction

Since Mishra and Koehler (2006) introduced the Technological Pedagogical and Content Knowledge (TPACK) framework, the effective use of technology in education has received increased attention. Several studies have used the TPACK framework to characterize pre-service and in-service teachers' technology integration in terms of the three basic TPACK elements (pedagogy, content, and technology) and their intersections (TPK, TCK, PCK, and TPCK[1]) (e.g., Koehler et al., 2011; Schmidt et al., 2009). Although the TPACK framework has proven to be successful in this respect, the framework does not offer specific guidelines to *support* teachers in integrating technology in their teaching practices. The goal of this chapter is to find out whether the TPACK framework could have prescriptive merits for the design of such support.

The term "support" refers to any kind of guidance that aims to assist teachers in integrating pedagogy, content, and technology during the planning and delivery of their lessons. This support can be offered in various ways, for example by written texts, modeling, or training activities, and ultimately aims to enable teachers to integrate all three basic TPACK elements. A recent review showed that there are three routes through which teachers can develop TPCK: either via PCK, via TPK, or simultaneously via PCK *and* TPCK (Koehler, Mishra, Kereluik, Shin, & Graham, 2014). Guidance along the way to TPCK can roughly be classified as pertaining to either the basic TPACK elements or their intersections.

Support on the basic TPACK elements aims to extend teachers' knowledge of technology, pedagogy, and content per se rather than their development of TPCK through a specific route. For example, in an online learning environment that enabled in-service teachers to create their own lessons, Doering, Koseoglug, Scharber, Henricksong, and Lanegrang (2014) offered in-service teachers information on geospatial technologies, subject matter, and pedagogical strategies. Graham, Borup, and Smith (2012) started their technology-integration course by specifying the technologies (e.g., Google Earth) and pedagogies (e.g., science inquiry) in order to facilitate pre-service teachers in their lesson planning. Both studies report positive effects of the support on technology integration. Doering et al. (2014) found that teachers' confidence concerning pedagogy, content, and PCK remained high throughout the study, and that their confidence in the technology-related TPACK components (TK, TPK, TCK, and TPCK) increased. Graham et al. (2012) assessed pre-service teachers' technological knowledge, TPK, and TPCK and found a decrease in the number of lesson planning justifications based on technology alone, and an increase in justifications related to TPK and TPCK.

Support on the intersections of the TPACK framework aims to assist teachers in integrating pedagogy, content, and technology. Research on this type of support illustrates how teachers can develop TPCK via the three routes mentioned by Koehler et al. (2014). Niess (2005) designed a one-year teacher preparation program that used PCK courses as the basis for developing TPCK. Koh and Divaharan (2011) modeled the pedagogical applications of the whiteboard to pre-service teachers prior to addressing the other TPACK components. In a more recent study, such TPK support was given to both in-service and pre-service teachers to demonstrate the use of ICT for several pedagogical approaches, such as authentic and self-directed learning (Koh & Chai, 2014). Even though these integrated programs intuitively seem beneficial to (learn to) integrate technology in education, results showed that integrated support does not necessarily lead to full technology integration. Koh and Chai (2014) found that the TPACK confidence of most pre-service and in-service teachers increased after the course, whereas Koh and Divaharan (2011) found that pre-service teachers' reflections on technology integration only increased in TPK-related justifications, and not in TCK or TPCK-related justifications. In the study by Niess (2005), most pre-service teachers managed to successfully develop TPCK, but some teachers were still oblivious to *how* to integrate technology.

Research comparing different types of TPACK-based support is scant. A notable exception is the study by Walker et al. (2012). They found that in-service teachers who received training on technology *and* were taught how this technology could be applied during problem-based learning (TPK) had more sophisticated statements on problem-based learning in their lesson plans than did teachers who merely received the technology training. However, no other TPACK element except pedagogy was assessed from the lesson plans, and even though both groups of teachers evidenced increased confidence in TK, PCK, and TPCK, differences between the two groups were not tested for statistical significance. The existing research therefore does not allow for any definitive conclusion on the design and effectiveness of TPACK-based support. Initial evidence suggests that support based on the TPACK framework can facilitate teachers' technology integration, but more research is needed to establish what type of support is most effective and whether and how the TPACK framework could serve as a basis to derive guidelines for teacher support.

This chapter presents two studies that examined two types of TPACK-based support for lesson planning. Contrary to the TPACK studies mentioned before, our studies did not employ a TPACK course but offered just-in-time support for the design and use of a technology-infused lesson plan. Lesson plans are prevalent in teachers' daily practice: they create lesson plans during lesson preparation and use them in class when delivering a lesson. Lesson plans therefore include information on the integration of pedagogy, content, and technology, as well as information on the actual classroom context (e.g., on students' prior knowledge, curriculum alignment, student materials, etc.), in this way showing TPACK integral to the context of teachers' actual classroom practice (cf. Porras-Hernandez & Salinas-Amescua, 2013).

The studies in this chapter start from the notion that teachers who are inexperienced in the integration of new technologies in their classes need support. This support should be aligned with the teachers' current TPACK level. In-service and pre-service teachers are generally unfamiliar with innovative technologies and even less knowledgeable of their educational use. Both groups of teachers would therefore benefit from support that offers information on the application of the technologies. However, pre-service and in-service teachers do differ considerably in teaching experience and, hence, in the extent to which they have developed and integrated pedagogical and content knowledge (PCK).

In-service teachers generally possess an advanced level of PCK. They have developed and integrated pedagogical and content knowledge in their teacher training and through professional experience (Gess-Newsome, 1999; Van Driel, Verloop, & De Vos, 1998). Pedagogical and content support for in-service teachers should therefore be offered in an integrated way, as this seems a fruitful route to develop TPACK (e.g., see Niess, Van Zee, & Gillow-Wiles, 2010). Pre-service teachers have a different TPACK starting position. Even though most teacher education programs focus on the development of PCK, not all pre-service teachers manage to acquire this knowledge (Hume & Berry, 2011; Van Driel, De Jong, & Verloop, 2002). This was also found in research on courses targeting the development of TPACK, in which a large share of the pre-service teachers did not fully develop PCK and TPACK (e.g., Pamuk, 2012; So & Kim, 2009). Pre-service teachers might therefore benefit more from support that contains separate pedagogical and content information, as it would enable them to extend their incomplete and fragmented pedagogical and content knowledge.

To summarize, we postulate that teachers' current TPACK level could serve as a vantage point for the design of support. We further assume that pre-service and in-service teachers differ with regard to their development and integration of pedagogical and content knowledge, and we predict that separate support for these components is more appropriate for pre-service teachers, whereas integrated support is more appropriate for in-service teachers. These expectations were investigated in two empirical studies that revolved around teachers' lesson planning. In the first explorative study, we asked teachers for their preference regarding either separate or integrated support materials; the second study was a controlled experiment that tested whether the most preferred type of support from the first study indeed led to higher quality lesson plans than the least preferred support.

Study 1: Teachers' Preference for Lesson Plan Support[2]

Based on the TPACK framework, we developed a technology-infused lesson plan for a secondary school biology unit using modeling software (technology) to investigate (pedagogy) the glucose–insulin regulation process (content). The lesson plan gave a description of the domain, learning goals, materials, and the learning activities. During the target lessons, students were first introduced to the software, then developed a glucose–insulin model, and finally tested the model in two scenarios (i.e., "eating a pizza" and "investigating the effects of Type 1 diabetes").

Additional technological, pedagogical, and content support was given in two types of support materials. Both variants offered the same technological information but differed with regard to the presentation of the pedagogical and content information. As shown in Table 8.1, the *integrated support* presented this information in a compact, integrated manner, whereas the *separate support* presented pedagogical and content information separately.

Additionally, student materials were given in order to mimic an authentic lesson preparation situation. These materials were complementary to the lesson plan and consisted of the modeling software, a model editor manual, a text about glucose–insulin regulation, and corresponding assignments.

To examine teachers' preferences for one of the two types of support, semi-structured interviews were held with 23 pre-service and 23 in-service biology teachers. In individual

Table 8.1 Pedagogical and Content Information in the Support Materials

Support	Description	Example
Integrated Support		
Content & Pedagogy	Information about glucose–insulin regulation and inquiry-based learning. Content information was purposefully integrated with pedagogical information.	"Based on what the students now know about eating a pizza and diabetes [content] they can formulate predictions for their experiment [pedagogy]."
Technology	Step-by-step description of the modeling software, supplemented with screenshots and a glossary of the symbols used.	"When clicking on a variable, the *start value* of that variable can be defined."
Separate Support		
Content	Information about glucose–insulin regulation. The main concepts were presented such that teachers could easily relate them to the variables in the model.	"After eating a pizza, the glucose spikes in an uncontrolled manner. The glucose level in the blood rises rapidly and the insulin level follows quickly."
Pedagogy	Information about the inquiry-based learning processes of orientation, hypothesis generation, experimentation, drawing conclusions, and the planning and monitoring process.	"Based on the classroom discussion... students can formulate predictions for their experiment."
Technology	*Identical to the integrated support.*	

45-minute sessions, we asked them to read all materials and then decide whether they would prefer the integrated or separate support when actually preparing the lesson. We predicted that pre-service teachers would prefer the separate support as they have incomplete and detached knowledge of pedagogy, content, and technology. In-service teachers were expected to choose the integrated support because they have extensive, integrated knowledge of pedagogy and content. To test these predictions, teachers were asked to choose either the separate or integrated support and to justify their choice.

All interviews were audio recorded and transcribed verbatim. Teachers' justifications were classified in five broad categories (i.e., amount of information, presentation format, transparency, concreteness, and theoretical rigor). Ten interviews were coded by two raters to establish that inter-rater agreement was satisfactory (Cohen's κ = .72). Additionally, detailed qualitative analyses were performed by the first author to relate the teachers' justifications to their level of teaching experience.

Results showed that pre-service and in-service teachers did not differ significantly in their preferences, χ^2 (1, N = 46) = 0.41, p = 0.52. A majority of both the in-service (73%) and pre-service teachers (65%) preferred the integrated support. Both pre-service and in-service teachers who preferred the integrated support felt that the amount of information was sufficient, that this support was more concrete and more closely related to the lesson plan and classroom practice. Similarly, the pre-service and in-service teachers who preferred the separate support believed it was concrete, but some of them also felt that this support was more theoretical, general, and abstract. Furthermore, they perceived this support as being more transparent, that is, clearer than the integrated support, which was probably because pedagogy and content were presented in separate sections.

There were also some notable differences between the responses of pre-service and in-service teachers. Regarding the amount of information in the separate support, pre-service teachers who chose this variant—as expected—appreciated the elaborate descriptions because they felt they needed a safety net in case they did not know or would forget certain information. In-service teachers who preferred this support, by contrast, appreciated the extensive information because it could serve as useful reference material. The separate presentation of content and pedagogy made it easier to find information so they could themselves single out the pieces of information they would need. This result was inconsistent with our expectation that in-service teachers would prefer integrated support. Still, as this was only a small group of in-service teachers who did not base their choice of support on their content and pedagogical knowledge, this result does not lead to implications for the TPACK framework.

The majority of the pre-service and in-service teachers liked the presentation format of the integrated support, albeit for different reasons. As predicted, in-service teachers preferred this presentation format because it matched their teaching practice. For example, one teacher stated:

> Especially because everything that is related is provided together. For example, content is content, but when you teach you do not talk only about content, but also about the pedagogy that relates to it.

Pre-service teachers liked this presentation format for a different reason: it supported them in the challenging process of integrating pedagogy and content. For example, one pre-service teacher said:

> I think that this [integrated support] will also take a lot less time. Because I think when you have to come up with this yourself, how will I do that, how should I guide the students, how will I increase students' understanding? When I have to think about that myself, what could be possible problems, how do I solve them, then this will take much more time than when I get examples like address the effect of eating or the effect of diabetes in this way.

This excerpt illustrates that pre-service teachers tended to be future-oriented and appreciated the support for the PCK they still need to develop rather than the separate pedagogical and content knowledge they currently have.

To conclude, although in-service teachers' responses largely correspond with the tenets of the TPACK framework, the preferences and justifications of the pre-service teachers did not. Most pre-service teachers preferred the integrated support because it assisted them in integrating pedagogy and content. Consequently, when using the TPACK framework as a guide to design support, a different interpretation should be considered, one where pre-service teachers are supported one step beyond their current TPACK level. Still, as this study merely addressed teachers' preferences, further research is needed to determine whether pre-service teachers indeed benefit more from integrated information than from separate information in preparing and delivering technology-infused lessons.

Study 2: Effectiveness of TPACK-Based Lesson Plan Support[3]

Having established teachers' support preferences, we shifted our attention to examining the effectiveness of this support. More specifically, we wanted to find out whether the perceived benefits of integrated pedagogical and content support maintain in an actual lesson-planning situation. Using the same support materials as in Study 1, we conducted a controlled experiment with 53 pre-service biology teachers; the reason for focusing exclusively on prospective teachers was motivated by the fact that in Study 1 their support preferences were least consistent with the tenets of the TPACK framework. That is, pre-service teachers preferred integrated pedagogical and content support over separate support because they argued it would assist them in the *integration* of pedagogy and content. During the experiment, pre-service teachers either received the integrated support ($n = 27$) or separate support ($n = 26$).

Our hypotheses relate specifically to the participants' justifications. Pre-service teachers who received integrated support were expected to include more PCK-related statements in their justifications than pre-service teachers who received separate support. As the integrated support is relatively closer to TPCK (i.e., pedagogy and content are already integrated), pre-service teachers who received this support were also expected to incorporate more TPCK-related statements in their justifications than pre-service teachers who received separate support.

The experiment was conducted in a single session that started with a brief hands-on tutorial on the modeling software. Following this activity, pre-service teachers were asked to use the separate or integrated support materials to design a lesson plan for an inquiry-based glucose–insulin regulation lesson. In addition to these resources, participants received complementary student materials consisting of a text about glucose–insulin regulation, assignments, and the model editor, its manual, and a fully worked-out glucose–insulin model. Additionally, they received a lesson plan template that outlined the organization of the lesson (content domain, learning goals, etc.) and the lesson itself (i.e., introduction, core, and closing). Part of the information was predefined (i.e., domain, subject, educational level, and prerequisite knowledge) so that the pre-service teachers would engage in similar lesson preparation activities. They were instructed to use this template to provide elaborate information on content, pedagogy, and technology and to justify their design decisions in the lesson-planning process.

Pre-service teachers' lesson plans were analyzed using a stepwise approach. First, the lesson plans were divided into learning activities that were checked to ensure that they reflected the information from the support materials and contained pedagogical, content, and technological information. Next, the information in each learning activity was classified as either descriptive information or justification; the justifications were further analyzed to determine whether pedagogy and content were integrated, and whether technology was integrated with pedagogy and/or content. For each step, two raters coded 12 lesson plans, yielding a Cohen's κ that ranged from .76 to .98. The first author coded the remaining lesson plans and consulted the second rater when in doubt.

Results showed that the lesson plans contained four learning activities on average (range: three to six). Three of these learning activities could readily be traced back to the information given in the available support materials, which means that approximately one learning activity was conceived by the pre-service teachers themselves. This relatively high coverage suggests that most pre-service teachers indeed used the support they received to design their lesson plan.

Closer inspection of the learning activities revealed that every single instance contained pedagogical information. Information about the learning content was present in approximately 75% of the learning activities, whereas technology was mentioned in nearly two-thirds of the learning activities. This indicates that there was sufficient opportunity for pre-service teachers to integrate pedagogy with content and/or technology.

Pre-service teachers' justifications were examined to find out whether and to what extent pedagogy, content, and technology were integrated. Pre-service teachers who received the integrated support included PCK-related statements in more than half of their justifications (52%), which proved to be significantly more than the 35% PCK-related statements found in the justifications of the pre-service teachers who received separate support, $U = 218.00$, $z = -2.38$, $p = .02$. This result confirms our first expectation that integrated support leads to higher integration of pedagogical and content information than does the separate support.

Next, we analyzed the justifications on TPCK-related statements, but the integration of all three TPACK elements proved to be slightly beyond the pre-service teachers' reach.

Pre-service teachers who received integrated support had 15% of these justifications on average, whereas the justifications of the pre-service teachers who received the separate support contained 9% of these statements, $U = 307.00$, $z = -0.89$, $p = .38$. These results contradict our second hypothesis and suggest that integrated support does not necessarily lead to significantly more integration of technology with pedagogy and content.

To conclude, the results of this study show that pre-service teachers generally use the support they receive, and that integrated support enhances the integration of pedagogical and content information in pre-service teachers' justifications. This substantiates the notion that the way that pedagogical and content information is provided affects the extent to which pre-service teachers integrate pedagogy and content in their lesson planning. When support is aimed at pre-service teachers' zone of proximal development (i.e., on the level of PCK), pre-service teachers are more successful in integrating pedagogical and content knowledge. This conclusion has direct implications for the prescriptive use of the TPACK framework: support on the TPACK intersections is more effective than support on the basic elements.

Discussion

In the studies described above, the TPACK framework was used to derive guidelines for the design of teacher support. In the first study, teachers' TPACK starting position was used as a basis to develop designated lesson plan support. Teachers were interviewed about their support preferences, which in turn served as input for the second study that investigated the effects of TPACK-based support on pre-service teachers' actual lesson planning.

The results of both studies point to one important guideline for supporting pre-service teachers' technology integration. Most pre-service teachers preferred support beyond their TPACK starting position, and the use of this integrated support enhanced the integration of pedagogy and content information. Instead of addressing pre-service teachers' current knowledge base, support should fall within their zone of proximal development (Vygotsky, 1987) so as to help them succeed in tasks that would otherwise be beyond reach. Even though pre-service teachers' pedagogical and content knowledge may be incomplete, they appear to be sufficiently knowledgeable to make productive use of integrated PCK support to consider pedagogical and content information in tandem during lesson planning.

Pre-service teachers who received integrated support had a similar percentage of TPCK-related statements as pre-service teachers who received separate support. In fact, they both had relatively few TPCK-related statements in their justifications, which confirms Mishra and Koehler's assertion that TPCK is "an emergent form of knowledge that goes beyond all three components" (Mishra & Koehler, 2006, p. 1028). Consequently, additional support for integrating technology with pedagogy and content seems needed in order for teachers to develop TPCK. Given that integrated support was found to be more effective than separate support, we postulate that pre-service teachers' should be offered support materials on the level of TPCK. Future research should examine whether such integrated support is equally effective for teachers' TPCK development as it was for pre-service teachers' integration of pedagogy and content in our studies.

Implications for in-service teachers are less apparent because we only know that most in-service teachers preferred integrated support over separate support. This finding could serve as a springboard for further investigations into the effectiveness of both types of support for in-service teachers' lesson planning. Future research could also examine whether the guideline we derived for pre-service teachers (i.e., support should fall within the teachers' zone of proximal development) also applies to in-service teachers. If so, this would result in support for TPCK. Further research comparing the effectiveness of this TPCK support with support on the level of PCK and technology should reveal which variant is most effective, and thus which guideline is most appropriate for in-service teachers' technology integration.

Future research should also investigate the effectiveness of support on the TPACK intersections *not* included in the present studies. The TPACK framework suggests that there are multiple "routes" to arrive at TPCK (Koehler et al., 2014). Our studies showed that PCK support is more effective than separate support for pedagogy and content. Whether this conclusion holds for the other two intersections (i.e., TPK and TCK) remains to be shown. In addition, it would be interesting to compare the relative effectiveness of integrated support for the three intersections to determine which "route" to TPCK support is most effective to promote teachers' technology integration.

To conclude, while previous TPACK research revolved around technology integration courses, our studies offered just-in-time TPACK-based support for lesson planning. This type of support seems particularly appropriate for in-service teachers who generally lack the time to attend extensive courses (Valcke, Rots, Verbeke, & van Braak, 2007) but do need guidance when using a new technology in their teaching. Just-in-time support is also deemed appropriate for use in teacher preparation programs. By offering just-in-time support on PCK and technology, teacher educators can focus directly on the technology integration process by having prospective teachers prepare or deliver TPACK-based lessons. Educational publishers and software designers could play a prominent role in the actual design of TPACK-based support. Supplementing a new (educational) technology with tailor-made lesson plan support might increase the successful uptake of that technology by educational practitioners. The productive use of existing technologies can be increased by having experienced TPACK teachers share their knowledge with less experienced teachers, for instance by uploading their own lesson plans on educational websites and portals. This sharing of teacher-made resources is already in vogue, and the challenge now becomes to add appropriate support for these materials. More research is therefore needed to find out which support most effectively enhances teachers' technology integration. The guideline derived from the studies presented in this chapter could function as an inspiration for researchers to further explore how the TPACK framework can guide the design of this support.

Notes

1 In this chapter, the acronym TPACK refers to the framework as a whole, whereas TPCK is used to indicate the core knowledge element within this framework.
2 This section is based on Janssen, N. & Lazonder, A.W. (2015). Implementing innovative technologies through lesson plans. What kind of support do teachers prefer? *Journal of Science Education and Technology*, 24, 910–920. doi:10.1007/s10956-015-9573-5
3 This section is based on Janssen, N. & Lazonder, A.W. (2015). Supporting pre-service teachers in designing technology-infused lesson plans. Manuscript submitted for publication.

References

Doering, A., Koseoglug, S., Scharberg, C., Henricksong, J., & Lanegrang, D. (2014). Technology integration in K–12 geography education using TPACK as a conceptual model. *Journal of Geography*, 1–15. doi:10.1080/00221341.2014.896393

Gess-Newsome, J. (1999). Pedagogical content knowledge: An introduction and orientation. In J. Gess-Newsome & N. Lederman (Eds.), *Nature, sources, and development of pedagogical content knowledge for science teaching* (pp. 3–17). Dordrecht: Kluwer Academic Publishers.

Graham, C. R., Borup, J., & Smith, N. B. (2012). Using TPACK as a framework to understand teacher candidates' technology integration decisions. *Journal of Computer Assisted Learning, 28*, 530–546. doi:10.1111/j.1365–2729.2011.00472.x

Hume, A., & Berry, A. (2011). Constructing CoRes—A strategy for building PCK in pre-service science teacher education. *Research in Science Education, 41*, 341–355. doi:10.1007/s11165–010–9168–3

Koehler, M. J., Mishra, P., Bouck, E. C., DeSchryver, M., Kereluik, K., Shin, T. S., & Wolf, L. G. (2011). Deep-play: Developing TPACK for 21st century teachers. *International Journal of Learning Technology, 6*. doi:10.1504/IJLT.2011.042646

Koehler, M. J., Mishra, P., Kereluik, K., Shin, T. S., & Graham, C. R. (2014). The technological pedagogical content knowledge framework. In J. M. Specter, M. D. Merrill, J. Elen, & M. J. Bishop (Eds.), *Handbook of research on educational communications and technology* (Vol. 4, pp. 101–111). New York: Springer.

Koh, J.H.L., & Chai, C. S. (2014). Teacher clusters and their perceptions of technological pedagogical content knowledge (TPACK) development through ICT lesson design. *Computers & Education, 70*, 222–232. doi:10.1016/j.compedu.2013.08.017

Koh, J.H.L., & Divaharan, S. (2011). Developing pre-service teachers' technology integration expertise through the TPACK-developing instructional model. *Journal of Educational Computing Research, 44*, 35–58. doi:10.2190/EC.44.1.c

Mishra, P., & Koehler, M. J. (2006). Technological pedagogical content knowledge: A framework for teacher knowledge. *The Teachers College Record, 108*, 1017–1054. doi:10.1111/j.1467–9620.2006.00684.x

Niess, M. L. (2005). Preparing teachers to teach science and mathematics with technology: Developing a technology pedagogical content knowledge. *Teaching and Teacher Education, 21*, 509–523. doi:10.1016/j.tate.2005.03.006

Niess, M. L., Van Zee, E. H., & Gillow-Wiles, H. (2010). Knowledge growth in teaching mathematics/science with spreadsheets: Moving PCK to TPACK through online professional development. *Journal of Digital Learning in Teacher Education, 27*, 42–52. doi:10.1080/21532974.2010.10784657

Pamuk, S. (2012). Understanding preservice teachers' technology use through TPACK framework. *Journal of Computer Assisted Learning, 28*, 425–439. doi:10.1111/j.1365–2729.2011.00447.x

Porras-Hernandez, L. H., & Salinas-Amescua, B. (2013). Strengthening TPACK: A broader notion of context and the use of teacher's narratives to reveal knowledge construction. *Journal of Educational Computing Research, 48*, 223–244. doi:10.2190/EC.48.2.f

Schmidt, D. A., Baran, E., Thompson, A. D., Mishra, P., Koehler, M. J., & Shin, T. S. (2009). Technological pedagogical content knowledge (TPACK): The development and validation of an assessment instrument for preservice teachers. *Journal of Research on Computing in Education, 42*, 123–149. doi:10.1016/j.compedu.2011.04.010

So, H. J., & Kim, B. (2009). Learning about problem based learning: Student teachers integrating technology, pedagogy and content knowledge. *Australasian Journal of Educational Technology, 25*, 101–116.

Valcke, M., Rots, I., Verbeke, M., & van Braak, J. (2007). ICT teacher training: Evaluation of the curriculum and training approach in Flanders. *Teaching and Teacher Education, 23,* 795–808. doi:10.1016/j.tate.2007.02.004

Van Driel, J. H., De Jong, O., & Verloop, N. (2002). The development of preservice chemistry teachers' pedagogical content knowledge. *Science Education, 86,* 572–590. doi:10.1002/sce.10010

Van Driel, J. H., Verloop, N., & De Vos, W. (1998). Developing science teachers' pedagogical content knowledge. *Journal of Research in Science Teaching, 35,* 673–695. doi:10.1002/(SICI)1098-2736(199808)35:6<673::AID-TEA5>3.0.CO;2-J

Vygotsky, L. (1987). *Mind in society: The development of higher psychological processes.* Cambridge, MA: Harvard University Press.

Walker, A., Recker, M., Ye, L., Robertshaw, M. B., Sellers, L., & Leary, H. (2012). Comparing technology-related teacher professional development designs: A multilevel study of teacher and student impacts. *Educational Technology Research and Development, 60,* 421–444. doi:10.1007/s11423-012-9243-8

9

Transforming Teachers' Knowledge for Teaching With Technologies

An Online Learning Trajectory Instructional Approach

Margaret L. Niess

Introduction

In this digital age, new and emerging technologies are more accessible and are potentially useful for teaching and learning (particularly when they are combined intelligently). While not typically designed for education, a careful examination suggests these technologies may guide students' learning in a variety of ways. Students might use probeware technology as an *inquiry tool* to dynamically explore scientific phenomena, such as monitoring environmental conditions with a temperature probe. Extending this exploration, they might use video applications, such as Jing, as a *communication tool* to share their spreadsheet data analyses. Finally, a small group of students might use Google Docs as a *collaborative* tool, where they cooperatively develop an essay that frames their combined results and learning.

Teachers who organize their instruction towards interweaving technologies for *inquiry*, *communication*, and *collaborative* actions are engaged in a *systems pedagogical approach* (Gillow-Wiles & Niess, 2014) for engaging their students in social constructivist learning with technologies. We argue that these teachers are, ultimately, relying on a more advanced, transformed form of Technological Pedagogical Content Knowledge (TPACK) (Mishra & Koehler, 2006; Niess, 2005).

Shifting to a systems pedagogical approach requires that teachers relearn, rethink, and redefine teaching and learning as they know and learned it. They need to confront their current conceptions for integrating technologies (Loughran, 2002). Yet, they need professional in-service learning experiences for transforming their TPACK to incorporate this systems approach. An increasingly important educational setting for such learning experiences now relies on online avenues. The challenge is to identify online learning trajectories that effectively transform teachers' TPACK for incorporating this systems pedagogical approach.

Margaret L. Niess

Conceptual Perspectives for the Design of Online Learning Trajectories

A significant amount of research supports online teacher education for reconceptualizing teaching and learning, drawing from a variety of learning perspectives (Chyung, 2007; Gabriel, 2004; Garrison, Anderson, & Archer, 2001; Guilar & Loring, 2008; Preece, Maloney-Krichmar, & Abras, 2003; Riverin & Stacey, 2008). Garrison, Anderson, and Archer (1999) describe online learning environments as dynamic relationships among three presences: *social, cognitive,* and *teaching*. The social presence leads to meaningful community participation and educational experiences for meaningful learning (Garrison & Cleveland-Innes, 2005; Hill, Song, & West, 2009; Rourke, Anderson, Garrison, & Archer, 1999; Sung & Mayer, 2012; Swan & Shih, 2005). Cognitive presences interact with active social presences to elevate community interactions to a higher level where students (the teachers) are "cognitively engaged in an educational manner" (Garrison & Cleveland-Innes, 2005, p. 135). The teaching presence concentrates on the design of the educational experiences, developing the structure, organization, and presentation of course content, activities, and assessments. These teaching presences facilitate the development of both the social and cognitive presences in meeting the educational goals and outcomes (Garrison et al., 1999; Garrison & Cleveland-Innes, 2005).

Social constructivist instructional strategies frame these trajectories as "ordered networks of experiences" (Confrey & Maloney, 2010, p. 968) for engaging a community of learners in discourse and critical reflection, where each participant's individual knowledge is expanded through the community's shared knowledge. The participants, as a community of learners, are guided in collectively for rethinking and relearning through higher order learning and reflection learning processes (Akyol & Garrison, 2008, 2010; Garrison & Cleveland-Innes, 2005; Sztajn, Confrey, Wilson, & Edgington, 2012).

Teacher educators need empirically supported online learning trajectories that identify learning experiences effective in transforming teachers' TPACK. The learning trajectories must guide participants in accommodating and assimilating their TPACK through "successive refinements of representation, articulation, and reflection, towards increasingly complex concepts" (Confrey & Maloney, 2010, p. 968). Such TPACK learning trajectories identify instruction for learning about the technologies as well as teaching with the technologies through more social, metacognitive, and constructivist higher order learning experiences. Beginning with four components of pedagogical content knowledge (Grossman, Wilson, & Shulman, 1989; Grossman, 1990), Niess (2005) expands the thinking about TPACK development experiences for engaging teachers in thinking about learning and teaching in four key ways, by suggesting that teachers are developing:

1. An overarching conception about the purposes for incorporating technology in teaching subject matter topics.
2. Knowledge of students' understandings, thinking, and learning in subject matter topics with appropriate technologies.
3. Knowledge of curriculum and curricular materials that integrate technology in learning and teaching subject matter topics.
4. Knowledge of instructional strategies and representations for teaching and learning subject matter topics with technologies.

Now, in recognition of the *pedagogical systems approach*, researchers must identify its effectiveness for guiding teachers toward examining their own thinking about teaching with technologies in ways that integrate and interweave *inquiry, communication,* and *collaboration* in their teaching and learning experiences. The challenge for this line of work is to provide the empirical support for such an online learning trajectory that uses the pedagogical systems approach to guide participants in inquiry, communication, and collaboration with multiple technologies in ways that effectively transform teachers' TPACK.

The Research: An Online TPACK Learning Trajectory Instruction

Previous research (Niess & Gillow-Wiles, 2013) proposed essential features of an online learning trajectory for using a social metacognitive constructivist instructional framework in online teacher education. The trajectory identified a process for participants moving from "informal ideas, through successive refinements of representation, articulation, and reflection towards increasingly complex concepts over time" (Confrey & Maloney, 2010). This trajectory proposed three primary components: (1) the necessary *tools for learning*; (2) the *learning processes* for using these tools; and (3) *learning content*.

This study extended that online learning trajectory by examining the influence of a systems pedagogical approach for transforming teachers' TPACK for teaching mathematics and science. The study (part of a larger study involving the three TPACK courses in the master's program) focused on the winter course in the second year of a three-year online master's program towards transforming practicing teachers' TPACK: *Technology and Literacy in Learning Mathematics and Science*. A multiple case study methodology was used to examine the influence of this systems approach on TPACK transformation. All nine K–12 teachers in the course (seven females and two males) consented to participate. The primary research question was, What is the influence of the online learning trajectory's systems pedagogical approach in guiding teachers in interweaving inquiry, communication, and collaboration with multiple technologies and transforming their TPACK? Three subquestions guided the data analysis:

1. What instructional features are essential for teachers' thinking through the systems pedagogical approach for teaching with multiple technologies?
2. How do these features interact to support teachers moving "from informal ideas through subsequent refinements or representation, articulation and reflection towards increasingly complex concepts over time" (Confrey & Maloney, 2010, p. 968)?
3. What combination of tools, learning processes, and learning outcomes support teachers in transforming their thinking for integrating and interweaving the technologies in inquiry, communication, and collaboration?

Course Design

The online course content used systems pedagogical strategies for integrating inquiry, communication, and collaboration actions with the multiple technologies for teaching

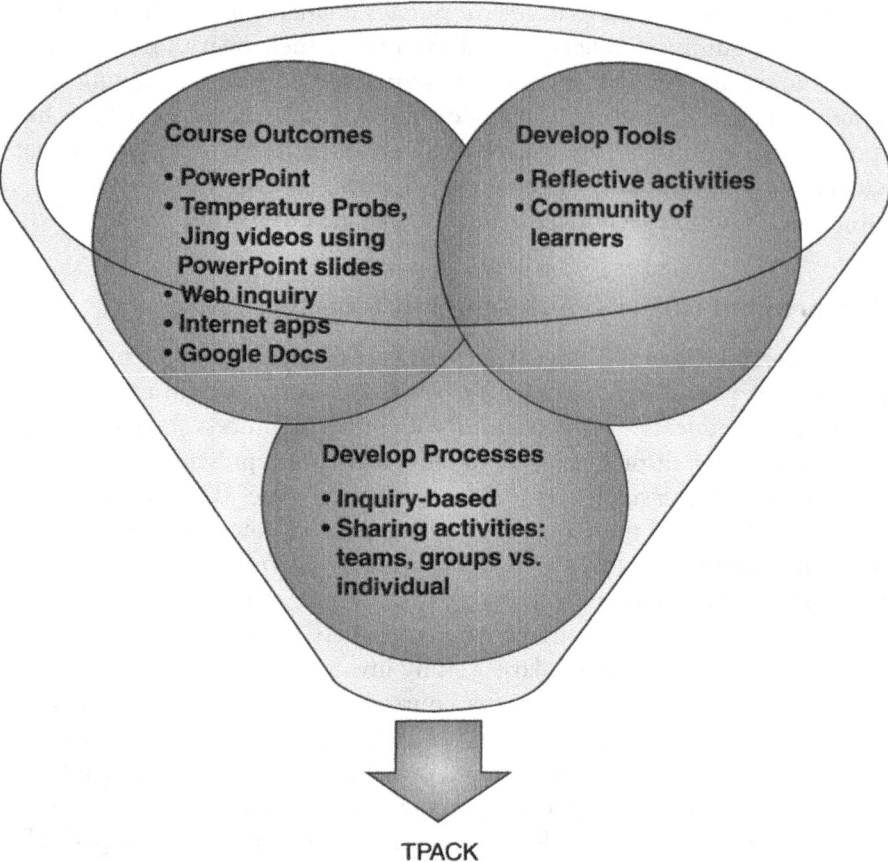

Figure 9.1 Designing the TPACK Learning Trajectory

mathematics and science. The course outcomes, tools, and processes were interactively and collectively framed to identify instructional actions leading toward Niess's (2005) four TPACK components. Figure 9.1 portrays the course design process.

We identified four kinds of basic technologies that would map onto the four TPACK components. Specifically, PowerPoint and Jing videos emphasized *communication*; probeware (temperature, Web inquiry, and Web applications) were added for the *inquiry* emphasis; and Google Docs emphasized *collaboration*. The *inquiry* emphasis throughout the course relied on an accepted science instructional model—the 5 E's Inquiry Instructional model (Engage, Explore, Explain, Elaborate, and Evaluate [Bybee et al., 2006]). Table 9.1 shows how the technologies were incorporated in each unit along with the 5 E's Inquiry emphasis and the challenges directing the primary actions in each unit.

Table 9.1 Course Outline: Technologies, Actions, and Challenges in Each of the Five Units

Unit	Technology	5 E's Inquiry Emphasis	Challenge
1	PowerPoint	Engage	Communicate ideas and reflections in ways that engage the listener in the ideas rather than in reading text.
2	Temperature probe; Jing videos using PowerPoint slides	Explore, Explain	Explore a technology with which you have no prior experience to consider its use in learning science/mathematics; explain your learning and students' learning through video reflection.
3	Web inquiry	Engage, Explore, Explain	Design a Web-based inquiry for science/mathematics that engages students in exploring a problem and explaining the solution.
4	Web applications	Engage, Explore, Explain, Elaborate	Design a lesson package to engage students in learning with a Web application for a science/mathematics topic.
5	Google Docs	Explain, Evaluate	Explain and evaluate the strengths, weaknesses, opportunities, and threats of collaborative writings.

Two essential components, *tools* and *learning processes*, were incorporated to actualize the social and cognitive presences (Garrison et al., 1999). The instructional actions purposefully framed the course content, to actualize the third presence, teaching. The three presences were then connected using an inquiry-based pedagogical systems approach.

A *community of learners* and *meaningful reflection* provided the learning tools. The community of learners was initiated in the first class with all students collaboratively developing a PowerPoint presentation that explored different Web 2.0 applications. Each participant created an informative slide on one application and an introductory slide to the community of learners.

Meaningful reflection in higher order thinking and learning (Lucey, O'Malley, & Jansem, 2009) provided the second key aspect of the approach. The participants consistently reflected on the instructional strategies and their learning experiences with the technologies. At the completion of each unit, they prepared reflective essays on the instructional strategies and how these strategies were useful in their knowledge development about learning and about teaching.

Inquiry and shared/individual knowledge development were the primary learning processes. The inquiry process engaged participants in constructing their understandings. They asked questions, gathered and analyzed information, generated solutions, made decisions, and justified their conclusions. The resulting actions interwove their learning about the multiple technologies through the instructional approaches and content. They communicated with multiple technologies and consistently engaged in thinking and reflecting about the dynamic interactions among content, pedagogy, and technology in their online learning experiences (Roberts, 2002).

The tools and learning processes collectively formed and sustained shared and individual knowledge construction. The participants engaged in dynamic interactions and metacognitive reflection as a community of learners. Both small group collaborative/cooperative activities, as well as large/whole group assignments throughout the trajectory, supported these interactions. Small group membership purposefully assured that every participant had an opportunity to work with every other participant, reinforcing the community of learners' relationships. The inquiry model framed the instructional strategies in these grouping structures, where small groups engaged at a virtual workbench to develop ideas and concepts. These ideas and concepts were brought to the larger community for a more thorough review and for integration into the commonly held body of shared knowledge. The large group discussions fostered relationships among students, facilitating the community of learners through engagement in common activities towards a common goal. As the participants became more comfortable moving between small and large group engagement, the focus of the activities transitioned away from the familiar (themselves) to the new, unfamiliar (the course content).

Data Sources and Analysis

Multiple data sources were gathered for examining the learning trajectory influence: online Blackboard Discussion Board interactions and discussions; unit products; unit reflective essays; and final audio Skype transcribed interviews. The members of the research team compiled electronic case binders for each participant (Meyers, Chappell, Elder, Geist, & Schwidder, 2003) to structure the data sources. Each case documented their knowledge progression; the final interviews summarized their thinking about teaching with technology with specific identification of tasks they found influential for their thinking. The cross-case analyses documented the patterns in their TPACK transitions throughout the course with specific attention to their changes in the four TPACK component areas (Niess, 2005).

Throughout the analysis, the *systems* lens was used to describe, analyze, and understand each participant's experiences and perceptions, revealing the interplay between the experiences and how the online learning trajectory influenced their TPACK. This intersection between their experiences, thinking, and TPACK context revealed the influence of the online learning trajectory's systems pedagogical approach.

Each researcher independently conducted the qualitative analysis of each case binder, using a whole-to-part inductive approach (Erickson, 2006) beginning with a first pass of an entire data set (e.g., assignments, transcriptions, etc.). Subsequent iterative reviews involved reviewing and confirming evidence significant to the description of the influence of the learning trajectory on each participant's learning progression using Niess' four TPACK components. As each subsequent case was analyzed, the description was modified to reflect the new understandings until each description was as complete as possible. Through this process, each researcher identified themes across all participants' discussions, unit products, unit reflections, and final interviews.

Next, the researchers collaborated until agreement on each participant's TPACK with respect to their progressions and the TPACK components, as well as the key themes across the cases. Using this qualitative analytic method, the researchers confirmed the influence of the online learning trajectory instructional approach in transforming the teachers' TPACK.

Online Learning Trajectory's Influence on TPACK Transformation

The online instruction engaged participants in ongoing inquiry, collaboration, communication, and reflection for thinking about teaching with these technologies. The analyses revealed three important themes with this learning trajectory. The individual cases provided detailed evidence of these themes (for individual case details, see Niess & Gillow-Wiles, 2014). The following discussion describes the resulting themes, using representative excerpts from the varied data sources in the case binders. The participants' identities are anonymized.

Theme One

The online learning trajectory is multifaceted, involving more than learning the content. It includes how to become an online student and how to become an online community member. Three instructional phases clearly emerged over this learning trajectory.

Phase One

The first phase immersed participants in learning experiences for working with and taking advantage of features of the *tools for learning* (community interactions and reflecting on their learning). Mary discovered:

> The various ways that people created their PowerPoint presentations helped me to realize features I had not discovered on my own. I was able to ask questions . . . that led me to even more new understandings of how to use this technology. I really can't believe how much I learned about a technology I thought I knew how to use pretty well.

Community feelings were initiated in the introductory activities. Lacey said, "Through the discussions I was also able to get a better sense of who my classmates are . . . I hope we all can take this opportunity to form a deeper bond with one another—a bond that will help us throughout the program and beyond as well."

In this phase, the participants began to value how consistent work with the trajectory *tools* engaged them in deeper reflection about the interactions among content, technology, and pedagogy, developing deeper understandings of the purposes and ways technologies are used in teaching. These initial experiences with the activities and instructional strategies engaged them in social metacognitive thinking about learning with technologies and supported their thinking about students' thinking and understanding using the technologies as learning tools.

Phase Two

As they gained skills with the tools, the trajectory transitioned to specific outcomes for the course (TPACK). Now, the tools were interjected with the *learning processes* (inquiry and shared/individual knowledge development). Through multiple tasks, the tools supported learning processes that in turn engaged participants in thinking about teaching with the technologies.

Mary rethought how she communicated and how technology supported new, richer ways of communicating ideas and the value of shared knowledge. "I am beginning to realize how different communication can be when you use other media . . . I rely much too heavily on words, when pictures and animated actions can convey some of the meaning for me." Her participation in the community extended her own learning and knowledge. Connecting her collaborative efforts with the assignments, she suggested, "When I went back to pull some of the ideas from our shared document to my essay, I found that it was impossible to provide credit to the thinking of my group colleagues. The document was changed and edited and elaborated upon so much by each of us, that the words were truly 'ours.'"

Lacey relied on the community interactions with her group members to support her TPACK thinking, developing her concepts of the role of technology in teaching as well as her understanding of student thinking with technology in learning science/mathematics concepts. "What helped me most with the TPK and TCK aspects was when I worked with two of my friends . . . Their reactions and questions gave me insight on learning and teaching mathematics with the temperature probe."

Reflecting about TPACK after the discussion forums, they shifted to valuing metacognitive thinking in learning. Sally concluded, "I have been reflecting on reflection :) Perhaps others have already considered this, but it occurred to me that reflection can involve a great deal of analyzing, evaluating, and synthesizing to arrive at new meaning."

Phase Three

The final phase brought closure to the ideas and concepts that emerged over the course. In this phase, the learning trajectory incorporated the *Explain* and *Evaluate* features in the 5 E's learning structure. This phase focused on a comparison of their individual knowledge development (in Unit 4) with shared knowledge development (in Unit 5). They began with an individual technology application where the instructors reduced the directions for interactions and engagement. The opportunities to engage remained but no assigned collaborative activities directed their engagement. Janice was clear about her feelings: "That was an awful unit. I felt really lost. It showed how much I depended on their responses as ways of helping me."

Now, the tools and learning processes had formed a solid platform from which the participants were able to engage in large and small group discussions as they reflected and expressed TPACK concepts and ideas demonstrating a transformed knowledge for teaching with technologies. The metacognitive thinking expectations during these two units directed their thinking toward learning with technology with and without the shared knowledge actions. Ronda addressed her perceptions this way:

> One of the most insightful concepts was the differences and similarities between the construction of individual and shared knowledge... scientists share, discuss, and analyze results collectively... individual knowledge can be developed in a variety of ways within the classroom. The use of collaboration is an effective method for the development of shared knowledge.

After the final collaborative activity, Mary's understanding about the dynamic between individual and shared knowledge matured:

> To build from all the pieces of individual knowledge that we as a group possessed, once again it proved that the collection was worth more than the sum of its parts. I am greatly appreciative of this knowledge of individual versus shared knowledge that I now possess, and will use it to my advantage when engaging my students in their own collaborative efforts.

Theme Two

The second theme highlighted technology as a critical component of the trajectory content. Technology needs to be introduced at the beginning, integrated in the activities for becoming an online student and a community member in the course. The technologies need to be included as a package, engaging the participants in the systems approach with communication, collaboration, and inquiry. This theme revealed that the participants used the technologies both as tools for sharing knowledge and for constructing knowledge.

Multiple examples indicated that participants valued Jing video as a communication tool. As soon as Alissa was comfortable with creating videos, she continued to post videos about what she had learned in multiple activities, sharing her insights from these activities. She noted, "Online collaboration is a great way to get new perspectives. I really enjoyed the hands-on lessons, such as... the Jing PowerPoint. This made me realize that students would be more interested in learning in this manner as compared to taking notes or listening to lectures." Their Jing creations incorporated PowerPoint slides and probeware graphical software to communicate their inquiries and collaborations in learning with and thinking about learning science/mathematics with this technology. Mary posted Jing videos describing her thinking about specific tasks, asking for help from other participants. Debbie described how sharing the videos enhanced her understanding of TPACK: "I enjoyed my classmates' Jing videos about TPACK. Again, I was single minded when I made mine, and the others added elements and depth to my understanding of this important concept."

Theme Three

The third theme focused on the activities and experiences important for building teachers' knowledge for teaching with the technologies. Influential tasks happened when they personally explored new technologies (such as the temperature probes), where they thought and reflected about their own developing understanding about the technologies, about student thinking and learning, and where they designed lessons and instructional activities for student exploration with technologies. They explored problems through hands-on, directed activities that required scientific/mathematical thinking as highlighted in the 5 E's. Joey said, "The action of collaboratively creating the Web-based inquiry gave me an experience of creating a learning task which included most of the levels of inquiry." Their personal experiences accompanied challenges to describe student thinking and understandings in similar experiences and in designing lessons for students. Joey continued: "I was able to experience how these open-ended activities provided opportunities for students to experience higher order thinking."

Their views on learning with technologies shifted toward application of technologies as higher order thinking tools. The participants then proclaimed the importance of placing control of the technologies in students' hands, developing student facility with technologies while engaging in inquiry-oriented, higher order thinking, and assuring students controlled the flow for developing the content ideas. "Sometimes less teacher direction is better, and students might just find their own ways without a strictly prescribed procedure" (Debbie).

This theme highlighted the importance of participants' personal experiences in learning with the technologies toward an understanding of student thinking with the technologies. Debbie indicated: "Instead of talking about student learning through collaboration using technology, we were forced to ... experience this from the viewpoint of a student." Their experiences in developing TPACK through their roles as "students" were instrumental in helping them transition to roles as "teachers" in crafting their thinking and understanding of creating learning experiences for their students where the technology was an essential thinking and learning tool.

Designing Courses With the TPACK Online Learning Trajectory

The question remains on how to use this learning trajectory for designing additional online courses directed toward TPACK development. A supportive community structure requires purposeful instructor actions in the design of courses and the facilitation of activities. Instructor actions frame and support the integration and interactions of the teaching, social, and cognitive presences. As in Figure 9.1, the process is an interactive immersion with course outcomes, tool development, and process development. Designers and researchers must clarify the primary intent of the course—the specific TPACK features to be emphasized. The technologies must be introduced early, as tools for collaboration and for teaching and learning. In this study, the course focused on building participants' facility in working with tools for communication and collaboration while concurrently exposing them to tools for teaching and learning within the context of the course concepts. Another important understanding is that the creation of a community of learners and a body of shared content knowledge are neither separate constructs nor separate endeavors. The creation of one requires dynamic interactions with the other. These constructs must be interconnected when designing the course.

Schoenfeld (2010) declares that identification of tasks or actions for such courses comprises important pieces of an instructional puzzle that requires continued research. The online learning trajectory provides one explanatory structure for integrating descriptive tasks into a purposefully designed instructional approach—the systems pedagogical approach. The key is the scaffolding of the learning platform, first guiding the participants in learning with the course tools and then merging tool experiences with learning process experiences while also integrating with the course content moving toward TPACK development. Through purposeful planning in the successive phases in the trajectory, the participants are then engaged in "predictable sequences of constructs that capture how knowledge progresses from novice to more sophisticated levels of understanding" (Confrey & Maloney, 2010).

References

Akyol, Z., & Garrison, D. R. (2008). The development of a community of inquiry over time in an online course: Understanding the progression and integration of social, cognitive, and teaching presence. *Journal of Asynchronous Learning Networks, 12*(3–4), 3–22.

Bybee, R. W., Taylor, J. A., Gardner, A., Van Scotter, P., Powell, J., Westbrook, A., & Landes, N. (2006). *The BSCS 5E Instructional Model: Origins and effectiveness.* Colorado Springs, CO: BSCS.

Chyung, S. (2007). Invisible motivation of online adult learners during contract learning. *The Journal of Educators Online, 4*(1), 1–22.

Confrey, J., & Maloney, A. (2010). The construction, refinement, and early validation of the equipartitioning learning trajectory. *Proceedings of the 9th International Conference of the Learning Sciences—Volume 1,* 968–975.

Erickson, F. (2006). Definition and analysis of data from videotape: Some research procedures and their rationales. In J. L. Green, G. Camilli, & P. B. Elmore (Eds.), *Handbook of complementary methods in educational research* (pp. 177–191). Washington, DC: American Educational Research Association.

Gabriel, M. A. (2004). Learning together: Exploring group interactions online. *Journal of Distance Education, 19*(1), 54–72.

Garrison, D. R., Anderson, T., & Archer, W. (1999). Critical inquiry in a text-based environment: Computer conferencing in higher education. *Internet and Higher Education, 2*(2–3), 87–105.

Garrison, D. R., Anderson, T., & Archer, W. (2001). Critical thinking, cognitive presence, and computer conferencing in distance education. *American Journal of Distance Education, 15*(1), 7–23.

Garrison, D. R., & Cleveland-Innes, M. (2005). Facilitating cognitive presence in online learning: Interaction is not enough. *American Journal of Distance Education, 19*(3), 133–148.

Gillow-Wiles, H., & Niess, M. (2014). A systems approach for integrating multiple technologies as important pedagogical tools for TPACK. In L. Liu & D. Gibson (Eds.), *Research highlights in technology and teacher education 2014* (pp. 51–58). Waynesville, NC: AACE.

Grossman, P. L. (1990). *The making of a teacher: Teacher knowledge and teacher education.* New York: Teachers College Press.

Grossman, P. L., Wilson, S. M., & Shulman, L. S. (1989). Teachers of substance: Subject matter knowledge for teaching. In M. C. Reynolds (Ed.), *Knowledge base for the beginning teacher* (pp. 23–36). New York: Pergamon Press.

Guilar, J. D., & Loring, A. (2008). Dialogue and community in online learning: Lessons from Royal Roads University. *Distance Education, 22*(3), 19–40.

Hill, J., Song, L., & West, R. (2009). Social learning theory and Web-based learning environments: A review of research and discussion of implications. *American Journal of Distance Education, 23*(2), 88–103.

Loughran, J. J. (2002). Effective reflective practice: In search of meaning in learning about teaching. *Journal of Teacher Education, 53*, 33–43.

Lucey, T. A., O'Malley, G. S., & Jansem, A. (2009). Using online reflection and conversation to build community. *Journal of Interactive Online Learning, 8*(3), 199–217.

Meyers, J. D., Chappell, A., Elder, M., Geist, A., & Schwidder, L. (2003). Re-integrating the research record. *Computing in Science and Engineering, 5*(3), 44–50.

Mishra, P., & Koehler, M. J. (2006). Technological pedagogical content knowledge: A framework for integrating technology in teacher knowledge. *Teachers College Record, 108*(6), 1017–1054.

Niess, M. L. (2005). Preparing teachers to teach science and mathematics with technology: Developing a technology pedagogical content knowledge. *Teaching and Teacher Education, 21*, 509–523.

Niess, M. L., & Gillow-Wiles, H. (2013). Developing asynchronous online courses: Key instructional strategies in a social metacognitive constructivist learning trajectory. *The Journal of Distance Education, 27*(1), 1–23.

Niess, M. L., & Gillow-Wiles, H. (2014). Transforming science and mathematics teachers' technological pedagogical content knowledge using a learning trajectory instructional approach. *Journal of Technology and Teacher Education, 22*(4), 497–520.

Preece, J., Maloney-Krichmar, D., & Abras, C. (2003). History of emergence of online communities. In K. Christensen & D. Levinson (Eds.), *Encyclopedia of community* (pp. 1–11). Thousand Oaks, CA: SAGE Publications.

Riverin, S., & Stacey, E. (2008). Sustaining an online community of practice: A case study. *Journal of Distance Education, 22*(2), 43–58.

Roberts, B. (2002). Interaction, reflection and learning at a distance. *Open Learning, 17*(1).

Rourke, L., Anderson, T., Garrison, D. R., & Archer, W. (1999). Assessing social presence in asynchronous, text-based computer conferencing. *Journal of Distance Education, 14*(3), 51–70.

Schoenfeld, A. H. (2010). *How we think: A theory of goal-oriented decision making and its educational applications.* New York: Routledge.

Sung, E., & Mayer, R. E. (2012). Five facets of social presence in online distance education. *Computers in Human Behavior, 28*(5), 1738–1747.

Swan, K., & Shih, L. F. (2005). On the nature and development of social presence in online course discussions. *Journal of Asynchronous Learning Networks, 9*(3), 115–136.

Sztajn, P., Confrey, J., Holt Wilson, P., & Edgington, C. (2012). Learning trajectory based instruction: Toward a theory of teaching. *Educational Researcher, 41*(5), 147–156.

10

Universal Design for Learning (UDL) Infused Technological Pedagogical Content Knowledge (TPACK) Model Prepares Efficacious 21st-Century Teachers

Beatrice Hope Benton-Borghi

Introduction

Mishra and Koehler (2006, 2008) developed the technological, pedagogical, content knowledge (TPACK) model (from a general education perspective) to integrate technology in teaching and learning, while on a parallel track, Rose and Meyer (2002) developed universal design for learning (UDL) (from a special education perspective) to integrate technology in teaching and learning. In the existing dual system of education, teacher educators, in-service teachers, and pre-service teachers continue to work to collaborate and communicate in these two parallel worlds, even as the lines have blurred with diverse student populations and students with disabilities being included in the general education classroom. Does the present TPACK model help to bridge the divide and prepare all teachers to meet the needs of all students in the 21st century?

Benton-Borghi (2013) posits TPACK alone does not meet the needs of general education teachers because they are expected to teach diverse and exceptional students in inclusive general education classrooms to meet the intent of legislative mandates (e.g., Individuals with Disabilities Education Act, 2004; Higher Education Opportunity Act, 2008; No Child Left Behind Act, 2002). This necessitates teaching *for* student learning, assessing *for* student learning, and engaging *for* student learning based on the conceptual framework of universal design for learning (UDL) (Rose & Meyer, 2002) along with the theoretically sound technological, pedagogical, content knowledge (TPACK) model (Mishra & Koehler, 2006). These two common sense conceptual frameworks enable both general and special education teachers to comprehend the need for technology and to become more confident in their ability to integrate technology.

Researchers (Angeli & Valanides, 2009; Cox & Graham, 2009; Schmidt et al., 2009) continue to search for clarification of the framework with a deeper understanding and practical measure of the components of TPACK. This research is an attempt to add to the discussion, because both models are essential to provide a clear roadmap for teacher educators to prepare efficacious teachers to teach all students and to prepare teachers to improve student performance, reducing the achievement gap reported by the NCES in 2012 (Aud et al., 2012). Researchers and teacher educators recognize the reciprocal nature between teacher efficacy and teacher performance (Bandura, 1989) and the need to eliminate the gap in efficacy to integrate technology to teach diverse and exceptional students (Benton-Borghi & Chang, 2012). This researcher challenges teacher educators and educational computing experts to consider this research approach to measure the impact of the UDL Infused TPACK model to reduce the gap in teachers' sense of efficacy to teach all students (Benton-Borghi, 2013, 2015).

Theoretical Framework: What Is a UDL Infused TPACK Practitioner's Model?

Universal design for learning began as equal access (to content in the general education classroom) at CAST in 1988 (CAST, 2015) and evolved into the coherent conceptual framework of UDL (Rose & Meyer, 2002). It has been widely accepted by special education teachers, who must consider multiple dimensions (e.g., need for technology to access curriculum content) to support the teaching and learning of diverse and exceptional students. Yet general education pre-service and in-service teachers have not been as quick to embrace UDL (Benton-Borghi & Chang, 2009, 2010), and they do not have the requisite efficacy to succeed in teaching all students (Benton-Borghi & Chang, 2012) even though they are expected to apply UDL principles (Higher Education Opportunity Act, 2008).

UDL permeates the entire TPACK model with all three elements or dimensions of UDL (representation of content, expression of knowledge, and engagement in learning) visually represented (Benton-Borghi, 2015) (see Figure 10.1). These layers provide deeper understanding and application for all aspects of TPACK and its components (CK, TK, PK, TCK, TPK, PCK, and TPACK). The merger of these two transformational frameworks into a UDL Infused TPACK model makes teaching and learning goals easier to accomplish—producing highly efficacious general and special education teachers who automatically consider all three elements of UDL and TPACK as part of any instructional decision-making.

The Universally Designed for Learning (UDL) Infused Technological Pedagogical Content Knowledge (TPACK) model finds the whole, the parts, and the intersections in the universally designed world of the learner (Benton-Borghi, 2015).

Context and Situational Background

Benton-Borghi and Chang (2010) found resistance to universal design for learning (UDL) and to teaching with technology. Attitudes were entrenched in the bifurcated

Universal Design for Learning (UDL)

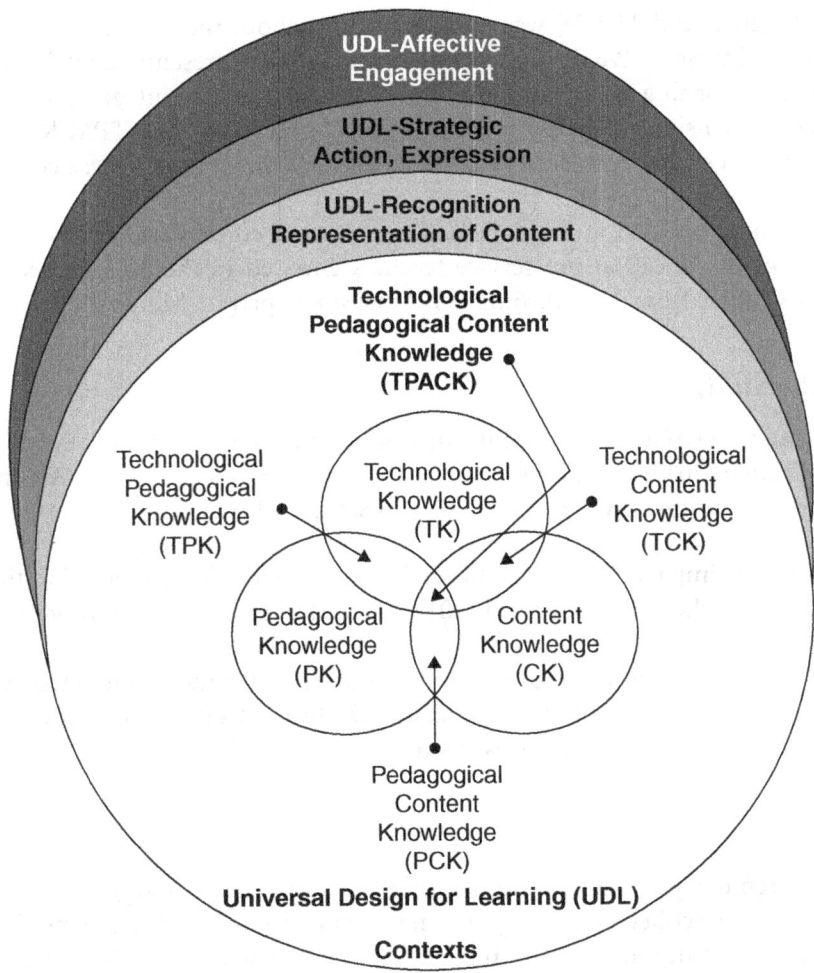

Figure 10.1 UDL Infused TPACK (adapted from http://www.tpack.org (Benton-Borghi, 2015), reprinted with permission Springer, Science + Business Media, New York, 2015)

system of education—UDL was meant only for special education teachers. This led to further research that identified a gap in efficacy among pre-service and in-service teachers, who did not feel efficacious about teaching students with disabilities or diversity, despite decades of focus with diversity courses and urban field experiences (Benton-Borghi & Chang, 2012). In 2011, this researcher learned about an innovative, logical, and coherent conceptual framework that might reduce resistance to UDL and technology and make them more palatable to secondary general education pre-service teachers: TPACK.

Would a UDL Infused TPACK model in the secondary general education methods course prepare efficacious teachers to teach the full spectrum of learners in the schools today? The course was redesigned and TPACK was integrated throughout the course with a strong focus on the UDL Infused TPACK model. The merged model presents the principles of universal design for learning as the rationale for why teachers need to integrate technology at three levels or dimensions (e.g., input, output, and engagement), and TPACK provides the robust theoretical structure at each of these levels, enriching both of these conceptual frameworks.

This research study on UDL Infused TPACK and teacher efficacy was conducted with 54 secondary general education pre-service teachers enrolled in the 3-credit secondary general methods course from 2011 through 2014 in a small, private Midwest university.

Purpose of the Study

Research examining TPACK domains inform teacher education (Schmidt et al., 2009; Hofer & Grandgenett, 2012; Shinas, Yilmaz-Ozden, Mouza, Karchmer-Klein, & Glutting, 2013). The purposes of this mixed methodology research study were:

1. To determine the impact of the UDL Infused TPACK model implemented in the secondary general methods courses (2011–2014) on the teachers' sense of efficacy to teach *every* student.
2. To hear the voices of these same pre-service teachers after they completed student teaching in order to understand the impact of UDL Infused TPACK on student teaching and the teacher performance assessment.

Method

The mixed research design included the collection of quantitative and qualitative data. Quantitative data were collected through online survey research to investigate the predictor variable, UDL Infused TPACK, and its relationship with the criterion variable Twenty-First Century Teachers' Sense of Efficacy Scale (T-TSES) and with the other predictor variables including the Teachers' Sense of Inclusion Efficacy Scale (I-TSES) and the Teachers' Sense of Diversity Efficacy Scale (D-TSES). Qualitative data were collected through one-on-one semistructured interviews with a convenience sample of participants to illuminate quantitative findings, providing a deeper understanding of the research questions.

Research Questions

What are the relationships and interrelationships among the predictor variables, Universal Design for Learning (UDL) Infused Technological Pedagogical Content Knowledge (TPACK), Teachers' Sense of Inclusion Efficacy, Teachers' Sense of Diversity Efficacy, and the criterion variable, the Twenty-First Century Teachers' Sense of Efficacy? Did secondary general education pre-service teachers become more efficacious to teach all students as a result of the UDL Infused TPACK model?

Data Analysis

Quantitative

The following analyses of quantitative data were performed using SPSS software: descriptive quantitative statistics, frequency distributions, means, standard deviation, principal component analyses, KMO sampling data, measure of internal consistency, paired sample statistics, and Cohen's d.

Qualitative

The following analyses of qualitative data were performed using HyperTRANSCRIBE and HyperRESEARCH: frequency, codings, and themes. Triangulation methods were used to analyze data collected (e.g., informal member checking, faculty/peer observer).

Participants

Quantitative Sample

The participants included fifty-four (54) pre-service teachers enrolled in the secondary general methods course from 2011 to 2014. The following demographic data were provided: (a) Content Major: Sciences (9.3%), Language Arts (35.2%), Mathematics (35.2%), Social Studies (13%), and Visual Arts (7.4%); (b) Race: African American/Black (1.9%), American Indian (1.9%), Caucasian (94.4%), Multi-Racial (1.9%); (c) Gender: Female (68.5%), Male (31.5%); (d) Grade Level: Seniors (64.8%), Continuing Education/Post Baccalaureate (22.2%), and Juniors (13%).

Qualitative Sample

A convenience sample of four (4) secondary general education pre-service student teachers and one (1) K–12 special education student teacher (comparison) participated in semi-structured one-on-one interviews. All secondary pre-service student teachers completed the general methods course prior to student teaching. Demographic data provided included (a) Content Major: Social Sciences (20%), Language Arts (20%), Mathematics (40%), and Special Education (20%); (b) Race: Caucasian (100%); (c) Gender: Female (60%), Male (40%); (d) Grade Level: Seniors (100%); (e) Submitted Teacher Performance Assessment/Completed Student Teaching: Yes (100%).

Program Description

Secondary general education pre-service teachers enrolled in the three-credit hour general methods course with urban field experiences the semester before student teaching. This course is taken concurrently with a content methods course. The course followed a blended

Table 10.1 Secondary General Education Methods Course (Blended Online and Face-to-Face Course with Field Component)

Course Content	Course Assignments and Assessments
UDL Infused TPACK and Instructional Methodologies	1. Complete online UDL, TPACK, and UDL Infused TPACK learning modules and activities and instructional methodologies.
	2. Create a digital book and apply UDL Infused TPACK principles.
	3. Complete the Classroom Learning Profile (CLP) (Benton-Borghi & Chang, 2012) for one class, applying UDL infused TPACK to create UDL Infused TPACK lesson plans with formative assessments to collect data for the case study.
	4. Videotape teaching of one of the lessons and provide a critical reflection and analysis of one's teaching with feedback from cooperating teacher (CT).
Assessment Value Added	5. Complete learning modules and activities on assessment and value added concepts. Create Case Study to represent assessment data and analysis of the impact of one's teaching on students' achievement (e.g., Excel file, graphed data, analysis of data, impact on secondary students' learning and samples of student work with feedback, and teaching solutions).
Project-Based Learning	6. Participate in large group online PBL experience with collaboration, communication, critical thinking, and creativity (e.g., Google documents, discussion boards, create a multimedia presentation of UDL Infused TPACK).

online and face-to-face delivery format, using a project-based learning teaching methodology, and the course content included assessment (value added), teaching methodologies, technology, and the UDL Infused TPACK model. Assignments and urban field placements provided opportunities for mastery experiences (see Table 10.1). At the beginning and end of each course, data were collected online using the three teacher efficacy scales along with the UDL Infused TPACK survey. This researcher and teacher educator redesigned and taught all course sections of this secondary general methods course, providing consistency in instruction and assessment across all sections of the course.

Data Collection Instruments

Two separate survey instruments were created through SurveyMonkey with informed consent information provided. A link was sent to each participant at the beginning and end of each semester asking them to take the survey online. All but one student completed the demographic data part of the survey instruments, and several failed to complete the entire survey; therefore, inferential statistics are not provided and descriptive statistics are used.

UDL Infused TPACK Survey

The Schmidt et al. (2009) survey to measure the TPACK conceptual framework with elementary teachers was adapted to measure UDL Infused TPACK with secondary general education pre-service teachers (Benton-Borghi, 2012, 2014).

TPACK Components

Twenty-nine (29) items were used to measure TPACK domains (TK, PK, CK, PCK, TCK, TPK, and TPACK). The only change was related to the items measuring content knowledge (CK). All content questions were included for items CK, PCK, and TCK, but respondents were asked to answer only the questions for their specific content area. The data collected included their answers as CK1, CK2, CK3, PCK1, and TCK1.

UDL Components

Fifteen (15) items were added to the instrument to measure universal design for learning (UDL) domains: TKU, PKU, TPKU, and TPACKU. Item example: "I know how to apply universally designed for learning (UDL) principles to assess for student learning."

UDL Infused TPACK Components

Forty-four (44) items were used to measure UDL Infused TPACK domains: 6 TK items, 7 TKU items, 7 PK items, 2 PKU items, 3 CK items (specific for each content area for secondary), 1 PCK item (content specific for secondary), 1 TCK (content specific for secondary), 6 TPK items, 5 TPKU items, 5 TPACK items, and 1 TPACK-UDL item. The first principal component analysis resulted in the relocation of four items (2 PKU items and 2 TPKU items) increasing TKU to 7 items. The same five-level Likert scale (i.e., strongly disagree, disagree, neither agree nor disagree, agree, and strongly agree) in the original survey was used.

Teachers' Sense of Efficacy Scales (I-TSES, D-TSES, T-TSES)

Benton-Borghi (2006) adapted the valid and highly reliable 12-item Teachers' Sense of Efficacy Scale (TSES) (Tschannen-Moran & Woolfolk Hoy, 2001), adding items to measure a technology construct and changing the word *student* to *student with disabilities*, and found the original TSES scale did not measure teachers' efficacy to teach students with disabilities. The new scale was called Teachers' Sense of Inclusion Efficacy Scale (I-TSES). Benton-Borghi and Chang (2009) adapted the I-TSES scale to measure the teachers' sense of efficacy to teach diverse student populations, the words *student(s) with disabilities* were changed to *diverse student populations*, and the new scale was called Teachers' Sense of Diversity Efficacy Scale (D-TSES). Benton-Borghi and Chang (2012) found a gap in efficacy when they used all three teachers' sense of efficacy scales (including the original TSES).

Benton-Borghi (2012, 2014) adapted the 18-item I-TSES scale by changing the words *student with disabilities* back to the word *student* and adding 2 items (to all scales) to improve the measure of the technology construct. The new scale was called Twenty-First Century Teachers' Sense of Efficacy Scale (T-TSES), replacing the original TSES (Tschannen-Moran & Woolfolk Hoy, 2001). The same nine-level Likert scale (i.e., nothing 1, very little 3, some influence 5, quite a bit 7, and a great deal 9) in the original survey was used. Item example: "How much can you do to integrate technology to provide student opportunities to develop 21st century skills?"

Data Analyses

Quantitative

SPSS Software

The principal component analysis (PCA) was used to determine how many underlying constructs (dimensions) account for the variance in the UDL Infused TPACK subscales and the teacher efficacy scales along with the KMO sampling data. Only the PCA data for the TPACK survey are provided. Reliabilities were calculated using Cronbach's alpha as a measure of the internal consistency of the TPACK instrument and subscales and each of the three (3) Teachers' Sense of Efficacy Scales and subscales based on the principal component analysis (PCA) data. Pretest and posttest data from both instruments were analyzed using paired samples statistics. Cohen's *d* effect size data were provided for each set of paired samples. Cohen's *d* was calculated using the mean of the differences data (mean of the differences data not provided).

Principal Component Analysis

Principal component analysis was used for data reduction of the UDL Infused TPACK model to determine whether these data supported the same theoretical constructs for TPACK components as found by Schmidt et al. (2009), along with the new universally designed for learning items. The PCA included only the posttest data.

The PCA provided strong support for the UDL Infused TPACK model similar to that found for the TPACK model (Schmidt et al., 2009). The PCA was very informative and provided data with strong factor loadings on items PKU3, PKU4, TPKU3, and TPKU4 that resulted in two-factor structures within these subscales. Closer examination revealed that these four (4) items dealt with assistive technology and these were moved to the subscale TKU, becoming TKU4 through TKU7. PCA data were used to improve the UDL Infused TPACK subscales.

A second principal component analysis (PCA) was run and the data were even stronger and eliminated the two-factor structures within PKU and TPKU. UDL Infused TPACK is stronger with these UDL items relocated to the TKU subscale. Only one TPACK subscale (PK) continued to have a two-factor structured subscale, but no further changes were made (see Table 10.2).

The UDL infused TPACK items (TKU, PKU, TPKU, and TPACKU) had strong factor loadings on all subscales ranging from .708 to .944, and strong Cronbach's coefficient alpha scores ranging from .87 to .95. The TPACK subscales items had similar strong factor loadings on all subscales ranging from .702 to .957, with outliers for two items with factor loadings of .504 in TPK and .584 in TK. Cronbach's coefficient alpha scores for the TPACK subscales were strong, ranging from .82 to .95 with only one outlier PCK/TCK with an alpha score of .41. The percent of total variance for all subscales with single-factor structure ranged from 57.76% to 91.97%, and the one subscale with the two-factor structure (PK) accounted for a total variance of 71.47%. The UDL Infused TPACK subscales are stronger with UDL items included in the survey.

Table 10.2 Principal Component Factor Analysis for UDL Infused TPACK Subscales. Rotation Method: Varimax with Kaiser Normalization

TPACK Components	Item and Factor Loading	Eigenvalues	No. Factor	% Variance	Alpha
TK***	TK1 .584, TK2 .866, TK3 .897, TK4 .900, TK5 .901, TK6 .715	4.03	1	67.16	.90
TKU***	TKU1 .708, TKU2 .815, TKU3 .805, TKU4 .852, TKU5 .737, TKU6 .835, TKU7 .777	4.38	1	62.60	.89
PK***	PK1 .698, PK2 .884, PK3 .843, PK4 .866, PK5 .727, PK6 .890, PK7 .757	3.35 1.60	2	47.97 23.50	.86
PKU*	PKU1 .944, PKU2 .944	1.77	1	88.56	.87
CK**	CK1 .957, CK2 .957, CK3 .957	2.75	1	91.97	.95
PCK/TCK*	PCK1 .905, TCK1 .905	1.63	1	81.86	.41
TPK**	TPK1 .743, TPK2 .828, TPK3 .504, TPK4 .803, TPK5 .806, TKP6 .767	3.46	1	57.76	.82
TPKU***	TPKU1 .871, TPKU2 .874, TPKU5 .955, TPKU6 .876, TPKU7 .947	4.09	1	81.96	.96
TPACK***	TPACK1 .827, TPACK2 .780, TPACK3 .838, TPACK4 .815, TPACK5 .727	3.18	1	63.77	.84
TPACK and TPACKU**	TPACK1 .793, TPACK2 .759, TPACK3 .851, TPACK4 .827, TPACK5 .702, TPACKU .740	3.18	1	63.77	.86

Note: Posttest data. Secondary general education pre-service teachers only answered CK, PCK, and TCK items for their specific content major for licensure (e.g., Mathematics, Science). SPSS software used. KMO measure of sampling adequacy: *** > .800 ** > .700 * > .500.

Reliability

The reliability tables are provided for pretests and posttests on both the UDL Infused TPACK and the Teachers' Sense of Efficacy instruments.

TPACK AND UDL INFUSED TPACK

In the TPACK survey (see Table 10.3), the entire UDL Infused TPACK scale had the strongest Cronbach's alpha score of .96 on the pretest and .94 on the posttest. Reliability was calculated for the TPACK scale with UDL items removed, and the Cronbach's alpha scores were equally strong with .93 on the pretest and .91 on the posttest.

Cronbach's alpha for each of the scales and subscales is above .80, and these are very good measures of the reliability of UDL Infused TPACK scale and the subscales. The subscale

Table 10.3 UDL Infused TPACK Survey Pretest and Posttest Reliabilities

Scales	Pretest				Posttest			
	N	Mean	Alpha	SD	N	Mean	Alpha	SD
Total Scales								
UDL-TPACK	43	3.59	.96	0.84	47	4.17	.94	0.63
TPACK	44	3.85	.93	0.80	48	4.24	.91	0.63
Subscales								
TK	50	3.61	.91	0.89	50	3.98	.90	0.85
TKU	49	2.99	.89	0.68	49	3.81	.89	0.57
TKU and TK	50	3.27	.90	0.59	49	3.89	.89	0.53
PK 7	48	3.86	.87	0.68	50	4.26	.86	0.55
PKU 2	48	2.80	.97	0.86	50	4.12	.87	0.56
PK and PKU	47	3.62	.88	0.53	50	4.23	.87	0.39
CK (CK1-CK3)	51	4.23	.94	0.56	50	4.61	.95	0.56
TCK/PCK	49	3.70	.77	1.09	50	4.37	.41	0.50
TPK	49	3.75	.90	0.81	49	4.23	.82	0.57
TPKU	49	3.33	.96	0.83	50	4.83	.96	0.44
TPK/TPKU	49	3.56	.93	0.66	49	4.21	.90	0.39
TPACK	46	3.62	.87	0.78	50	4.22	.84	0.56
TPACK/TPACKU	46	3.50	.85	0.84	50	4.21	.87	0.44

Note: All scales and subscales are measures on a 5-point scale. Total Scales: UDL-TPACK 44 items, TPACK 29 items. Subscales: TK 6 items, TKU 7 items, TKU/TK 13 items, PK 7 items, PKU 2 items, PKU/PK 9 items, CK 3 items, TCK/PCK 2 items, TPK 6 items, TPKU 5 items, TPKU/TPK 11 items, TPACK 5 items, TPACK and TPACKU 6 items. SPSS used with listwise deletion based on variables.

PCK/TCK was the one exception with an alpha score of .77 on the pretest and .41 on the posttest. Except for this one outlier, these data were very good reliability measures of the internal consistency in the UDL Infused TPACK scale and the subscales, with alpha scores ranging from .82 to .96.

TEACHERS' SENSE OF EFFICACY SCALES

The efficacy scales used in this study included Twenty-First Century Teachers' Sense of Efficacy Scale (T-TSES), Teachers' Sense of Inclusion Efficacy Scale (I-TSES), and the Teachers' Sense of Diversity Efficacy Scale (D-TSES). Reliability scores were calculated for all scales (T-SES, I-TSES, and D-TSES) and subscales: Classroom Management, Instructional Strategies, Student Engagement, and Technology (UDL) (see Table 10.4). All Cronbach's alpha scores ranged from .83 to .97, which are very good to excellent measures of internal reliabilities. Reliability data for these scales continue to be strong because they are based on the robust TSES scale (Tshannen-Moran & Woolfolk Hoy, 2001).

Table 10.4 Three Teacher Efficacy Scales Pretest and Posttest Reliabilities

Scales and Subscales	Pretest				Posttest			
	N	Mean	SD	Alpha	N	Mean	SD	Alpha
T-TSES 20	22	6.34	1.47	.96	18	7.17	1.04	.97
T-TSES 18	40	6.50	1.59	.96	37	7.11	1.18	.97
SE	44	6.75	1.29	.89	39	7.19	1.22	.92
IS	42	7.02	1.31	.89	38	7.38	1.08	.90
CM	44	5.86	1.41	.90	39	7.19	1.12	.92
Tech 8	25	5.90	1.59	.94	18	7.02	1.00	.95
Tech 6	43	5.91	1.59	.93	37	6.84	1.23	.94
I-TSES 20	23	5.72	1.40	.96	17	6.77	0.96	.96
I-TSES 18	41	5.85	1.40	.96	36	6.71	1.16	.97
SE	44	6.11	1.32	.88	37	6.77	1.18	.91
IS	43	6.19	1.49	.92	39	6.85	1.16	.93
CM	44	5.86	1.41	.90	38	6.65	1.09	.93
Tech 8	25	5.59	1.53	.92	18	6.56	0.94	.91
Tech 6	45	5.50	1.41	.91	39	6.53	1.19	.93
D-TSES 20	23	6.31	1.48	.96	17	7.04	1.13	.94
D-TSES 18	42	6.31	1.40	.93	36	6.96	1.19	.94
SE	45	6.48	1.33	.85	38	6.94	1.26	.87
IS	45	6.61	1.48	.83	39	7.26	1.04	.87
CM	44	6.42	1.36	.87	39	7.02	1.15	.86
Tech 8	26	6.01	1.50	.91	17	7.00	1.04	.90
Tech 6	46	5.85	1.50	.87	37	6.72	1.07	.92

Note: All scales are measured on a 9-point scale. Total scales include: 20 items with 8 Tech items or 18 items with 6 Tech items. Subcales include: SE Student Engagement (items 2, 3, 4, 11), IS Instructional Strategies (items 5, 9, 10, 12), CM Classroom Management (items 1, 6, 7, 8), and Tech Technology with Tech 8 (items 13–20), and Tech 6 (items 13–18). SPSS used with listwise deletion based on variables.

Qualitative

HyperTRANSCRIBE and HyperRESEARCH Software

Audiotapes of student teacher interviews were transcribed and analyzed to code and determine common themes (see Table 10.5). Four (4) semi-structured one-on-one interviews were conducted with pre-service secondary general education teachers who had taken the secondary general methods course. Interviews were conducted after these student teachers submitted their teacher performance assessments and completed student teaching. One (1) comparison interview was conducted with a special education student teacher, completing an inclusion course with UDL infused TPACK taught by this teacher educator.

Beatrice Hope Benton-Borghi

Table 10.5 Interviews: HyperTRANSCRIBE and HyperRESEARCH Codings and Themes

Codings	Themes	
	Secondary Pre-service Teachers (4)	*Special Education Pre-service Teacher (1)*
Teaching and UDL Infused TPACK	UDL essential to TPACK and teaching	UDL essential to teaching and learning
UDL and understanding TPACK	UDL supports and deepens understanding of TPACK	UDL supports and deepens understanding of TPACK
Teacher performance assessment and UDL Infused TPACK	UDL/TPACK supports teacher performance assessment	UDL knowledge supports teacher performance assessment
Classroom Learning Profile, CLP (UDL), and teaching every student	CLP and UDL support teacher performance and teaching every student	CLP and UDL support teacher performance
UDL and Diversity	UDL principles support diverse students	UDL principles support diverse students

Note: Comparison special education pre-service student teacher did not take the secondary methods course but had the same instruction on UDL by this researcher in another course for the other program areas. All completed student teaching and submitted teacher performance assessments.

These data provided a different dimension and the opportunity to gain insight through interpretation of the impact of UDL Infused TPACK on teachers' sense of efficacy to teach every student. Several triangulation methods were used to analyze data collected (e.g., informal member checking, comparison interview). The prompts for the semistructured interviews focused on the impact of UDL and UDL Infused TPACK on these student teachers' confidence to teach every student, on their understanding of TPACK, and on their teacher performance assessments.

Results

Quantitative

UDL Infused TPACK

The data show secondary general education pre-service teachers self-reported a strong UDL Infused TPACK at the end of the semester (see Table 10.6). The data show pre-service teachers scored higher on the posttests on TPACK and UDL Infused TPACK total scales and on all subscales with a larger effect size Cohen's $d = 1.25$ for the UDL Infused TPACK scale and a Cohen's $d = 1.04$ for the TPACK scale. The largest gains were found on subscales with UDL (TKU changed from 2.97 to 3.83 with a strong effect size Cohen's $d = 1.12$, PKU

Table 10.6 UDL Infused TPACK Survey Pretest and Posttest Paired Samples Statistics

Scales and Subscales	Pretest				Posttest				Effect
	N	Mean	SD	Std Error Mean	N	Mean	SD	Std Error Mean	Cohen's D
Total Scales									
UDL-TPACK**	50	3.53	.48	.06	50	4.16	.35	.05	1.25
TPACK**	50	3.78	.45	.06	50	4.23	.35	.05	1.04
Subscales									
TK**	48	3.59	.73	.10	48	3.96	.69	.10	.71
TKU**	48	2.97	.67	.09	48	3.83	.57	.08	1.12
TKU/TK**	50	3.39	.53	.07	50	3.89	.52	.07	1.12
PK**	48	3.82	.49	.07	48	4.28	.40	.05	.89
PKU**	48	2.77	.86	.12	48	4.13	.56	.08	1.32
PK/PKU**	48	3.59	.51	.07	48	4.24	.39	.05	1.20
CK*	49	4.51	.64	.09	49	4.60	.54	.07	.14
TCK/PCK**	48	3.67	1.08	.15	48	4.39	.47	.06	.65
TPK**	47	3.75	.63	.09	47	4.23	.42	.06	.78
TPKU**	47	3.33	.84	.12	47	4.19	.45	.06	.98
TPK/TPKU**	47	3.56	.65	.09	47	4.21	.39	.05	.99
TPACK**	48	3.59	.61	.08	48	4.21	.45	.06	.99
TPACK/TPACKU**	48	3.46	.61	.08	48	4.21	.44	.06	1.18

Note: All scales and subscales are measures on a 5-point scale. Total Scales: UDL Infused TPACK 44 items, TPACK 29 items. Subscales: TK 6 items, TKU 7 items, TKU/TK 13 items, PK 7 items, PKU 2 items, PKU/PK 9 items, CK 3 items, TCK/PCK 2 items, TPK 6 items, TPKU 5 items, TPKU/TPK 11 items, TPACK 5 items, TPACK and TPACKU 6 items. Cohen's *d* was calculated using the mean differences data. SPSS used for paired samples statistics. **$p < .000$. *$p < .310$.

changed from 2.77 to 4.13 with a strong effect size Cohen's $d = 1.32$). The only outlier was CK with an effect size Cohen's $d = .14$. Secondary pre-service teachers did not indicate that they were any stronger in content knowledge after taking the methods course.

The paired samples data indicate that PK, TK, and TPK have a stronger effect when UDL items are included. For example, the effect size for TK was .71 and for TK and TKU was 1.12. These data support a UDL Infused TPACK scale because the effect size is stronger with UDL items included.

Teachers' Sense of Efficacy Scales

The data show secondary pre-service teachers self-reported a strong sense of efficacy to teach at the end of the semester. They scored higher on the posttests on all three instruments and all subscales (see Table 10.7). The highest efficacy mean scores were on the

Table 10.7 Teacher Efficacy Scales: Pretest and Posttest Paired Samples Statistics

Scales	Pretest				Posttest				Effect
	N	Mean	SD	Std Error Mean	N	Mean	SD	Std Error Mean	Cohen's d
T-TSES 20***	37	6.63	1.09	.18	37	7.22	.84	.13	.61
T-TSES 18***	37	6.62	1.10	.18	37	7.22	.84	.13	.62
SE**	37	6.82	1.19	.19	37	7.31	1.00	.16	.47
IS*	37	7.03	1.12	.18	37	7.45	.86	.14	.41
CM*	37	6.84	1.16	.19	37	7.31	.91	.14	.39
Tech 8***	37	6.17	1.30	.21	37	6.98	.98	.16	.66
Tech 6***	37	6.08	1.35	.22	37	6.96	.99	.16	.69
I-TSES 20***	38	5.87	1.13	.18	38	6.70	.93	.15	.73
I-TSES 18***	38	5.86	1.14	.18	38	6.71	.93	.15	.74
SE*	38	6.11	.87		38	6.77	.91	.91	.52
IS***	38	6.10	1.34	.21	38	6.90	1.02	.16	.62
CM**	38	5.86	1.30	.21	38	6.66	.97	.15	.60
Tech 8***	38	5.67	1.15	.18	38	6.58	.99	.16	.73
Tech 6***	38	5.53	1.20	.19	38	6.57	1.00	.16	.82
D-TSES 20***	40	6.31	.91	.14	40	6.92	.85	.13	.60
D-TSES 18***	40	6.29	.93	.14	40	6.91	.86	.13	.61
SE**	39	6.48	1.13	.18	39	6.95	1.06	.17	.42
IS***	39	6.60	1.01	.16	39	7.26	.88	.14	.63
CM*	39	6.48	1.10	.17	39	6.97	1.10	.16	.37
Tech 8***	39	6.00	1.06	.16	39	6.77	1.02	.16	.59
Tech 6***	39	5.90	1.11	.17	39	6.71	1.01	.16	.63

Note: All scales are measured on a 9-point scale. Total scales: 20 items with 8 Tech items or 18 items with 6 Tech items. Subcales: SE Student Engagement, IS Instructional Strategies, CM Classroom Management, and Tech Technology. Cohen's *d* was calculated using the mean differences data. SPSS used for paired samples statistics. Missing values excluded listwise. ***$p < .000$. **$p < .010$. *$p < .050$.

T-TSES scale followed by the D-TSES scale, and the lowest mean scores were on the I-TSES scale. These data were similar to other findings by Benton-Borghi and Chang (2012) and indicate a continuing gap in efficacy, even though it was smaller in this study. Although the mean scores were higher for the T-TSES and D-TSES scales, the strongest gains from pretest to posttest with Cohen's *d* values of .73 and .74 were on the I-TSES total scale. For all three scales, Cohen's *d* values ranged from .60 to .74 for the total scales (T-TSES, I-TSES, and D-TSES). The strongest gains on the subscales pretest to posttest were on technology with Cohen's *d* values ranging from .59 to .82 with the I-TSES technology subscale having the strongest effect sizes with .73 and .82.

Qualitative

Voices of Pre-Service Teachers

The voices of these teachers supported the need for a UDL Infused TPACK model to prepare efficacious teachers. Mary explained during student teaching, "I need to reach every student and TPACK alone helps me with those steps, but the final step is UDL... without UDL, I might reach some students, but with UDL I am able to reach the entire classroom." John indicated, "It [UDL] made TPACK easier to understand and to see how all of the connections were being made. I don't know if we would have the same understanding of TPACK without UDL." Their voices support teacher confidence in UDL and TPACK as a merged model. Elizabeth said, "I think that your methods course prepared us so much for edTPA. You know that they (edTPA) don't refer to it as UDL, but essentially everything it is referring to is UDL or parts of UDL." Harrison also reinforced the impact of UDL Infused TPACK on the teaching performance assessment: "I think without UDL, it is difficult to respond to any of the edTPA prompts... without UDL and understanding UDL... you are going to lose that in the edTPA and it is going to show that you probably aren't teaching all of your students." These interviews provided positive feedback on the impact of UDL Infused TPACK on teacher efficacy and confidence to teach and to complete the teacher performance assessment.

Discussion

Quantitative

Did UDL Infused TPACK have a relationship or impact on teacher efficacy? Were participants more efficacious after completing the secondary methods course with UDL Infused TPACK? The sample of 54 participants in the online surveys was not sufficient to allow the use of inferential statistics because the researcher cannot be sure that respondents were representative of the population. This study cannot generalize to the target populations of secondary pre-service teacher candidates, but it can provide a rich source of descriptive quantitative data to support the reliability and validity of the instruments and the predictability of the variables to increase 21st-century teachers' sense of efficacy in the sample of secondary pre-service teachers who participated in the survey research.

The UDL Infused TPACK instrument was valid based on the principal component analysis (PCA) data and highly reliable based on strong Cronbach's alpha scores. It was difficult to capture PCK and TCK with secondary pre-service teachers, but the instruments did measure the TPACK components and the UDL-TPACK components.

The UDL-TPACK instrument was developed for this research study and provided valuable data to support TPACK components (Schmidt et al., 2009) and to support a merged model of UDL and TPACK.

The teacher efficacy scales were valid and reliable with strong Cronbach's alpha scores. The PCA data (although not provided) resulted in strong support for all efficacy scales. The gap in efficacy on the three Teachers' Sense of Efficacy Scales was smaller compared to other studies (Benton-Borghi & Chang, 2012), but the gap still exists with pre-service teachers feeling less efficacious about teaching the full spectrum of students.

Qualitative

The student teachers who participated in the one-on-one interviews were confident in their understanding and application of UDL infused TPACK and the impact on their student teaching, sense of efficacy, and successful completion of the teacher performance assessment.

Limitations

Pre-service general education teachers may not have self-reported honest responses on the two instruments, UDL Infused TPACK and Teachers' Sense of Efficacy Scales. The number of participants was too small to consider or to report the multiple regression analysis data with confidence. A control group was not possible inasmuch as there is only one secondary general education method course offered each semester at this small, private Midwest university.

The sample size was small, and in the future, a larger sample size would allow a principal component analysis on the entire UDL Infused TPACK instrument. Participants in the survey research do not always complete every item, which has an impact on the data and analyses; only valid percentages and data were used—average means were not used to replace missing data.

Implications/Recommendations

Implications for Practice

The results from this study indicate that UDL Infused TPACK is a reliable and valid measure of secondary pre-service teachers' knowledge of UDL and TPACK knowledge domains, and teacher efficacy scales were reliable and valid measures of teacher efficacy to teach students with and without diversity and disability. UDL Infused TPACK had a moderate impact on the teachers' sense of efficacy to integrate technology and to reduce the gap in efficacy to teach every student, but the voices of pre-service teachers after student teaching demonstrate the promise of and need for a UDL Infused TPACK model.

These data informed other licensure programs and resulted in the development of a new course on assessment and technology by this researcher. This course is now required by all teacher candidates in all licensure programs at this private, Midwest university beginning in 2014.

The new assessment and technology course will teach UDL Infused TPACK and will be taken concurrently with one methods course the semester before student teaching. Hofer and Grandgenett (2012) found an educational technology course taught like a methods course provides more opportunities for candidates to apply and learn TPACK. This teacher educator's experience supports their findings, because the evolution of the secondary general methods course from 2006 to 2014 also resulted in a technology and assessment methods course.

TPACK should be viewed from a transformative perspective (Shinas et al., 2013) and to identify items that capture TPACK. This researcher agrees and challenges teacher educators to research the UDL Infused TPACK model and the Teachers' Sense of Efficacy using all three scales until the gap in efficacy is eliminated.

References

Aud, S., Hussar, W., Johnson, F., Kena, G., Roth, E., Manning, E., Wang, X., & Zhang, J. (2012). *The condition of education 2012* (NCES 2012–045). U.S. Department of Education, National Center for Education Statistics. Washington, DC. Retrieved May 1, 2013, from http://nces.ed.gov/pubsearch

Angeli, C., & Valanides, N. (2009). Epistemological and methodological issues for the conceptualization, development, and assessment of ICT-TPCK: Advances in technological pedagogical content knowledge (TPCK). *Computers & Education, 52*(1), 154–168. doi:10.1016/j.compedu.2008.07.006

Bandura, A. (1989). Human agency in social cognitive theory. *American Psychologist, 44*(9), 1175–1184.

Benton-Borghi, B. H. (2006). Teaching every student in the 21st century: Teacher efficacy and technology. Doctoral dissertation. Columbus, OH: Ohio State University. Retrieved from Proquest Digital Dissertations Database (AAT3226460).

Benton-Borghi, B. H. (2012). The intersection, and impact of universal design for learning (UDL) and technological, pedagogical, content knowledge (TPACK) on 21st century teachers' sense of efficacy to teach every student. Paper presented at the Association of Teacher Educators (ATE) Annual Conference, San Antonio, TX, February.

Benton-Borghi, B. H. (2013). A universally designed for learning (UDL) infused technological pedagogical content knowledge (TPACK) practitioners' model essential for teacher preparation in the 21st century. *Journal of Educational Computing Research, 48*(2), 245–265. Retrieved from http://dx.doi.org/10.2190/EC.48.2.g

Benton-Borghi, B. H. (2014). The intersection of universal design for learning (UDL) and technological, pedagogical, content knowledge (TPACK) and 21st century teachers' sense of efficacy to teach every student. 66th American Association of Colleges of Teacher Education (AACTE) Annual Conference, Indianapolis, IN, February.

Benton-Borghi, B. H. (2015). Intersection and impact of universal design for learning (UDL) and technological, pedagogical, content knowledge (TPACK) on 21st century teacher preparation: UDL infused TPACK practitioner's model. In C. Angeli-Valanides & N. Valanides (Eds.), *Technological pedagogical content knowledge: Exploring, developing, and assessing TPCK* (pp. 287–304). London, UK: Springer.

Benton-Borghi, B. H., & Chang, Y.M. (2009). P-12 teachers inform teacher education: Overcoming resistance to universally designing instruction for student learning. Paper presented at the Ohio Confederation of Teacher Education Organizations (OCTEO) Spring Conference, Columbus, OH, April.

Benton-Borghi, B. H., & Chang, Y. (2010). Achieving inclusivity and equity for diverse student populations: Increasing teacher efficacy to teach every student using universal design for learning principles. Paper presented at the 62nd Annual Conference of the American Association of Colleges for Teacher Education (AACTE), Atlanta, GA, February.

Benton-Borghi, B. H., & Chang, Y. (2012). Critical examination of candidates' diversity competence: Rigorous and systematic assessment of candidates' efficacy to teach diverse student populations. *The Teacher Educator, 47*(1), 29–44. doi:10.1080/08878730.2011.632472

CAST. (2015). *About CAST: Timeline 1988*. CAST. Retrieved October 15, 2015, from http://www.cast.org/about/timeline.html#.Vh_nR7TFtmA

Cox, S., & Graham, C. R. (2009). Diagramming TPACK in practice: Using an elaborate model of the TPACK framework to analyze and depict teacher knowledge. *Tech Trends, 53*(5), 60–69.

Hofer, M., & Grandgenett, N. (2012). TPACK development in teacher education: A longitudinal study of pre-service teachers in a secondary M.A.Ed. program. *Journal of Research on Technology in Education, 45*(1), 83–106.

Higher Education Opportunity Act. (2008). Retrieved from the U.S. Department of Education on May 1, 2012, from http://ed.gov/policy/highered/leg/hea08/index.html

Individuals with Disabilities Education Act (IDEA). (2004). Public Law 108–446. Washington DC: U.S. Congress. Retrieved May 1, 2012, from http://idea.ed.gov/

Koehler, M. J., & Mishra, P. (2008). Introducing TPCK. In AACTE Committee on Innovation and Technology (Ed.), *The handbook of technological pedagogical content knowledge (TPCK) for educators* (pp. 3–29). Mahwah, NJ: Lawrence Erlbaum Associates.

Mishra, P., & Koehler, M. J. (2006). Technological, pedagogical content knowledge: A framework for teacher knowledge. *Teachers College Record, 108*(6), 1017–1054. Retrieved on May 1, 2012, from http://www.tcrecord.org/content.asp?contentid=12516

No Child Left Behind Act of 2001. (2002). Public Law 107–110. Washington, DC: U.S. Congress. Retrieved on May 1, 2012, from http://www.ed.gov/policy/elsec/leg/esea02/index.html

Rose, D. H., & Meyer, A. (2002). *Teaching every student in the digital age: Universal design for learning*. Alexandria, VA: ASCD.

Schmidt, D. A., Baran, E., Thompson, A. D., Mishra, P., Koehler, M. J., & Shin, T. S. (2009). Technological pedagogical content knowledge (TPACK): The development and validation of an assessment instrument for pre-service teachers. *Journal of Research on Technology in Education, 42*(2), 123–149.

Shinas, V. H., Yilmaz-Ozden, S., Mouza, C., Karchmer-Klein, R., & Glutting, J. J. (2013). Examining domains of technological pedagogical content knowledge using factor analysis. *Journal of Research on Technology in Education, 45*(4), 339–360.

Tschannen-Moran, M., & Woolfolk Hoy, A. (2001). Teacher efficacy: Capturing an elusive construct. *Teaching and Teacher Education, 17*, 783–805.

Appendices

Appendix A: UDL Infused TPACK Survey

Adapted TPACK survey by Schmidt et al. (2009).

UDL Infused TPACK

Technology is a broad concept that can mean many different things. For the purpose of this questionnaire, technology is referring to digital technology/technologies. That is, the digital tools we use such as computers, laptops, iPods, handhelds, interactive whiteboards, software programs, etc. Please answer all of the questions and if you are uncertain of or neutral about your response, you may always select "Neither Agree or Disagree"

Strongly Disagree (SD) = 1 Disagree (D) = 2 Neither Agree/Disagree (N) = 3 Agree (A) = 4 Strongly Agree (SA) = 5

TK	**Technological Knowledge**
TK1	I know how to solve my own technical problems.
TK2	I can learn technology easily.
TK3	I keep up with important new technologies.
TK4	I frequently play around with the technology.
TK5	I know about a lot of different technologies.
TK6	I have the technical skills I need to use technology.
TKU	**UDL Infused Technological Knowledge**
TKU1	I know how to use/choose technology that is universally designed for student learning.
TKU2	I know about different assistive technologies.
TKU3	I know how to use technologies that support students' learning to meet the intent of Section 504, 508, and IDEA.

(Continued)

TKU4	I can use assistive technology in teaching and learning.
TKU5	I know information about assistive technology and access to curriculum content (e.g., NIMAS and NIMAC).
TKU6	I can select assistive technologies that support student access to the curriculum content.
TKU7	I can select assistive technologies that support access to the curriculum content for the full spectrum of learners.
PK	**Pedagogical Knowledge**
PK1	I know how to assess student performance in a classroom.
PK2	I can adapt my teaching based upon what students currently understand or do not understand.
PK3	I can adapt my teaching style to different learners.
PK4	I can assess student learning in multiple ways.
PK5	I can use a wide range of teaching approaches in a classroom setting.
PK6	I am familiar with common student understandings and misconceptions.
PK7	I know how to organize and maintain classroom management.
PKU	**PCK/TCK Pedagogical Content Knowledge and Technological Content Knowledge**
PKU1	I know how to apply universally designed for learning (UDL) principles to teach for student learning.
PKU2	I know how to apply universally designed for learning (UDL) principles to assess for student learning.
CK	**Secondary Education Content Knowledge**
	Secondary pre-service teachers should answer only the questions for their content areas (literacy [language arts], social studies, mathematics, science, and art).
CK1	I have sufficient knowledge about mathematics (or language arts, social studies, mathematics, science, or art).
CK2	I can use a mathematical (or scientific, historical, literary, or artistic) way of thinking.
CK3	I have various ways and strategies of developing my understanding of mathematics (or literacy, social studies, science, or art).
PCK1	**PCK/TCK Pedagogical Content Knowledge and Technological Content Knowledge**
TCK1	I can select effective teaching approaches to guide student thinking and learning in mathematics (or literacy, social studies, science, or art).
	I know about technologies that I can use for understanding and doing mathematics (or literacy, social studies, science, or art).
TPK	**Technological Pedagogical Knowledge**
TPK1	I can choose technologies that enhance the teaching approaches for a lesson.
TPK2	I can choose technologies that enhance students' learning for a lesson.

TPK3	My teacher education program has caused me to think more deeply about how technology could influence the teaching approaches I use in my classroom.
TPK4	I am thinking critically about how to use technology in my classroom.
TPK5	I can adapt the use of the technologies that I am learning about to different teaching activities.
TPK6	I can choose technologies that enhance the content for a lesson.
TPKU	**UDL Infused Technological Pedagogical Knowledge**
TPKU1	I can universally design instruction for student learning.
TPKU2	I can universally design assessments for student learning.
TPKU5	I can universally design instruction to represent content and information
TPKU6	I can universally design instruction for student expression in multiple ways.
TPKU7	I can universally design instruction for student engagement.
TPACK	**Technological Pedagogical Content Knowledge**
TPACK1	I can select technologies to use in my classroom that enhance what I teach, how I teach, and what students learn.
TPACK2	I can use strategies that combine content, technologies, and teaching approaches that I learned about in my coursework in my classroom.
TPACK3	I can provide leadership in helping others to coordinate the use of content, technologies, and teaching approaches at my school and/or district.
TPACK4	I can teach lessons that appropriately combine content, technologies, and teaching approaches.
TPACK5	I can teach lessons that appropriately combine mathematics (or literacy, art, science, or social studies), technologies, and teaching approaches.
TPACKU	**UDL Infused TPACK**
TPACKU6	I can teach lessons that appropriately combine content, technologies, and teaching approaches infused with principles of universal design for learning.

Appendix B: Twenty-First Century Teachers' Sense of Efficacy Scale

Three Teachers' Sense of Efficacy Scales were administered, but only the Twenty-First Century Teachers' Sense of Efficacy Scale is provided below. The other two scales are exactly the same except the word "student" reads "student with disabilities" in the Teachers' Sense of Inclusion Efficacy Scale (I-TSES) (Benton-Borghi, 2006, 2012, 2014), and the word "student with disabilities" reads "diverse student populations" in the Teachers' Sense of Diversity Efficacy Scale (D-TSES) (Benton-Borghi & Chang, 2009, 2012).

Twenty-First Century Teachers' Sense of Efficacy Scale (T-TSES)

Based on the Teachers' Sense of Inclusion Efficacy Scale (I-TSES) (Benton-Borghi, 2006, 2012, 2014), originally adapted from the Teachers' Sense of Efficacy Scale (TSES) developed by Tschannen-Moran and Woolfolk Hoy (2001)

> Directions: This questionnaire is designed to help us gain a better understanding of things that create difficulty for teachers in their school activities. Please indicate your opinion about each of the statements below. Your answers will be kept confidential.

How much can you do? (1) Nothing (3) Very little (5) Some influence (7) Quite a bit (9) A great deal

1. How much can you do to control disruptive behavior of students in the classroom?
2. How much can you do to motivate students who show low interest in school work?
3. How much can you do to get students to believe they can do well in school work?
4. How much can you do to help students to value learning?
5. To what extent can you craft good questions for students?
6. How much can you do to get students to follow classroom rules?

(Continued)

7. How much can you do to calm students who are disruptive or noisy?
8. How well can you establish a classroom management system with students in your classroom?
9. How much can you use a variety of assessment strategies for students?
10. To what extent can you provide alternative explanations or examples when students are confused?
11. How much can you assist families in helping their children do well in school?
12. How well can you implement alternative strategies in your classroom?
13. How well can you motivate students who require assistive technologies in your classroom?
14. To what extent can you implement accommodations for assistive and accessible technology for students in your classroom?
15. How much can you do to provide students who require text readers and accessible digital content access to the curriculum content?
16. How much can you do to provide universally designed (digital) assessments to evaluate learning of students in your classroom?
17. How much can you do to provide the curriculum content in specialized formats [Braille, digital, audio] for students who require them?
18. How much can you do to provide Web 2.0 and 3.0 tools for students to develop collaboration, communication, critical thinking, and creativity skills?
19. How much can you do to integrate technology to provide students opportunities to develop 21st-century skills?
20. How much can you do to provide universally designed instruction for students to learn?

Section III
Implications for Practice

11

Developing and Assessing TPACK Among Pre-Service Teachers
A Synthesis of Research

Chrystalla Mouza

Introduction and Purpose

There is wide recognition that technology plays a crucial role in preparing students for a global knowledge-based economy (Partnership for 21st Skills & AACTE, 2010; UNESCO, 2011). Effective use of technology in teaching and learning, however, hinges on teachers' ability to develop knowledge and skills required to match digital tools with content and pedagogy. This knowledge is represented in the framework of Technological Pedagogical Content Knowledge (TPACK), which has been used to conceptualize effective teaching with technology (Mishra & Koehler, 2006).

Increasingly, teacher preparation programs are considered a key catalyst in helping new teachers acquire the knowledge and skills illustrated in the TPACK framework (Tondeur et al., 2012). As a framework of teacher knowledge, however, TPACK does not offer recommendations on the kinds of learning experiences that are conducive to TPACK development among pre-service teachers (Niess, 2012). As a result, helping pre-service teachers develop this complex and interconnected knowledge base presents significant challenges for teacher education programs (Hofer & Grandgenet, 2012). These challenges are further exacerbated by the lack of consensus on how to define and assess TPACK through reliable instruments (Shinas, Karchmer-Klein, Mouza, Yilmaz Ozden, & Glutting, 2015).

This chapter provides a synthesis of existing approaches used to develop and assess pre-service teachers' TPACK by addressing three questions:

1. What are the characteristics and current experiences of pre-service teachers' regarding technology?
2. What types of instruments have been used to date to document and assess pre-service teachers' TPACK?
3. What specific pathways and strategies have been used to date to help pre-service teachers develop knowledge and skills associated with the TPACK framework? What evidence do we have on their effectiveness?

The purpose of this chapter is not to present an exhaustive review of the literature. Rather, the focus is on synthesizing the literature on promising approaches published since the initial release of the *Handbook of TPACK for Educators* (AACTE, 2008). Further, the chapter focuses exclusively on the assessment and development of pre-service teachers' TPACK. Readers interested in broader issues related to measuring TPACK should read the chapter by Archambault describing qualitative TPACK measures and the chapter by Chai, Koh, & Tsai reviewing quantitative TPACK measures. Readers may also be interested in the chapter by Harris outlining approaches to developing TPACK among in-service teachers.

Three criteria were used to select studies for this review of pre-service approaches to developing and assessing TPACK. First, studies had to be published in peer-reviewed journal articles or books. For the most part, doctoral dissertations and conference proceedings were eliminated. Second, selected studies had to focus on pre-service teachers exclusively and provide empirical data. Third, selected studies had to be explicit about the ways in which the TPACK framework informed teacher preparation efforts, data collection, and analysis. Typical electronic search procedures were used to identify the literature, including scientific databases (e.g., ERIC), the TPACK bibliography on the Mendeley social network, and the author's personal knowledge of key studies in the field. To narrow the search, a number of keywords were used, including "pre-service teachers" AND "technological pedagogical and content knowledge" OR "TPACK" or "TPCK."

Pre-Service Teacher Characteristics and Current Experience With Technology

Technology is rapidly shifting how we teach and how we learn (Dilworth et al., 2012). Although there are different conceptions and definitions of technology, the focus of the TPACK framework is on emerging technologies (Cox, 2008). According to Cox, *emerging technologies* (e.g., digital tools, computers, etc.) are different from *transparent technologies* (e.g., pencil, chalkboard), which are already within teachers' existing pedagogical repertoire. Mouza and Lavigne (2012) identified four types of emerging technologies that have potential to significantly influence the processes and outcomes of teaching and learning. These include technologies that support (a) learning to understand and create (graphical tools, modeling and visualization tools, and digital fabrication tools); (b) learning by collaborating (handheld devices, classroom networks, Web 2.0 tools, and social networks); (c) anytime, anyplace learning (mobile devices and augmented reality); and (d) learning by gaming (educational and commercial virtual worlds and programming tools for game development).

Given the range of available tools, pre-service teachers are confronted with challenges and questions related to how and when to incorporate emerging technologies for teaching and learning (Niess, 2011). This generation of pre-service teachers, referred to as *digital natives* to indicate the fact that they grew up with access to computers and Internet, is often considered savvy with technology (Prensky, 2001). Empirical studies examining college students' use of technology, however, failed to provide support for such notions.

The majority of the studies examining the technological familiarity of digital natives found that college students are only familiar with a narrow range of mostly established technologies such as email, instant messaging, mobile phones, and social networking sites (Kennedy, Judd, Churchward, Gray, & Krause, 2008). Familiarity and use of more advanced technologies, such as blogs, wikis, and virtual worlds, was found to be limited (Jones & Cross, 2009; Margaryan, Littlejohn, & Vojt, 2011).

Specifically regarding pre-service teachers, Lei (2009) found that digital-native pre-service teachers were proficient with basic technologies but were not familiar with more advanced technologies, particularly Web 2.0 technologies. Although they used such technologies for social networking, they lacked the experience and expertise in using Web 2.0 technologies with potential for classroom applications. Lei concluded that the technology proficiency of this generation of pre-service teachers is limited and lacks depth. She suggested that teacher education programs help pre-service teachers make connections between technology and teaching and make the transition from "digital native students to digital native teachers" (p. 92).

Similarly, So, Choi, Lim, & Xiong (2012) examined pre-service teachers' past experiences, pedagogical beliefs and attitudes towards technology, and prospective uses of computers in education. Data collected from 225 pre-service teachers in Korea and Singapore revealed a heterogeneous composition and cautioned teacher educators about making generational assumptions. Specifically, despite positive beliefs and attitudes towards technology, So et al. found that pre-service teachers did not use computers frequently for a wide variety of purposes (e.g., communication, information production, etc.). Further, findings indicated that using computers for personal purposes did not appear to be a strong predictor for prospective use of computers in teaching. So et al. recommended that teacher educators help this generation of pre-service teachers strengthen the connections among their technical skills and pedagogical knowledge.

The above findings make it necessary for teacher education programs to play a more active role in the preparation of pre-service teachers for the use of technology. Accreditation and national organizations also make it necessary for teacher education programs to help pre-service teachers acquire this body of knowledge prior to graduation. The Council for the Accreditation of Educator Preparation (CAEP, 2013), for example, includes technology as a cross-cutting theme and a critical area requiring "substantial innovation by preparation providers." More specifically, CAEP standards require teacher educators to ensure that graduates can "model and apply technology standards as they design, implement, and assess learning experiences to engage students and improve learning and enrich professional practice" (p. 32). Further, standards related to clinical preparation refer to technology-enhanced learning opportunities, while standards on pre-service teacher quality expect teacher education programs to present multiple forms of evidence related to pre-service teachers' developing knowledge and skills, including the integration of technology in all knowledge domains.

To accomplish these complex tasks, Niess (2008) argues for the need to provide specialized instruction that helps this generation of pre-service teachers learn *about* new forms of technology while simultaneously learning *how* to teach their core content with technology.

Additionally, Tondeur et al. (2012) emphasize the importance of focusing on institutions of teacher education as a unit of change and paying attention to institutional conditions needed to support technology integration efforts. This chapter examines opportunities situated within teacher education settings that hold promise for helping pre-service teachers learn how to teach with technology.

Using TPACK to Inform Pre-Service Teacher Preparation

Building upon Shulman's (1987) work, the TPACK framework includes three core categories of knowledge: content knowledge (CK), pedagogical knowledge (PK), and technological knowledge (TK). CK refers to subject matter knowledge. PK refers to the theoretical and methodological knowledge needed to develop appropriate instruction. TK refers to knowledge and proficiency with emerging technology tools. By combining these three core knowledge types, the framework introduces four additional constructs: pedagogical content knowledge (PCK), technological pedagogical knowledge (TPK), technological content knowledge (TCK), and finally TPACK. PCK is the amalgam of CK and PK that illustrate teachers' professional understanding of how to help students learn specific subject matter (Shulman, 1987). TCK refers to the reciprocal relationship between technology and content (Mishra & Koehler, 2006). TPK relates to the understanding of how technology can influence teaching and learning. When technology, content, and pedagogy blend effectively the result is TPACK. These seven constructs capture the different types of teachers' professional expertise needed for effective technology integration.

As a conceptual framework, TPACK has been widely used to inform teacher preparation and measure teacher learning outcomes. Nevertheless, the framework is complex and multifaceted, often resulting in different epistemological perspectives ranging from integrative to transformative (Graham, 2011). The *integrative* perspective views TPACK as a body of knowledge that develops by integrating the three contributing knowledge bases of content, pedagogy, and technology. The *transformative* perspective views TPACK as a synthesized and unique body of knowledge that can be developed and assessed on its own (Angeli & Valanides, 2009).

Understanding whether the constructs in the TPACK framework are integrative or transformative has implications for the construct validity of instruments that measure TPACK and the ways in which researchers examine the development and assessment of TPACK among pre-service teachers (Graham, 2011). Researchers adopting the integrative perspective tend to measure individual knowledge constructs independently (e.g., Koehler, Mishra, & Yahya, 2007), while researchers adopting the transformative perspective typically examine TPACK development more holistically (e.g., Angeli & Valanides, 2009). Other researchers follow a combination of methods examining both the individual knowledge constructs that contribute to TPACK development as well as TPACK as a unique knowledge base (e.g., Mouza, Karchmer-Klein, Nandakumar, Yilmaz Ozden, & Hun, 2014). This chapter includes studies that examine TPACK more holistically (transformative perspective) and studies that examine the ways in which individual knowledge constructs support overall TPACK development (integrative perspective). Specifically, the following questions were used to frame the presentation and discussion of the literature:

- How is TPACK conceptualized in the instructional strategies utilized in the study?
- What types of data were collected and what instruments were used to collect the data?
- How were data analyzed and how did TPACK conceptualization influence the analysis of the data?

Measures for Assessing Pre-Service Teachers' TPACK

The wide adoption of TPACK as a theoretical frame of teacher knowledge necessitated the need to develop techniques and instruments that help document pre-service teachers' learning. To date, five commonly used techniques for measuring TPACK among pre-service teachers have been used: surveys, performance assessments, interviews, observations, and open-ended questionnaires (Abbit, 2011; Koehler, Shin, & Mishra, 2012). This section summarizes these techniques and associated instruments to help readers evaluate the efficacy of the strategies used to develop TPACK among pre-service teachers presented in the next section.

Surveys

According to Koehler et al. (2012), most frequently researchers measure TPACK through surveys. The most widely used survey instrument for pre-service teachers is the "Survey of Pre-service Teachers for Teaching with Technology" (Schmidt, et al., 2009). The survey consists of 8 items designed to collect demographic data and 55 items focusing on pre-service teacher' self-assessed levels of knowledge in each of the TPACK domains (CK, TK, PK, PCK, TCK, TPK, and TPACK). Additionally, three open-ended questions ask pre-service teachers to describe specific episodes where university faculty, cooperating teachers in their field placement or themselves, effectively combined content, technology, and teaching approaches in a classroom lesson.

A number of studies utilized this survey to assess pre-service teachers' TPACK development using a pre–post methodology (e.g., An, Wilder, & Lim, 2011; Mouza et al., 2014). In all instances, the survey was found to be valid and reliable for the sample and provided an efficient tool for research and evaluation related to TPACK from an integrative perspective (Abbit, 2011). Nevertheless, some authors questioned the construct validity of the instrument. A number of studies, for example, revealed that the knowledge domains of TPACK could not be reproduced through exploratory factor analysis, indicating that pre-service teachers may have difficulty distinguishing among TPACK constructs (Koh, Chai, & Tsai, 2010; Shinas, Yilmaz-Ozden, Mouza, Karchmer-Klein, & Glutting, 2013). Despite these limitations, the Survey of Pre-service Teachers' Knowledge of Teaching and Technology is the most mature instrument developed to date that can be used to collect quantitative data among large samples of pre-service teachers.

Building on the work of Schmidt et al. (2009), Chai, Koh, Tsai, and Tan (2011) developed a 46-item survey instrument designed to measure TPACK constructs. To contextualize the survey for their sample, Chai et al. amended some of the subject specific items. Further, additional items were generated related to PK, focusing on five dimensions of meaningful learning emphasized in the teacher education program under study, namely active, cooperative, constructive, intentional, and authentic. These items were labelled "pedagogical knowledge for meaningful learning" (PKML). Further, these items included pre-service teachers' Web-based learning as they adopt more Web 2.0 technologies. Web-based competencies were also added in the technology knowledge (TK) scale. Exploratory factor analysis conducted with pre-service teachers in Singapore revealed five factors that fit with the conceptions of the TPACK framework. Results from the study indicated that pre-service teachers were able to distinguish between several TPACK domains, and the authors concluded that the generation of more contextualized items (e.g., PKML) contributed to better factor structures.

While the above surveys utilized an integrative perspective, measuring all constructs associated with the TPACK framework, Yurdakul et al. (2011) utilized a transformative perspective to develop the TPACK-deep scale. Yurdakul et al. began by identifying competencies and indicators associated with effective technology integration, which were used to create the items for the scale. To examine the validity and reliability of the scale, the authors utilized the survey with 995 pre-service teachers in Turkey. Both exploratory and confirmatory factor analysis were utilized, which resulted in a 33-item scale including 4 factors: design (creating and developing curriculum plans), exertion (implementing design plans and facilitating a variety of effective assessments), ethics (exhibiting legal and ethical behavior in the use of technology), and proficiency (exhibiting teacher leadership ability to integrate technology into the teaching and learning process). The survey as a whole was also found to be valid and reliable for measuring TPACK, therefore offering another instrument for examining TPACK from a transformative perspective.

Performance Assessments

As with other self-report measures, the ability of the above survey instruments to represent knowledge is highly influenced by the ability of the pre-service teachers to assess their knowledge and respond accurately to the survey items (Koehler et al., 2012). As a result, some studies have attempted to triangulate survey data with performance assessments using artifacts created by pre-service teachers during their coursework or teacher education program. These artifacts are seen as evidence of pre-service teachers' instructional design and planning process, as well as their knowledge of TPACK domains (Abbit, 2011). For the most part, researchers using performance assessments utilized coding schemes mapped onto the TPACK framework to code for specific TPACK constructs and for TPACK more holistically (e.g., Graham, Borup, & Smith, 2012; Mouza et al., 2014).

In an effort to provide a more systematic evaluation of pre-service teachers' performance assessments, Harris, Grandgenett, and Hofer (2010) developed a rubric that measures the quality of TPACK-based technology integration lessons. The rubric asks scorers to rate lesson plans on four dimensions: (a) curriculum goals and technologies, (b) instructional strategies and technologies, (c) technology selection, and (d) "fit" of content, pedagogy, and technology. Each dimension is scored on a range of one through four, with four providing the highest rating. To strengthen the construct and face validity of the instrument, Harris et al. (2010) solicited reviews from several experts who were both TPACK researchers and teacher educators. Additionally, they asked experienced teachers and district-based teacher educators to score pre-service teachers' lesson plans following a training session on using the rubric. Comments provided by reviewers supported the face validity of the instrument, while reliability was assessed through measures of internal consistency and test–retest reliability. Findings indicated that the instrument has adequate validity and reliability and can be used to score pre-service teachers' technology-integrated lesson plans, in line with the TPACK framework.

Questionnaires, Interviews, and Observations

In their review of assessment instruments, Koehler et al. (2012) noted that *open-ended questionnaires, interviews,* and *observations* were used less frequently in efforts to measure TPACK. Hofer, Grandgenett, Harris, and Swan (2011) developed a TPACK-based instrument that can be used to assess observed evidence of TPACK during classroom instruction. Seven TPACK experts confirmed the rubric's construct and face validity. Further, 12 experienced technology-using teachers and district-based teacher educators tested and retested the reliability of the instrument by using it to assess 12 video-recorded lessons. The lessons were taught in elementary, middle, and high school classrooms in a variety of content areas, including mathematics, language arts, science, and social studies. Findings indicated that this is a valid and reliable instrument that can be used to assess enacted TPACK in observed lessons taught by either pre-service or in-service teachers. The authors noted, however, the challenge in training scorers to consider the important TPACK-related aspects of the lessons. As a result, they developed a scoring guide to assist researchers with using the instrument in a consistent manner. The authors concluded that, "using this instrument can help researchers and teacher educators to assess the quality of technology integration envisioned as a teacher's TPACK-in-action" (p. 4357).

Pathways to TPACK Development

A review of existing literature identified three potential pathways to the development of TPACK among pre-service teachers: (a) a stand-alone educational technology course, (b) instructional strategies embedded within an educational technology course or content-specific method courses, and (c) instructional strategies implemented in the context of entire teacher education programs. This section reviews research studies focusing on the development of TPACK (integrative and transformative perspectives) among pre-service teachers within each pathway, including the methods and data collection instruments used to assess their effectiveness.

Pathway 1: The Stand-Alone Educational Technology Course

The most commonly used pathway for developing pre-service teachers' TPACK is the delivery of a stand-alone educational technology course consistently offered since the

1990s (Niess, 2012; Polly, Mims, Shepherd, & Inan, 2010). Typically, this course focuses on learning about different technologies (e.g., word processors, presentation software, the Internet) along with their affordances and constraints and subsequently examining how the technologies can be used in teaching and learning by having pre-service teachers design lessons or projects for specific subject matter (Chai, Koh, & Tsai, 2013). The literature focusing on the stand-alone educational technology course to date reveals many benefits associated with this approach, including the ability to improve pre-service teachers' self-efficacy, provide a good overview of the use of technology in teaching, and develop a strong foundation of technology skills (Kay, 2006; Niess, 2012).

Nevertheless, a focus on technology alone is not sufficient to the development and application of TPACK in practice. To address this challenge, Mishra, Koehler, Shin, Wolf, and DeSchryver (2010) suggest retaining the technology course but reconsidering its curriculum to place more emphasis on the interconnections among technology, content, and pedagogy. A number of studies to date attempt to reconsider the curriculum of the educational technology course, make it more meaningful, and help pre-service teachers identify connections among content, pedagogy, and technology.

Wetzel, Foulger, and Williams (2009) used the TPACK framework as a guide to rethink the design of the stand-alone technology course and redesign assignments to make the interconnections highlighted in the TPACK framework explicit. As such, TPACK in this study was treated as a unique knowledge base. More specifically, Wetzel et al. introduced two assignments that fostered the development of pre-service teachers' TPACK. The first assignment engaged small groups of pre-service teachers learning about a new technology tool, teaching other classmates about it, providing a picture of its use in their future classrooms, and beginning to use the new tool to accomplish learning goals. According to Wetzel et al., in this assignment the content and technology constructs largely overlapped, as students learned to use new technologies and discussed where to use them in PK–12 academic areas. The second assignment interweaved all aspects of TPACK, including content, pedagogy, and technology. This project focused on state historical content (content), project-based pedagogy (pedagogy), and video-editing technology (technology). In particular, the students assumed the roles of historians responsible for documenting the lives of elders in their family through digital stories that featured edited video, audio, and digital images.

To examine the effectiveness of the redesigned educational technology course, Wetzel et al. (2009) adopted an action research methodology, collecting data through surveys, focus groups, and performance assessments (e.g., class wiki and student work). Analysis did not focus explicitly on knowledge development but rather on the manner in which pre-service teachers learned new tools used in the course, as well as their perceptions on the influence of the projects for their future teaching. As such, the study focused primarily on the skills needed to directly apply technology in classroom settings rather than on the individual knowledge components of TPACK. Findings indicated that participants were successful in learning new technologies independently (TK), but concerns were raised by some pre-service teachers indicating resistance to collaborative work and applicability of those models to their future classrooms. Wetzel et al. indicated that the technology course could help as the first stop to redesigning teacher education experiences based on the TPACK framework. The authors acknowledged that the TPACK framework should help us "think broadly at the program level rather than just at the course level" (p. 5).

In a similar effort, Chai et al. (2011) used the TPACK framework as a theoretical lens to the design of a 12-hour module entitled "Information Communication Technology (ICT) for Meaningful Learning in Singapore." The first half of the module aimed at building pre-service teachers' PK and TPK by focusing on the development of a theoretical understanding of what constituted meaningful learning with technology. The second half of the module aimed at building pre-service teachers' TK, TCK, TPK, and TPACK through a series of technology-enhanced lessons that explored how technology could be used to foster meaningful learning.

In the case of spreadsheets, for instance, pre-service teachers first engaged with spreadsheets as learners through exercises that modeled the relationship between distance traveled by a projectile and the velocity of the projectile represented in Microsoft Excel. Subsequently, they learned the technology skills (TK) of building representations or models with Excel. Based on these experiences, they analyzed the pedagogical affordances of the technology (i.e., TPK) and difficulties they anticipated their students might face in understanding concepts or theories in their subject area (i.e., TPACK). In the end, they worked in groups to propose lesson ideas on how this technology tool could be used to engage their students in meaningful learning supported by technology.

To examine the effectiveness of this approach, Chai et al. utilized a 46-item survey instrument adapted from Schmidt et al. (2009) designed to measure TPACK constructs. Unlike the work of Wetzel et al. (2009), Chai et al. (2011) focused explicitly on pre-service teachers' knowledge development, examining both the individual domains that fuel TPACK (integrative perspective), as well as TPACK as a unique knowledge construct (transformative perspective). Findings from this work indicated significant gains in all TPACK domains, and the authors concluded that the redesigned module was effective in improving pre-service teachers' knowledge for teaching with technology. The results also affirmed that engaging teachers in designing technology-integrated lessons was an effective pedagogical approach in developing not only the individual knowledge bases of content, pedagogy, and technology, but also the knowledge constructs that promote professional understanding in using technology, such as TPK and TPACK.

Similar to Chai et al. (2011), An et al. (2011) developed a two-stage curriculum intended to help elementary pre-service teachers understand technology integration. The curriculum consisted of two courses: a basic technology course and an educational technology course covering both general principles of teaching with technology and assistive technology. Both courses were offered early in the education program so pre-service teachers could apply their learning in subsequent methods courses. Data were collected through a technology competency survey, a modified version of the Survey of Pre-Service Teachers Knowledge of Teaching and Technology, pre-service teacher reflections, and course assignments. Survey data were analyzed quantitatively, while reflection data were analyzed using a rubric mapped onto the TPACK framework, illustrating a focus on both TPACK as a distinct knowledge construct (transformative perspective) and its individual domains of content, pedagogy, and technology (integrative perspective). Findings from this work indicated that the educational technology course contributed to pre-service teachers' development of TPACK and improved their attitudes and beliefs on their technology integration practices.

Rather than separating the educational technology course from methods courses, Mouza et al. 2014 examined an integrated pedagogical approach, which juxtaposed an educational technology course with methods courses and field experience. This integrated approach aimed at fostering both TK and knowledge related to the intersections of technology, content, and pedagogy (TPACK). Through careful instructional design, Mouza et al. described the redesign of the educational technology course in line with markers of effective teacher preparation articulated in the literature, including: (a) theory to practice connections, (b) opportunities for instructional design, (c) modeling by faculty and cooperating teachers, (d) authentic experiences, and (e) opportunities for enactment and reflection (Tondeur et al., 2012).

To investigate the effectiveness of this integrated approach, Mouza et al. utilized both survey data focusing on knowledge development (integrative perspective) and performance assessments that examined application of knowledge in practice (transformative perspective). Specifically, using pre and post data collected through the Survey of Pre-Service Teachers Knowledge of Teaching and Technology, findings from this work indicated that participants experienced significant gains in all TPACK constructs and that effect sizes were large in all areas except content knowledge (CK), which was not particularly targeted in this approach. Further, analysis of performance assessments indicated that all participants were able to apply their learning to classroom practice as they implemented technology-integrated lessons in their field placement classrooms and reflected on their experience.

Building more heavily on the role of field experience, Habowski and Mouza (2014) combined a content-specific technology integration course with extensive field experience in a secondary science teacher education program. The course focused on the importance of incorporating appropriate and effective technology applications in the science classroom and was built around markers of effective teacher preparation (Tondeur et al., 2012). While enrolled in the course, pre-service teachers in the program engaged in extensive field experience following a co-teaching model, which allowed them to spend 150 hours in the field. During that time, they worked with a cooperating teacher to identify curricular goals, design technology-integrated lessons, and reflect on their practice.

Similar to other efforts, data examining the effectiveness of this approach were collected through the Survey of Pre-Service Teachers Knowledge of Teaching and Technology and focus groups with pre-service teachers (integrative perspective). Findings from this work indicated that participants improved their understanding of combining technology with science content and pedagogy and experienced significant gains in their TPACK. Further, the content-specific nature of the course encouraged pre-service teachers to consider the interactions among technology and content (TCK) more frequently compared to technology and pedagogy (TPK).

Pathway 2: Instructional Strategies Embedded Within the Educational Technology Course or Content-Specific Methods Courses

A number of studies so far have examined the potential and efficacy of specific instructional strategies that can foster pre-service teachers' TPACK development in the context of the educational technology course or content-specific methods courses. In particular, four approaches appear to hold promise: instructional design, TPACK-based case development, reflection, and technology-rich field placements.

Instructional Design

Angeli and Valanides (2009) introduced an instructional design framework called technology mapping (TM) to guide teacher thinking about the ill-defined problem of designing technology-enhanced learning. Using this framework, Angeli and Valanides asked pre-service teachers to map software affordances with content representations and pedagogical issues as they designed lessons that integrate technology. Subsequently, participants worked in peer-assessment groups using TPACK-based criteria to examine and provide feedback on each other's work. In the process of design, TM allows pre-service teachers to identify the dynamic transactions among TPACK knowledge constructs, while simultaneously acknowledging the role of context in instructional decision-making.

In an empirical investigation of the TM approach in the context of a required educational technology course for pre-service teachers, Angeli and Valanides (2009) reported promising findings. Specifically, participants in the study were asked to follow TM in two design tasks. Findings indicated that pre-service teachers' performance on the second design tasks was significantly better than their performance on the first design task. Further, examining TPACK holistically using a transformative perspective, findings indicated that participants' TPACK related competencies significantly improved during the course of a semester. The authors concluded that the teaching of the TM instructional design process in combination with the peer-and-instructor assessment model had a positive impact on the development of pre-service teachers' TPACK.

Similarly, Graham et al. (2012) engaged pre-service teachers in three instructional design tasks that asked them to describe how they would teach particular curricular standards using technology. The instructional design tasks were administered at the beginning and end of an educational technology course for elementary and early childhood pre-service teachers. For each design task, participants were asked to describe specific instructional strategies or activities that used technology to help students learn knowledge and skills related to the identified curricular standard. Further, they were asked to provide a rationale for why they chose to use technology in the way described in their design task.

Subsequently, Graham et al. (2012) used the TPACK framework as a lens for examining how pre-service teachers make decisions related to the use of technology in teaching, focusing on both the individual knowledge bases fueling TPACK (integrative perspective) and TPACK as a unique construct (transformative perspective). Findings from this work indicated that initially pre-service teachers provided a limited number of rationales, focusing on surface-level general PK. In contrast, rationales provided at the end of the course were detailed and sophisticated with multiple overlapping reasons. Nevertheless, findings indicated that many rationales failed to connect directly to content-specific uses of technology as expected by the TPACK framework. Graham et al. identified the need for exposing pre-service teachers to more content-specific technology integration examples (TPACK), compared to examples that link technology to general pedagogical practices (TPK).

татраск-Based Case Development

While in the above studies pre-service teachers engaged in instructional design tasks, Mouza and Karchmer-Klein (2013) investigated TPACK-based case development as an approach that goes beyond design to include enactment and reflection upon technology-integrated lessons. The process of case development progressed incrementally throughout pre-service teachers' participation in an educational technology course offered in conjunction with methods courses and field experience. This process was divided in four stages. In stage 1, participants developed a technology inventory for their field placement. In stage 2, participants selected a technology-integrated lesson developed through their participation in the course that they wished to implement in their field placement. In stage 3, participants enacted the identified technology-integrated lesson in their field placement. Finally, in stage 4, participants wrote a case report based on the cycle of preparation, enactment, and reflection on the technology-integrated lesson in their field placement.

To assess the effectiveness of TPACK-based case development Mouza and Karchmer-Klein (2013) used performance assessments, including technology-integrated lessons and case reports collected from 58 participants. Technology-integrated lessons were scored using the four-point rubric developed by Harris et al. (2010), while case reports were holistically assessed for evidence of TPACK (transformative perspective). Findings indicated that TPACK-based case development provided a fruitful context for helping pre-service teachers bring together different knowledge bases to design and implement technology-integrated lessons, as well as engage participants in the type of analysis and reflection that fosters practical wisdom. Results, however, indicated that some participants have demonstrated only emergent TPACK, as well as a disconnect between knowledge evidenced in their lesson plans and application of knowledge evidenced in their case reports. Mouza and Karchmer-Klein argued for the need to consider pre-service teachers' development of TPACK not only at a theoretical level, but also in relation to practice.

Reflection

Focusing more specifically on reflection, Jang and Chen (2010) developed a transformative model and online system for building TPACK among science pre-service teachers based on four main activities that included comprehension of TPACK, observation, practice, and reflection. During comprehension, participants learned about concepts and technologies around e-learning in collaborative groups. During observation, participants observed experienced mentor science teachers demonstrate their teaching of integrating technology in a specific science unit. During practice, participants designed and demonstrated lesson plans that integrated computer activities with appropriate topic-specific pedagogy. Finally, during reflection, participants shared videos of their lesson implementation and reflected on their performance. After each activity, participants answered questions and maintained reflective journals. Data included written assignments, online work, reflective journals, videos of their own practice, and interviews. Findings indicated that the model was successful in helping participants better understand PCK and TPACK. Participants were able to model their own technology integration lessons after those of their mentors. Further, analysis and reflection video helped participants "explicate and further integrate their TPACK about students' learning difficulties, instructional strategies and technology" (p. 562).

Along the same lines, Kopcha, Ottenbreit-Leftwich, Jung, and Baser (2014) engaged pre-service teachers in decision-making around technology integration and reflection using lesson-planning vignettes and e-portfolios. Specifically, students completed two lesson-planning vignettes that challenged them to integrate technology around content- and context-specific constraints. Further, they created end-of-course e-portfolios that included multiple artifacts and in-depth reflections that summarized their perceptions of their own TCK, TPK, and TPACK. Data were collected using two popular measures of TPACK, including the Survey of Pre-Service Teachers for Teaching with Technology and the lesson-planning rubric developed by Harris et al. (2010), reflecting a focus on both the integrative and transformative perspectives. Findings indicated that participants were able to articulate their understanding of TPACK in their end-of-course portfolio written reflections, but struggled to create planning documents that used technologies that were appropriate for their given audience and supported the content standards. Further, survey data were not always aligned with lesson planning scores, raising concerns about the instruments and the discriminatory validity of the TPACK framework.

Field Experience

Looking specifically at TPACK in relation to practice, Meagher, Ozgün-Koca, and Edwards (2011) examined the role of two separate field experiences in promoting use of technology in a mathematics methods course for pre-service teachers through the TPACK lens. In particular, this study examined pre-service teachers' evolving relationships with technology in their teaching and the interplay between their field placements and the quality of their own use of technology in inquiry-based lessons. Findings from this work highlighted the "decisive effect" of modeling of exemplary practice in technology-rich environments on pre-service teachers' attitudes and the quality of their lesson plans in terms of inquiry. More specifically, the study noted the difficulty of making connections between practices promoted in methods classes and practice without exemplary experiences provided by practicing teachers.

Pathway 3: TPACK Development in the Context of Teacher Education Programs

Studies investigating methods for integrating the development of TPACK within entire teacher preparation programs were scarce in the literature. In one of the earliest studies, Niess (2005) examined TPACK development among pre-service teachers in a multidimensional science and mathematics teacher preparation program that integrated teaching and learning with technology. The teacher education program in this study was a one-year, graduate-level program focused on the preparation of science and mathematics teachers. The program employed a multidimensional approach guided by four themes, including research-based teaching and learning, technology integration (TPACK), development of pedagogical content knowledge, and instructional practice integrated with campus-based coursework. Technology preparation in the program took various forms, including an educational technology course, microteaching, and practical experiences in the design, teaching, and reflection on hands-on lessons with technology.

Analysis provided by Niess (2005) examined TPACK holistically (transformative perspective) and indicated that only some of the pre-service teachers recognized the interplay of technology and science, despite the emphasis throughout the program. Through a set of five individual cases, Niess illustrated pre-service teachers' decision-making process when choosing to use or not use technology in their field practicum and described the difficulties and successes experienced by participants in molding their TPACK. Specifically, Niess found that dispositions for how a subject matter is typically taught, the complexity of technology use by students, and lack of clear understanding related to the impact of technology on student understanding of subject matter influenced pre-service teachers' technology use. Findings from this work highlighted important issues in the development of pre-service teachers' TPACK, including the interactions of the content (e.g., science and mathematics) with the content of specific technologies.

While the work of Niess (2005) focused on a small number of qualitative case studies, Hofer and Grandgenett (2012) employed a mixed-methods approach to look more closely into the development of pre-service teachers' TPACK over time, combining the integrative and transformative perspectives. This work was conducted in the context of an 11-month master's program in secondary (grades 6–12) education. The teacher preparation program spanned three semesters. In the first semester, participants enrolled in foundational coursework focusing on social and historical foundations of education, curriculum, and instruction, educational psychology, and research. In the second semester, participants enrolled in content-based teaching methods courses in conjunction with a 20-hour practicum, educational technology coursework, and coursework on classroom management and students with special needs. In the third semester, participants completed coursework on assessment, collaboration with families and school personnel, and content-based instructional planning, as well as 11 weeks of student teaching. Technology preparation in this program was addressed through the educational technology course offered in the second semester, as well as to varying degrees in the required teaching methods courses.

Using survey data collected through the Survey of Pre-Service Teachers for Teaching with Technology, structured reflections, and instructional plans at four points in time spanning the three-semester program, Hofer and Grandgenett (2012) measured both individual TPACK components and TPACK as a unique knowledge base. Results revealed significant development in participant's TPK and TPACK. The largest knowledge gains were documented during the second semester in the program, when pre-service teachers completed educational technology coursework and teaching methods for the first time. Similarly with Niess (2005), however, they found limited growth in participants' knowledge of the interactions among technology and content (TCK). Further, Hofer and Grandgenett noted that pre-service teachers found it difficult to maintain what they learned about pedagogy in the realities of classroom practice as illustrated in their instructional planning documents.

More recently, Mouza, Nandakumar, Yilmaz Ozden, and Karchmer-Klein (2015) used longitudinal data collected from freshman to junior/senior year to investigate the development of pre-service teachers' TPACK throughout their initial four-year teacher preparation program. The program curriculum for this teacher education program was divided into three areas: the *general studies* (i.e., content) courses, the *professional studies* courses (i.e., methods), and the *concentration* courses, which help pre-service teachers' develop expertise in a middle school concentrations area (e.g., English, mathematics) or special education. Additionally, the program required a range of field experiences in a variety of classroom settings, beginning with the general studies courses, moving into methods field experience, and culminating with student teaching. Technology preparation in the program was addressed intentionally in two required educational technology courses offered at the freshman and junior or senior year. The first course (freshman year) was designed to prepare incoming pre-service teachers to use educational technology techniques and methods in their own learning and their future teaching. The second course (junior/senior year) emphasized use of technology for designing and implementing technology-integrated instruction aligned with the TPACK framework. Additionally, the program addressed technology to varying degrees in methods courses and field experience.

Survey data and performance assessments were used to examine pre-service teachers' knowledge development over time. Specifically, survey data were collected from 120 participants using the Survey of Pre-Service Teachers for Teaching with Technology at four key points: before and after each technology course (integrative perspective). Further, blog entries collected during the first technology course (freshman year) and case reports collected during the second technology course (junior/senior year) were used to examine TPACK development more holistically at different time points (transformative perspective). Findings indicated that educational technology coursework, content, methods courses, and field experience collectively provided pre-service teachers' with opportunities to develop their knowledge of teaching with technology. Specifically, pre-service teachers significantly improved their TPACK knowledge components from their freshman to junior/senior year. Findings, however, indicated that with the exemption of CK, knowledge gains from the freshman year were not maintained to junior/senior year in the absence of intentional educational technology coursework. The authors noted that intentional coursework in technology might be more effective when spaced throughout teacher education programs to ensure that knowledge gains are retained over time.

Discussion and Directions for Future Research

The synthesis of research presented in this chapter demonstrated the increased interest around the TPACK framework and the ways in which it has been used to inform teacher preparation. Specifically, the studies reviewed in this chapter revealed three important insights. First, there are multiple pathways to TPACK development that include both stand-alone courses and more integrated approaches through methods courses and entire teacher education programs. While all three pathways hold promise, much of the empirical literature has examined the efficacy of stand-alone educational technology courses. Fewer studies examined integrated approaches in the context of content-specific methods courses. Even fewer studies have examined TPACK development throughout teacher education programs.

Second, there is variability in the instruments and methods used to document TPACK development. Research with stand-alone educational technology courses tends to utilize self-reported surveys, measuring TPACK from an integrative perspective. In contrast, research with specific instructional strategies or content-specific methods tends to utilize performance assessments and interviews, measuring TPACK more holistically from a transformative perspective. The variability in TPACK conceptualization and assessment makes it difficult to compare TPACK-related outcomes as a result of the different instructional approaches.

Third, there is variability in the technology focus, with many studies lacking explicit discussion around the types of technologies utilized by pre-service teachers. Those studies that specifically discuss their technology focus typically use productivity, Internet, and other types of Web 2.0 tools. Studies addressing novel technologies such as mobile tools, games, and programming environments were absent from the literature. Collectively, these findings illuminate significant insights for future research, which are presented below.

Future Research: Instructional Strategies and Process for Developing TPACK

Although a number of instructional interventions related to TPACK development have been presented in the chapter, the literature revealed little attention to the *process* of TPACK development among pre-service teachers. Working with in-service teachers, for example, Niess (2012) proposed a developmental view of TPACK which progresses through five different levels: recognizing (knowledge), accepting (persuasion), adapting (decision), exploring (implementation), and advancing (confirmation). While this view is promising, little empirical evidence supports this trajectory among pre-service teachers (e.g., Mouza et al., 2014).

One way to examine the process of TPACK development is to study TPACK-related outcomes associated with the sequence of the educational technology course in teacher preparation. While some programs offer the educational technology course prior to methods courses to help develop TK and TPK first (see An et al., 2011), other programs offer the educational technology course in conjunction with methods courses and field experience to foster simultaneous development of TK, TPK, and TPACK (see Mouza et al., 2014). Examining more closely the unique advantages and drawbacks of placing educational technology coursework before, during, or after methods courses could help illuminate the ways in which individual knowledge domains contribute to TPACK development more holistically. Recently, for instance, Shinas et al. (2015) used quantitative data from a large number of pre-service teachers to tease out the contributions of each knowledge domain in the development of TPACK. Findings from this work emphasized the foundational role of PK in TPACK development, but noted that TPK made the largest impact on TPACK development. More studies like this are needed to identify the unique contributions of each knowledge construct on pre-service teacher learning in ways that point to specific pathways and course sequence in teacher preparation programs.

Further, research revealed little attention around content-specific approaches to TPACK development. As Koehler, Mishra, Kereluik, Shin, and Graham (2014) note, a key distinction between TPACK and traditional technology integration efforts is a focus on content-specific pedagogies as opposed to general pedagogies. Yet, the majority of efforts to develop TPACK among pre-service teachers focus on technology tools that span all content areas (Koehler et al., 2014). Few studies report on content-specific efforts for TPACK development, with the majority of them conducted in secondary teacher education settings (e.g., Habowski & Mouza, 2014). Future research can examine TPACK-related outcomes for elementary pre-service teachers as a result of completing methods courses that explicitly target technology in the context of specific disciplines.

Future Research: Assessment of TPACK

As Young, Young, and Hamilton (2013) point out, the TPACK framework is by design fluid and, thus, there are a number of instruments and variations used to examine the nuances of TPACK development. Clearly, identifying a single measurement instrument is not consistent with the content- and context-specific nature of the TPACK framework. Further, the ever-changing nature of technology and the continuous emergence of new tools make it necessary to continuously update TPACK-domains dependent on technology (e.g., TK, TCK, and TPK) to avoid the risk of losing validity (Koehler et al., 2012). Nevertheless, more valid and reliable instruments are needed that would enable researchers to compare TPACK-related outcomes as a result of different instructional approaches. Young et al. (2013), for example, noted that TPACK-related inferences from meta-analytic statistical methodologies are not feasible due to the current lack of relevant TPACK data. As a result, researchers should focus on developing both survey instruments and observation and performance assessment instruments that would enable consistent data collection and triangulation.

Further, researchers must move beyond pre–post designs in the context of single courses to focus on longitudinal research that captures triangulated representations of pre-service teachers' TPACK before, during, and after university coursework (Hofer & Grandgenett, 2012). To date, few studies utilized triangulated measures to examine levels of discrimination and convergence among TPACK constructs as assessed by existing TPACK measures

(Agyei & Keengwe, 2014; Hofer & Grandgenett, 2012; Kopcha et al., 2014). For the most part, these studies found low levels of convergence among the measured constructs. Kopcha et al., for instance, found that in many cases survey and rubric scores were clearly misaligned and correlations between similar constructs were weak. Similarly, Agyei and Keengwe (2014) found that teachers' learning outcome measures as indicated by performance assessments did not correlate with their self-reported TPACK measure. Collectively, these studies indicate that while self-reported survey measures are useful for examining participants' awareness and confidence, additional measures must be utilized to triangulate survey data and examine concrete representations of pre-service teachers' TPACK (Agyei & Keengwe, 2014). As Hofer and Grandgenett point out, "triangulated study designs that include both self-report and performance measures that span multiple years in the field will help us to not only better understand how TPACK develops, but also know what contextual factors support and inhibit this growth" (p. 103).

Future Research: New Technologies and TPACK

As indicated, a number of studies reviewed in this work utilized productivity and Internet-based technologies. Yet, novel technologies such as tablets, games, programming environments (e.g., Scratch), and digital fabrication tools make it necessary to identify the type of teacher knowledge required to respond to the affordances and constraints associated with these technologies. Recent industry efforts, for example, have generated increased interest related to the role of computer science principles in K–12 settings with a number of organizations (e.g., Code.org) providing free curricular resources for teachers. Given that such tools are not yet widely utilized in K–12 settings, pre-service teachers may not have adequate opportunities to experience or observe their use in authentic settings. As a result, researchers must identify alternative approaches to the development of TPACK-related knowledge and skills needed for the integration of these novel tools with content-specific pedagogical practices.

To date, only a handful of studies reported on TPACK-related outcomes as a result of using novel technologies. Hutchison, Beschorner, & Schmidt-Crawford (2012), for example, used the TPACK framework as a lens for understanding the viability of integrating mobile technologies (i.e., tablets) into literacy instruction. Similarly, guided by the TPACK framework, Smith (2013) explored one middle school teacher's yearlong journey as she integrated digital fabrication technology to create pop-up books in an afterschool program with a language arts focus. Both of these studies, however, were conducted with in-service teachers. As a result, future research must identify pedagogical practices that meaningfully prepare pre-service teachers to transform novel technology tools to meaningful educational technology experiences for K–12 learners in the spirit of the TPACK framework.

Conclusion

This chapter provided a thoughtful overview of existing approaches used to assess and develop pre-service teachers' TPACK. Although researchers and teacher educators have embraced the TPACK framework with excitement, this review indicated great variability in the instruments and strategies used to assess and develop TPACK, making it difficult to draw comparisons around the efficacy of these strategies. While much-needed insights into the development of TPACK have been identified so far, we must continue investigating methods and learning trajectories for integrating and assessing the development of TPACK within teacher education programs, while also strengthening the construct validity of the TPACK framework.

References

AACTE Committee on Innovation and Technology. (2008). *Handbook of technological pedagogical content knowledge (TPCK) for educators*. New York: Routledge.

Abbit, J. (2011). Measuring technological pedagogical content knowledge in pre-service teacher education: A review of current methods and instruments. *Journal of Research on Technology in Education, 43*(4), 281–300.

Agyei, D.D., & Keengwe, J. (2014). Using technology pedagogical content knowledge development to enhance learning outcomes. *Education and Information Technology, 19*(1), 155–171.

An, H., Wilder, H., & Lim, K. (2011). Preparing elementary pre-service teachers from a non-traditional student population to teach with technology. *Computers in the Schools, 28*(2), 170–193.

Angeli, C., & Valanides, N. (2009). Epistemological and methodological issues for the conceptualization, development, and assessment of ICT-TPCK: Advances in technology and pedagogical content knowledge (TPCK). *Computers & Education, 52*, 154–168.

CAEP 2013 Standards for Accreditation of Educator Preparation. (2013). Council for the Accreditation of Educator Preparation. Retrieved on July 15, 2014, from http://caepnet.org

Chai, C.S., Koh, J.H.L., & Tsai, C.C. (2013). A review of technological pedagogical content knowledge. *Educational Technology & Society, 16*(2), 31–51.

Chai, C.S., Koh, J.H.L., Tsai, C., & Tan, L.L.W. (2011). Modeling primary school pre-service teachers' technological pedagogical content knowledge (TPACK) for meaningful learning with information and communication technology (ICT). *Computers & Education, 57*(1), 1184–1193.

Cox, S. (2008). A conceptual analysis of technological pedagogical content knowledge. Unpublished doctoral dissertation. Provo, UT: Brigham Young University.

Dilworth, P., Donaldson, A., George, M., Knezek, D., Searson, M., Starkweather, K., Strutchens, M., Tillotson, J., & Robinson, S. (2012). Preparing teachers for tomorrow's technologies. *TechTrends, 56*(4), 11–14.

Graham, C.R. (2011). Theoretical considerations for understanding technological pedagogical content knowledge (TPACK). *Computers & Education, 57*, 1953–1960. doi:10.1016/j.compedu.2011.04.010

Graham, C.R., Borup, J., & Smith, N.B. (2012). Using TPACK as a framework to understand teacher candidates' technology integration decisions. *Journal of Computer Assisted Learning, 28*(6), 530–546. doi:10.1111/j.1365-2729.2011.00472.x

Habowski, T., & Mouza, C. (2014). Pre-service teachers' development of technological pedagogical content knowledge (TPACK) in the context of a secondary science teacher education program. *Journal of Technology and Teacher Education, 22*(4), 471–495.

Harris, J., Grandgenett, N., & Hofer, M. (2010). Testing a TPACK-based technology integration assessment rubric. In C. D. Maddux, D. Gibson, & B. Dodge (Eds.), *Research highlights in technology and teacher education 2010* (pp. 323–331). Chesapeake, VA: Society for Information Technology in Teacher Education (SITE).

Hofer, M., & Grandgenett, N. (2012). TPACK development in teacher education: A longitudinal study of pre-service teachers in a secondary M.A.Ed. Program. *Journal of Research on Technology in Education, 45*(1), 83–106.

Hofer, M., Grandgenett, N., Harris, J., & Swan, K. (2011). Testing a TPACK-based technology integration observation instrument. In C. D. Maddux, D. Gibson, B. Dodge, M. Koehler, P. Mishra, & C. Owens (Eds.), *Research highlights in technology and teacher education 2011* (pp. 39–46). Chesapeake, VA: Society for Information Technology in Teacher Education (SITE).

Hutchison, A., Beschorner, B., & Schmidt-Crawford, D. (2012). Exploring the use of the iPad for literacy learning. *The Reading Teacher, 66*(1), 15–23.

Jang, S.-J., & Chen, K. C. (2010). From PCK to TPACK: Developing a transformative model of pre-service science teachers. *Journal of Science Education and Technology, 19*(6), 553–564.

Jones, C., & Cross, S. (2009). Is there a new generation coming to university? In Proceedings of the Association of Learning Technology Conference (ALT-C) "In dreams begins responsibility: Choice, evidence and change," Manchester, UK, September 8–10, 2009.

Kay, R. (2006). Evaluating strategies used to incorporate technology into pre-service education: A review of the literature. *Journal of Research on Technology in Education, 38*(4), 383–408.

Kennedy, G., Judd, T., Churchward, A., Gray, K., & Krause, K.L. (2008). First year students' experiences with technology: Are they digital natives? *Australasian Journal of Educational Technology, 24*(1), 108–122.

Koehler, M. J., Mishra, P., Kereluik, K., Shin, T. S., & Graham, C. R. (2014). The technological pedagogical content knowledge framework. In J.M. Specter, M.D. Merrill, J. Elen, & M.J. Bishop (Eds.), *Handbook of research on educational communications and technology* (pp. 101–111). New York: Springer.

Koehler, M. J., Mishra, P., & Yahya, K. (2007). Tracing the development of teacher knowledge in a design seminar: Integrating content, pedagogy and technology. *Computers & Education, 49*(3), 740–762.

Koehler, M.J., Shin, T.S., & Mishra, P. (2012). How do we measure TPACK: Let me count the ways. In R.R. Ronau, C.R. Rakes, & M.L. Niess (Eds.), *Educational technology, teacher knowledge, and classroom impact: A research handbook on frameworks and approaches* (pp. 16–31). Hershey, PA: IGI Global.

Koh, J.H.L., Chai, C.S., & Tsai, C.C. (2010). Examining the technological pedagogical content knowledge of Singapore pre-service teachers with a large-scale survey. *Journal of Computer Assisted Learning, 26*, 563–573.

Kopcha, T.J., Ottenbreit-Leftwich, A., Jung, J., & Baser, D. (2014). Examining the TPACK framework through the convergence and discriminant validity of two measures. *Computers & Education, 78*, 87–96. Retrieved from http://dx.doi.org/10.1016/j.compedu.2014.05.003

Lei, J. (2009). Digital natives as pre-service teachers: What technology preparation is needed? *Journal of Computing in Teacher Education, 25*(3), 87–97.

Margaryan, A., Littlejohn, A., & Vojt, G. (2011). Are digital natives a myth or reality? University students' use of digital technologies. *Computers & Education, 56*, 429–440.

Meagher, M., Ozgün-Koca, S. A., & Edwards, M. T. (2011). Pre-service teachers' experiences with advanced digital technologies: The interplay between technology in a pre-service classroom and in field placements. *Contemporary Issues in Technology and Teacher Education, 11*(3), 243–270.

Mishra, P., & Koehler, M.J. (2006). Technological pedagogical content knowledge: A framework for teacher knowledge. *Teachers College Record, 108*(6), 1017–1054.

Mishra, P., Koehler, M. J., Shin, T. S., Wolf, L. G., & DeSchryver, M. (2010). Developing TPACK by design. In J. Voogt (Chair), Developing TPACK. Symposium conducted at the Annual

Meeting of the Society for Information Technology and Teacher Education (SITE), San Diego, CA, March 2010.

Mouza, C., & Karchmer-Klein, R. (2013). Promoting and assessing pre-service teachers technological pedagogical content knowledge in the context of case development. *Journal of Educational Computing Research, 48*(2), 127–152.

Mouza, C., Karchmer-Klein, R., Nandakumar, R., Yilmaz Ozden, S., & Hun, L. (2014). Investigating the impact of an integrated approach to the development of pre-service teachers' technological pedagogical content knowledge (TPACK). *Computers & Education, 71,* 206–221. doi:10.1015/j.compedu.2013.09.020

Mouza, C., & Lavigne, N. (2012). *Emerging technologies for the classroom: A learning sciences perspective.* New York: Springer.

Mouza, C., Nandakumar, R., Yilmaz Ozden, S., & Karchmer-Klein, R. (2015). A longitudinal investigation of pre-service teachers' technological pedagogical content knowledge (TPACK) in the context of a teacher preparation program. Annual Meeting of the American Educational Research Association, Chicago, IL, April.

Niess, M. L. (2005). Preparing teachers to teach science and mathematics with technology: Developing a technology pedagogical content knowledge. *Teaching and Teacher Education, 21,* 509–523.

Niess, M.L. (2008). Guiding pre-service teachers in developing TPCK. In AACTE Committee on Innovation and Technology (Ed.), *The handbook of technological pedagogical content knowledge (TPCK) for educators* (pp. 223–250). New York: Routledge.

Niess, M. L. (2011). Investigating TPACK: Knowledge growth in teaching with technology. *Journal of Educational Computing Research, 44*(3), 299–317.

Niess, M. L. (2012). Teachers knowledge for teaching with technology: A TPACK lens. In R. R. Ronau, C. R. Rakes, & M. L. Niess (Eds.), *Educational technology, teacher knowledge, and classroom impact: A research handbook on framework and approaches* (pp. 1–15). Hershey, PA: IGI Global.

Partnership for 21st Century Skills & American Association of Colleges of Teacher Education (AACTE). (2010). *21st century knowledge and skills in teacher educator preparation.* Retrieved in October 2014 from http://www.p21.org/storage/documents/aacte_p21_whitepaper2010.pdf

Polly, D., Mims, C., Shepherd, C., & Inan, F. (2010). Evidence of impact: Transforming teacher education with preparing tomorrow's teachers to teach with technology (PT3) grants. *Teaching and Teacher Education, 26,* 863–870.

Prensky, M. (2001). Digital natives, digital immigrants: Do they really think differently? *On the Horizon, 9*(6), 1–6.

Schmidt, D.A., Baran, E., Thompson, A.D., Mishra, P., Koehler, M.J., & Shin, T.S. (2009). Technology pedagogical content knowledge (TPACK): The development and validation of an assessment instrument for pre-service teachers. *Journal of Research on Technology in Education, 42*(2), 123–149.

Shinas, V. H., Karchmer-Klein, R., Mouza, C., Yilmaz Ozden, S., & Glutting, J. (2015). Analyzing pre-service teachers' TPACK development in the context of a multi-dimensional teacher preparation program. *Journal of Digital Learning in Teacher Education, 31*(2), 47–55.

Shinas, V.H., Yilmaz Ozden, S., Mouza, C., Karchmer-Klein, R., & Glutting, J. (2013). Examining domains of technological pedagogical content knowledge using factor analysis. *Journal of Research on Technology in Education, 45*(4), 339–360.

Shulman, L.S. (1987). Knowledge and teaching: Foundations of the new reform. *Harvard Educational Review, 57*(1), 1–22.

Smith, S. (2013). Through the teacher's eyes: Unpacking the TPACK of digital fabrication integration in middle school language arts. *Journal of Research on Technology in Education, 46*(2), 207–227.

So, H., Choi, H., Lim, W.Y., & Xiong, Y. (2012). Little experience with ICT: Are they really the Net Generation student-teachers? *Computers & Education, 59,* 1234–1245. doi:10.1016/j.compedu.2012.05.008

Tondeur, J., van Braak, J., Sang, G., Voogt, J., Fisser, P., & Ottenbreit-Leftwich, A. (2012). Preparing pre-service teachers to integrate technology in education: A synthesis of qualitative evidence. *Computers & Education, 59,* 134–144.

UNESCO. (2011). *UNESCO ICT competency framework for teachers.* Paris, France: UNESCO. Retrieved on October 2014 from http://unesco.org

Wetzel, K., Foulger, T. S., & Williams, M. K. (2009). The evolution of the required educational technology course. *Journal of Computing in Teacher Education, 25*(2), 67.

Young, J.R., Young, J.L., & Hamilton, C. (2013). The use of confidence intervals as a meta-analytic lens to summarize the effects of teacher education technology courses on pre-service teacher TPACK. *Journal of Research on Technology in Education, 46*(2), 149–172.

Yurdakul, I.K., Odabasi, H.F., Kilicer, K., Coklar, A.N., Birinci, G., & Kurt, A.A. (2011). The development, validity and reliability of TPACK-deep: A technological pedagogical content knowledge scale. *Computers & Education, 58,* 964–977. doi:10.1016/j.compedu.2011.10.012

12

In-Service Teachers' TPACK Development

Trends, Models, and Trajectories

Judith B. Harris

Introduction

Ways of helping experienced teachers develop TPACK (Koehler & Mishra, 2008) have proliferated since the construct was introduced more than a decade ago. Even some of TPACK's first appearances as technological pedagogical content knowledge (TPCK) recommended particular strategies for its development: a collaborative learning-by-design approach for in-service teachers (Koehler & Mishra, 2005) and university faculty (Koehler, Mishra, Hershey, & Peruski, 2004), and instructional systems design (Angeli & Valanides, 2005) and collaborative reflection-upon-practice (Niess, 2005) approaches for pre-service teachers. During subsequent years, 12 different ways of helping teachers to develop this particular type of contextualized and applied knowledge have emerged. In this chapter, these 12 strategies are overviewed and situated within the larger teacher professional development literature, noting trends in TPACK-related teacher learning during the past decade and probable directions for future TPACK development methods and research.

Professional Development for Teachers

Research about teachers' professional learning shows that it is most effective when it is active, reflective, sustained, job-embedded, coherent, in-depth, and focused upon students' curriculum-based learning. In particular, the success, advisability, and challenges of using collaborative and learning community-based models for professional development (PD) have been documented during the past two decades (Darling-Hammond & Richardson, 2009). Other PD models—such as coaching, mentoring, and teacher inquiry—have also been shown to be successful (Joyce & Calhoun, 2010). This literature is far from conclusive, however; teacher-learner, organizational, and contextual factors combine to form complexities that complicate what Opfer & Pedder (2011) critique as a "process-product conceptualization of causality" (p. 384) within teacher professional development research that attempts to link particular characteristics of PD to improved student learning, but fails to do so consistently across multiple teacher learning contexts and systems. The efficacy of different types of professional learning approaches may well depend upon how well their content, structure, and timing fit the needs, preferences, and contextual affordances and constraints experienced by different teachers working within differing educational contexts (e.g., Pea & Wojnowski, 2014). Given this variability, it may be advisable—at least for now—to consider the full range of types of professional development for teachers, so that teacher learning can be customized for maximal efficacy.

Which approaches comprise the gamut of options for teacher PD? Few authors have attempted to organize and describe extant models for systematic, intentional teacher learning comprehensively. Joyce and Calhoun (2010) group PD types into five categories: those that support the individual teacher; those that task another teacher or administrator to provide customized professional learning opportunities; those that situate active learning within professional learning communities; those that are organized around school- or district-based curricular and/or instructional initiatives; and those that provide single-opportunity, workshop-based learning experiences for individual teachers. Kennedy (2005), situating her work within the UK's continuing professional development (CPD) movement that is occurring within multiple professions (Friedman & Phillips, 2004), organizes PD for teachers into nine models. Whereas Joyce & Calhoun's five models reference structural features of PD primarily, Kennedy's nine models focus mostly upon general purposes for teachers' learning. Kennedy's nine approaches include training, award-bearing (e.g., certification), deficit-focused, cascading (in which teachers participating in PD teach others what they have learned), standards-based (i.e., government-specified standards for teachers' practice), coaching/mentoring, community of practice, action research, and transformative PD. Kennedy explains that transformative PD is actually a combination of several PD models, encompassing goals for school organizational and/or contextual change in addition to teacher learning. Park Rogers et al. (2010) classify PD approaches by their "orientations," which reflect their designers' PD knowledge, experience, and beliefs. These researchers identified five such orientations within science education PD: activity-driven, content-driven, pedagogy-driven, curriculum materials-driven, and needs-driven.

Although overall structure, purpose, and orientation for PD are important to consider, specifying particular *processes* for professional learning might be even more helpful with the logistics of planning PD, especially as it relates to a particular focus, such as developing teachers' TPACK. How might classifications of professional learning processes be described so that the full range of PD approaches that can help teachers to develop their TPACK can be considered?

To answer this question, the contents of 23 issues of the *TPACK Newsletter* (http://www.matt-koehler.com/tpack/tpack-newsletters/), dating from January 2009 (the inaugural issue) through May 2015, plus a Web-based compilation of TPCK/TPACK publications appearing prior to 2009 that was distributed prior to the first issue of the newsletter, were screened to identify all articles, chapters, conference papers, and dissertations that addressed the development of in-service teachers' TPACK or TPCK. The

TPACK Newsletter is a freely available publication that is distributed by email to approximately 1,200 subscribers several times each year. It contains citations and abstracts of TPACK-related articles, chapters, books, dissertations, conference presentations, and commentaries and aims to be comprehensive in its contents. One hundred seventy-nine publications that addressed the development of in-service teachers' TPACK were found. Their contents were reviewed to identify those pieces that provided enough detailed information to deduce the design and specific processes used within the TPACK-related PD for in-service teachers that the publications were describing. Of the 179 publications, 63 contained enough information to discern the specific ways in which teachers' TPACK-related learning was supported. Thirty-five of these were selected to illustrate the distinct models of professional development that emerged from analysis of the 63 publications, based upon the clarity and comprehensiveness of the information provided in each. These 35 publications are referenced in Table 12.1 on page 198, grouped according to general type of and specific strategy for TPACK development. These classifications are described in detail below.

Types of TPACK Development

As the analysis of extant TPACK PD literature described above demonstrates, many approaches to TPACK development have been created and explored in the decade since the construct was named and defined. Koehler, Mishra, and Cain (2013) and Koehler, Mishra, Kereluik, Shin, and Graham (2014) classify these approaches in terms of teacher knowledge-building origins and sequences. According to these authors, "PCK to TPACK" approaches help teachers to build upon existing pedagogical content knowledge to develop technological pedagogical content knowledge. "TPK to TPACK" approaches suggest that teachers begin instead with existing technological knowledge, learning to analyze and apply particular technologies in educational environments, then use that technological pedagogical knowledge to teach specific content that is well enhanced with the use of digital tools and resources. Simultaneous PCK and TPACK development approaches encourage teachers to work collaboratively in design-based ways on problems of practice with colleagues with differing sets of expertise, developing all of the aspects of TPACK interactively and emergently (Koehler et al., 2013, p. 18).

This three-category way of conceptualizing TPACK development approaches is helpful in understanding the nature of the technology integration knowledge that teachers build when participating in these three general types of professional learning experiences. To examine the particular *strategies* that can be used to help teacher-learners to develop their TPACK, however, a more fine-grained classification system is needed. Focusing upon the different *processes* for professional learning that have been used to assist teachers' TPACK growth, in addition to the sequences of the different types of knowledge developed (Koehler et al., 2013) and the overarching structures (Joyce & Calhoun, 2010), purposes (Kennedy, 2005), and orientations (Park Rogers et al., 2010) to PD design can help researchers and teacher educators to build more comprehensive and pragmatic knowledge about approaches to and specific methods for TPACK development.

TPACK Development Approaches

At present, there are at least 12 process-based methods of TPACK-related professional learning that have surfaced in TPACK scholarship. These are overviewed in Table 12.1 on page 198 and introduced in the paragraphs that follow. The 12 processes for TPACK development can be classified into 8 general approaches: collaborative instructional design, pedagogical content knowledge (PCK)-focused learning, technological pedagogical knowledge (TPK)-focused learning, reflective/reflexive learning, problem-based learning, computer-adaptive learning, instructional planning, and workplace learning.

Collaborative Instructional Design

Instructional design strategies for developing teachers' TPACK (e.g., Boschman, McKenney, & Voogt, 2015; Koehler & Mishra, 2005; Koehler, Mishra, & Yahya, 2007) are typically constructivist in orientation, design-based in procedure, and collaborative. Using these strategies, a small group of professionals with differing and complementary expertise in curriculum/content, instruction, and educational technology typically work together to design and test an educational project, unit, or course in which students will engage. Teams using this approach often revise what they have created based upon results from formative assessments of successive implementations of what the group designed. Learning occurs for the group's participants in a "just-in-time" fashion, as designs are created, tested, and revised, according to individual professional development needs and interests.

Pedagogical Content Knowledge (PCK) Methods

TPACK development that is PCK-focused includes methods such as instructional modeling (e.g., Jaipal-Jamani & Figg, 2014; Niess, 2005), lesson study (e.g., Groth, Spickler, Bergner, & Bardzell, 2009), peer coaching (e.g., Jang, 2010), and the collaborative development and vetting of curriculum-based instructional materials (e.g., Allan, Erickson, Brookhouse, & Johnson, 2010). These methods situate the development of teachers' TPACK within a detailed, often collaborative, analysis of teaching practice that incorporates digital tools and resources in ways that assist students' learning directly and within particular curriculum areas. PCK-focused approaches to TPACK development are often more overtly structured than collaborative instructional design approaches. Outcomes of PCK-based approaches to TPACK development can include video-recorded microteaching, constructive critique of instruction, or curriculum-based, technologically infused materials to use in the classroom.

Technological Pedagogical Knowledge (TPK) Methods

TPK-focused approaches to teachers' TPACK development are grounded in the specific educational affordances and constraints of particular digital tools, as they can be best used for content-based teaching and learning in particular disciplines. Technology mapping (Angeli & Valanides, 2009), for example, directs teachers to identify particular content-based problems of practice (e.g., concepts that students find difficult to understand and apply) as learning objectives, then use their knowledge of available technological tools' affordances and constraints, situated within the teachers' PCK and contextual knowledge, to transform the confusing content into powerful and understandable representations for their students. TPK-focused approaches, in short, help teachers to "develop technological solutions to pedagogical problems" (Ioannou & Angeli, 2014, p. 228).

Reflective/Reflexive Methods

Three types of reflective/reflexive strategies for teachers' TPACK development have been documented to date. These include action research/teacher inquiry (e.g., Pierson & Borthwick, 2010); meta-analytic reflection techniques such as pedagogical practice-focused case development (e.g., Mouza & Wong, 2009) or TPACK-based learning trajectories (e.g., Niess & Gillow-Wiles, 2014); and TPACK self-assessment (e.g., Foulger, 2015; Roblyer & Doering, 2010), which can be used formatively by teachers to identify and address TPACK-related professional learning needs and progress. Although these strategies can be enacted in communication with other educators, reflective/reflexive TPACK development tends to be more focused upon a particular teacher's in-depth and ongoing reflections within a specific teaching context, while instructional design and PCK-focused TPACK development efforts are often more collaborative in process.

Problem-Based Methods

Similar to reflective/reflexive approaches, problem-based strategies for TPACK development often situate the focus for teachers' learning within authentic classroom and school environments. Tee & Lee (2011, 2014), for example, ask in-service teachers who are enrolled in a graduate course to work in small teams that are formed based upon common and complex problems they are experiencing in their classrooms. Each team then identifies multiple approaches to addressing the problem, selects/designs a solution to try, then implements it, reflecting with the group and adjusting the approach as they do so. To complete the learning cycle, team members share outcomes and reflections with all of the groups in the class in which the problem-based learning project was assigned. Although Tee & Lee (2014) reported one learning cycle in which TPACK development was the aim of their students' collaborative problem solving, this approach to professional learning typically addresses other authentic problems of practice that are focused upon particular curricula and types of instruction into which educational technology use can be well infused.

Computer-Adaptive Methods

The newest approach to TPACK development is software-based, computer-adaptive, and personalized. GeoThentic (Doering, Scharber, Miller, & Veletsianos, 2009), for example, an online geography learning environment for both students and teachers that utilizes geospatial technologies, includes a three-part teacher interface that analyzes teacher-reported, program-assessed, and user-path data to produce individualized TPACK professional learning profiles and recommended emphases for continued development. e-TPACK (Angeli, Valanides, Mavroudi, Christodoulou, & Georgiou, 2014) is a self-paced, adaptive series of curriculum- and classroom-based design scenarios at varying levels of completion that are presented to teacher-learners within a virtual environment. Users' responses to a sequence of personalized prompts about specific, contextualized instructional designs and users' self-regulated learning guide the program's selection of scaffolding for professional learning within the system. These early explorations of personalized TPACK development show considerable promise for the role of data analytics in future TPACK-based professional learning.

Instructional Planning Methods

The final two approaches to TPACK development are designed to occur within the scope of teachers' daily work, rather than within a separately scheduled professional development activity, such as a graduate course or a series of after-school meetings. Bos (2011), for example, described how elementary-level teachers designing mathematics units for their students, focusing upon the pedagogical, mathematical, and cognitive fidelity of the educational resources and activities incorporated, were able to hold themselves to rigorous quality standards, despite initial frustration in locating appropriately complex and cognitively focused math online tools and resources. Their processes of problem-based unit development, plus self- and peer evaluation, helped to develop their TPACK in a holistic way.

Harris and Hofer (2006, 2009) draw upon research about teachers' planning practices to suggest a learning activities selection approach to planning lessons, projects, and units that focuses first upon curriculum-based learning goals and last upon the digital technologies to incorporate. In this on-the-job approach to teachers' TPACK development, educational technologies are chosen according to the instructional content and processes incorporated into the activity-structured learning experience being planned. Using comprehensive, freely available taxonomies of learning activity types (LATs) and corresponding recommended technologies in nine different curriculum areas (Harris et al., 2010), teachers select, combine, and sequence multiple learning activity types based upon knowledge of their students' learning needs and preferences, curricular standards, and contextual affordances and constraints. Teachers' TPACK is built in the process of using the LAT taxonomies to plan lessons, projects, and units that incorporate educational technologies in curriculum- and pedagogically focused, educationally sound ways (Harris & Hofer, 2011).

Workplace Learning Methods

Along with computer-adaptive methods, contextually focused workplace-learning strategies for teachers' TPACK development (e.g., Phillips, 2014) have emerged recently. Like the instructional planning methods described above, workplace learning TPACK development occurs within and is shaped by the micro, meso, and macro contexts (Porras-Hernández & Salinas-Amescua, 2013) of teachers' and students' everyday work together in schools and communities. Unlike all of the methods described above, however, workplace TPACK learning is inherent in the "processes of identity development and practice" (Phillips, 2014, p. 254) that characterize a professional community of practice within a particular educational context. TPACK in a community of practice is "knowledge in the making" (Phillips, 2014, p. 256); it is ever-emerging, negotiated and changing among community members, and is not always coherent, consensual, or consistently enacted. As such, workplace learning may be one of the most authentic forms of TPACK development, but its progress is challenging to document and to assist, due to differing interpretations and enactments of TPACK among and between the members of a professional community.

These 12 strategies and 8 approaches to in-service teachers' TPACK development are abstracted in Table 12.1, with sample references provided for each. As the paragraphed summaries and table contents illustrate, TPACK development strategies have proliferated in the ten years since the TPCK/TPACK construct's first appearance in research publications. What might the future of TPACK development be? Are there patterns that can be discerned from the first decade of work with experienced teachers?

TPACK Development Trends and Trajectories

The contents of Table 12.1 and their explanations suggest that, as TPACK development work has progressed over time, approaches for experienced teachers have become increasingly situated and contextualized (e.g., Phillips, 2014; Porras-Hernández & Salinas-Amescua, 2013), curriculum- and pedagogically focused (e.g., Kafyulilo, Fisser, & Voogt, 2014; Niess & Gillow-Wiles, 2014), and reflective/reflexive (e.g., Mouza & Wong, 2009; Foulger, 2015), while remaining largely collaborative (e.g., Groth et al., 2009; Koehler & Mishra, 2005) and pragmatic (e.g., Harris et al., 2010; Tee & Lee, 2014). These trends mirror documented developments in teacher PD overall (e.g., Opfer & Pedder, 2011) and specifically within PD for technology integration (e.g., Vrasidas & Glass, 2007). The more sustained, collaborative, and situated nature of TPACK PD that has been reported especially in recent years may indicate that shorter-term, larger-group, top-down, and technocentric (Papert, 1987) approaches are being eschewed in favor of more personalized (e.g., Angeli et al., 2014; Roblyer & Doering, 2010), curriculum-based (e.g., Jaipal-Jamani & Figg, 2014; Kafyulilo, Fisser, & Voogt, 2014) and authentic-to-the-classroom (e.g., Bos, 2011; Harris et al., 2010) methods, given researchers' and teacher educators' growing awareness of TPACK as a highly contextualized construct (e.g., Phillips, 2014).

Does this mean that we should jettison some types of TPACK PD, perhaps those approaches that are used by individual teachers instead of collaborating groups or those that emphasize the development of TPK over TPACK? Although some PD literature might imply such action, doing so would ignore the uniqueness of different educational contexts and the differing preferences and professional learning needs of individual teachers. As

Table 12.1 TPACK Development Approaches and Strategies

TPACK Development Approach	TPACK Development Strategy	Description	Sample References
Collaborative instructional design	Learning by design	Educators, content experts, and technology specialists design instruction recursively, often collaboratively	Antonenko (2013); Boschman, McKenney, & Voogt (2015); Koehler & Mishra (2005); Koehler, Mishra, & Yahya (2007)
PCK-focused approach	Instructional modeling; TPACK-in-practice	Teacher educator models curriculum-based, tech-infused learning experiences for students	Jaipal-Jamani & Figg (2014); Niess (2005)
PCK-focused approach	Collaborative lesson study; peer coaching	Educators plan, observe, critique, and revise each others' teaching collaboratively	Groth, Spickler, Bergner, & Bardzell (2009); Jang (2010); Ndongfack (2015)
PCK-focused approach	Collaborative curriculum materials development	Educators co-construct tech-enhanced or -infused curriculum materials for themselves and others to use	Allan, Erickson, Brookhouse, & Johnson (2010); Kafyulilo, Fisser, & Voogt (2014); Polly (2011)
TPK-focused approach	Technology mapping; game-based learning; deep-play	Educational affordances and constraints of particular devices and software applications are explored and applied to content-specific teaching and learning	Angeli & Valanides (2009, 2013); Duran, Brunvand, Ellsworth, & Sendag (2012); Hsu, Liang, & Su (2014); Koehler et al. (2011)
Reflective/reflexive approach	Teacher inquiry/action research	Data-based, systematic exploration of teacher-identified focus in teaching and/or learning	Dawson, Cavanaugh, & Ritzhaupt (2013); Pierson & Borthwick (2010)
Reflective/reflexive approach	Case development; learning trajectory	Meta-analytic reflection upon use of technologies in teaching, with a group of educators and/or a researcher	Mouza & Wong (2009); Niess & Gillow-Wiles (2014)
Reflective/reflexive approach	TPACK self-assessment; just-in-time professional development	Periodic self-assessment of extant and desired TPACK levels (all components), used to direct individualized professional learning	Foulger (2015); Roblyer & Doering (2010)

Approach	Description	Key idea	References
Problem-based approach	Curriculum-based, authentic problem solving; solving problems of practice	Authentic, contextualized problem solving using content-related technologies and/or repurposed general-purpose devices and applications	Tee & Lee (2011, 2014)
Computer-adaptive approach	Software-based, interactive, formative assessments of TPACK	Interactive, online software assesses teachers' TPACK formatively, as professional learning progresses	Angeli, Valanides, Mavroudi, Christodoulou, & Georgiou (2014); Doering, Veletsianos, Scharber, & Miller (2009)
Instructional planning approach	Learning activity types; fidelity-based unit design	Developing TPACK while focusing upon instructional planning of curriculum-based lessons, projects, or units	Bos (2011); Harris & Hofer (2006, 2009); Harris et al. (2010); Polly (2011); Roblyer & Doering (2013)
Workplace learning approach	Community of practice	Teachers' TPACK is shaped by processes of identity development and practice that are contextually and communally effected and held	Phillips (2014); Porras-Hernández & Salinas-Amescua (2013)

Joyce and Calhoun (2010) argue, after presenting, explaining, and illustrating their five models of PD for teachers:

> Central is the idea that there are numerous legitimate approaches to generating growth opportunities for educators. Second is the assertion that these approaches, while often having overlapping goals, such as helping all of us attain higher states of growth, favor certain goals of their own. We are not going to have "one best model," but a variety that can, in combination, have a fine impact.
>
> (p. 129)

Perhaps all of the models for TPACK PD presented in this chapter, plus those that may emerge as TPACK work continues, should be considered and used in the customized ways that Joyce and Calhoun suggest.

TPACK Development Research Trajectories

Does this recommendation contradict research results that identify common attributes of effective PD for teachers? At first, it may seem to do so. With a list of 12 strategies for developing teachers' TPACK that have emerged during the past decade now available for researchers' use, the temptation to test, contrast, and rank-order these PD methods in terms of comparative efficacy may seem like a logical next step. Before such studies are designed, however, please remember that although teacher PD literature seems to be reaching consensus about specific characteristics of effective professional development, these characteristics do not predict measurable teacher learning consistently, and some PD that is *not* characterized by many of these attributes has been empirically successful. Moreover, multiple studies of similarly structured teacher learning do not often produce replicable results across different contexts; they usually conflict in their findings (Opfer & Pedder, 2011).

Why is this so? Opfer and Pedder (2011) explain that our conceptualizations of teacher learning and the conditions that support it have, overall, been much too simplistic:

> In the context of current research on professional development and teacher learning, misunderstanding the nature of teacher learning by underplaying the complexity of the problem leads to focus on the micro context (individual teachers or individual activities or programs) to the exclusion of influences from meso (institutional) and macro (school system) contexts.... As a complex system... teacher learning becomes hard to define by aggregation and generalities because the nature of learning depends on the uniqueness of the context, person, and so on.... Relationships between elements in the system vary in scale and intensity, come together in different combinations depending on the situation, are often reciprocal, and are always nested.
>
> (pp. 378–379)

Some researchers are even beginning to suggest that teachers' knowledge (such as TPACK) is not only highly contextualized, as Opfer and Pedder explain, but also highly individualized and uniquely experientially formed. For example, Hashweh (2013), one of Shulman's doctoral students whose 1985 dissertation predated Shulman's often-cited articles about pedagogical content knowledge, asserts that PCK is not a form of knowledge that is objectively generalizable across teachers. Rather, he says that it is a collection of "private and personal," "content-specific," both general and "story-based" "pedagogical constructions" (p. 121). Specifically, Hashweh says that:

1. PCK represents personal and private knowledge.
2. PCK is a collection of basic units called teacher pedagogical constructions.
3. Teacher pedagogical constructions result mainly from planning, but also from the interactive and postactive phases of teaching.
4. Pedagogical constructions result from an inventive process that is influenced by the interaction of knowledge and beliefs from different categories.
5. Pedagogical constructions constitute both a generalized event-based and a story-based kind of memory.
6. Pedagogical constructions are topic specific.
7. Pedagogical constructions are (or should ideally be) labeled in multiple interesting ways that connect them to other categories and subcategories of teacher knowledge and beliefs.

(p. 121)

Given this highly individualized and active interpretation of PCK—extrapolated to TPCK/TPACK—the ways in which TPACK PD for teachers is offered needs to be similarly differentiated, personalized, and adaptive, which argues for the potential use of a full range of different types of PD approaches and methods, as presented in this chapter.

Also, if these researchers are correct, the content of their assertions may explain some of the reasons why many studies of both PCK and TPACK have been unable to distinguish empirically among the constructs' subcomponents, such as TPK, TCK, and PK (e.g., Archambault & Barnett, 2010). Perhaps teachers' PCK and TPCK/TPACK—and the ways in which these types of professional knowledge are developed—are too contextualized and personalized to be generalizable across educators or educational contexts. This suggests that future studies of TPACK PD should describe the nature of the complex systems in which the studies are situated in enough detail so that the reported results can be appropriately and sufficiently contextualized by readers. Perhaps some of this work could focus upon ways to determine the "fit" of particular TPACK development approaches and strategies to particular combinations of individual teacher characteristics and micro, meso, and macro workplace attributes.

Given the complexity and time-consuming nature of the research sketched tentatively above, the question of whether TPACK as an identifiable type of knowledge for teachers will disappear with time, and with it the need for explicit TPACK development, should be addressed. Doering et al. (2009), for example, assert that

> despite the framework's potential usefulness, TPACK should be a temporary construct.... As technology becomes entwined in classrooms and schools, it will become

braided into pedagogical knowledge, content knowledge, and pedagogical content knowledge such that the focus on technology will no longer be needed.

(p. 318)

This view is in sharp contrast with that of Angeli and Valanides (2009), who see ICT-TPCK as a unique and distinct body of knowledge that requires understanding of different techologies' specific educational affordances and constraints. Cox and Graham (2009) remind us that PCK has always included technologies, and that as particular digital tools and resources become more ubiquitous in schools (and in society in general), their TPACK will be subsumed within an expanded notion of PCK. However, Cox and Graham also predict that "there will always be a need for TPACK as long as there are new, emergent technologies that have not yet become a transparent, ubiquitous part of the teaching profession's repertoire of tools" (p. 64).

Given the rapid emergence of digital technologies within the first ten years of the TPCK/TPACK construct's influence upon educational research and practice, it seems probable that for at least the next ten years of TPACK development, in-service teachers will continue to require—and benefit from—focused, situated, authentic, and personalized ways to develop their technological pedagogical content knowledge. By purposefully choosing among and combining the strategies and approaches classified and presented here, perhaps the design and crafting of specific TPACK development efforts can become even better matched to particular teachers' professional learning needs and preferences and the contextual realities of their workplaces.

References

Allan, W. C., Erickson, J. L., Brookhouse, P., & Johnson, J. L. (2010). Teacher professional development through a collaborative curriculum project—An example of TPACK in Maine. *TechTrends, 54*(6), 36–43. doi:10.1007/s11528-010-0452-x

Angeli, C., & Valanides, N. (2005). Pre-service teachers as ICT designers: An instructional design model based on an expanded view of pedagogical content knowledge. *Journal of Computer-Assisted Learning, 21*(4), 292–302.

Angeli, C., & Valanides, N. (2009). Epistemological and methodological issues for the conceptualization, development, and assessment of ICT-TPCK: Advances in technological pedagogical content knowledge (TPCK). *Computers & Education, 52*(1), 154–168.

Angeli, C., & Valanides, N. (2013). Technology mapping: An approach for developing technological pedagogical content knowledge. *Journal of Educational Computing Research, 48*, 199–221. doi:10.2190/EC.48.2.e

Angeli, C., Valanides, N., Mavroudi, A., Christodoulou, A., & Georgiou, K. (2014). Introducing e-TPCK: An adaptive e-learning technology for the development of teachers' technological pedagogical content knowledge. In C. Angeli & N. Valanides (Eds.), *Technological pedagogical content knowledge* (pp. 305–317). New York: Springer.

Antonenko, P. D. (2013). Two heads are better than one: Inservice teachers engaging in instructional design 2.0. *Journal of Digital Learning in Teacher Education, 29*(3), 72–81.

Archambault, L. M., & Barnett, J. H. (2010). Revisiting technological pedagogical content knowledge: Exploring the TPACK framework. *Computers & Education, 55*(4), 1656–1662.

Bos, B. (2011). Professional development for elementary teachers using TPACK. *Contemporary Issues in Technology and Teacher Education, 11*(2). Retrieved from http://www.citejournal.org/vol11/iss2/mathematics/article1.cfm

Boschman, F., McKenney, S., & Voogt, J. (2015). Exploring teachers' use of TPACK in design talk: The collaborative design of technology-rich early literacy activities. *Computers & Education, 82,* 250–262. doi:10.1016/j.compedu.2014.11.010

Cox, S., & Graham, C. R. (2009). Diagramming TPACK in practice: Using an elaborated model of the TPACK framework to analyze and depict teacher knowledge. *TechTrends: Linking Research & Practice to Improve Learning, 53*(5), 60–69.

Darling-Hammond, L., & Richardson, N. (2009). Teacher learning: What matters? *How Teachers Learn, 66*(5), 46–53.

Dawson, K., Cavanaugh, C., & Ritzhaupt, A. D. (2013). ARTI: An online tool to support teacher action research for technology integration. In R. Hartshorne, T. Heafner, & T. Petty (Eds.), *Teacher education programs and online learning tools: Innovations in teacher preparation* (pp. 375–391). Hershey, PA: Information Science Reference. doi:10.4018/978–1–4666–1906–7.ch020

Doering, A., Scharber, C., Miller, C., & Veletsianos, G. (2009). GeoThentic: Designing and assessing with technology, pedagogy, and content knowledge. *Contemporary Issues in Technology and Teacher Education, 9*(3), 316–336.

Doering, A., Veletsianos, G., Scharber, C., & Miller, C. (2009). Using the technological, pedagogical, and content knowledge framework to design online learning environments and professional development. *Journal of Educational Computing Research, 41*(3), 319–346.

Duran, M., Brunvand, S., Ellsworth, J., & Sendag, S. (2012). Impact of research-based professional development: Investigation of inservice teacher learning and practice in wiki integration. *Journal of Research on Technology in Education, 44*(4), 313–334.

Foulger, T. S. (2015). Graphic assessment of TPACK instrument (GATI) as a professional development tool. In D. Slykhuis & G. Marks (Eds.), *Proceedings of Society for Information Technology & Teacher Education International Conference 2015* (pp. 3157–3168). Chesapeake, VA: Association for the Advancement of Computing in Education (AACE).

Friedman, A., & Phillips, M. (2004) Continuing professional development: Developing a vision. *Journal of Education and Work, 17*(3), 361–376.

Groth, R., Spickler, D., Bergner, J., & Bardzell, M. (2009). A qualitative approach to assessing technological pedagogical content knowledge. *Contemporary Issues in Technology and Teacher Education, 9*(4). Retrieved from http://www.citejournal.org/vol9/iss4/mathematics/article1.cfm

Harris, J., & Hofer, M. (2006). Planned improvisations: Technology-supported learning activity design in social studies. Session presented at the National Educational Computing Conference, San Diego, CA, July. Retrieved from http://center.uoregon.edu/ISTE/NECC2006/program/search_results_details.php?sessionid=13514149

Harris, J., & Hofer, M. (2009). Instructional planning activity types as vehicles for curriculum-based TPACK development. In C. D. Maddux (Ed.), *Research highlights in technology and teacher education 2009* (pp. 99–108). Chesapeake, VA: Society for Information Technology & Teacher Education (SITE).

Harris, J. B., & Hofer, M. J. (2011). Technological pedagogical content knowledge (TPACK) in action: A descriptive study of secondary teachers' curriculum-based, technology-related instructional planning. *Journal of Research on Technology and Education, 43*(3), 211–229.

Harris, J. B., Hofer, M. J., Blanchard, M. R., Grandgenett, N. F., Schmidt, D. A., van Olphen, M., & Young, C. A. (2010). "Grounded" technology integration: Instructional planning using curriculum-based activity type taxonomies. *Journal of Technology and Teacher Education, 18*(4), 573–605.

Hashweh, M. (2013). Pedagogical content knowledge: Twenty-five years later. In C. J. Craig, P. C. Meijer, & J. Broeckmans (Eds.), *From teacher thinking to teachers and teaching: The evolution of a research community (Advances in Research on Teaching, Vol. 19*, pp. 115–140). Bingley, UK: Emerald Group Publishing.

Hsu, C. Y., Liang, J. C., & Su, Y. C. (2014). The role of the TPACK in game-based teaching: Does instructional sequence matter? *Asia-Pacific Education Researcher*. Advance online publication. doi:10.1007/s40299-014-0221-2.

Ioannou, I., & Angeli, C. (2014). Technological pedagogical content knowledge as a framework for integrating educational technology in the teaching of computer science. In C. Angeli & N. Valanides (Eds.), *Technological pedagogical content knowledge* (pp. 225–237). New York: Springer.

Jaipal-Jamani, K., & Figg, C. (2014). The framework of TPACK-in-practice: Designing content-centric technology professional learning contexts to develop teacher knowledge of technology-enhanced teaching (TPACK). In C. Angeli & N. Valanides (Eds.), *Technological pedagogical content knowledge* (pp. 137–163). New York: Springer.

Jang, S.-J. (2010). Integrating the interactive whiteboard and peer coaching to develop the TPACK of secondary science teachers. *Computers and Education, 55*, 1744–1751.

Joyce, B., & Calhoun, E. (2010). *Models of professional development: A celebration of educators*. Thousand Oaks, CA: Corwin.

Kafyulilo, A., Fisser, P., & Voogt, J. (2014). Teacher design in teams as a professional development arrangement for developing technology integration knowledge and skills of science teachers in Tanzania. *Education and Information Technologies, 19*(2), 1–18. doi:10.1007/s10639-014-9321-0

Kennedy, A. (2005). Models of continuing professional development: A framework for analysis. *Journal of In-Service Education, 31*(2), 235–250.

Koehler, M. J., & Mishra, P. (2005). Teachers learning technology by design. *Journal of Computing in Teacher Education, 21*(3), 94–102.

Koehler, M. J., & Mishra, P. (2008). Introducing TPACK. In AACTE Committee on Innovation & Technology (Eds.), *Handbook of technological pedagogical content knowledge for educators* (pp. 3–29). New York: Routledge.

Koehler, M. J., Mishra, P., Bouck, E. C., DeSchryver, M., Kereluik, K., Shin, T. S., & Wolf, L. G. (2011). Deep-play: Developing TPACK for 21st century teachers. *International Journal of Learning Technology, 6*(2), 146–163.

Koehler, M. J., Mishra, P., & Cain, W. (2013). What is technological pedagogical content knowledge (TPACK)? *Journal of Education, 193*(3), 13–19.

Koehler, M. J., Mishra, P., Hershey, K., & Peruski, L. (2004). With a little help from your students: A new model for faculty development and online course design. *Journal of Technology and Teacher Education, 12*(1), 25–55.

Koehler, M., Mishra, P., Kereluik, K., Shin, T., & Graham, C. (2014). The technological pedagogical content knowledge framework. In J. M. Spector, M. D. Merrill, J. Elen, & M. J. Bishop (Eds.), *Handbook of research on educational communications and technology* (pp. 101–111). New York: Springer Science+Business Media. doi:10.1007/978-1-4614-3185-5_9

Koehler, M. J., Mishra, P., & Yahya, K. (2007). Tracing the development of teacher knowledge in a design seminar: Integrating content, pedagogy, and technology. *Computers and Education, 49*(3), 740–762.

Mouza, C., & Wong, W. (2009). Studying classroom practice: Case development for professional learning in technology integration. *Journal of Technology and Teacher Education, 17*(2), 175–202.

Ndongfack, M. N. (2015). Mastery of active and shared learning processes for techno-pedagogy (MASLEPT): A model for teacher professional development on technology integration.

Niess, M. L. (2005). Preparing teachers to teach science and mathematics with technology: Developing a technology pedagogical content knowledge. *Teaching and Teacher Education, 21*, 509–523.

Niess, M. L., & Gillow-Wiles, H. (2014). Transforming science and mathematics teachers' technological pedagogical content knowledge using a learning trajectory instructional approach. *Journal of Technology and Teacher Education, 22*(4), 497–520.

Opfer, V. D., & Pedder, D. (2011). Conceptualizing teacher professional learning. *Review of Educational Research, 81*(3), 376–407.

Papert, S. (1987). *A critique of technocentrism in thinking about the school of the future* (Epistemology and Learning Memo No. 2). Cambridge, MA: Massachusetts Institute of Technology, Media Lab. Retrieved from http://www.papert.org/articles/ACritiqueofTechnocentrism.html

Park Rogers, M. A., Abell, S. K., Marra, R. M., Arbaugh, F., Hutchins, K. L., & Cole, J. S. (2010). Orientations to science teacher professional development: An exploratory study. *Journal of Science Teacher Education, 21*, 309–328.

Pea, C., & Wojnowski, B. (2014). Introduction to models and approaches to STEM professional development. In B. Wojnowski & C. Pea (Eds.), *Models and approaches to STEM professional development* (pp. 3–8). Arlington, VA: NSTA Press.

Phillips, M. (2014). *Teachers' TPACK enactment in a community of practice* (Doctoral dissertation, Monash University). Retrieved from http://arrow.monash.edu.au/hdl/1959.1/981787

Pierson, M., & Borthwick, A. (2010). Framing the assessment of educational technology professional development in a culture of learning. *Journal of Digital Learning in Teacher Education, 26*(4), 126–131.

Polly, D. (2011). Teachers' learning while constructing technology-based instructional resources. *British Journal of Educational Technology, 42*(6), 950–961. doi:10.1111/j.1467-8535.2010.01161.x

Porras-Hernández, L. H., & Salinas-Amescua, B. (2013). Strengthening TPACK: A broader notion of context and the use of teacher's narratives to reveal knowledge construction. *Journal of Educational Computing Research, 48*(2), 223–244. doi:10.2190/EC.48.2.f

Roblyer, M. D., & Doering, A. H. (2010). *Integrating educational technology into teaching* (5th ed.). Boston: Allyn & Bacon.

Roblyer, M. D., & Doering, A. H. (2013). *Integrating educational technology into teaching* (6th ed.). Boston: Allyn & Bacon.

Tee, M. Y., & Lee, S. S. (2011). From socialisation to internalisation: Cultivating technological pedagogical content knowledge through problem-based learning. *Australasian Journal of Educational Technology, 27*(1), 89–104.

Tee, M. Y., & Lee, S. S. (2014). Making tacit knowledge and practices more explicit for the development of TPACK. In C. Angeli & N. Valanides (Eds.), *Technological pedagogical content knowledge* (pp. 269–283). New York: Springer.

Vrasidas, C., & Glass, G. G. (2007). Teacher professional development and ICT: Strategies and models. In L. Smolin, K. Lawless, & N. D. Burbules (Eds.). *Information and communication technologies: Considerations of current practice for teachers and teacher educators* (National Society for the Study of Education Yearbook Vol. 106, No. 2, pp. 87–102). doi:10.1111/j.1744-7984.2007.00116.x

13

TPACK Development in Higher Education

Mary C. Herring, Sohyun Meacham, Daniel Mourlam

Introduction

The development of TPACK in higher education has taken many forms given the multiple layers within institutions. These layers extend from students to faculty to the leadership structures that enable TPACK development across institutions. Much of the work surrounding TPACK in higher education has focused on teacher education, specifically with the development of pre-service teacher TPACK. Given the prevalence of publications in the literature on pre-service teacher TPACK, a chapter in this book has been devoted to reviewing those practices and will not be repeated here (see the chapter by Mouza). Rather, the focus of this chapter will be on the issues unique to higher education outside of pre-service teacher education. These issues center on two key areas. The first key area is the creation of leadership structures that promote the development of TPACK. The second is faculty development for both teacher education and nonteacher education faculty.

TPACK and Leadership Structures

Technological Pedagogical Content Knowledge (TPACK) development in higher education has been emphasized mostly in teacher preparation programs, as TPACK built off Schulman's (1987) concept of pedagogical content knowledge (Polly, Mims, Shepherd, & Inan, 2010), which has been an important theoretical framework for teacher education programs. Between fall 2005 and spring 2007, the American Association of Colleges for Teacher Education Committee on Innovation and Technology (AACTE I&T Committee) implemented a consensus panel on the role of technology in the classroom, with a focus on acquisition and exhibition of teachers' instructional skill and knowledge, which led to the publishing of the *Handbook of Technological Pedagogical Content Knowledge for Educators*. This preliminary work increased interest in TPACK's applicability in higher education (Brown & Canto, 2008) with those involved looking for a home for continued work in this area.

An arena for TPACK scholarship was established within the Society for Information Technology & Teacher Education (SITE) and at the SITE 2007 and SITE 2008 conferences, where Harris, Koehler, Kelly, and Mishra launched the Technology, Pedagogy, and Content Knowledge (TPACK) special interest group (SIG). Its intent was "to bring together researchers, developers, and teacher educators interested in exploring technological pedagogical content knowledge . . . for use in all content areas and educational contexts" (Society for Information Technology & Teacher Education, 2014, para. 1). Present TPACK SIG activities include a TPACK newsletter, TPACK.org wiki, and several SIGs within the SIG with the foci of TPACK research, teaching, grants, and future (Society for Information Technology & Teacher Education, 2014). The SIG established a TPACK Mendeley group, which by August 2014 had 948 papers and 478 group members. It also hosts the TPACK Academy website, which offers extensive information on TPACK and access to TPACK resources. Additionally, SITE has developed a TPACK topic conference presentation thread. Between 2012 and 2014, 448 TPACK presentations have been accepted for the annual SITE conference (D. Slykhuis, personal communication, August 8, 2014). The SIG also notes that TPACK has been featured at ten other national and international conferences. SITE leaders have also been involved in the development and delivery of Microsoft's Technology Enriched Instruction workshops given to higher educators around the world. See Chapter 14 by Hofer et al. for more information.

In 2011, the AACTE I&T Committee began identifying a leadership module and formative assessment for use by teacher education leaders as they initiated transformation of teacher preparation programs into fully realized TPACK environments. This work, targeted at deans and educational leaders, identified necessary learning opportunities and support needed to motivate college leaders and faculty to participate in the change process. To develop a systematic, coordinated approach for programs to use, the committee collaborated with the National Technology Leadership Coalition (NTLC) and Microsoft's Partners in Learning Higher Education Teacher Education Initiative (see chapter by Hofer et al.). The outcome of this work was a set of materials for teacher education leaders' use to guide the process of creating TPACK-aligned teacher education programs (Thomas, Herring, Redmond, & Smaldino, 2013). While this work was centered on pre-service programs, it would work with any program interested in TPACK-based initiatives. The following section is a synopsis of the committee's findings as identified within the aforementioned article.

During the committee's vetting process, it was identified that a change process should be guided by a theory of action that identifies the components of a change process. Drawing upon the work of Argyris and Schön (1974) and Hill and Celio (1998), identification of (a) how change should happen, (b) what is within the leader's control, and (c) what needs to be in place if change is to occur but is not under the leader's control, needed to be addressed. Table 13.1 depicts a TPACK Leadership Theory of Action that can be used to guide the change process through thorough reviews of each indicated area in relationship to a TPACK initiative.

Focus group and vetting discussions were organized around three key leadership functions (Day, Sammons, Leithwood, & Kington, 2008; Leithwood, Harris, & Hopkins, 2008; Leithwood & Jantzi, 2008; Leithwood & Riehl, 2003) associated with improving student

Table 13.1 TPACK Leadership Theory of Action

How will change happen?	What can we control?	Zone of wishful thinking
Leadership Team's Learning (TPACK) ↓	Human Resources (faculty, staff, etc.)	Favorable policy environment (institutional & external)
Leadership Practice ↓	Fiscal Resources (allocation & incentives)	Additional resources (incentives, operating funds, etc.)
Faculty Learning (TPACK) ↓	Personal Resources (time, messages, political capital, attention, etc.)	Faculty willing to allocate time & attention necessary
Faculty Practice ↓	Engagement with internal/ external/initiatives/partners	Culture of partner schools conducive to goal
Goal: Pre-service teachers' learning and practice (TPACK)		Scalability
Underlying Theory of Change		

outcomes. The functions were: (a) establish a vision to set direction; (b) develop faculty members to accomplish vision; and (c) redesign the organization to support members' work toward the vision. National level supports, professional development resources, and college-level, context-specific products and processes needed were identified for each of the three areas (Thomas et al., 2013). The following addresses the three areas and the requisite processes to be followed by teacher education leaders as identified during the vetting process to successfully incorporate TPACK into their programs.

Establish a Vision to Set Direction

All system stakeholders should be engaged in setting a vision that is seen as personally compelling and achievable. Faculty expected to implement the work are best positioned to define the TPACK knowledge and skills that best fit in program components and that meet their needs to create effective TPACK-based student learning experiences. Expectations for performance and progress monitoring by leaders are needed at both the faculty and student levels. Leadership teams composed of deans, faculty leaders, department and program directors, instructional support specialists, and students should be part of creating the change rationale and shared TPACK-based outcomes. Developing the vision should be based upon two questions:

1. What are we trying to do?
2. What will our institution look like when TPACK is embedded into teacher education programs?

Answers to these questions, a review of the institution's values, and the education unit's basic assumptions and artifacts will allow the leadership team to identify the outcomes for incorporating and modeling TPACK. Special attention should be given to the mapping of TPACK to accreditation standards.

Develop Faculty Members to Accomplish the Vision

Teacher education leaders must identify the compelling rationale and action plan that guides faculty learning and practice. Items they control, and those they cannot, must be considered (see Table 13.1). Attention to tenure and promotion guidelines can assist in this endeavor. The following are suggestions for components of a TPACK-focused action plan:

- Identify the areas over which deans and administrators have control and those that need collaboration in order to be successful.
- Work with a Chair in one program area and discuss how to construct an innovative collaborative (e.g., use of video cases/case studies) as a pilot.
- Identify program areas across institutions so that there is a larger community that involves faculty from colleges of education as well as colleges of arts and sciences faculty.
- Develop a university-school community collaboration as well as pre-service, induction, or professional development opportunities to consider different platforms (online, face-to-face, blended) to expand the work.
- Create or join a peer network of support locally, regionally, and/or nationally.

(Thomas et al., 2013, p. 59)

Redesign the Organization to Support Members' Work Toward the Vision

To facilitate and inspire change, the dean or educational leader should address resources that can be controlled (see Table 13.1), as well as opportunities for the whole organization to participate in the process. External requirements, such as a university's strategic plan and program accreditation requirements, must be considered as they can serve as compelling motivators to the change process. These materials can be used as part of a curricula redesign process. Redesign offers an opportunity to better align all components of the program (e.g., foundational courses or field experiences). Alignment of resources used to program goals and the restructuring of department leadership roles will assist with the successful members' work towards the established vision.

The AACTE I&T Committee started this process focused on what leaders needed to do to transform teacher education programs into fully realized TPACK-based programs. The developed framework for leading change provides leaders with an action plan for change that ultimately results in pre-service teachers learning about, creating, and implementing TPACK-based learning environments.

Apply TPACK in Broader Higher Education Contexts

Higher education institutions have emphasized the importance of quality instruction. As technology integration in instruction is considered to be effective for engaging students (Kushner Benson & Ward, 2013), researchers have studied TPACK application in nonteacher education programs as well as in teacher education programs. The overall success of any higher education program is held within faculty members' hands (Donovan & Green, 2010). The applicability of TPACK in broader higher education contexts relates to the development of faculty members in teacher education programs (e.g., college of education) as well as nonteacher education programs (e.g., college of arts and science). Knowles (1973) states, "our traditional educational system is progressively regressive. The best education . . . takes place in the nursery school and kindergarten, and tends to get progressively worse on climbing up the educational ladder, reaching its nadir in college" (p. 41). While highlighting the need for improved classroom instructional practices, Knowles' statement can be applied to university faculty development. Meacham and Ludwig (2001) describe what likely is common at many institutions, where one or two individuals come to an institution and present on a topic during a one- or two-day workshop. Often these presentations are highly attended with faculty leaving inspired; however, rarely are these experiences effective unless there is follow-up with both support from a varied social system and targets for meeting goals. Even though the content of workshops such as those described by Meacham and Ludwig may be critical in advancing educational practice in higher education, the assumptions about the learners fail to move the content into practice.

Faculty's TPACK Development in Higher Education

In this section, we review literature addressing faculty's TPACK development in higher education. We used the Academic Search Elite and ERIC databases to search for adequate literature to review. Descriptors for the database searches were as follows: TPACK AND higher education, leadership, TPACK AND faculty development. TPACK and technology integration were also searched individually to ensure an exhaustive exploration of potential articles. Then we sorted chosen articles into two categories based on the study contexts: teacher education program versus nonteacher education program. The following criteria were used to select articles to include in the literature review, coming up with 25 chosen articles.

The chosen studies were published in a peer-reviewed journal or reported in a completed doctoral dissertation at a nationally accredited university. We did not limit the publication date because of the general scarcity of published articles about TPACK development in higher education, particularly in nonteacher education programs. We also included articles published before the TPACK framework was developed. We searched these articles using the term "technology integration" to provide a comprehensive review and robust recommendations for future directions of research and practice.

The study participants must have used computers or technology for instructional (learning) purposes. All studies chosen took place in a higher education institution. We

TPACK in Teacher Education Programs

The Development of TPACK in Faculty

Even though programs have invested in faculty development around integrating educational technologies, there is currently very little available in the literature as to best practices and processes. Yet, developing faculty TPACK so that faculty can model effective technology integration is critical for students' TPACK development (Figg & Jaipal, 2013; Koh & Divaharan, 2011). Professional development of instructors is an important vehicle for making changes (Teclehaimanot & Lamb, 2005), yet too often the development opportunities available are insufficient to meet the demands faced by faculty (Yilmazel-Sahin & Oxford, 2010). Faculty must have opportunities to learn about the TPACK framework for them to reflect upon and think through their content knowledge and teaching practice using the lens of technology to identify what TPACK can mean in their discipline. However, faculty also need opportunities to enhance their instruction through the purposeful integration of each TPACK domain in their own instruction. Faculty can advance the integration of technology within subject matter and pedagogy, as an outcome of professional development (Scott, 2009), but development activities must afford faculty these opportunities.

The most common current approach for faculty development combined the workshop approach and the mentoring approach (Brush et al., 2003; Ludwig & Booz, 2003; Polly et al., 2010; Schaffer & Richardson, 2004). Polly et al.'s (2010) review of the various U.S. Department of Education–funded PT3 projects, where this workshop–mentoring hybrid approach was widely used, found that different aspects in the TPACK framework were evidenced in this approach. Workshops focused on the development of faculty knowledge of technology and pedagogies relevant to their technology use in their courses to teach, which relates to technological knowledge (TK) and technological pedagogical knowledge (TPK). On the other hand, individual mentoring could address content needs and the overlap among technology, content, and pedagogies (TPACK), as faculty members could develop TK and TPK in workshops. As workshops usually include faculty members who teach different subject matters, it can be a challenge for a workshop to address TPACK, which encompasses each technology, pedagogy, and content knowledge for all workshop attendees. Types of professional development in TPACK should be more diversified in research to capture more complex details regarding what elements of the TPACK framework are more strongly addressed in different approaches for faculty development.

While the workshop and mentoring approaches have been relatively frequent, other common faculty development approaches, such as co-teaching, professional learning communities, book clubs, lesson study, action research, and curriculum development initiatives, were rarely documented in literature. Although overall there is little in the literature on specific TPACK development approaches, perhaps the most prevalent in what currently was available was the Learning Technology by Design approach (Koehler & Mishra, 2005;

Koehler et al., 2011; Koehler, Mishra, Hershey, & Peruski, 2004; Koehler, Mishra, & Yahya, 2007). In this approach, faculty worked with graduate students as part of design teams creating instruction for their courses, where faculty experienced "negotiating the interactions between pedagogy, content, and technology by developing their competencies with technology, and by giving them experiences with the interactions of the three components (technology, pedagogy, content)" (Koehler et al., 2004, p. 31). Koehler and his colleagues went on to explain that engaging faculty in such a design process immerses them in a process "that is spontaneous, unpredictable, messy, creative, and hard to define. It is a dialogue between constraints and tradeoffs. It is a process that does not offer easy solutions" (p. 32).

In two early studies of faculty TPACK development using the Learning Technology by Design approach (Koehler & Mishra, 2005; Koehler, Mishra, & Yahya, 2007), it was found that this approach encouraged faculty to consider the interactions amongst each of the TPACK domains. Koehler and Mishra (2005) found that participants recognized changes in their thinking about TPACK and that in order to have success teaching online, there had to be a change in their PCK. Koehler, Mishra, and Yahya (2007) then found that as members of the design team worked together, they moved from conversations of content, pedagogy, and technology as isolated entities to conversations that integrated each domain in transactional ways. This integrative dialogue among members of the design team was indicative of the dynamic relationship within TPACK. As such, the Learning Technology by Design faculty development approach, as evidenced in these two studies, highlights the need for a shift from traditional technology focused workshops to a process by which the connections between each content, pedagogy, and technology can be supported in ways that hone faculty knowledge and skills.

In a similar approach to Learning Technology by Design, Archambault, Wetzel, Foulger, and Williams (2009) sought to help faculty leverage the affordances of Web 2.0 technologies in their courses. Archambault and her colleagues used a workshop approach to developing faculty knowledge. However, as faculty embarked upon an eight-hour initial workshop, other faculty and faculty developers were available to interact with as they developed a unit of instruction. Faculty then implemented and evaluated their instruction and reflected with other faculty participants at the conclusion of the study. Just as Koehler and his colleagues found that faculty began integrating content, pedagogy, and technology, faculty in Archambault et al.'s study had a similar experience. Faculty explained that they wanted to have a unit with a "smooth relationship between pedagogy, content and technology so that pre-service and in-service teachers feel empowered to use their final projects in their [classrooms]" (p. 8). Characteristic of both the Learning Technology by Design approach and the approach used by Archambault et al. was that faculty worked with a purpose in mind. While both approaches used workshop-style experiences to engage faculty, they did so with a clear purpose in mind: the development of instruction that leveraged the use of technologies.

The success of both approaches should come as no surprise given the context of working with adult learners. Adult Learning Theory (Knowles, 1973) asserts that as adult learners, in this case faculty, engage in learning experiences, they do so both prepared to learn and of their own free will in self-directed ways that allow them to leverage their experiences and knowledge. The approaches of both Koehler and his colleagues (2005, 2007) and Archambault et al. (2009) provided faculty with exactly those opportunities. Faculty, presumably so since they self-selected to participate, were interested in exploring the role of technologies in their instruction and could do so in ways that built on what they knew and in some cases did so to solve very authentic problems of practice.

Non-TPACK Faculty Development Approaches

Given the lack of faculty TPACK development literature available, our inquiry extended to what is currently known about effective faculty development for technology integration. Yilmazel-Sahin and Oxford (2010) compiled criteria based on findings from the literature that has the potential to guide faculty development practices where technology integration is the goal. Their criteria for excellence in faculty development for technology integration included:

- Alignment to institutional goals so as to encourage continuous improvement;
- Based on needs assessment where participants have opportunities to provide input that is then used for planning purposes;
- Experiential for participants in ways that allow for hands-on learning;
- Implementation promotes collaboration;
- Includes ongoing technical support that mitigates delays and frustration;
- Targets faculty attitudes and beliefs;
- Provides multiple levels of support and incentives for faculty;
- Promotes ongoing learning in sustainable ways; and
- Acknowledges the value of faculty efforts to improve their practice.

It is possible that many of the faculty development opportunities available embody some if not many of these qualities, however, it is unknown the extent to which faculty knowledge is impacted.

An example of some of the criteria identified by Yilmazel-Sahin and Oxford (2010) is in the study conducted by Devlin-Scherer and Sardone (2013) that investigated two faculty members' team teaching as professional development. These two faculty members (one late adopter and one educational technology specialist) in a teacher education program were involved in a multiyear collaboration. They began with the basic training relationship for instructional technology tools, such as the curriculum-based learning game Oregon Trail, software programs Inspiration and FrontPage, instructional websites, and hardware tools like digital cameras and scanners. The relationship expanded into co-teaching. They collaborated on redesigning a teacher education course to provide students with experiences of new technology tools and digital learning games that could serve their future students of the digital age. In this collaborative process, they widened their knowledge of resources (new affordable technology tools) and teaching strategies and developed innovative assignments and projects for their students.

The co-teaching relationship in Devlin-Scherer and Sardone's (2013) study was similar to the mentoring relationship that Polly et al.'s (2010) earlier review study described, as one of the two faculty members was an expert in educational technology whereas the other was a late adopter. The professional development of the late-adopter faculty started from learning about the new technology tools and teaching strategies for the technology tools (TK and TPK) to advancing into course transformation that required TPACK. This finding is also similar to Polly et al.'s finding regarding more TPACK-oriented development at the mentoring approach.

Teclehaimanot and Lamb (2005) studied faculty development in technology integration during a three-year-long process. Initially during the program development period, they identified nine ways to support the professional development of faculty: (a) depth, (b) hands-on practice, (c) project-based approach, (d) modeling, (e) examples, (f) ongoing assessment, (g) timesavers, (h) differentiation, and (i) expanded opportunities. Then in the following years, these strategies were implemented in workshop and individualized formats such as mentoring and professional sharing. As a result of the professional development program, faculty members updated their syllabi with more technology use, demonstrating they were prepared to integrate technology in their teaching.

TPACK in Higher Education Exclusive of Teacher Education

Higher education in nonteacher education programs has explored the TPACK framework less well than K–12 education has, and professors' TPACK development has rarely been discussed outside of teacher education programs (Kushner Benson & Ward, 2013). The TPACK framework can increase the range of faculty's instructional methods with the support of technology among the faculty in various colleges as well as colleges of education. However, because of a prevailing sentiment among higher education faculty members that subject matter knowledge is sufficient for college-level teaching, particularly among noneducation faculty, there can be at least two hurdles for the faculty TPACK development: in promoting awareness of pedagogical content knowledge and in providing guidance for technology integration pertaining to pedagogical content knowledge (TPACK).

In the available literature about the faculty's TPACK development in nonteacher education programs, three trends are observed. First, learner-centered pedagogy is emphasized in faculty's technology integration in their face-to-face instruction (Kahveci et al., 2008). Second, TPACK was used as a theoretical framework for developing faculty's online instruction competency (Arinto, 2013; Meyer & Murrell, 2014; Scott, 2009). Third, the evaluation of faculty's technology integration in their pedagogy and content knowledge teaching was aligned with the TPACK framework (Shih & Chuan, 2013). The following section will discuss the literature in these three trends.

University educators have used lecturing as a central instructional method in the United States (Cuban, 2001). Pedagogical content knowledge that emphasizes the learner's side in teaching and learning can be structurally and culturally foreign among general higher education faculty members (Kahveci et al., 2008). In this circumstance, the big portion of technology-oriented investment in colleges of arts and sciences has been emphasizing the embellishment of wide lecture halls with multiple high-definition screens and high-quality acoustic systems, which supports lecturing for a large number of students rather than individual students' learning and development.

Kahveci, Gilmer, and Southerland (2008) studied two university chemistry professors' technology integration that was not far from the lecturing-centered instruction. As a part of the findings of this study, the chemistry professors experienced challenges such as lack of communication and collaboration among faculty members, constraints for innovative chemistry teaching, large class sizes, and poor technology environments in classrooms. Kahveci et al. investigated these two faculty members' teaching beliefs and professors' own learning experiences. A senior professor with plenty of teaching awards exhibited his teaching beliefs that emphasized lecturing rather than learner-centered instruction. His meaning of interactions in teaching related to the instructor's proximity to tell students what to learn and what to do, indicating which information is more important than the other. His way of teaching, broadly recognized in his institution and beyond, was similar to what his undergraduate professors had practiced. The other chemistry professor in the study also used to emphasize lecture-based instruction, which was similar to the senior chemistry professor in the study and to his own undergraduate professor. Interestingly, however, after his tenure was ensured, he started employing the learner-centered teaching approach that was influenced from his middle school science teacher. This professor's new learner-centered teaching approach guided him to more frequent use of various technology tools in his instruction. The authors suggested that openness to examining the efficacy of teaching practices could naturally lead to implementing technology-enhanced teaching strategies. Use of these strategies can shift a classroom to a more learner-centered approach even at the university level or beyond. Although Kahveci et al.'s study provided insights for applying the TPACK framework in nonteacher education faculty development, it did not explicitly discuss the TPACK framework.

There are some studies available that used the TPACK framework with nonteacher education faculty development for online teaching, whereas the literature about faculty's TPACK development for traditional face-to-face instruction is very rare. In Scott's (2009) case study with two professors who taught online classes, one of her two participants was from outside of the college of education, teaching sociology with a limited online teaching experience, whereas the other participant was teaching special education with more than five years of online teaching experience. Both of these participants attended a faculty workshop on best practices in teaching online. The results of this study indicated that TPACK was evidenced in both participants' online courses when they were examined after the workshop. This result implies that the TPACK framework can be applied to nonteacher education faculty members' teaching practices. In addition, while the mastery of the basic technology elements was found to be necessary, options of teaching strategies for communicating with students online were important elements for these professors. This finding implies that pedagogical knowledge became transferrable between online teaching and face-to-face teaching.

Arinto (2013) used TPACK in the process of developing a framework for faculty development of online instruction competencies. In a traditional campus-based university in the Philippines, eight regular faculty members and two affiliate faculty administrators from various disciplines (biology, nursing, reading education, media studies, development communication, public management, R&D management, and environment and natural resources management) were interviewed for the investigation of impact of teaching with Web technologies on distance education course design. Working with these research participants, Arinto proposed a framework that included four important areas: content development, design of learning activities, teaching strategies, and assessment. A notable aspect of this TPACK-based comprehensive framework emphasizes participatory pedagogies that encourage students' collaborative learning activities and reduce lecturing modes of online instruction, which was an important stepping-stone for nonteacher education faculty.

Alsofyani, bin Aris, and Eynon (2013) evaluated training workshops for faculty's TPACK development designed to support their online instruction. Twenty-five faculty members from education, English teaching, computer science, physics, and dentistry at different universities participated in the workshops. In their findings, technological and pedagogical knowledge were mainly addressed. The main topics addressed were as follows: Theory and practice of online learning, instructional design tips, JISC e-learning models, IDMM design model, learning styles, modeling pedagogy and practice, evaluation models, and rubric for online instruction.

While the majority of available literature regarding TPACK development in higher education is based upon small-scale case studies, Meyer and Murrell's (2014) national study investigated multiple higher education institutions' faculty development for online teaching, focusing on their theoretical framework. They collected data using surveys responded by a coordinator, director, dean, and vice president affiliated in various units in their institutions (e.g., Academic Affairs, Chief Information/Technology Officer, a Department, a College, Central/System Office). A small number of the institutions (13%) employed TPACK as their theoretical framework for content and training activities for faculty development in online teaching, whereas other theories such as the learning styles theory, self-directed learning theory, adult learning theory, and multiple intelligences theory were more frequently observed among the responses. Meyer and Murrell (2014) argued that faculty developers have to be more explicit about their theoretical framework to make changes more sustainable among faculty. They stated that faculty understand theories, and it would shortchange them if training does not explicitly address learning theories.

Assessments of faculty's technology integration can be another consideration in applying the TPACK framework in nonteacher education programs in higher education. While there is a myriad of criticisms about any self-reported survey instruments of affects, skills, and academic performances (Fulmer & Frijters, 2009), Shih and Chuang (2013) recently reported in their study about an author-developed instrument, which sought to capture the students' evaluation of their instructors' TPACK. A notable aspect of this study was that participating undergraduate students were not from the college of education but from various disciplines (e.g., engineering, liberal arts, social sciences, marine sciences, science, and management). Their instrument assessed students' perceptions of college teachers' knowledge in technology-supported classroom environments. They integrated the criteria

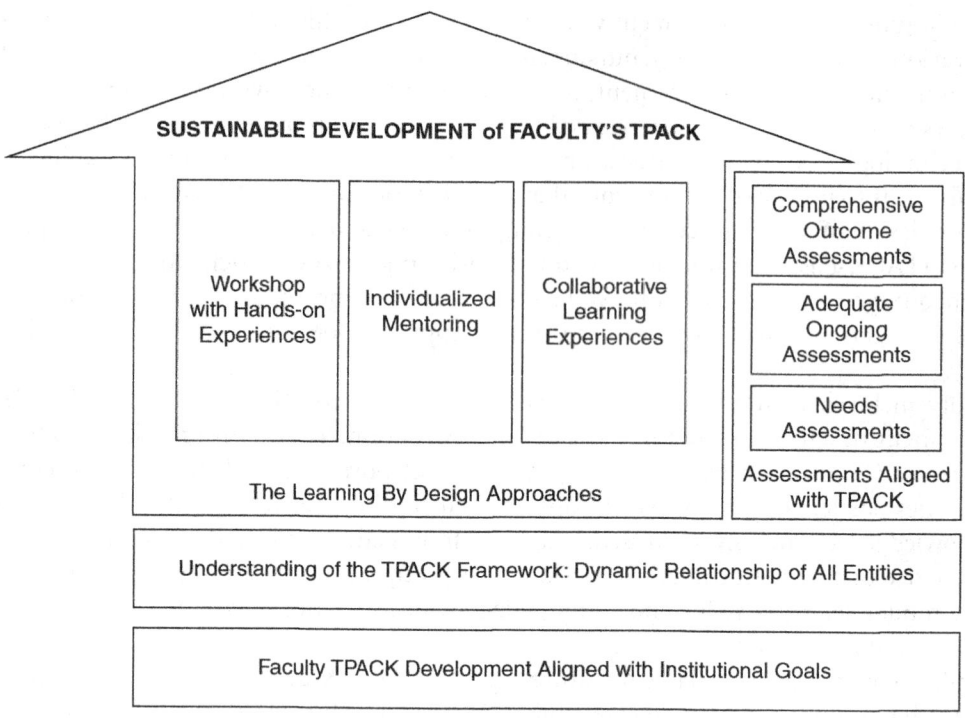

Figure 13.1 Sustainable Development of Faculty's TPACK

of PCK (Jang, 2011; Tuan, Chang, Wang, & Treagust, 2000) and of TPACK (Angeli & Valanides, 2009). While the reliability for each subscale and the survey construct validity of their measures were supported through the confirmatory factor analysis, the authors cautioned about the utility of this instrument because of a couple of unresolved issues: (a) a complicated process for composite score calculation and (b) the lack of items developed by the authors. In addition to these author-addressed issues, their survey items put too much emphasis on instructors' presentation mode for technology integration rather than students' learning activities with technology. Only a few items out of 24 TPACK items were addressing students' problem-solving or creativity-oriented activities (e.g., "My teacher uses an online student learning portfolio to assess my learning," p. 117). More items that can exemplify diverse, pedagogically progressive, learner-centered, or problem-solving oriented technology integration should be developed in order to be able to sensitively capture the faculty's advanced level of TPACK.

Based on the review of the literature, we provide synthesis of suggestions for faculty's TPACK development in higher education, which can be applied for both teacher education and nonteacher education faculty. In addition, the diagram in Figure 13.1 depicts the summary of the process of faculty's TPACK development.

- Faculty TPACK development should be aligned with institutional goals.
- A sound theoretical framework should be provided for faculty's sustainable change.

- Faculty (particularly nonteacher education faculty) has to have opportunities to understand the importance of pedagogical knowledge to facilitate learner-centered instruction using technology.
- The Learning Technology by Design approach can be helpful for faculty to understand the dynamic relationship of all entities in the TPACK framework.
- Individualized mentoring as well as workshops for TPACK development can support individual faculty members' ongoing learning.
- Collaborative learning experiences (e.g., co-teaching relationships) can be helpful for sustainable development.
- Faculty's individual needs have to be assessed. Faculty can have vast knowledge of content-specific technology tools, although generic instructional technology tools can be new.
- Adequate ongoing assessments have to be developed for progress monitoring.
- Comprehensive outcome assessments can include students' evaluation as well as faculty's self-reported survey.
- Assessments need to be aligned with the TPACK framework.

Discussion

Higher education leadership attention to systemic issues to support TPACK-based initiatives can serve to promote faculty members' awareness and capacity to implement the use of the TPACK framework. In the TPACK development process, building a solid conceptual framework with a comprehensive picture for the development of TPACK among faculty members is substantial in leadership efforts to make a change. Within the conceptual framework to promote faculty members' participation and engagement in the initiative, individual faculty members' concerns, perspectives, and learning needs should be respected. In addition, the leadership efforts can be invested in creating an environment that sustains TPACK-based initiatives by providing faculty members with professional development opportunities, environmental support, faculty networking, and rewards for TPACK integration, as well as in developing adequate evaluation methods.

The studies presented in this chapter point to areas where some work has been completed that sought to develop teacher educator TPACK. Primarily this has been through development opportunities that engaged faculty in lesson development. In both of the two faculty development approaches presented, lesson development was a common theme. Yet, lesson development was only part of the development experience. There was also a collaborative and reflective component throughout both approaches, likely providing faculty with a sense of support and collegiality, giving the work they were engaged in additional value. The qualities embedded in these approaches to TPACK development align very well with effective faculty development for technology integration as well. Yet, there was very little in the literature in terms of best practices for faculty TPACK development, which is an indicator of one of two potential phenomena. The first is that faculty TPACK development has not been studied and, therefore, there is very little in the literature to draw upon. The second, and perhaps most concerning, is that current faculty development practices in teacher preparation programs are not targeting faculty TPACK development and are instead treating technology integration and the development of faculty knowledge about technologies as an isolated activity from what and how faculty teach. If the latter proves to be true, then a disservice is being paid to both faculty and students enrolled in their courses, because without the proper support and learning opportunities, there can be no expectation that faculty will enhance their instruction to target key competencies and literacies that are critical for success through the use of educational technologies.

Similar to the trends of literature regarding teacher education faculty's TPACK development, the amount of literature about nonteacher education faculty's TPACK development is limited. While this literature is emerging and requires additional empirical studies, our current review can provide the following summary of accumulated information. To begin with, the literature has emphasized the importance of having a theoretical framework in leadership efforts to make sustainable changes in nonteacher education faculty's instruction. Some universities have adopted the TPACK framework for this purpose. As the TPACK framework integrates all three important aspects, TPACK-based approaches for making changes in faculty's instruction can be comprehensive. Meanwhile, nationwide data indicates that the TPACK framework is adopted in a small number of universities; there is still room for growth. Moreover, contexts of faculty's TPACK development are predominantly online instruction settings. Not only online instruction, but also traditional face-to-face instruction can be enhanced by faculty's TPACK development, particularly among the faculty of arts and sciences, where lecturing has been the most prominent mode of instruction. Pedagogical knowledge among seven aspects of the TPACK framework has been emphasized in the literature about the nonteacher education faculty's TPACK development. On the other hand, the content-specific technology tools have rarely been discussed in this literature. We need more information regarding the technological content knowledge aspect to delineate a more comprehensive framework for nonteacher education faculty's TPACK development.

Recommendations

In the context of what the authors have shared, the following recommendations are put forth. Foremost, more studies about TPACK in teacher education, and higher education in general, are needed. There is a double deficit in the literature body of TPACK studies in higher education. One deficit relates to the lack of empirical studies with solid research methods and systematically collected data. Additional empirical studies, including replication studies of previous studies with different populations in various contexts, can test current findings and yield more detailed knowledge. The other deficit relates to the rarity of studies about higher education faculty development. TPACK studies have been focusing on pre-service or in-service teachers. While working with faculty provides for a new context, researchers should examine the lessons learned from studies with foci on pre-service and in-service teachers to determine if they are applicable with higher education faculty members as well.

While more studies about TPACK application in nonteacher education courses are called for, studies about TPACK application in teacher education courses can still provide a rationale for the extrapolation of TPACK among various courses in higher education. A university is an organization that comprises departments or schools of technology, pedagogy, and various content areas. Bull, Bell, and Hammond (2008) reminded us of Koehler and Mishra's (2005) earlier endeavors for developing the idea of TPACK by establishing a coalition for several teacher educator content associations and educational technology associations. In this way, the review of knowledge constructed in Bull, Bell, and Hammond's chapter in the first *Handbook of Technological Pedagogical Content Knowledge (TPCK) for Educators* can provide an important foundation to understand TPACK levels in arts and sciences, technology, and education faculties. They suggest that the activities of the National Technology Leadership Coalition (NTLC) in creating networks among various higher education people participating in teacher education organizations was the most important aim in ensuring that pre-service and in-service teachers develop TPACK and that technology's potential to facilitate learning across content areas be realized.

Based upon the existing literature about the development of faculty's TPACK, regardless of the rarity of the literature, methods of monitoring and evaluating faculty's performance in regards to TPACK are emerging. As the faculty member is the unit of change in the development of faculty's TPACK (Kahveci et al., 2008), it makes sense that monitoring faculty's performance is a primary concern. However, there are claims that the promotion of faculty's technology integration in instruction will lead to enhanced students' learning outcomes, although these claims are difficult to justify (Cope & Ward, 2002). Literature about the relationships between higher education faculty's performance in regards to TPACK and their students' learning outcomes in higher education is currently unavailable, and requires additional systematic research.

References

Alsofyani, M. M., bin Aris, B., & Eynon, R. (2013). A preliminary evaluation of a short online training workshop for TPACK development. *International Journal of Teaching and Learning in Higher Education, 25*(1), 118–128.

Angeli, C., & Valanides, N. (2009). Epistemological and methodological issues for the conceptualization, development, and assessment of ICT-TPCK: Advances in technological pedagogical content knowledge (TPCK). *Computers & Education, 52*(1), 154–168.

Archambault, L., Wetzel, K., Foulger, T. S., & Williams, M. K. (2009). Professional development 2.0: Transforming teacher education pedagogy with 21st century tools. *Journal of Digital Learning in Teacher Education, 27*(1), 4–11. doi:10.1080/14759390300200149

Argyris, C., & Schön, D. (1974) *Theory in practice: Increasing professional effectiveness*. San Francisco: Jossey-Bass.

Arinto, P. (2013). A framework for developing competencies in open and distance e-learning. *International Review of Research in Open and Distance Learning, 14*(1), 167–185. Retrieved from http://www.irrodl.org/index.php/irrodl/article/view/1393/2433

Brush, T., Glazewski, K., Rutowski, K., Berg, K., Stromfors, C., Van-Nest, M. H., et al. (2003). Integrating technology into a field-based teacher training program: The project. *Journal of Educational Technology Research and Development, 51*(1), 57–72.

Brown M.C., II, & Canto, B., Jr. (2008). In AACTE Innovation & Technology Committee (Eds.), *Handbook of technological pedagogical content knowledge (TPCK) for educators* (pp. vii-ix). New York: Routledge.

Bull, G., Bell, L., & Hammond, T. (2008). Advancing TPCK through collaborations across educational associations. In AACTE Committee on Innovation and Technology (Eds.), *The handbook of technological pedagogical content knowledge for teaching and teacher educators* (pp. 273–287). New York: Routledge.

Cope, C. M., & Ward, P. (2002). Integrating learning technology into classrooms: The importance of teachers' perceptions. *Educational Technology & Society, 5*(1), 67–74.

Cuban, L. (2001). *Oversold and underused: Reforming schools through technology, 1980–2000*. Cambridge, MA: Harvard University Press.

Day, C., Sammons, P., Leithwood, K., & Kington, A. (2008). Research into the impact of school leadership on pupil outcomes: Policy and research contexts. *School Leadership & Management: Formerly School Organization, 28*, 5–25.

Devlin-Scherer, R., & Sardone, N. B. (2013). Collaboration as a form of professional development: Improving learning for faculty and students. *College Teaching, 61*, 30–37.

Donovan, L., & Green, T. (2010). One-to-one computing in teacher education: Faculty concerns and implications for teacher educators. *Journal of Digital Learning in Teacher Education, 26*(4), 140–148.

Figg, C., & Jaipal, K. (2013). Using TPACK-in-practice workshops to enable teacher candidates to create professional development workshops that develop tech-enhanced teaching. In R. McBride & M. Searson (Eds.), *Proceedings of Society for Information Technology & Teacher Education International Conference 2013* (pp. 5040–5047). Chesapeake, VA: AACE.

Fulmer, S. M., & Frijters, J. C. (2009). A review of self-report and alternative approaches in the measurement of student motivation. *Educational Psychology Review, 21*, 219–246.

Hill, P. T., & Celio, M. (1998). *Fixing urban schools*. Washington, DC: Brookings Institution Press.

Jang, S. (2011). Assessing college students' perceptions of a case teacher's pedagogical content knowledge using a newly developed instrument. *Higher Education, 61*(6), 663–678.

Kahveci, A., Gilmer, P. J., & Southerland, S. A. (2008). Understanding chemistry professors' use of educational technologies: An activity theoretical approach. *International Journal of Science Education, 30*(3), 325–351. doi:10.1080/09500690601188638

Knowles, M. (1973). *The adult learner: A neglected species*. Houston, TX: Gulf Publishing Company.

Koehler, M. J., & Mishra, P. (2005). What happens when teachers design educational technology? The development of technological pedagogical content knowledge. *Journal of Educational Computing Research, 32*(2), 131–152.

Koehler, M. J., Mishra, P., Bouck, E. C., DeSchryver, M., Kereluik, K., Shin, T. S., & Wolf, L. G. (2011). Deep-play: Developing TPACK for 21st century teachers. *International Journal of Learning Technology, 6*(2), 146–163. doi:10.1504/IJLT.2011.042646

Koehler, M. J., Mishra, P., Hershey, K., & Peruski, L. (2004). With a little help from your students: A new model for faculty development and online course design. *Journal of Technology and Teacher Education, 12*(1), 25–55. Retrieved from http://www.jcu.edu/education/dshutkin/ed586/techdesign.pdf

Koehler, M. J., Mishra, P., & Yahya, K. (2007). Tracing the development of teacher knowledge in a design seminar: Integrating content pedagogy and technology. *Computers & Education, 49*(3), 740–762. doi:10.1016/j.compedu.2005.11.012

Koh, J.H.L., & Divaharan, S. (2011). Developing pre-service teachers' technology integration expertise through the TPACK-developing instructional model. *Journal of Educational Computing Research, 44*(1), 35–58. doi:10.2190/EC.44.1.c

Kushner Benson, S. N., & Ward, C. L. (2013). Teaching with technology: Using TPACK to understand teaching expertise in online higher education. *Journal of Educational Computing Research, 48*(2), 153–172.

Leithwood, K., Harris, A., & Hopkins, D. (2008). Seven strong claims about successful school leadership. *School Leadership and Management, 28*(1), 27–42.

Leithwood, K., & Jantzi, D. (2008). Linking leadership to student learning: The contributions of leader efficacy. *Educational Administration Quarterly, 44*(4), 496–528.

Leithwood, K., & Riehl, C. (2003). *What we know about successful school leadership*. Philadelphia, PA: Laboratory for Student Success, Temple University.

Ludwig, M., & Booz, W. H. (2003). *Teacher technology leaders*. Washington, DC: George Washington University, Department of Teacher Preparation and Special Education.

Meacham, J., & Ludwig, J. (2001). Faculty and students at the center: Faculty development for general education courses. *The Journal of General Education, 50*(4), 254–269.

Meyer, K. A., & Murrell, V. S. (2014). A national study of theories and their importance for faculty development for online teaching. *Online Journal of Distance Learning Administration, 17*, 1–19. Retrieved from http://www.westga.edu/~distance/ojdla/summer172/Meyer_Murrell172.html

Polly, D., Mims, C., Shepherd, C. E., & Inan, F. (2010). Evidence of impact: Transforming teacher education tomorrow's teachers to teach with technology (PT3). *Teaching and Teacher Education, 26*, 863–870.

Schaffer, S., & Richardson, J. (2004). Supporting technology integration across the teacher education system. In R. Ferdig et al. (Eds.), *Proceedings of Society for Information Technology & Teacher Education International Conference 2004* (pp. 1383–1388). Chesapeake, VA: Association for the Advancement of Computing in Education (AACE).

Schulman, L. S. (1987). Knowledge and teaching: Foundations of the new reform. *Harvard Educational Review, 57*(1), 1–22.

Scott, L. C. (2009). Through the wicked spot: A case study of professors' experiences teaching online. Doctoral dissertation. Available from ProQuest Dissertation and Theses database (Publication No. AAT3379753).

Shih, C., & Chuang, H. (2013). The development and validation of an instrument for assessing college students' perceptions of faculty knowledge in technology-supported class environments. *Computers & Education, 63*, 109–118.

Society for Information Technology & Teacher Education. (2014). Technology, pedagogy and content knowledge (TPACK) SIG. Retrieved from http://site.aace.org/sigs/tpack-sig/

Teclehaimanot, B., & Lamb, A. (2005). Technology-rich faculty development for teacher educators: The evolution of a program. *Contemporary Issues in Technology and Teacher Education, 5*(3/4), 330–344.

Thomas, T., Herring, M., Redmond, P., & Smaldino, S. (2013). Leading change and innovation in teacher preparation: A blueprint for developing TPACK ready teacher candidates. *Techtrends: Linking Research & Practice to Improve Learning, 57*(5), 55–63.

Tuan, H., Chang, H., Wang, K., & Treagust, D. F. (2000). The development of an instrument for assessing students' perception of teachers' knowledge. *International Journal of Science Education, 22*(4), 385–398.

Yilmazel-Sahin, Y., & Oxford, R. L. (2010). A comparative analysis of teacher education faculty development models for technology integration. *Journal of Technology and Teacher Education, 18*(2010), 693–720.

14

Opportunities and Challenges of TPACK-Based Professional Development on a Global Scale

Mark Hofer, John K. Lee, David A. Slykhuis, James Ptaszynski

Introduction

Since the initial publication introducing the TPACK (then TPCK) framework in 2006, this new way of conceptualizing teacher knowledge for technology integration has spurred a flurry of research and development activity in the educational technology community. Much of this work has focused upon efforts to develop and measure TPACK with pre-service and in-service K–12 teachers. These efforts are synthesized in the chapters by Archambault and Chai, Koh, and Tsai in this book. This work has contributed significantly to how we design, structure, implement, and assess TPACK development in K–12 and related contexts.

While much of the literature reports on TPACK research and development efforts in K–12 contexts, Koehler & Mishra's (2005) study focused on the development of faculty members' TPACK in a learning-by-design experience. As the TPACK framework has matured, new efforts build on this work to explore the development of higher education faculty knowledge about teaching with technology. The TPACK framework has shown promise in recent research framing professional development for higher education faculty as they expand their knowledge and practices using technology. Rienties, Brouwer, and Lygo-Baker (2013) examined an online professional development program instituted at multiple institutions in the Netherlands and determined that faculty benefited from exposure to methods designed to introduce TPACK. The authors found success in using the TPACK framework to measure faculty beliefs about teaching using technology. In particular, they were able to show that among 33 participants, exposure over time to the TPACK model decreased participants' reliance on knowledge transmission pedagogies (see also Rienties et al., 2013).

The TPACK framework is often represented with a Venn diagram as way of understanding how the three domains of technological, pedagogical, and content knowledge intersect. Benson and Ward (2013) examined the nature of these intersecting domains in a study of TPACK profiles among faculty in a college of education. They found that knowledge of pedagogy was the most dominant domain of knowledge in terms of predicting high capacity for TPACK among the participants. In related research, Anderson, Barham, and Northcote (2013) used TPACK as a theoretical lens to examine higher education faculty perceptions of online and blended instruction and found that the instructors focused primarily on recreating face-to-face learning experiences online, but were unable or unwilling to consider the technologies that enabled those shifts without a parallel consideration of pedagogy. The professional development initiative we introduce below is one such effort, undertaken on a global scale.

Initial Development of the Technology Enriched Instruction (TEI)

In 2011, the education team at Microsoft reached out to the National Technology Leadership Coalition (NTLC), its representatives from ten specialty professional associations, and the Society for Information Technology for Education (SITE) to help design the strategy for a new initiative aimed to assist faculty in appropriately integrating technology into their teaching. The primary focus at the time was to support faculty in colleges and schools of education. Twenty individuals, initially led by Glen Bull of the Curry School at the University of Virginia and Jim Ptaszynski of Microsoft, comprised the original Microsoft Higher Education Advisory Board commissioned to start this initiative.

This design effort resulted in two approaches, both of which are referred to by the acronym TEI: the Teacher Education Initiative and the Technology Enriched Instruction workshop, respectively. This chapter is designed to provide an overview of the development of TEI and to report on evaluation findings from around the world. For a more in-depth understanding of the evolution of TEI, readers should consult the previously published overview, "Preparing Teachers for Tomorrow's Technologies" (Dilworth et al., 2012) and "Implementing the Teacher Education Initiative" (Bull et al., 2012).

The Teacher Education Initiative (TEI)

A planning meeting with representatives of the NTLC and SITE was held in October 2011 at the Microsoft Campus in Redmond, Washington. The purpose of this initial meeting was to acquaint the Higher Education Advisory Board with leading-edge and yet-to-be-released technology to expand their thinking on the technology tools that were, or soon would be, available for use by students, teachers, and faculty.

The primary purpose of the meeting was to identify the audience for the workshop and the best approach to structure it to help faculty more effectively integrate technology in their teaching. After lengthy discussion, the group determined that the biggest impact on changing how K–12 teachers use technology would be made if the focus was on changing the practice of how faculty use technology when they educate pre-service teachers. The Board agreed that the most effective approach would be to design a workshop where faculty participants were involved in active and inquiry-based learning. Further, it was decided that collaboration throughout the workshop with other faculty members, as well as significant hands-on practice with the technology, would also be beneficial.

Although not a part of the original discussion, Board members discussed the importance of assisting faculty with the difficult task of navigating the selection of technology that "fit" with the content they were teaching and the pedagogy they employed. TPACK met both of our requirements and has been integral in bringing the different elements of the workshop together. It has always been the intent of the TEI workshop to be more than a random series of technology demonstrations, simple product training (e.g., how to use advanced program features), or worse, a promotional/sales event. TPACK provided a robust, academic framework upon which to build a rigorous, but flexible, workshop that integrated three of the most fundamental building blocks of teaching: content, pedagogy, and technology.

Perhaps the most vociferous debate came when the Board discussed whether the focus of the workshop should be discipline specific (i.e., science, social studies, math, English) or more general in approach. Given our focus on teacher educators, the group ultimately decided to develop content-focused approach. It was decided that workshop would follow this outline:

- Welcome, introductions, and workshop overview
- Introduction to technology to be used during the workshop and the TPACK framework
- Concurrent discipline-specific sessions
- Integration of the day and evaluation

The resulting workshop was designed to help participants develop competencies that would enable them to effectively select, use, and evaluate technology tools and resources in their teaching. The Board decided to acknowledge the commitment the workshop participants exhibited by offering them Microsoft Faculty Fellows status and a certificate from Microsoft and the Society of Information Technology and Teacher Education (SITE). They would also receive a digital badge that would acknowledge their accomplishment.

Shifting to Technology Enriched Instruction

Following three "beta" offerings of the workshop in this content-specific model, the TEI Leadership Team made several important changes to the workshop. First, due to the challenges of recruiting and equally distributing faculty from four disciplines in the content-focused model, we decided to develop a more general focus to appeal to a wider audience. We knew that we needed to create a workshop that would still be TPACK-focused while remaining flexible enough for faculty from a range of disciplines (including those outside education) to benefit from the workshop and materials to inform their teaching. This shift challenged our notions of TPACK as a framework for professional development. Rather than structuring the content according to discipline, our challenge was to design experiences that would enable participants to draw on their already strong content knowledge to identify pedagogical strategies and educational technologies that would enhance their teaching practice. In this approach, participants would build their TPACK through a process of bridging their own experience with new insights and ideas provided in the workshop. This approach mirrors the design-based approach discussed by Koehler and Mishra (2005), the originators of the TPACK construct. Like in their model, the faculty participants in the TEI workshop would leverage their deep content expertise through a scaffolded experience to identify appropriate technology tools and resources to enhance their practice.

One challenge that we encountered in early iterations of this redesign was the need for an additional organizing framework. Conceptual frameworks can be powerful tools to enable participants to consider a complex issue or challenge from a similar perspective. When the focus of the workshop was limited to teacher education, the faculty participants shared a broad set of assumptions and foci. While education faculty might focus on teaching methods, educational psychology, or historical foundations, many of the teaching strategies and the content in the field of education are more similar than different. When we expanded the audience for the workshop to include faculty from arts and sciences as well as other professional schools, it was important for us to incorporate an organizing framework or set of values/approaches that would work in concert with TPACK to help provide faculty with a vision for technology integration.

After considering several options, Board members decided to include the 21st Century Learning Design (21CLD) framework. Designed by SRI International (ITL Research, 2012), it provided a research-based framework that allowed for the consideration, discussion, and integration of the potential skills and abilities that would be needed to be successful in the 21st century. While not assumed to be the definitive model of 21st-century skills, it was decided that 21CLD was robust enough to be a valuable framework for TEI facilitators and workshop participants, as they considered what frame was important to teaching in the longer term.

The framework identifies six 21st-century learning skills (21CLS), including:

- Collaboration
- Construction of knowledge
- Real-world problem solving and innovation
- Use of ICT for learning
- Self-regulation
- Skilled communication

This framework provides the kind of broad applicability and concrete guidance for the use of technology to support learning for the workshop setting. The 21CLD framework helps to provide faculty with a vision for how the integration of technology might support or enhance student learning. The common language embodied in the framework enables faculty from disparate disciplines to have productive and generative conversations about teaching and learning.

We designed the new version of the workshop in a guided inquiry approach, in which participants begin and end with the challenge of redesigning one course activity or assignment to leverage 21st-century skills and technology-enhanced learning (21CLD) within the context of their own disciplines and courses (TPACK). Rather than focusing on the tools or specific pedagogical approaches, we designed a spiraling inquiry sequence that challenges participants to move from a common challenge to a more specific challenge that they encounter in a course they teach. As they progress through the following series of activities, participants engage in this guided inquiry process:

- Introduction to the workshop and design challenge
- Changing conditions of teaching and learning
- New literacies and technologies for the 21st century
- 21st Century Learning Design
- Introduction to TPACK and the TPACK game
- Instructional design
- Sharing new approaches

Brief Description of Final Workshop Content

Beginning with an email prior to the workshop, participants are encouraged to identify an instructional problem or opportunity in their teaching that they would like to focus on during the workshop. Beginning in the first activity and repeatedly throughout the workshop, we encourage the participants to come back to this focus as they move through the day. This focus provides a concrete and specific goal, in which the participants can anchor their learning, and appeals to the adult learner's emphasis on connecting new ideas to their prior knowledge and experience to inform their professional practice.

The focus on helping participants to develop their TPACK takes place primarily in activities four, five, and six. We begin with 21CLD to help them broaden their vision of how technology can support student learning. As we formally introduce TPACK, we encourage them to begin to connect these emerging ideas with their disciplinary focus and the particular courses they teach in the context of the instructional problem or opportunity they previously identified. As they are introduced to TPACK, they have an opportunity to discuss connections they see with the other participants at their table. They also post these ideas on a collaborative whiteboard Web application (Padlet) in order to share them with the larger group to encourage cross-pollination of ideas. We have found that these table conversations are critical in helping participants make sense of the new ideas to which they are exposed.

The two frameworks really begin to crystallize for participants in the fifth activity—the TPACK game. Based on the version of the game originally developed by Judi Harris, Punya Mishra, and Matthew Koehler for the 2007 National Technology Leadership Summit (Mishra, 2010), we provide participants with a set of three different types of playing cards: blank content topic cards, pedagogy cards with one of a range of different pedagogical strategies (e.g., group discussion, simulation, presentation) on each card, and cards with different technology options (e.g., word processing, videoconferencing, data analysis, etc.). The TPACK game cards are available online for customization and printing (http://1drv.

ms/1pM2YC0). Through a series of three increasingly complex rounds, participants reason through a process of finding a "fit" between the content topic they have selected and one or more pedagogy and technology cards. This activity often leads to robust and protracted discussions of optimal combinations of content, pedagogy, and technology. In the process of playing the game, participants often begin to formulate ideas for the instructional design activity that follows.

After exploring the changing nature of teaching and learning, 21st-century literacies and learning designs, and the TPACK framework, participants are challenged to redesign a course experience or assignment that draws on what they have learned in the workshop. They have an extended period to plan individually or collaboratively to design an experience they can take back with them to implement in their teaching. We find that the participants often refer back to the 21CLD rubrics and cards from the TPACK game as they approach this problem. We provide a Word document template that requires the participants to identify the course topic, learning goal, pedagogical strategies and technologies of their original approach, as well as their redesigned vision. We encourage the participants to present their new designs using a technology of their choice (e.g., PowerPoint, Glogster, video). They then share these approaches in their small group, discussing how 21CLD and TPACK are represented in their designs. Each group then identifies one example at their table that they agree best exemplifies 21CLD and TPACK to share with the larger group via the workshop Yammer network. This process of sharing both affirms the faculty participant who created the activity and provides additional ideas and approaches for the other participants to consider.

Workshop Outcomes and Evaluation

As we have evolved the program and offered workshops around the world, we have attempted to measure their effectiveness in terms of both participants' satisfaction and knowledge development and application. In the limited space we have in this chapter, we offer the following brief analysis of the workshop evaluation data.

Workshop Survey Evaluation Data

The workshop evaluation data has consistently been positive for events offered around the world. The TEI workshops have always received high evaluations, perhaps best illustrated by two questions, "Will your experience today influence your future teaching?" and "Would you recommend the TEI workshop to a colleague?" In workshops in the United States and Canada, 91% of the participants indicated the workshop would influence their teaching practice. Evaluation data from workshops in the United States, Canada, and Korea indicated that 96% would recommend the workshop to a colleague.

In particular, the TPACK activity and game rated as one of the highest, if not the highest, component of the overall TEI workshop. For example, in the Thailand workshop, all the responses rated the TPACK activity as effective (16.1%) or very effective (83.9%). Similar results were found in other workshops as well, in Korea (61.8% very effective, 35.3%

effective) and in the United States at William and Mary (67.9% very effective, 25.0% effective). The participants' appreciation of the TPACK activity and game also was displayed in the comments section of the evaluation with statements such as "Great activity," "Card game a hit!" "Love these exercises," "The cards were extremely useful," and "I think it would be great for participants to walk away with a copy of the TPACK card game."

Analysis of Yammer Network Feed

One of the central features of the TEI workshop is the use of the Yammer online social network. Yammer is an enterprise social network designed to support collaborative activities at large-scale organizations. The Yammer network provides participants with an environment to enhance face-to-face activities as well as an opportunity to extend and support participants after the workshop.

The TEI workshop leaders have used Yammer successfully to organize participants in regional and local TEI workshops. TEI has leveraged three Yammer features in the delivery and support of project goals: (1) the capacity for participants to create personal accounts and post information to those accounts, (2) the establishment of smaller Yammer groups built around TEI workshops, and (3) the staging of specific TEI workshop activities.

There are currently over 2,500 members in the TEI Yammer network. These members have used, and in some cases continue to use, a wide range of Yammer tools. Most importantly, TEI Yammer members have posted over 10,000 messages using the Update feature. TEI participants have used the communication feature to post responses about specific workshop activities, as well as to share their general observations and questions related to using technology in their teaching.

Yammer supports a wide range of grouping functions. Twenty public workshop groups have been created to support activities connected to face-to-face workshops. The most common use of Yammer in these groups has been to facilitate activities and extend discussion during the workshops. Beyond these workshop groups another 200 smaller, private groups related to TEI have been created to facilitate various collaborative activities.

One of the most important uses of Yammer has been to support workshop activities. These activities include member reflections on the changing conditions of teaching and learning in the 21st century and the two theories informing TEI: 21CLD and TPACK. TEI workshop activities build toward a cumulative activity where participants reconsider an activity from their teaching experiences. TEI workshop participants are asked to upload a final product of their work. This activity and others have resulted in participants uploading over 1,600 files. An example and analysis of the Yammer feed from one workshop illustrates how it is integrated into the TEI workshop.

In-Depth Findings from Sydney

In April 2014, we conducted a workshop in Sydney, Australia, for 35 faculty members and instructional designers. Participants represented an interesting mix of faculty that taught either fully face-to-face or fully online. The instructional designers in the group typically worked with faculty to support online teaching efforts. The participants included faculty from Australia, New Zealand, and Malaysia.

The Yammer feed for this workshop included three "required" posts. In the first part of the day, participants worked in small groups to identify how the conditions of teaching and learning had changed in the 21st century. The second post focused on participants' perceptions of students' changing expectations for their learning experience. These posts focused primarily on how students had become more distracted amid the constant flow of information and social network activity and how they were more demanding and selective in the courses and learning experiences in which they were engaged. Four of the groups noted that even though class sizes were increasing, fewer students were opting to come to class to attend lectures. One group noted, "Drops in class attendance as students opt for streamed lectures etc.," while another suggested that, "Students pick and choose which offerings they want to consume, i.e., which lecture to attend, which one to view the recording of." Several groups noted how students often preferred social and collaborative learning experiences. One group commented, "they expect to be co-creators of authentic meaningful activity, more student centred, more creative, need meaning, interested in linking it with their career goals." They all seemed to agree that students were increasingly expecting more flexible and relevant learning experiences. This perceived shift in preferred pedagogies seemed to drive a great deal of the discussion in the Yammer feed and in the workshop itself.

As groups were posting these "required" responses, they also used the Yammer feed to share resources including multiple links to information on new literacies, different 21st-century skill frameworks, and a number of different technology tools and resources related to the discussions in both the large and small group settings. Three posts answered specific questions that came up in whole group discussions, including the compatibility of tools that we modeled in the workshop on different types of digital devices. These kinds of technology-centric posts demonstrated ways in which the instructional designers were able to share their technological knowledge with their faculty colleagues.

The final "required" post was connected with the final workshop activity, in which participants shared their revised course activities or assignments with the rest of the group. Using a Word document template, participants worked on reimagining a class activity in which they drew on the 21CLD and TPACK frameworks to inform their thinking. Participants posted completed versions of the Word document template and PowerPoint slides to share their work. Of the 12 posted activities (participants in this workshop worked in small groups), all but one demonstrated a shift to significantly greater emphasis on active learning and the integration of 21st-century learning skills. All of the activities included multiple technologies that were well integrated with the selected content focus and pedagogies employed. One interesting example focused on genetic mutations in a biology course. Specifically, the activity was designed to help students "understand the ways that various mutations can occur" and "investigate the impact of mutations on individuals and populations." In the original version of the activity, the instructor relied primarily on lecturing, videos for demonstration, and a student seminar for discussion. In the new version, the instructor had revised the experience to move the lecture portion of the class as prework and used the class time to challenge students to "Collaboratively design and evaluate an experiment to investigate the impact of a mutation on individuals or a population." This new version of the activity demonstrated strong TPACK "fit" by utilizing data collection, analysis, and presentation tools. This new design provided opportunities to engage students in high levels of three 21st-century skills: knowledge construction, self-regulation, and collaboration. In each of these final posts, the participants referenced TPACK and 21CLD to represent their instructional choices.

The Future of TEI

TEI evolved to address an important need in higher education. Workshops have circled the globe with events in Stockholm, Sweden; Seattle, USA; Sharjah, UAE; Budapest, Hungary; Wuhan, China; Jakarta, Indonesia; Kiev, Ukraine; Niagara Falls, Canada; Alberta, Canada; Atlanta, USA; Williamsburg, USA; Doha, Qatar; Sydney, Australia; and Monterrey, Mexico. In addition, many of the faculty completing the workshop quickly went back to their home countries and conducted their own workshop in places such as Vietnam, Brunei, Malaysia, Egypt, Lebanon, Russia, Poland, and Norway.

As the workshop structure and content has changed in the three years we have been active, we assume that it will continue to evolve to meet the changing needs of faculty. We are also currently developing an online version of the course to help bring the workshop content and learning to faculty in underserved parts of the world. In preparing for these new opportunities, the TEI Board and leadership team must strike a balance between the existing affordances of the face-to-face workshops and the new opportunities that online delivery offers. Vaughan and Garrison (2006) describe the challenges that programs face when delivering blended programs in terms of needing to "recognize the changing dynamics of the faculty learning communities over time and the need to adjust social, cognitive and teaching presence strategies to meet the evolving demands of inquiry for faculty development" (p. 150). Balancing the social and cognitive experiences of TEI participants is critical given the importance of teaching practice and intellectual engagement (i.e., TPACK and 21CLD frameworks) inherent in the workshop. However, these experiences cannot come at the cost of neglecting the social and collaborative aspects of TEI. Presently, the TEI experience takes advantage of face-to-face grouping and other in-person peer dynamics to support the social dynamic of the work. As TEI relies more heavily on an online delivery, new attention will need to be given to nurturing the social aspects of the participant experience.

Conclusion

The findings shared here are limited in a number of ways. First, not all participants from the workshops completed the evaluation survey and the final assessment. Therefore, it is reasonable to assume that those who took the time to respond were perhaps more invested in the content of the workshop. Second, the impact demonstrated in the form of the instructional design element of the workshop is limited to a single course session or topic. There is no way to predict whether the new understandings developed will transfer or scale beyond this scope. The intent behind the inquiry-driven approach is to focus on the process that should, in theory, be replicable. There is no guarantee, however, of any impact beyond this limited measure. Finally, it is well documented in the literature that professional development is optimally sustained over time to significantly impact instructional practice. Even the best one-day workshop cannot hope to effect the same level of change as an ongoing initiative.

Despite these varied and significant limitations, the evaluation data we have assessed is positive. We have repeatedly witnessed faculty from different countries in a range of disciplines actively engage in vibrant and sustained discussion and application of 21st-century skills and TPACK. They leave the workshop with ideas that they can take back with them and implement in their courses. The development of their TPACK is a journey that will last for one's entire career. We hope that the TEI workshop is the first step on the journey for some of our participants.

References

Anderson, A., Barham, N., & Northcote, M. (2013). Using the TPACK framework to unite disciplines in online learning. *Australasian Journal of Educational Technology, 29*(4), 549–565.

Benson, S.N.K., & Ward, C. L. (2013). Teaching with technology: Using TPACK to understand teaching expertise in online higher education. *Journal of Educational Computing Research, 48*(2), 153–172. Retrieved from http://baywood.metapress.com/openurl.asp?genre=article&id=doi:10.2190/EC.48.2.c

Bull, G., George, M., Shoffner, M., Bolick, C., Lee, J., Anderson, J., Slykuis, D., Garofalo, J., Angotti, R., McKenna, M., West, E., Dexter, S., Herring, M., Hofer, M., and Brown, A. (2012). Editorial: Implementing the teacher education initiative. *Contemporary Issues in Technology and Teacher Education, 12*(2), 115–121. Retrieved from http://www.citejournal.org/articles/v12i2editorial1.pdf

Dilworth, P., Donaldson, A., George, M., Knezek, D., Searson, M., Starkweather, K., Strutchens, M., Tillotson, J., & Robinson, S. (2012). Editorial: Preparing teachers for tomorrow's technologies. *Contemporary Issues in Technology and Teacher Education, 12*(1). Retrieved from http://www.citejournal.org/vol12/iss1/editorial/article1.cfm

ITL Research. (2012). 21CLD learning activity rubrics. Retrieved from http://www.pil-network.com/pd/21CLD/Overview

Koehler, M.J., & Mishra, P. (2005). What happens when teachers design educational technology? The development of technological pedagogical content knowledge. *Journal of Educational Computing Research, 32*(2), 131–152.

Mishra, P. (2010). TPACK game, the Matt Koehler version. Retrieved from http://punya.educ.msu.edu/2010/08/13/tpack-game-the-matt-koehler-version/

Rienties, B., Brouwer, N., Bohle Carbonell, K., Townsend, D., Rozendal, A.-P., van der Loo, J., Dekker, P., et al. (2013). Online training of TPACK skills of higher education scholars: A cross-institutional impact study. *European Journal of Teacher Education, 36*(4), 480–495.

Rienties, B., Brouwer, N., & Lygo-Baker, S. (2013). The effects of online professional development on higher education teachers' beliefs and intentions towards learning facilitation and technology. *Teaching and Teacher Education, 29*(1), 122–131.

Vaughan, N., & Garrison, D. R. (2006). How blended learning can support a faculty development community of inquiry. *Journal of Asynchronous Learning Networks, 10*(4), 139–152.

15

Understanding the Role of a School Principal in Setting the Context for Technology Integration
A TPACK Perspective

Vinesh Chandra

Introduction

A holistic approach needs to be adopted when teachers' Technological Pedagogical Content Knowledge (TPACK) is under the microscope. The context in which a teacher develops and demonstrates this knowledge can vary markedly. Thus, understanding the complexity of the context is very important. In many developing countries (e.g., Fiji), technology integration is just beginning to occur. A number of unique factors come into play before technology reaches classrooms. For example, many schools are at the mercy of the donors—the frequency at which they receive the technology (which varies in both in quality and quantity) can fluctuate significantly. This has an impact on what teachers can and cannot do.

Within this mix of factors are the school principals. They can have a significant influence on how the contexts for technology innovation and reform are set up and managed. Without their vision and direction, many initiatives within schools fail. This chapter investigates the role of a school principal in facilitating a context that enables teachers to teach with technology. The contextual factors associated with the principal are presented. Krishna (pseudonym) is a high school principal in a rural area in Fiji. The journey that he undertakes over a 12-month period is discussed. Field notes, conversational interviews, reports, and a survey inform this investigation.

The Context in the TPACK Framework

For teachers to integrate digital technology, the learning environment has to be both a catalyst and conducive to facilitate the design, development, and delivery of appropriate classroom activities. This is based on the assumption that teachers have the appropriate technological pedagogical content knowledge (TPACK) (Mishra & Koehler, 2006). Two points are significant here—the learning environment and teachers' TPACK. The context determines the type of learning environment within which teachers are immersed. This will in turn influence how their technological pedagogical content knowledge manifests and evolves within the learning environment.

According to Kincheloe (2008), "each teaching and learning context has its unique dimensions that must be dealt with individually. Our understanding of educational purpose is also shaped by the complexity of these contextual appreciations" (p. 32). Kincheloe also acknowledged that the context might be more important than the content itself. Rosenberg and Koehler (2014) pointed out that there was a need for a better understanding of "the relationship between context and contextual factors and the knowledge needed to teach with technology as understood through the TPACK framework" (p. 2391). Despite the obvious importance of the context, researchers have given it little significance (Porras-Hernandez & Salinas-Amescua, 2013; Rosenberg & Koehler, 2014). In a content analysis of 170 TPACK focused publications, Rosenberg and Koehler (2014) reported that there was a wide variation in terms of how the context was explained and interpreted. This can impact how the technology is integrated.

According to Porras-Hernandez and Salinas-Amescua (2013), the "context is conceived as a complex element, not only because of its multilevel nature, but also because of its double directional nature" (p. 231). They proposed the incorporation of two additional "dimensions" to the TPACK framework—actor and scope. The scope was represented by macro, meso, and micro level contexts. The macro level context was defined by "social, political, technological, and economic conditions" (p. 228) that affect schools. The meso level involved the role that the school leadership and the community (parents, peers, superintendents, and school principals) "played in maintaining a good attitude toward the use of technology for learning to integrate ICT" (p. 230) into teachers' classroom practices. The micro level was represented by the "in-class conditions for learning," which encompassed the day-to-day variables such as resources, norms, practices, and so on.

There is some overlap between Porras-Hernandez and Salinas-Amescua's (2013) propositions and some of the barriers to technology integration that have been identified in educational contexts. For example, a poor attitude of the school leadership towards ICT can be a barrier and impact on "in-class conditions" (e.g., availability of technology). Hew and Brush's (2007) analysis of a large number of studies into the integration of technology in K–12 learning environments showed that there were 123 barriers. They grouped the barriers into six categories. Barriers in the following four categories were cumulatively mentioned in more than 90% of the studies that they reviewed: resources (40%), knowledge and skills of teachers (23%), institution (14%), and attitudes and beliefs (13%).

The school principal can have a direct influence on how these barriers (Hew & Brush, 2007) and the two additional dimensions proposed by Porras-Hernandez and Salinas-Amescua (2013) play out in a teacher's development and demonstration of their technological pedagogical content knowledge. In terms of the barriers, the principals determine the types of resources that teachers can have access to. Motivated principals can implement strategies that lead to the development of teachers' knowledge and skills, which can in turn affect their attitudes and beliefs and vice-versa. Principals who are well grounded in the rationale of technology integration can influence the key stakeholders in institutions, such as school management boards and parents. They also have the power to bring about a change. In so doing, the principals have a positive influence on the meso and micro context levels.

The SEE Project

The Share, Engage, and Educate (SEE) Project (http://theseeproject.org) has worked proactively with schools in Fiji and other countries to develop their technology capacity (Chandra, Chandra, & Nutchey, 2014). I lead this unfunded project with the support of a handful of like-minded individuals. In the past three years, class sets of computers and hardware such as digital cameras and data projectors (secondhand) have been donated to more than 30 schools. Initiatives to building teacher capacity have also been undertaken by the SEE Project in some schools.

Our experience thus far has shown that the donated resources are effectively integrated in schools, which has a tech-savvy principal. Where this is not the case, the resources are of limited value. They occupy space in classrooms and eventually become a wasted resource. As a consequence, no one benefits.

Smart High School

Smart High School (pseudonym) has benefitted through our support. It is situated in a rural area on the island of Viti Levu in Fiji. The school has 18 staff with 235 students in forms 3 to 7 (aged 13–18 years). Most classes have up to 30 students on the roll. We have noticed a change in terms of how teaching and learning occur at the school with technology.

The principal has been a significant driver and catalyst of this change. Krishna (pseudonym) is the school principal with 14 years of teaching experience. Over this time, he was promoted from classroom teacher to the positions of head of department, vice principal, and principal. Smart High School was his second appointment as principal where he started two years earlier. He had a strong track record in the first school where the majority of the students succeeded in external exams. This is sometimes considered as a benchmark of good leadership in Fijian schools.

Understanding the Role of Krishna

In order to understand the role of the principal, answering the question "What role does Krishna play in technology integration at Smart High School?" was very important. Given the nature of the SEE Project, a multiple case studies with an ethnographic action research design was considered to be the most appropriate method (Tacchi, Slater, & Hearn, 2003; Thomas, 2007). The school principal is the "case" in this case study. The context provides an ethnographic insight into how the principal navigates through the school culture to facilitate technology integration that can develop teachers' TPACK. Tacchi et al. (2003) proposed four key questions on action research. These were used to develop these subquestions:

(a) What is the principal's technology background? (b) What procedure(s) did the principal follow to facilitate technology integration? (c) What are some of successes/challenges associated with the principal's initiatives in terms of developing teachers' TPACK?

A number of different strategies were used to gather data. My visits to the school enabled me to gather field notes and conduct conversational interviews with the principal. These sources together with reports and a survey completed by the principal triangulated the data. The content analysis method was used to analyze the data. I read and reread the data sources before it was coded. The codes were grouped to identify the key themes (Tacchi et al., 2003).

Krishna's Technology Background

School leadership and teachers' attitudes and beliefs play a significant role in making technology integration possible (e.g., Hew & Brush, 2007). A school principal is both a teacher and a leader. How a principal responds to technology integration depends on his/her attitudes and beliefs, which in turn is influenced by his/her background.

Krishna began his career in a school that had 40 computers that were only for students studying specific subjects (e.g., office management, typing). The school also had a lecture theatre with a data projector and it catered to 250 students. The provision of these resources made this school unique and one of the leaders in technology-supported learning in Fiji. The teachers were not allowed to use the computers, so the school typist acted like an interface between the teachers and the computer. She did what the teachers wanted done (e.g., type exam papers). Krishna could only use the computers when he was given the task of editing the school magazine. However, from time to time he was able to get his drama classes into the lecture theatre. This led "to a small change in my teaching—it enabled me to change my strategies to involve students and move away from 'chalk and talk' teaching with the teacher being on stage for 100% of the lesson."

Krishna later moved to another school where there were two desktop computers in his staff room for teacher use. He began "typing lesson notes, current affairs quiz questions and started using Microsoft PowerPoint and Publisher." Working with students, he produced the school's newsletters. All these opportunities had a positive impact on him. "My interest grew as I could see the potential of computers from an educational perspective." However, he could not access the computers in the staff rooms after hours because "the management made a rule that the school gates will close at 4:00 pm each day and will not open on weekends." Therefore, the teachers were locked out. Consequently, he had to buy his own desktop (20GB hard disk, 256 MB RAM, DVD writer, 15" CRT screen). Krishna later purchased his own cameras (still and digital), and these gave him opportunities to explore the technologies even further. He became passionate about moviemaking. He engaged his students, who earned awards in local short film competitions. Krishna developed his knowledge of the Adobe Suite. This enabled him to work with his staff and students to produce a school magazine. All these experiences had an impact on Krishna. He strongly believes that "children love ICT, and they have more to offer when ICT is used in the learning process."

There were no technology courses in Krishna's teacher training program. His knowledge and understanding developed through his own initiatives as he dabbled with technology.

Most importantly, he engaged his students along the way as well. Krishna's proactive engagement with technology over time enabled him to see the value it can add to the teaching and learning process. It was also evident that these experiences had a positive influence on his attitudes and beliefs towards technology.

Krishna's Approach to Advancing the Technology Agenda

When Krishna became the principal at Smart High School, his immediate challenge was to implement strategies that would arrest the dwindling student enrollment figures. Students were opting to enroll in neighboring schools because Smart High School lacked innovation and variety in terms of teaching and learning opportunities:

> There was a need to market the school. . . . With my interest in ICT and knowing that other schools in the district did not focus on ICT, we prepared a list of 10 key development areas to market the school to improve enrolment . . . at the top of the list was the integration of ICT. . . . We wanted to modernize education and focus on student centred learning at the school.

For this strategy to be implemented, Krishna had to undertake the following tasks to transform his vision to reality:

1. Convince the School Management Board

Like all schools in Fiji, Smart High School has a management board. The members of these boards are stakeholders because they have a significant input into the management and directions of school policies (Hollows, 2010). However, they have varied educational, professional, and experiential backgrounds. Therefore, principals need to understand their backgrounds and then clearly articulate their vision and rationale about school reform at an appropriate level (Mitchell & Sackney, 2000). Such an approach can have a significant impact on the longevity and success of new initiatives (Nyika et al., 2010). The "management board members had little knowledge of ICT." Consequently, this new and innovative approach to learning "did not make much sense." For the management board members, the only expectation in terms of learning outcomes was "good results in external exams"—this is part of the school culture in Fiji. Through dialogue and active engagement in the technology integration process, the management team was convinced. Krishna took time to demonstrate the value of ICT though hands-on engagement. This facilitated their understanding of the technology. As a consequence, they supported many of his decisions on technology integration.

2. Set the Learning Environment to Acquire and Accommodate the Resources

The physical environment is important for technology-driven reforms. When Krishna started at the school, he realized that in terms of the physical space for computer labs, there were no problems because there were rooms that could be remodeled for this purpose. However, there were only eight computers and three were relatively old. Internet connectivity to the school was poor. Limited funding was available for paying Internet bills and computer repairs. There were no additional funds for purchasing new computers. Severe floods and cyclones are relatively common in Fiji. At the start of Krishna's tenure, Smart High School was extensively damaged in a cyclone, resulting in four rooms that needed extensive repairs. In order to get the school operations back to normal, repair of the buildings was a priority and this drained the school's financial resources even further.

The school did not have the financial capability to purchase new or secondhand computers and accessories. It is important to highlight that more than 95% of the schools in Fiji are run and managed by the local communities and religious organizations. There is a huge divide in the income and lifestyles of urban and rural dwellers (Narsey, 2012). Given the financial position of the parents, they could not be approached for donations to buy the technology. One of the few alternatives that Krishna had was to approach external donor agencies. The SEE Project initially supported the school with ten laptops and a data projector (all secondhand), with the school meeting the cost of freight. The Ubuntu/Edubuntu operating system was installed on the machines. A YouTube video (https://www.youtube.com/watch?v=AmqUXZL4NNI) was created and this enabled the installation of the Edubuntu image to occur at the school with ease. One of requirements of the SEE Project is that the recipients provide feedback on how the resources are used and how they are impacting classroom activities. Krishna's feedback on how the laptops were used was very encouraging (http://theseeproject.org/2014/01/27/2014-a-story-of-success-at-balata-high-school/). This led to the donations of more laptops, desktops, data projectors, and digital video cameras. At the start of Krishna's tenure, the school had a student to computer ratio of 1:30. Through the partnership with the SEE Project, this ratio dropped to 1:4.

Over time, existing spaces in the school buildings were remodeled to accommodate the new technologies. Students enrolled in vocational education courses at the school built security screens for the rooms. Two new spaces—a computer lab and media room—were created with appropriate electrical and networking capability. A part of the building was renovated to create a new teachers' staff room, where teachers could readily access computers.

3. Convince Teachers to Embrace Technology

The success of school reforms is dependent upon how teachers embrace and implement the opportunities that technology presents to them. They are the most significant stakeholders in terms of technology-related reforms (Hollows, 2010). Their knowledge, attitudes, beliefs, success, and values can have a significant influence on how ICT is integrated (Chandra & Mills, 2014; Starkey, 2010; Wozney, Venkatesh, & Abrami, 2006). Krishna had a number of challenges as he grappled with his vision of technology integration. One of the core issues was that some "teachers had hardly used computers and more than 50% of the teachers were not computer literate." Others saw ICT integration as an added workload. A number of strategies were put in place to advance the technology agenda:

a) A policy was drafted for technology integration. As part of this policy, teachers had to take students to the computer lab at least once a week and they had to provide written reports and evidence of technology use in students' assignments and classroom tasks.
b) In-house professional development workshops (led by Krishna) were offered to the teachers after school.
c) In order to acknowledge teachers' work, the school provided Internet access and refreshments during many of the professional development sessions.
d) The school's Academic Committee designed a criterion for identifying the technology teacher of the month as a way to encourage and motivate the teachers.

Despite the implementation of these strategies, a number of other new challenges emerged. There were times when other activities got in the way. This either disrupted the existing routines or prevented some of the teachers from participating in technology-related activities; also, even after participating in professional development activities, some teachers were still either shy, frightened, or challenged and did not use technology in their classrooms. Prestridge (2012) investigated teacher beliefs ($n = 48$) and their use of ICT and reported that teachers do not need to possess high levels of ICT competency before they have the confidence to use it in their classrooms. However, some teachers perceive competency and confidence differently. They believe that a high level of technology competency is a prerequisite to embedding technology effectively in classroom activities. Such fear of inadequacy leads to avoidance of using technology. This was possibly the case with some teachers at Smart High School.

The new initiatives also facilitated the emergence of the ICT champions (OECD, n.d.). These teachers were "very dedicated and gave their reports on time. They also put in extra hours to do research and prepare for lessons. In addition they trained other teachers at the Smart High School and surrounding schools." It was evident that their positive attitudes and beliefs towards technology were likely to not only influence their own practices, but that they also became catalysts for change in their peers. Such teachers can "intentionally make thing(s) happen" through their "own actions" (Bandura, 2001, p. 2). This in turn impacts positively on their behavior in the classroom.

Developing Teachers' TPACK: Challenges and Successes

The Ubuntu operating system initially presented a challenge, as none of the teachers (who had computers) had used it before. However, the professional development workshops that were conducted by Krishna made a difference. They buoyed the knowledge and confidence of many teachers. As a consequence, "they were able to take at least one [40-minute] lesson a week in the Computer Lab." With 35 desktops in this lab, every child in class got a chance to use a computer. "The Vice Principal and Heads of Departments monitor these activities and they forward a monthly report with evidence of lesson plans and completed student tasks to me [Principal]." Of significance here is that for many children, computers are a wholly new experience. Given that nationally only 5% of the households in rural areas have computers (Narsey, 2012), in the student catchment area for Smart High School, the percentage of students who have computer access at home would be a lot lower. This applied to the teachers as well—few had access to a computer at home. Therefore, it was a giant leap to use a tool that they were unfamiliar with. For some it was too big a risk to take in front of their students.

Other strategies were also put in place. For example, the Year 13 (last year of high school, 18–19 year-old students) classroom has a data projector and each of the 21 students has access to a donated laptop. Teachers have uploaded external exam papers with solutions from the previous ten years in PDF format. According to Krishna, students go through these papers individually, in small groups, or as part of their classroom activities. Teachers who taught in the disciplines of home economics, industrial arts, and agriculture also started to video record their practical lessons. Teachers in the home economics department were working towards creating a database of local recipes. Some other teachers were using the technology in other creative ways to produce online quizzes, e-books, e-newsletters, newspapers, and MP3 music files with local content. A change fueled by technology was evident at Smart High School.

Lessons Learned from Krishna's Experiences

Krishna's engagement as a key driver within the context appears to have occurred at four levels. These have been identified as alpha, beta, gamma, and delta levels in Figure 15.1.

School principals are the gatekeepers of change. At the alpha level is the principal's background. His or her abilities and vision to innovate and lead the community can make or break school reform agendas. For this to occur, school leaders have to be excited about innovation and reforms themselves before they can invite others to be partners in such initiatives (OECD, n.d.; Stuart, Mills, & Remus, 2009). In the case of Smart High School, the role of Krishna in driving the technology agenda was crucial. He was excited about the reform because his prior experiences over many years had shown him the potential of technology. However, very few principals in the Fijian context (and possibly in other developing countries) can demonstrate this capability. There are limited opportunities for principals to be up skilled. Unless a principal is intrinsically motivated towards technology integration, reform is unlikely to happen.

At the beta level, school management boards have to be convinced about the reforms. Unless the school principal is excited and understands the rationale of technology integration, he or she is unlikely to convince the management with clear and concise messages. One of the strategies used by Krishna was to engage the members "hands-on" with the technologies. In the Fijian context, where many in the community do not have a good understanding of the technologies, this is a useful approach. It develops a partnership, which adds weight to the reform agenda. Success at this level enabled Krishna to convince the management to meet the cost of freight (from Australia) for transporting the donated technologies. He was also able to convince the school management board to remodel and renovate existing classrooms.

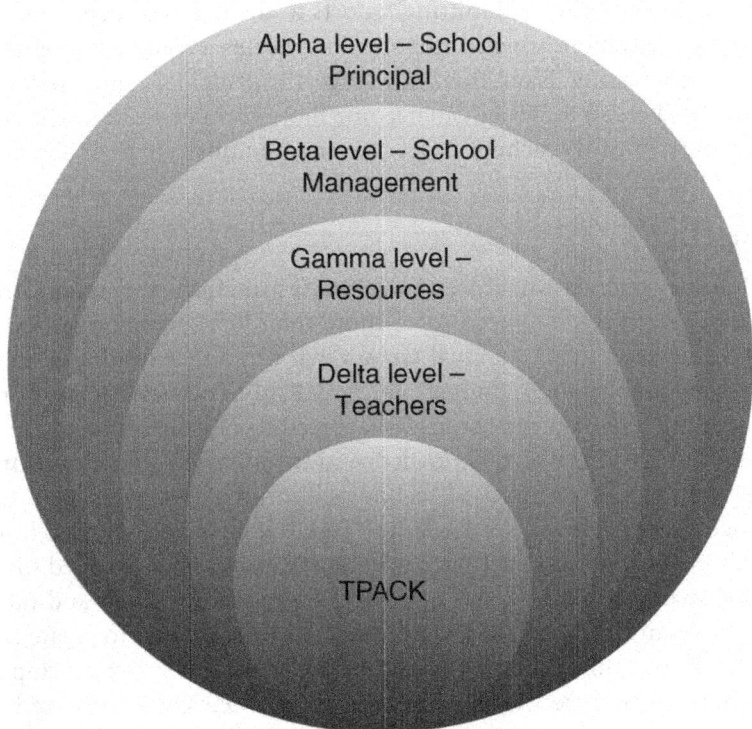

Figure 15.1 The Four Contextual Factors Influenced by the School Principal

The gamma level is about resources. Krishna's role at this level was crucial. He partnered with a donor and the school management to get technology to his school. This would otherwise not have been possible. Krishna did not have any influence on what was donated to his school. The equipment was all secondhand, with an operating system that even he was not familiar with. Yet he was able to improvise and optimize its use for teaching and learning purposes. Krishna's good knowledge of technology and his prior experiences were valuable here. His hands-on engagement was critical. According to Stuart, Mills, and Remus (2009), school leaders "need to be more practically involved in the ICT projects in their school and in ICT management" (p. 740). Such engagement will "not only enhance their ICT competence" (p. 740) but will provide opportunities for the leaders to be "role models to others in the use of ICT" (p. 740). Their conclusions were based on an investigation of school leaders in New Zealand (n = 64).

A principal's ability to be a role model for his teachers is important at the delta level. At Smart High School, Krishna acts as a good role model, and this has a positive influence on his staff. He developed strategies to support the teachers through professional development, which he conducted himself. Such proactive action builds confidence in teachers because they know that they have an expert who is on site and someone they can lean on. He set clear and doable goals for the teachers, such as mandating teachers to conduct lessons in the computer lab and then submitting reports to the heads of department and the vice principal, which are then submitted to him. This creates a feedback loop that shows how the initiative is progressing. From this knowledge, the principal can then develop strategies to support the teachers so that they can become more competent in teaching with technology. This sets the scene for teachers to develop and demonstrate their TPACK.

Conclusion

For the technology agenda to succeed in schools, principals and school leaders need to become more proactive—they need to be more than just spectators. They play a significant role in influencing the contextual factors that can either hinder or support teachers to teach with technology and demonstrate TPACK in their classrooms. For principals to exert a positive influence on the context, they need to not only understand the potential of technology, but also have some knowledge of having used it in classrooms. There was strong evidence that as Krishna used technologies in his classrooms as a teacher, he not only developed his technological knowledge (TK), but he got a chance to immerse himself in different facets of the TPACK framework. For example, he developed his technological pedagogical knowledge (TPK) as his approach shifted from "chalk and talk" teaching to using a data projector. He used cameras and related technologies to create content-related movies. In the process, his technological content knowledge (TCK) developed further.

Principals need such experiences, because it buoys their confidence and they can then influence school management boards, teachers, and donor agencies, as was the case in this investigation. It also enables them to understand the resources that teachers need to teach with technology. However, in many developing countries, principals with Krishna's background and leadership qualities are rare. Thus, before any attempt is made to integrate technology in schools, principals need to be "educated" first. Professional development should be structured in a way that immerses a principal in hands-on activities in much the same way as Krishna dabbled with technology. Thus, through this immersion, they need to develop technology-based classroom activities and implement these themselves. Such an experience will give them a true appreciation of what TPACK entails. This in turn will enable principals to engage with all the key contextual factors, including school management, resources, and teachers.

References

Bandura, A. (2001). Social cognitive theory: An agentic perspective. *Annual Review of Psychology, 52*(1), 1–26.

Chandra, V., Chandra, R., & Nutchey, D. (2014) Implementing ICT in schools in a developing country: A Fijian experience. In H. Kaur & X. Tao (Eds.), *ICTs and the millennium development goals: A United Nations perspective* (pp. 139–159). New York: Springer US.

Chandra, V., & Mills, K. A. (2014). Transforming the core business of teaching and learning in classrooms through ICT. *Technology, Pedagogy and Education, 24*(3), 285–301.

Hew, K., & Brush, T. (2007). Integrating technology into K–12 teaching and learning: Current knowledge gaps and recommendations for future research. *Educational Technology Research and Development, 55*(3), 223–252.

Hollows, D. (2010). Evaluating ICT for education in Africa. Retrieved from http://pure.rhul.ac.uk/portal/files/1773319/DavidHollowThesisFinalCopy.pdf

Kincheloe, J. L. (2008). *Critical pedagogy primer*. New York: Peter Lang.

Mishra, P., & Koehler, M. J. (2006). Technological pedagogical content knowledge: A framework for teacher knowledge. *Teachers College Record, 108*(6), 1017–1054.

Mishra, P., & Koehler, M. J. (2007). Technological pedagogical content knowledge (TPCK): Confronting the wicked problems of teaching with technology. In C. Crawford et al. (Eds.), *Proceedings of Society for Information Technology and Teacher Education International Conference 2007* (pp. 2214-2226). Chesapeake, VA: Association for the Advancement of Computing in Education.

Mitchell, C., & Sackney, L. (2000). *Profound improvement: Building capacity for a learning community*. Lisse, NL: Swets & Zeitlinger.

Narsey, W. L. (2012). Poverty in Fiji: Changes 2002–03 to 2008–09 and policy implications. Retrieved from http://researchonline.jcu.edu.au/23801/1/Poverty_in_Fiji.pdf

Nyika, A., et al. (2010). Engaging diverse communities participating in clinical trials: Case examples from across Africa. Retrieved from http://www.malariajournal.com/content/pdf/1475-2875-9-86.pdf

OECD. (n.d.). ICT in innovative schools: Case studies of change and impacts. Retrieved from http://www.oecd.org/site/schoolingfortomorrowknowledgebase/themes/ict/41187025.pdf

Prestridge, S. (2012). The beliefs behind the teacher that influences their ICT practices. *Computers & Education, 58*(1), 449–458.

Porras-Hernandez, L. H., & Salinas-Amescua, B. (2013). Strengthening TPACK: A broader notion of context and the use of teacher's narratives to reveal knowledge construction. *Journal of Educational Computing Research, 48*(2), 223–244.

Rosenberg, J., & Koehler, M. (2014). Context and technological pedagogical content knowledge: A content analysis. In M. Searson & M. Ochoa (Eds.), *Proceedings of Society for Information Technology & Teacher Education International Conference 2014* (pp. 2626-2631). Chesapeake, VA: Association for the Advancement of Computing in Education.

Starkey, L. (2010). Teachers' pedagogical reasoning and action in the digital age. *Teachers and Teaching: Theory and Practice, 16*(2), 233–244.

Stuart, L. H., Mills, A.M., & Remus, U. (2009). School leaders, ICT competence and championing innovations. *Computers & Education, 53*(3), 733–741.

Tacchi, J. A., Slater, D., & Hearn, G. N. (2003). *Ethnographic action research: A user's handbook*. New Delhi, India: UNESCO.

Thomas, D. R. (2007). A general inductive approach for analyzing qualitative evaluation data. *American Journal of Evaluation, 27*(2), 237–246.

Wozney, L., Venkatesh, V., & Abrami, P. (2006). Implementing computer technologies: Teachers' perceptions and practices. *Journal of Technology and Teacher Education, 14*(1), 173–207.

16

Making Meaningful Advances
TPACK for Designers of Learning Tools

Karin Forssell

New Tools for Learning

Before teachers can use new digital tools in the classroom, designers must create those tools. Aspiring designers in the field of education technology are typically eager to make a big impact on the experience of future students by designing tools that enhance learning. It is crucial that they leverage teacher knowledge to enable their vision. In this chapter, I argue that the Technological Pedagogical Content Knowledge (TPACK) of teachers informs the core interactions and substance of successful learning tools. Attending to the domains in the TPACK framework helps designers articulate their goals and suggests indicators of whether the design is on the path to success. Ultimately, using the TPACK framework increases the likelihood that technology designers will produce tools for learning that teachers will choose to use.

Choosing to Use New Tools

Researchers have sought to identify critical factors that contribute to the intention to use new tools in work settings. The most salient factors in the technology adoption model (TAM) are that a tool be perceived as both *useful* and *easy to use* (Venkatesh & Davis, 2000). Knezek and Christensen's (2008) "will, skill, and tool" model captures similar constructs, where seeing the tool as useful is akin to *will* and ease of use maps onto *skill*. They further point out that not all teachers have ready access to tools. Zhao and Cziko (2001) identify positive and negative sides of usefulness, when they propose three necessary conditions for teachers to use technology:

- The teacher must believe that technology can more effectively meet a higher-level goal than what has been used.

- The teacher must believe that using technology will not cause disturbances to other higher-level goals that he or she thinks are more important than the one being maintained.
- The teacher must believe that he or she has or will have sufficient ability and resources to use technology (p. 6).

Although technology has made possible some real advances in education, all too many of the new, digital tools teachers encounter are not perceived as useful or do not improve on current practices. Many are unreliable or difficult to use. Others are not designed for the needs or constraints of the school or classroom. Teachers frequently repurpose tools that were designed for other tasks.

There is a great need for tools that are designed to address the real instructional problems that educators find difficult to solve, but designing them well is a challenge. To increase the likelihood that a learning tool will be successful in schools, designers must gain insight into teachers' goals, constraints, and assets. Informed by teachers, they can uncover opportunities in the form of unmet needs and possibilities presented by new technologies.

Designing for Schools

There are abundant opportunities to design new tools that will help students and teachers, in part because technologies are always changing and in part because the needs are great, with a wide variety of learners, levels, topics, approaches, and conditions. Koehler and Mishra (2008) call teaching with technology a "wicked problem" as defined by Rittel and Webber (1973). Such problems are fraught with interdependent and ever-changing variables. Making a similar argument, Cuban (2013) argues that there is a difference between "complicated" and "complex" systems. While complicated systems have many parts and require leadership, knowledge, and resources, complex systems are all that and also decentralized and dynamic. Schools fall into the latter category (p. 156). When the teacher and student change over time or as a result of interacting with the tool, the design task presents further challenges (Peters, 2014).

Embracing this complexity opens the doors to a great many opportunities to create meaningful new educational technologies. Once designers accept that "the formulation of a wicked problem is the problem!" (Rittel & Webber, 1973, p. 161), they embrace the task of understanding the many players and their ever-shifting realities in schools. The preeminent approach to human–computer interface design, the "human-centered" approach, is "centered on the exploration of new forms of living with and through technologies that give primacy to human actors, their values, and their activities" (Bannon, 2011, p. 50). Such exploration is especially important in designing for schools. Designers have spent years as students, observing teachers at work. Yet this "apprenticeship of observation" (Lortie, 1975, p. 61) provides little insight into the decisions that teachers make about when, whether, and why they employ a particular tool for learning in class.

Working closely with teachers, designers can uncover opportunities in the form of unmet needs and the possibilities presented by new technologies. Teachers can play several different roles in this design process, providing inspiration, features, feedback, edits, and information about enactment of lessons (Cober, Tan, Slotta, So, & Könings, 2015). Participating in this way can have very positive implications for the teachers involved, as well as their students (Cviko, McKenney, & Voogt, 2014). Designers must be aware, however, that teachers are experience designers. When the finished tool is in the classroom, teachers will redesign the technology-enhanced learning (TEL) experiences, which the tool is meant to enable, as needed for their situation (Matuk, Linn, & Eylon, 2015; McKenney, Kali, Markauskaite, & Voogt, 2015). Respecting this role of teachers, tool designers must consider how teachers might use it to realize their goals for their students, to increase the likelihood that the new learning technology will be chosen over other tools.

Using the TPACK framework to guide design helps to keep the use of technology closely tied to the work of teachers. From the beginning, research around the TPACK framework has been closely aligned with co-design with teachers (Mishra & Koehler, 2006), and design activities are often employed in TPACK assessment (Koehler, Shin, & Mishra, 2012). In a recent review, Chai and colleagues note the potential for the framework to guide software development (Chai, Koh, & Tsai, 2013), an idea that has begun to be explored in practice (e.g., Wong, Chai, Zhang, & King, 2014; Wu, Chen, Wang, & Su, 2008). The purpose of this chapter is to articulate the specific contributions of the TPACK framework to the technology design process, encouraging more informed design efforts. In the next section, I illustrate how the knowledge of teachers as organized by the TPACK framework can inform the design of valuable new learning tools.

Looking Through the TPACK Lens

The TPACK framework directs our attention to different design goals and measures of success, inspiring features of the final tool that make it useful in the classroom. To illustrate, I present the examples of "Catherine" and "Gina," two teachers who participated in a study of teachers' choices in using new technologies for teaching. Both were middle school teachers (grades 8 and 7, respectively) with more than a dozen years of classroom experience who had taken on leadership roles within their respective schools. Both worked in a community with high levels of computer access in homes and at school. However, they differed in that Catherine described herself as "low-tech," while Gina was an eager adopter of new digital methods.

Designers may use a variety of tools to understand and observe the people they seek to serve. The examples presented here were gathered through observations of the schools and classrooms; interviews focused on the teachers' goals and definitions of "good teaching"; their technobiographies (Barron, 2006); and their responses to hypothetical scenarios. For the purposes of design, it is productive to take a broad view of the "will" and "skill" (Knezek & Christensen, 2008) that contribute to teaching with new tools. Beliefs, attitudes, and orientation are closely linked to technology use in classrooms (Ertmer & Ottenbreit-Leftwich, 2010; Hermans, Tondeur, van Braak, & Valcke, 2008). Therefore, I include beliefs and pedagogical orientation in my examination of teachers' knowledge. Other chapters of this handbook provide examples of additional methods that can be used to uncover relevant teacher knowledge.

Knowledge of Context

Much relevant information about the context in which a potential learning tool would be implemented can be found online or observed relatively quickly in the classroom. It is helpful for designers to know, for example, the size of the school; the levels of language proficiency among students; how many minutes of instruction are available for a given activity; what types of devices and platforms are available and familiar; and the funding structures that make new tools available. Other relevant information may include existing infrastructure, such as wireless Internet access, reservation processes, and user authentication systems; the level of resources available in students' homes; or parents' orientations toward acceptable amounts of so-called "screen time."

The TPACK framework, however, considers context as teacher knowledge. A teacher knows how the funding structures, parental pressures, or authentication systems affect her decisions in the classroom. Culture and policies can impact how, when, or where particular devices will be used. Looking through the lens of teacher knowledge of context reminds the designer to dig deep into the interactions that at first might not be visible, learning how contextual factors interact with the teacher's choices about what tools to use, for what purposes.

Constraints can be generative in providing guidelines for the design challenge. For the designer, context is essentially answering the questions: What are some of the boundaries of the design challenge and the solution space? How applicable is this solution to other teachers or students? Ultimately, the answers will identify potential populations who would find a particular tool useful, beyond the individuals contributing to the initial design. The degree to which those populations are served by the tool will constitute a measure of its success.

Knowledge of Technology

The designer of learning tools may be well informed about existing and emerging technologies and may possibly be more knowledgeable than the teachers she is designing for. Nevertheless, leveraging teachers' knowledge of technology (TK) plays an important role in designing for classroom adoption.

A well-designed tool should reach the majority of teachers, not just the "early adopters" (Rogers, 2003). Therefore, it is important to understand what "low-tech" teachers know and do. The example of Catherine is illustrative. When asked about her use of technology outside of work, she first indicated she didn't use it:

> I'm sure a lot of why I don't do stuff more with technology is just because I don't know it myself, I'm not . . . I don't use it myself at home. I mean . . . we just got our HDTV the other day, and I don't want to try and figure it out. Somebody else do it. Don't even talk to me about it.

But later Catherine shared that she did have experience using her computer at home:

> I use [my home computer] for iPhoto, I use it for Google stuff, I have a couple little blogs that I like to read, not too many . . . We use it for like when we're planning vacation . . . oh, e-mail! Too much!

Close attention to teacher knowledge of technology is motivated by the hope that the technology will cease to become an object to be learned in itself. Experiences with other tools provide many suggestions for making new tools easier to use. Prior experience with similar tools facilitates intuitive interactions and lowers the barrier to learning (Blackler, Popovic, & Mahar, 2010). Familiarity may help to explain why recent learning management systems (LMSs) that leverage the look and feel of familiar social media such as Facebook have seen rapid adoption (Empson, 2012). When tools look familiar, transferring interaction patterns from similar tools becomes intuitive. The teachers and students may also perceive the usefulness of the tool from the design of its interface, understanding the types of activities it is meant to facilitate. This lowers the amount of time spent on training for both teachers and students, freeing up time to focus on the learning activities. A successful design will be recognized by the ease with which a wide range of teachers and students can engage with it.

Technology in the Service of Pedagogy

Knowledge of pedagogy—the practice of teaching—plays an important role in the design of new learning tools. The pedagogical knowledge (PK) of teachers includes the goals of schooling or education, strategies for organization and management of the classroom, developmental levels and capabilities of students, and special challenges or needs that must be addressed. Designers can mine these insights for opportunities for technology to support valuable pedagogical interactions (generating technological pedagogical knowledge, or TPK). When creating digital tools for classroom use, designers must look for ways in which they can provide valuable activity, management, and organizational support.

Gina provides an illustrative example of the interaction between pedagogy and technology use. When asked about her access to computers in her classroom, she reflected that she often preferred to have two students working together on one computer while watching videos.

> I could fudge the scheduling so I could get two laptop carts, but I think maybe working in pairs is better. One student saying to the other "I need to pause" is great . . . I think even if I could get enough computers I'd still do it in pairs.

Gina wanted her students to monitor their own learning and to self-advocate when they needed more time to process. A self-paced pair activity using the computer became an opportunity to put the responsibility for learning and communication into the hands of learners.

New technologies can introduce problems, however, making it harder to use digital tools than to continue with existing analog practices. Catherine was frustrated by the loss of instructional time when going to a computer room and by the lack of control she felt over the storage of digital files. When asked about her use of computers, she explained,

> And to go to the computer lab . . . I just don't want to do all that. You know, sign up for it, and take the kids there, and you lose 10 minutes. And you lose 10 minutes at the end. And yuck, maybe I just don't feel like I can manage it as well as I should . . . they lose things on the computer, and they don't save it, and it just drives me crazy.

For Catherine, taking the students to the computer lab means disrupting key organizational and managerial functions in the classroom workflow. The designer needs to address the perception of wasted time and effort. This might take the form of software that saves students work automatically and documents progress in a form visible to the teacher, or an activity designed to be accessed on a limited number of computers at an activity center within the classroom. Success would be indicated when the perceived risks are less than the perceived advantages of the interactions that the tool facilitates.

In both these examples, focusing on the pedagogical knowledge of teachers helps designers find ways to create technology-based tools that add valuable interaction patterns in the classroom. The pedagogical examples above suggest features that are valuable to teachers, but they are not specific to any particular content. To build only "content-free" tools is to miss a huge opportunity for impact on learning. It is productive to focus specifically on teachers' content knowledge as well.

Technology Connecting to Content

The topic or concept that is the focus of any given lesson is part of a larger subject area being taught. The content knowledge of teachers (CK) includes the major questions and approaches to understanding the subject, the nature of argument and controversies in the field, and how the target learning fits in the overall landscape of the discipline.

Further, technological developments have led to new tools, representations, and data, which have impacted practices and knowledge in the field (represented by technological content knowledge, or TCK). When documenting her use of technology across time and settings in her technobiography, Gina shared, "After college, my first job . . . I used a device that would count the number of cells that had a fluorescent marker on them, a flow cytometer it was called." She also made several mentions of the importance of visualizing phenomena in her reflections on teaching science. This theme of "making the invisible visible" appears often in the history of scientific progress. A designer might leverage this theme to design a learning tool that helps students "see" scientific concepts in powerful new ways.

It is important that designers understand the ways in which technologies afford or constrain the representation of specific ideas. Both content knowledge and technological content knowledge can serve to identify opportunities for learning tools to create connections between the target learning activity and the larger academic field. By focusing on content, the designer identifies ideas that serve as catalysts for relevant learning tools. Tools that successfully leverage content knowledge will use technology to provide powerful representations and exploration of content, building bridges between student learning and expert practice in the field.

Extending Pedagogical Content Knowledge Through Technology

In the late 1980s, Shulman argued that there is a professional knowledge of teachers that is neither pedagogy nor content, but rather "that special amalgam of content and pedagogy" that represents "an understanding of how particular topics, problems, or issues are organized, represented, and adapted to the diverse interests and abilities of learners, and presented for instruction" (1987, p. 8). Many scholars have since explored pedagogical content knowledge (PCK), discussing what it might include, how it can be measured, and how it impacts practice. The knowledge, beliefs, and orientations of teachers have been examined, as have strategies for instruction and assessment (Magnusson, Krajcik, & Borko, 1999). This research has served to describe many ways in which teachers provide key support to students' developing understanding of topics and concepts. The discourse around the Technological Pedagogical Content Knowledge (TPACK) framework has addressed the ways in which new technologies can be used to enhance and extend the pursuit of the same goal.

In working with teachers, the designer is looking for existing teaching strategies (evidence of PCK) that can be incorporated into the design of a new tool, as well as opportunities to extend, enhance, or create new learning experiences through the use of technologies (leveraging TPACK). Designers derive key insights into how to support the development of content knowledge through effective instructional activities and assessments. For example, when interviewed about how she had grown as a teacher over time, Catherine shared,

> Now I let them create their [reading response] questions. . . . They ask fantastic questions and if some of their questions are not as deep as maybe something I would have asked, that's okay. That just tells me where they are as readers, and I can encourage them to maybe ask deeper questions.

This could inspire a designer to create a tool that prompted students to ask questions, allowing the teacher to view them and gain insight into students' thinking. The teacher could then engage the student or class in conversation, or the tool might let a teacher respond digitally outside of class time.

Needs that cannot easily be met with teachers' current tools are also often generative for designers. For example, Catherine explained,

> Why did I want them to write it by hand? Because I think that for many of them, the act of typing becomes more important to them than what they're saying. . . . their typing can't keep up with their thinking almost.

Catherine resolved this tension by having her students turn in a hand-written first draft of each assignment. Using this comment as a starting place, a designer might look for technologies that would allow students to capture their initial ideas at the speed of thought, such that they could revise or expand them more fully later. Alternatively, a designer might explore ways of making typing easier for children. Even one short comment such as this can lead to multiple design opportunities.

The practices of high-TPACK teachers can also provide examples of how to use new technologies to enhance learning of content. Creative repurposing of existing tools can inspire features of new tools. When explaining how she used technology to engage her students with content, Gina stated,

> I used to use Brain-Pop cartoons for a quick wrap-up. But then I decided to have them answer questions based on the content of the video. I made them work in pairs, and turn on the closed-captioning [to keep noise levels down]. If they didn't get it, they had to pause. And then, Hello! The students are now in control of their own learning. They stop when they're confused, not when I think they're confused, or when I see someone else in the classroom looks confused. The students are so much farther along with getting it.

Gina's creative use of video controls prompts designers to consider including features such as scrubbing and subtitles, supporting interactions that are difficult or impossible without the use of technology.

A final example comes from Catherine. Despite her initially hesitant attitude toward the use of digital technologies, she had applied for a grant to fund a class set of digital cameras. She explained that

> it would be a fun way for them to do some authentic writing that was meaningful to them, because it would be about them . . . You usually write better, write more effectively, if you write about what you know. So if they're taking pictures of their world, and then writing about a picture that they took, chances are they would be better pieces of writing.

This example underscores the importance of attending to the paramount motivation for the use of a new tool in the classroom: better student outcomes. The key is to leverage teachers' knowledge of powerful ways to enhance learning. Whereas other parts of the TPACK framework focus on scale, usability, organization, and connections to content, this domain prompts the question: "How can technology help students *learn*?" A successful tool will be recognized by its contribution to student learning of content.

Making Meaningful Advances

Gawande (2002), writing about professional development for doctors, reflects on the importance of adopting new techniques to ensure the best care: "To fail to adopt new techniques would mean denying patients meaningful medical advances" (p. 26). Similarly, some might argue that teachers who fail to adopt new learning tools are denying students the best possible education. Before we demand that teachers adopt new tools, however, we must ensure that the tools make a meaningful contribution to teachers' work with students.

For teachers to choose to use a learning tool, they need to see it as serving a useful purpose and easy enough to use for teaching. A new tool is more likely to be both useful and usable if the designer has leveraged the knowledge of teachers to inform the design. The TPACK framework focuses the designer's efforts on key questions:

- Knowledge of Context: How likely is it that a tool will meet the needs of a range of target learners? Leveraging teachers' knowledge of how their specific contexts impact technology use can help designers gauge where or under what conditions a tool will be successful.
- Knowledge of Technology: How can a new tool be made easy to use? Building on the tools that teachers already know can minimize the learning required to use a new tool.
- Knowledge of Pedagogy and Technological Pedagogical Knowledge: How might a new tool support existing or new interaction patterns in learning activities? How might technology be used to provide opportunities to manage the work of the classroom? By understanding how teachers orchestrate the interplay of students and materials, designers can provide tools that facilitate valuable interactions.
- Knowledge of Content and Technological Content Knowledge: How do the topics or concepts addressed by new tools connect to other subject area content? Are there opportunities to leverage the specialized tools used in the field to inspire meaningful experiences for the classroom? Designers can build bridges that make learning the target content more relevant.
- Pedagogical Content Knowledge and Technological Pedagogical Content Knowledge (TPACK): How can designers leverage teachers' knowledge of how to support student learning of content? How might new technologies help learning activities become more efficient, effective, or creative? Focusing on these knowledge domains helps designers create tools that support students' learning outcomes.

Each part of the TPACK framework contributes a unique perspective on what it is important for designers to know and do. Across all of these areas, the goal is to design tools that employ new technologies in ways that teachers and students will find valuable.

The questions above provide an additional benefit in that they imply successful outcomes of using that tool. Designers can look for evidence of success on these dimensions all along the development process. By the same token, this becomes a list by which teachers and administrators can describe the desired effect of tools used in the classroom. Will it serve students in a school like ours? Will it be easy for our teachers and students to use? Does it support desirable interactions without creating new problems? How does the tool connect content to the larger subject area discipline? How might it lead to learning?

Not every tool will address every one of these questions or leverage all the domains of teacher knowledge in the TPACK framework. In those cases, the framework helps designers explain where they seek to make a contribution. For designers of tools aimed at enhancing learning, however, attending to all the knowledge domains in the TPACK framework enables designs that make a significant impact. By identifying ways for tools to be useful and easy to use, this approach increases the opportunities for designers to create learning tools that make meaningful advances.

References

Bannon, L. (2011). Reimagining HCI: Toward a more human-centered perspective. *Interactions, 18*(4), 50–57.

Barron, B. (2006). Interest and self-sustained learning as catalysts of development: A learning ecologies perspective. *Human Development, 49*, 193–224.

Blackler, A., Popovic, V., & Mahar, D. (2010). Investigating users' intuitive interaction with complex artefacts. *Applied Ergonomics, 41*(1), 72–92.

Chai, C. S., Koh, J.H.L., & Tsai, C. C. (2013). A review of technological pedagogical content knowledge. *Educational Technology & Society, 16*(2), 31–51.

Cober, R., Tan, E., Slotta, J., So, H. J., & Könings, K. D. (2015). Teachers as participatory designers: Two case studies with technology-enhanced learning environments. *Instructional Science*, 203–228.

Cuban, L. (2013). *Inside the black box of classroom practice: Change without reform in American education*. Cambridge, MA: Harvard Education Press.

Cviko, A., McKenney, S., & Voogt, J. (2014). Teacher roles in designing technology-rich learning activities for early literacy: A cross-case analysis. *Computers & Education, 72*, 68–79.

Empson, R. (2012). 1M users strong, Schoology grabs $6M to take on Blackboard, Moodle. *TechCrunch*. Retrieved in April 2012 from http://techcrunch.com/2012/04/16/schoology-series-b/

Ertmer, P. A., & Ottenbreit-Leftwich, A. T. (2010). Teacher technology change: How knowledge, confidence, beliefs, and culture intersect. *Journal of Research on Technology in Education, 42*(3), 255–284.

Gawande, A. (2002). *Complications: A surgeon's notes on an imperfect science*. New York: Metropolitan Books.

Hermans, R., Tondeur, J., van Braak, J., & Valcke, M. (2008). The impact of primary school teachers' educational beliefs on the classroom use of computers. *Computers & Education, 51*(4), 1499–1509.

Knezek, G., & Christensen, R. (2008). The importance of information technology attitudes and competencies in primary and secondary education. In J. Voogt & G. Knezek (Eds.), *International Handbook of Information Technology in Primary and Secondary Education* (pp. 321–331). New York: Springer US.

Koehler, M. J., & Mishra, P. (2008). Introducing TPCK. In AACTE (Ed.), *Handbook of technological pedagogical content knowledge (TPCK) for educators* (pp. 3–29). New York: Routledge.

Koehler, M. J., Shin, T. S., & Mishra, P. (2012). How do we measure TPACK? Let me count the ways. In R. Ronau, C. Rakes, & M. Niess (Eds.), *Educational technology, teacher knowledge, and classroom impact: A research handbook on frameworks and approaches* (pp. 16–31). Hershey, PA: Information Science Reference. doi:10.4018/978-1-60960-750-0.ch002

Lortie, D.C. (1975). *Schoolteacher: A sociological study*. Chicago: University of Chicago Press.

Magnusson, S., Krajcik, J., & Borko, H. (1999). Nature, sources, and development of pedagogical content knowledge for science teaching. In J. Gess-Newsome & N. G. Lederman (Eds.), *Examining pedagogical content knowledge* (pp. 95–132). Dordrecht, The Netherlands: Springer Netherlands.

Matuk, C. F., Linn, M. C., & Eylon, B. S. (2015). Technology to support teachers using evidence from student work to customize technology-enhanced inquiry units. *Instructional Science*, 229–257

McKenney, S., Kali, Y., Markauskaite, L., & Voogt, J. (2015). Teacher design knowledge for technology enhanced learning: An ecological framework for investigating assets and needs. *Instructional Science*, 181–202.

Mishra, P., & Koehler, M. J. (2006). Technological pedagogical content knowledge: A framework for teacher knowledge. *Teachers College Record, 108*, 1017–1054.

Peters, D. (2014). *Interface design for learning: Design strategies for learning experiences.* San Francisco, CA: New Riders.

Rittel, H. W., & Webber, M. M. (1973). Dilemmas in a general theory of planning. *Policy Sciences, 4*(2), 155–169.

Rogers, E. M. (2003). *Diffusion of innovations* (5th ed.). New York: Free Press.

Shulman, L. S. (1987). Knowledge and teaching: Foundations of the new reform. *Harvard Educational Review, 57*(1), 1–23.

Venkatesh, V., & Davis, F. D. (2000). A theoretical extension of the technology acceptance model: Four longitudinal field studies. *Management Science, 46*(2), 186–204.

Wong, L., Chai, C., Zhang, X., & King, R. (2014). Employing the TPACK framework for researcher-teacher co-design of a mobile-assisted seamless language learning environment. *IEEE Transactions on Learning Technologies, 8*(1), 31–42.

Wu, W. H., Chen, W. F., Wang, T. L., & Su, C. H. (2008). Developing and evaluating a game-based software engineering educational system. *International Journal of Engineering Education, 24*(4), 681–688.

Zhao, Y., & Cziko, G. A. (2001). Teacher adoption of technology: A perceptual control theory perspective. *Journal of Technology and Teacher Education, 9*(1), 5–30.

17

Designing Professional Development to Support Teachers' TPACK in Elementary School Mathematics

Drew Polly, Chandra Hawley Orrill

Leveraging Professional Development to Develop TPACK in Mathematics

Learner-Centered Professional Development

One approach to deepening teachers' TPACK is to provide rich professional development opportunities. Guidance for such professional development has been consistent over the past decade and a half in its call for learner-centered professional development (LCPD) approaches (Orrill, 2001; Polly & Hannafin, 2010; National Partnership for Education and Accountability in Teaching, 2000). LCPD approaches have potential to increase teachers' TPACK related to mathematics instruction. Based on the literature, LCPD approaches (a) focus teachers on addressing student learning deficiencies and carrying out a plan to address student learning (Loucks-Horsley, Stiles, Mundry, Love, & Hewson, 2009); (b) provide teachers with opportunities to choose learning activities and take ownership of professional development activities (Hawley & Valli, 2000); (c) promote collaboration among teachers and with related educational personnel (Loucks-Horsley et al., 2009); (d) provide ongoing and comprehensive learning opportunities (Heck, Banilower, Weiss, & Rosenberg, 2008); (e) deepen knowledge related to content, pedagogy, and the intersection of content and pedagogy (Jaquith, Mindich, Wei, & Darling-Hammond, 2010); and (f) support reflection of practice and student learning through the use of records of practice and student data (Garet, Porter, Desimone, Briman, & Yoon, 2001). In this chapter, we describe LCPD approaches that have been used to deepen teachers' TPACK related to their mathematics teaching.

One of the overarching characteristics of learner-centered professional development is its attention to the development of knowledge for teaching (Jaquith et al., 2010), which aligns closely to the TPACK model. Rather than focusing solely on the content knowledge a teacher needs or only the pedagogies teachers need to know, knowledge for teaching combines these two along with knowledge of how to put them together to create a meaningful learning environment (e.g., pedagogical content knowledge [PCK], Shulman, 1986). A small but growing body of research demonstrates that in mathematics, this specialized knowledge is both measurable and important for student performance (e.g., Baumert et al., 2010; Hill, Rowan, & Ball, 2005). A recent review of large-scale PD studies found that focusing on specialized content knowledge is one way to influence student achievement (Yoon, Duncan, Lee, Scarloss, & Shapley, 2007). This emphasis on knowledge for teaching and PCK means that learner-centered professional development approaches are fertile ground for exploring how these approaches can support teachers' development of TPACK as it relates to their mathematics teaching.

Learner-centered PD approaches are also socioculturally grounded, relying on communities of practice, lesson study, and other collaborative approaches that have been shown to promote school change rather than impacting only a single teacher's classroom (Darling-Hammond et al., 2009). Further, these and other learner-centered approaches are ongoing rather than short-lived workshop-based efforts. Such ongoing approaches have been demonstrated to generally be more effective for promoting change than shorter efforts (Yoon et al., 2007). Effective PD should address the everyday classroom needs of the teachers and model the desired practices for the teachers. This supports teachers in becoming increasingly precise about the kinds of concepts and skills they want their own students to know and understand (Darling-Hammond et al., 2009). After all, to effectively impact student learning, LCPD efforts should support teachers' efforts to apply new ideas into their teaching (Polly & Hannafin, 2010, 2011; Yoon et al., 2007). In terms of TPACK in mathematics, professional development efforts should support teachers' development and application of knowledge and skills related to technology, mathematics, and effective pedagogies.

Examining Approaches to Developing TPACK Related to Mathematics Teaching

In this section, we describe three learner-centered professional development approaches that we have employed in an effort to develop teachers' TPACK related to mathematics teaching. Our discussion of these approaches centers on the role of the technology. We chose this organization to highlight the differences in approaches to technology integration in supporting TPACK.

Fully Integrated Technology and Mathematics PD

In fully integrated technology PD, technology is used to support teachers in developing meaningful understandings of the mathematics content influencing multiple dimensions of TPACK. In this approach, participants are immersed as learners in a technology-rich environment. The discussions and activities related to their roles as teachers arise out of their own questions rather than being planned by a facilitator. The assumption of this approach is that teachers will engage in meaning-making through the technology and will use reflection on their own learning processes to generate questions about teaching in this way.

The NSF-supported InterMath project (Orrill & the InterMath Team, 2006) deepened teachers' TPACK by having teachers use technology to explore rich mathematical tasks. Teachers participated as mathematics learners, engaging with investigations individually or in pairs (teacher's choice) to explore the ideas of the mathematics. The project was designed for middle grades teachers, and the available set of investigations or tasks (http://intermath.coe.uga.edu) include all of the strands of middle school mathematics.

The goals of InterMath were threefold. First and foremost, InterMath sought to support teachers as mathematical learners. InterMath also sought to support teachers in using more technology in their mathematics classrooms by providing them with experiences using the technology as learners. Finally, InterMath attempted to support the inclusion of cognitively demanding tasks (Smith & Stein, 1998) into classrooms by providing opportunities for teachers to develop comfort with them as learners before trying to teach with them.

Technology was used to support the Common Core Standards of Mathematical Practice (Common Core State Standards Initiative, 2010). For example, spreadsheets were used to find patterns and look for and make meaning of structure. Microworlds and Geometer's Sketchpad were used to make and test conjectures, as well as to support mathematical argument. After all, it is far easier to explain an idea if there is an image of that idea available for everyone to see.

In our studies of several years of InterMath implementation, we found that teachers learned content (e.g., Orrill & the InterMath Team, 2006). As an example, in one recent InterMath course focused on fractions and proportions, we administered matched forms for a pretest and posttest (see Izsák, Orrill, Cohen, and Brown, 2010, for more information on the assessment). We saw a 0.5 standard deviation growth in our PD participants (0.3 standard deviations is considered significant) and we noted that 10 of the 14 participants showed significant gain, while only 2 of 9 teachers in a control group showed significant gain from the pretest to the posttest. We also found mixed responses to the use of technology in teachers' classrooms. Some of the teachers adopted just the idea of mathematical investigations, while others adopted technology and investigations and some were reluctant to try either (e.g., Orrill & InterMath Team, 2006; Orrill & Kittleson, in press).

Technology-Integration Focused Professional Development

Technology-integration focused approaches to professional development develop teachers' TPACK in terms of specific tools rather than broad, comprehensive efforts. In these models, technological tools are the focus of teachers' learning and content is often secondary to learning how to use technology. In light of the TPACK framework, most of these types of professional development programs address technology knowledge (TK), the intersection of technology and content (TCK), and the intersection of technology and pedagogy (TPK); if the programs address the design or implementation of technology-rich activities for specific topics, teachers' TPACK will also be developed.

Most professional development programs that focus on technology integration situate the teacher in the role of an instructional designer who sets up the learning environment and as a facilitator who supports students' exploration of technology-rich activities. While these models emphasize the role of a facilitator, teachers often attend workshops such as these and return to their classroom as a teacher who uses technology to support traditional pedagogies (Polly, 2011a; Polly & Hannafin, 2011).

The Technology Integration in Mathematics (TIM) project was a multi-year series of efforts initially funded by the Eisenhower Title IID grant program in Georgia and, later, the Teacher Quality program that replaced it. The goal of the professional development was to support teachers' use of technology in a student-centered, investigation-focused ways in their mathematics classrooms. This program employed a site-based model in which professional development was offered throughout the year in the teachers' schools and included classroom-based follow-up support for teacher-participants.

Project funds provided resources to purchase software packages that included problem-solving activities. Project staff created a website that included links to free Internet-based activities that promoted problem solving and mathematical reasoning. In the early years of the TIM project, technology integration was the primary thrust for workshop activities. As project developers, we assumed that by modeling technology integration using learner-centered, standards-based mathematical software, teachers would engage in mathematics in new ways that would enhance their own understandings and therefore their teaching. As the project evolved, based on feedback from district leaders and teachers, we focused more on mathematics supported by the same technologies and with manipulatives. In the final years of the project, teachers also engaged with vignettes of mathematics teaching that focused on standards-based pedagogies. These changes were in response to the needs of the elementary teachers with whom we were working. Like many elementary teachers (Ball, Lubienski, & Mewborn, 2001), participants did not feel confident enough with their mathematics background to focus on the technology without additional content support. Based on the TPACK model, teachers reported that their content knowledge inhibited them from teaching with technology in ways that were emphasized.

As an example, in one of the later implementations of the PD, the project staff decided to address all aspects of the TPACK model by supporting teachers in learning to use technology, allowing teachers to explore teaching with technology in a more standards-based manner, and to use technology to more deeply explore mathematical concepts. For example, in one lesson, we had them work with virtual tangrams to explore the potential of technology for supporting communication, as well as doing the tangram puzzles. Through this approach, the professional development workshops focused on technology integration, but the facilitators in Year 3 were able to integrate mathematics content and pedagogy into the workshops. In every session, teacher-participants explored numerous technology-rich mathematical tasks and discussed with each other the mathematics that was embedded in the tasks. Teachers also analyzed vignettes of mathematics teaching that focused on standards-based pedagogies.

The results of surveys collected from all the TIM participants indicated that teachers integrated more technology into their teaching, but teachers self-reported a range of technologies and ways that technology was used (Orrill & Polly, 2006; Singleton, Orrill, Rich, & Shepherd, 2004). In a more intensive research study, three teacher-participants from Year 3 of the project attempted to teach with technology in a standards-based manner—they struggled early in the year to use technology in ways that were not teacher-directed (Polly & Hannafin, 2011). There was a slight increase in the frequency of technology use and the types of technologies that teachers used. In some cases, teachers directly adopted technology-rich activities from workshops and tried them with their students if they matched their grade-level content standards.

Some teachers began adopting more standards-based pedagogies throughout the year after taking time to gain confidence with technology on their own prior to having their students use it. The largest adoption of technology-rich activities that embodied standards-based instruction occurred when a few teachers co-planned lessons with project staff. This co-planning process provided intensive support to teachers for integrating technology and standards-based pedagogy to teach content, in essence TPACK (Polly, 2011a). On the whole, an analysis of teachers' instructional practices indicated that the teachers observed lessons that demonstrated knowledge of technology and content (TCK), but teachers did not consistently demonstrate TPACK since technology was used in very teacher-centered ways in some lessons (Polly, 2011a).

Professional Development Focused on Mathematics Teaching Enhanced by Technology

This approach to professional development primarily leverages technology as a tool to facilitate PCK and TPACK development as teachers use technology to explore and learn mathematics content and pedagogies. When professional development is focused primarily on the mathematics content (CK) and mathematics pedagogies (PCK), participants can engage with mathematics-specific technologies, such as spreadsheets and graphing calculators, to simultaneously explore the mathematics and consider pedagogies to support mathematics learning with technology. Professional development focused on teacher-participants' mathematics teaching has goals of preparing teachers to become more confident in their mathematics knowledge, enacting standards-based pedagogies, and designing instruction to best meet their students' needs. Through participating in professional development focused on mathematics learning, teachers can deepen their knowledge of MKT and TPACK through their use of technologies to explore and solve mathematical tasks.

Through a state-wide Mathematics Science Partnership (MSP) grant, the Content Development for Investigations (CoDe-I) project provided over 80 hours of professional development focused on standards-based mathematics pedagogies (PCK) for teachers in kindergarten through Grade 5. Technology integration was a focus of the professional development as teachers considered how to use technologies in their classroom, such as interactive whiteboards, calculators, and virtual manipulatives, to support teaching and learning. CoDe-I was implemented as a series of three one-year cohorts in two high-need school districts. It included over 400 teachers across three years. During the workshops, participants explored cognitively demanding mathematical tasks (Smith & Stein, 1998), analyzed the district's standards-based curriculum, Investigations in Number, Data, and Space (TERC, 2007), and explored various technologies that aligned to their standards and the curriculum.

Teachers developed TPACK in Year 1 by exploring virtual manipulatives and software included with Investigations in Number, Data, and Space. The professional development engaged teachers in using technology to solve mathematical tasks and considering how to use the technology with their own students. In Years 2 and 3, the teacher-leaders looked for opportunities in the workshops to provide teachers with more opportunities to explore technologies and design technology-rich activities that could further support the teaching of specific mathematics concepts. Most of these technologies were virtual manipulatives or mobile iPad applications focused on mathematical reasoning.

During workshops teacher-participants, teacher-leaders, and project staff frequently discussed characteristics of effective technology-based activities, thus attending explicitly to TPACK for mathematics. Initially, many teachers were familiar with Internet-based mathematics games that solely focused on basic facts or drill and practice. The goal of the MSP grant, however, was to support standards-based mathematics pedagogies, such as reasoning, problem solving, and higher-level mathematical thinking. As a result, facilitators provided teacher-participants with opportunities to examine and compare various websites that had a range of reasoning and problem types, before discussing them. Teachers acknowledged that they enjoyed the benefit of technology-rich activities to give students more basic skills practice and noted that they were intrigued and interested in trying some of the websites sponsored by the National Council of Teachers of Mathematics, which include more higher-level thinking activities. While the professional development was designed to focus on PCK, TPACK was developed as teachers consistently engaged in technology-rich activities related to their PCK and mathematics teaching.

Another technological tool that teacher-participants examined during the workshops was interactive whiteboards, which were available in the teachers' classrooms in both districts. During workshops in Years 2 and 3, teachers spent time examining interactive whiteboard activities, discussing their features, and creating activities to use in their classroom that promoted problem solving and/or mathematical reasoning.

The evaluation and research studies from the grant indicate that the professional development influenced teachers' adoption of more standards-based pedagogies, as well as a shift for most participants towards more standards-based beliefs about learning mathematics (Polly et al., in press; Wang et al., 2013). Through this project, we saw teachers using technology more in their mathematics classroom, but demonstrating inconsistencies in the level of mathematical tasks that their students explored (Polly et al., in press).

Implications

The Significance of Technology in Professional Development

To support teachers' development of TPACK, professional development designers and facilitators need to examine the role that technology plays in the professional development activities. The TPACK construct calls for an intersection between educational technologies, content, and pedagogies (Mishra & Koehler, 2006). In terms of mathematics professional development, such as the examples described above, technology, pedagogy, and content are intertwined as teachers engaged in activities using technology to explore mathematical tasks and considering how technology and mathematics intersect from a pedagogical perspective (Polly, 2011b).

For TPACK to be developed in such a way as to be implemented in classrooms, teachers need professional development that is designed at the intersection of the TPACK framework and learner-centered professional development principles. Teachers need time in professional development to participate in technology-rich experiences as learners, in ways similar to those that they should implement in their own classroom (Polly et al., 2010). Regardless of the role of technology in professional development, having teachers use technology as learners has shown promise in supporting teachers' development of TPACK. In our own work, we have seen positive results, whether for technology integration (Polly, 2011a, 2011b) or for teaching in standards-based ways (Polly et al., in press; Polly, 2013). Technology also supported learning during professional development focused on teachers' content development during the InterMath project; the primary TPACK-related outcome of that project was teachers' technological content knowledge (TCK) (Polly & Orrill, 2012).

Professional development designers and facilitators should continue to explore ways to immerse teachers in technology-rich learning environments during professional learning experiences (Lawless & Pellegrino, 2007; Polly & Hannafin, 2010). Such professional development should aim to deepen teachers' TPACK by providing experiences that allow teachers' to simultaneously develop their knowledge of technology, pedagogy, and content and attend to the intersections between each of these kinds of knowledge.

The Tension of Technology in Content-Focused Professional Development

Despite the promise of technology-based PD for supporting teachers in moving toward becoming more learner centered, a number of tensions must be acknowledged and planned around. First, working in content areas in which teachers have well-known issues with the content is a challenge. As noted in the description of the TIM project above, over time we moved away from technology-focused PD and toward technology-enhanced PD because it proved to be too cognitively challenging for teachers to simultaneously learn how to implement technology in their classrooms and focus on mathematics topics. By shifting the focus to content, rather than technology, the TIM team was able to focus the teachers on the mathematics and pedagogy with the technology being used as a support tool. This seemed to allow teachers to engage with technology to learn the content and then start to think about using it in their classrooms. While this is a subtle shift, it was needed for the TIM project to meet the needs of the teachers. Worth noting, in InterMath the stress level related to technology learning was lower than in TIM. This may be because it was focused on middle school teachers rather than elementary teachers or because it focused on learning mathematics for oneself. We posit that this may indicate that PD should either initially focus on only two of the three facets of TPACK (technology, pedagogy, and content) or that technology be integrated in all aspects of the professional development from the onset.

A second tension is the need for classroom-based support. In the TIM and CoDe-I examples, there was tremendous support for the teachers to implement technology-rich mathematical tasks even after working with them in their classroom. Without adequate support, students explored technology-rich mathematical tasks, but teachers modified their pedagogy to be more directive and procedural (Polly & Hannafin, 2011). The support provided during the projects ranged from identifying resources to co-planning and co-teaching with project personnel who were comfortable with technology. In our experience, once teachers start to have successful implementations of TPACK-based lessons, they develop the confidence to do more on their own. However, support in the early efforts is critical to success.

A final tension is the perceived alignment of the technologies to the curriculum being promoted by the district. In TIM, we saw mixed adoption from one implementation to the next based largely on the level of support the district offered in helping the participants see alignment between the work of the PD and the goals for classroom teaching in that district. Similarly, in CoDe-I, the effort was absolutely tied to the curricular materials being used in the district. Even more important, CoDe-I aligned to the principles underlying those materials and not just to the activities. In contrast, InterMath was largely divorced from discussions of classroom implementation other than those discussions opened up by the teachers. This led to extremely varied levels of integration of technology in the teachers' classrooms and varied levels of learner-centered problem-solving activities resulting from InterMath. We saw a continuum of influence ranging from the adoption of an investigation here or there (e.g., Orrill & Kittleson, in press) to wholesale application of InterMath tasks with technology in teachers' classrooms.

These tensions are very important to consider in planning a project and in identifying the goals of the project. Even with extended PD, it is unlikely that teachers will develop all aspects of TPACK through a single course or one-year project. However, such projects, as described above, can have a significant impact on laying the groundwork for teachers to take their first steps into learner-centered, technology-rich mathematical practices.

Conclusion

Our examples offered here are built intentionally upon the principles of learner-centered professional development. They were designed to support teachers' development of TPACK, even in cases in which the primary goal may have been developing PCK and improving the way students learn mathematics. Since technology permeates instruction, PCK professional development in our cases focused on and developed teachers' TPACK through the various activities in which the teachers engaged. We assert that these experiences may have applications for other teacher educators who may be considering how to design courses to develop teachers' TPACK. Pre-service teachers lack classroom experience, so pre-service teachers' TPACK development is best supported by a comprehensive program including multiple experiences, which could include a technology integration course, content methods courses that include experiences to learn about technology integration in light of that content area, and classroom-based experiences that include sound examples of technology integration (Schrum, 1999). It is unlikely that pre-service teachers can develop the pedagogical content knowledge necessary for practicing teachers without extensive fieldwork. However, teacher preparation programs can prepare pre-service teachers to take their first steps into TPACK with confidence.

References

Ball, D. L., Lubienski, S., and Mewborn, D. (2001). Research on teaching mathematics: The unsolved problem of teachers' mathematical knowledge In V. Richardson (Ed.), *Handbook of research on teaching* (4th ed.). New York: Macmillan.

Baumert, J., Kunter, M., Blum, W., Brunner, M., Voss, T., Jordan, A., & Tsai, Y. M. (2010). Teachers' mathematical knowledge, cognitive activation in the classroom, and student progress. *American Educational Research Journal*, 47(1), 133–180.

Common Core State Standards Initiative. (2010). Common core state standards. Retrieved from http://http://www.corestandards.org/the-standards

Darling-Hammond, L., Wei, R. C., Andree, A., Richardson, N., & Orphanos, S. (2009). *Professional learning in the learning profession: A status report on teacher development in the United States and abroad*. Dallas, TX: School Redesign Network at Stanford University and the National Staff Development Council.

Garet, M., Porter, A., Desimone, L., Birman, B., & Yoon, K. (2001). What makes professional development effective? Analysis of a national sample of teachers. *American Educational Research Journal*, 38(4), 915–945.

Hawley, W. D., & Valli, L. (2000). Learner-centered professional development. *Research Bulletin*, August 2000, No. 27. Phi Delta Kappa Center for Evaluation, Development, and Research. Retrieved from http://www.paadultedresources.org/uploads/8/6/3/4/8634493/learner_centered_pro.pdf

Heck, D. J., Banilower, E. R., Weiss, I. R., & Rosenberg, S. L. (2008). Studying the effects of professional development: The case of the NSF's local systemic change through teacher enhancement initiative. *Journal for Research in Mathematics Education*, 39(2), 113–152.

Hill, H. C., Rowan, B., & Ball, D. L. (2005). Effects of teachers' mathematical knowledge for teaching on student achievement. *American Educational Research Journal*, 42(2), 371–406.

Izsák, A., Orrill, C. H., Cohen, A., & Brown, R. E. (2010). Measuring middle grades teachers' understanding of rational numbers with the mixture Rasch model. *Elementary School Journal*, 110(3), 279–300.

Jaquith, A., Mindich, D., Wei, R. C., & Darling-Hammond, L. (2010). *Teacher professional learning in the United States: Case studies of state policies and strategies*. Oxford, OH: Learning Forward.

Lawless, K. A., & Pellegrino, J. W. (2007). Professional development in integrating technology into teaching and learning: Knowns, unknowns, and ways to pursue better questions and answers. *Review of Educational Research*, 77(4), 575–614.

Loucks-Horsley, S., Stiles, K. E., Mundry, S. E., Love, N. B., & Hewson, P. W. (2009). *Designing professional development for teachers of science and mathematics* (3rd ed.). Thousand Oaks, CA: Corwin.

Mishra, P., & Koehler, M. J. (2006). Technological pedagogical content knowledge: A new framework for teacher knowledge. *Teachers College Record*, 108(6), 1017–1054.

National Partnership for Education and Accountability in Teaching. (2000). *Revisioning professional development: What learner-centered professional development looks like.* Oxford, OH: National Assessment of Educational Progress.

Orrill, C. H. (2001). Building technology-based, learner-centered classrooms: The evolution of a professional development framework. *Educational Technology Research and Development, 49*(1), 15–34.

Orrill, C. H., & the InterMath Team. (2006). What learner-centered professional development looks like: The pilot studies of the InterMath professional development project. *The Mathematics Educator, 16*(1), 4–13.

Orrill, C. H., & Kittleson, J. (in press). Translating learning into practice: Considering the relationship between teachers' professional development and teaching. *Journal of Mathematics Teacher Education.* doi:10.1007/s10857-014-9284-5

Orrill, C., & Polly, D. (2006). Using data to design and refine a technology-integrated professional development model. Paper presented at the 2006 Convention of the Association for Educational Communications and Technology, Dallas, TX.

Polly, D. (2011a). Examining teachers' enactment of TPACK in their mathematics teaching. *International Journal for Technology in Mathematics Education, 18*(2), 83–96.

Polly, D. (2011b). Examining teachers' enactment of technological pedagogical content knowledge (TPACK) in their mathematics teaching after technology integration professional development. *Journal of Computers in Mathematics and Science Teaching, 30*(1), 37–59.

Polly, D. (2013). The influence of an online elementary mathematics pedagogy course on teacher candidates' performance. *Journal of Distance Education, 27*(2). Retrieved from http://www.jofde.ca/index.php/jde/article/view/854

Polly, D., & Hannafin, M. J. (2010). Reexamining technology's role in learner-centered professional development. *Educational Technology Research and Development, 58*(5), 557–571. doi:10.1007/s11423-009-9146-5

Polly, D., & Hannafin, M. J. (2011). Examining how learner-centered professional development influences teachers' espoused and enacted practices. *Journal of Educational Research, 104*(4), 120–130.

Polly, D., McGee, J. R., & Martin, C. S. (2010). Employing technology-rich mathematical tasks to develop teachers' technological, pedagogical, and content knowledge (TPACK). *Journal of Computers in Mathematics and Science Teaching, 29*(4), 455–472.

Polly, D., & Orrill, C. H. (2012). Developing technological pedagogical and content knowledge (TPACK) through professional development focused on technology-rich mathematics tasks. *The Meridian, 15.* Retrieved from http://ced.ncsu.edu/meridian/index.php/meridian/article/view/44/43

Polly, D., Wang, C., McGee, J.R., Lambert, R.G., Martin, C.S., & Pugalee, D.K. (in press). Examining the influence of a curriculum-based elementary mathematics professional development program. *Journal of Research in Childhood Education.*

Schrum, L. (1999). Technology professional development for teachers. *Educational Technology Research and Development, 47*(4), 83–90.

Shulman, L. S. (1986). Those who understand: Knowledge growth in teaching. *Educational Researcher, 15*(2), 4–14.

Singleton, E., Orrill, C., Rich, P., & Shepherd, C. (2004, October). Math and technology for young learners. Presentation at Georgia Mathematics Conference, Eatonton, GA.

Smith, M.S., & Stein, M.K. (1998). Selecting and creating mathematical tasks: From research to practice. *Mathematics Teaching in the Middle School, 3*(5), 344–350.

TERC. (2007). *Investigations in number, data, and space* (2nd ed.). New York: Pearson.

Wang, C., Polly, D., Lehew, A., Pugalee, D., Lambert, R., & Martin, C. S. (2013). Supporting teachers' enactment of elementary school student-centered mathematics pedagogies: The evaluation of a curriculum-focused professional development program. *New Waves—Educational Research and Development, 16*(1), 76–91. Available at http://www.caerda.org/journal/index.php/newwaves/article/view/97/46

Yoon, K. S., Duncan, T., Lee, S. W., Scarloss, B., & Shapley, K. L. (2007). Reviewing the evidence on how teacher professional development affects student achievement. (Issues & Answers Report, REL 2007-No. 033). Washington, DC: U.S. Department of Education, Institute of Educational Sciences, National Center for Education Evaluation and Regional Assistance, Regional Education Laboratory Southwest. Available at http://ies.ed.gov/ncee/edlabs

18

TPACK-Based Professional Development Programs in In-Service Science Teacher Education

Evrim Baran, Sedef Canbazoglu-Bilici, Erdem Uygun

Introduction

With the recent emphasis on using technologies in education, particularly in science instruction and scientific inquiry, the need has emerged to prepare science teachers with effective classroom technology integration skills. Science teachers' Technological Pedagogical Content Knowledge (TPACK) builds on the interactions between knowledge of the subject matter, pedagogical strategies, and technologies, as well as the contexts that they transform with technology (Yeh, Hsu, Wu, Hwang, & Lin, 2013). To build this unique knowledge, in-service teachers require training, including continuous and usable professional development (PD) and support opportunities beyond technocentric approaches that are disconnected from practice. New PD models are needed to develop teachers' competencies of integrating technologies into discipline-specific pedagogical approaches and addressing students' learning needs within classroom contexts.

Conceptualizing Science Teachers' TPACK

Knowledge about how technology facilitates domain-specific teaching methods (e.g., inquiry-based teaching) and general pedagogical strategies, such as classroom management, is essential for effective use in the classroom. To promote students' engagement with science, teachers also need to know how content representations can be transformed with technologies (Williams, Linn, Ammon, & Gearhart, 2004). Teachers need to be equipped not only with teacher-centered technology integration methods but also student-centered technology use to promote inquiry-learning processes (Maeng, Mulvey, Smetana, & Bell, 2013). Science teachers' TPACK, therefore, can be defined as understanding how technology transforms (a) students' learning (e.g., misconceptions), (b) representations of science content (e.g., examples, scientific models, analogies), (c) domain-specific science teaching methods (e.g., inquiry-based teaching) and general teaching methods (e.g., classroom management), (d) standards and objectives of curriculum, and (e) context, whether classroom, school, or community (Jimoyiannis, 2010; Yeh et al., 2013). To develop science teachers' TPACK, a variety of PD models has been implemented within in-service teacher education programs.

PD Strategies and Models for Developing Science Teachers' TPACK

Recent design reforms of PD programs call for situated, reflective, and authentic models that directly impact teachers' classroom practices (Valanides & Angeli, 2008). Higgins and Spitulnik (2008), in their review of PD approaches for supporting teachers' learning of technology integration, highlighted social support mechanisms such as mentoring, peer interaction, learning communities, and sharing evidence of student learning through teaching replays and rehearsals in workgroups. Jimoyiannis (2010) further listed learning strategies for science teachers' PDs that include practical training, collaboration, debate, discussion, learning by design, feedback, and grounding learning in classroom practice. Our review of empirical research on TPACK-based PDs implemented within in-service science teacher education contexts revealed a number of relevant strategies. These methods included direct instruction, scientific fieldwork, lesson plan development, reflection on practice, teaching, peer coaching, participation in online communities, and teacher design teams. These methods are presented in Table 18.1 with examples.

Technologies integrated into PD programs have included tools for recording and analyzing data, digital microscopes, probeware, mind-mapping tools, simulations, spreadsheets, digital images, videos, animations, interactive whiteboards, and concept mapping. The majority of the TPACK-based PD programs were short, intense programs that lasted about one week, while a small number lasted as long as one year (e.g., Guzey & Roehrig, 2009).

Several data sources were used to evaluate the impact of the PD programs on science teachers' TPACK: questionnaires, interviews, technology integration lesson plans, and classroom observations. However, these measures were generally applied before, during, or right after the programs, failing to obtain information about the long-term impact. While surveys were common modes of collecting data about teachers' TPACK, teacher action research studies have also been used to help teachers document their progress (e.g., Guzey & Roehrig, 2009). Observation tools designed specifically for TPACK in science education have also provided information on how teachers enact technology lessons in classrooms (e.g., Kafyulilo et al., 2014).

Increases in teachers' confidence and TPACK levels while teaching with technology as a result of attending PD programs have been frequently reported in the literature. Graham et al. (2009), who reported lower scores in teachers' technological content knowledge (TCK) compared to TPACK, revealed teachers' limited experience "doing" science, especially in the context of elementary science education. Another finding was the positive correlation between teachers' TPACK and teaching experience. The school context was reported as a contributing or constraining factor according to teachers' implications of

Table 18.1 Teacher Learning Methods Used Within TPACK-Based In-Service Science Teacher Education PDs

Teacher Learning Methods	Examples
Direct instruction	Instruction about inquiry-based learning and biology/earth content (e.g., Graham et al., 2009)
Technology demonstrations	Demonstrations of technological tools (e.g., Valanides & Angeli, 2008)
Scientific field work	Practicing scientific inquiry in a national park (e.g., Graham et al., 2009)
Designing lesson plans	Designing technology-integrated lesson plans (e.g., Guzey & Roehrig, 2009)
Reflections	Writing reflections on lessons and classroom practices (e.g., Valanides & Angeli, 2008)
Teaching	Enacting TPACK lessons in classrooms (e.g., Graham et al., 2009)
Feedback	Giving and receiving feedback with colleagues and experts (e.g., Jimoyiannis, 2010)
Peer coaching	Observing peer teachers' use of ICTs (e.g., Jang, 2010)
Online communities	Engaging in online conversation, attending to online discussions, reflecting on and sharing lessons (e.g., Guzey & Roehrig, 2009)
Teacher action research	Reflecting on teaching practices and learning about technology integration (e.g., Guzey & Roehrig, 2009)
Teacher design teams	Designing and enacting technology integration materials within teacher design teams (e.g., Kafyulilo, Fisser, & Voogt, 2014)

what they learned in the PD programs (e.g., Guzey & Roehrig, 2009). For example, availability of technologies and administrative and collegial support positively impacted teachers' motivation and level of technology integration into their science classrooms.

While some initial work has been conducted to identify science teachers' TPACK (e.g., Jimoyiannis, 2010), the current research lacks (a) frameworks for conceptualizing how this unique body of knowledge represents science teachers' domain-specific knowledge about technology integration (Jang & Tsai, 2012) and (b) models for supporting teacher learning about TPACK and technology integration. Understanding how teachers transfer their learning from the PDs to their teacher practice over time is crucial for determining the conditions for sustained learning and teaching with technology. Our recent review on the TPACK research in Turkey revealed a lack of research on TPACK-based PD models and in-service teacher training in Turkey (Baran & Canbazoglu-Bilici, 2015). With this in mind, we designed and implemented a TPACK-based PD program in Turkey to foster science teachers' classroom practices with technology. The purpose of this research was to investigate the impact of a TPACK-based PD program on science teachers' perceptions on their TPACK development as a result of attending the TPACK-based PD program.

Methods

This study followed qualitative case study methodology to collect evidence on science teachers' perceptions about their TPACK development before and after they attended a TPACK-based PD.

Participants

A total of 109 science teachers nationwide applied to participate in the PD program. Twenty-four elementary science teachers were selected according to the following criteria: (a) diversity in the different regions and cities the teachers came from, (b) diversity in levels of teaching experience, (c) knowledge of basic Office applications, and (d) relatively limited knowledge and usage of technologies in science classrooms. The final list of 24 teachers (12 female, 12 male) came from 21 provinces in 7 regions of Turkey. Their teaching experience ranged from 1 to 20 years with an average of 8 years.

The Design of a TPACK-Based PD Program

The TPACK-based PD program (total 80 hours) was conducted at a public university in Ankara, Turkey, in the summer of 2013. Integrating technology into classrooms in Turkey has gained great attention over the last ten years. Particularly after the initiation of the Movement of Enhancing Opportunities and Improving Technology project in 2006, large investments toward building an infrastructure for computerized classrooms all around Turkey have created an urgent demand to prepare teachers for using technologies effectively. However, teacher education programs, especially in-service PDs, still lack robust opportunities for developing technology integration practices. To respond to this need, we developed and implemented a TPACK-based PD program funded by the Scientific and Technological Research Council of Turkey under Science and Society Innovative Educational Applications. The grant covered all teachers', trainers', and guides' accommodation costs, visits to science museums, and trainers' and guides' daily expenses, as well as equipment purchases such as probeware and clickers.

The TPACK-based PD program aimed to increase teachers' awareness about domain-specific technologies that can be used for learning and teaching science, develop their knowledge about integrating technology into science classrooms, and increase their self-efficacy towards designing technology-enhanced science classrooms. The PD program featured three sections: introductions, modules, and final remarks. A total of 13 modules were implemented by 18 trainees who worked as faculty members at universities around the country and had expertise in related topics. Each module lasted 90–180 minutes, and 2–3 modules were conducted each day. The modules consisted of hands-on explorations of TPACK within science content domains and with technology tools such as SMART Boards, clickers, Web 2.0 tools, mobile apps, spreadsheets, cloud computing, concept maps, probeware, and simulations. During this 8-day intensive PD program, science teachers attended the sessions from 9:00 am until 6:30 pm every day. Ninety minutes each day was reserved for TPACK lesson plan design activity.

The PD started with introductory activities to acquaint teachers with TPACK and the content and format of the program. We first evaluated teachers' pre-knowledge and expectations about the PD with KWL (Know/Want to Know/Learned) charts. We then conducted creative drama warm-up activities to get to know each other and create a trustful group atmosphere. Presentations followed about the importance of technology integration in science classrooms. To help teachers understand TPACK deeply, we played the TPACK game, which was first developed at the National Technology Leadership Summit's annual gathering in 2007 (Richardson, 2010). The game included the selection of technology, pedagogy, and science content items drawn randomly from pools prepared beforehand. We modified the original game to allow for a two-hour session where groups designed science-learning activities using randomly and nonrandomly selected items. Finally, we introduced a project that entailed the design and presentation of a technology-integrated TPACK lesson in groups of four. Six teacher groups were assigned specific science topics and were guided to work on these projects during designated hours. Teachers were expected to implement their learning about technology integration into their lesson designs. Figure 18.1 presents teachers engaging in TPACK-based science education explorations.

The module topics were selected based on our review on the needs of science teachers. Each module consisted of activities for developing teachers' TPACK, such as technology presentations and demonstrations, technology exploration, design of technology-enriched

Figure 18.1 TPACK-Based Science Education Explorations

lesson materials via collaborative group work, presentation of technology-enriched materials, and discussion and feedback with the trainer and colleagues. Because initial technical training about the technologies was necessary for understanding their affordances and limitations (Valanides & Angeli, 2008), each module first started with a presentation and demonstration of the technologies followed by individual or group technology explorations. Then, science teachers designed content-specific examples. For example, after a 30-minute presentation and exploration of Animoto, science teachers prepared a video presentation on a science topic they selected. After designing these examples, science teachers presented their work to the group, discussed potential classroom implementations, and gave feedback to each other's materials. The final day included project presentations, feedback, discussions, and evaluation forms. The PD program outline and module details are presented in Table 18.2.

Table 18.2 The TPACK-Based PD Program Outline and Modules

Day	Hands-on Activity
Introduction	
1	Warm up activities
	Introduction to the importance of technology integration in science classrooms
	What is TPACK?
	Presentation of the TPACK lesson design project
	TPACK lesson design project group formation
Modules	
2	Using spreadsheets and Google Docs to analyze scientific data and create graphs
	Preparing presentations on science topics (e.g., water cycle, circulatory system) using Prezi and Animoto
	Using videos in science classrooms (e.g., downloading, editing, and sharing videos)
	Using cloud-based applications (e.g., Google Drive and Dropbox) in science classrooms
3	Using SMART Board and clickers in science classrooms
	Creating science blogs and videocasts (e.g., Blogspot, Voicethread)
4	Using simulations (e.g., PhEt, Stellarium, Algodoo) for physics, chemistry, biology, and astronomy topics
	Using probeware (e.g., conductivity probe, temperature probe, gas pressure sensor, pH sensor) to develop scientific inquiry process skills (e.g., predict, observe, explain)
5	Using concept mapping in science classrooms and constructing science specific concept maps with a software (e.g., Inspiration)
	Visiting a science museum and exploring hands-on exhibits (e.g., liquid nitrogen show, Van de Graaff generator)

Day	Hands-on Activity
6	Preparing online science puzzles (e.g., Crosswordlabs, Puzzle-Maker)
	Using tablets and educational mobile apps (e.g., Spacecraft, Anatomy 4D, The Elements by Theodore Gray) in science classrooms
7	Preparing public service announcements (PSAs) in science classrooms using Movie Maker
	Examining technology classrooms' physical layouts for different activities
8	Presenting group TPACK lesson design projects
	Evaluation of the PD program

Data Sources

Science teachers' perceptions of their TPACK development were investigated with (a) KWL charts that teachers completed on the first and last days, (b) PD evaluation forms, and (c) one-year follow-up evaluation forms. KWL charts were collected to gather teachers' prior knowledge, expectations, and learning about the TPACK-based PD program. Participants answered first two questions on the first day and a third question on the last day of the PD program. Open-ended questions included:

1. What do you know about the TPACK-PD program topics and activities?
2. What do you want to learn about the TPACK-PD program topics and activities?
3. What did you learn about the TPACK-PD program topics and activities?

The PD evaluation form was presented to participants on the last day of the program and included open-ended questions about how TPACK-based activities impacted their development of content knowledge (CK), pedagogical knowledge (PK), technological knowledge (TK), technological content knowledge (TCK), technological pedagogical knowledge (TPK), and TPACK by providing examples.

One year after the completion of the program, teachers were asked to complete another evaluation form online, asking how and why they used the things they learned in their teaching, barriers they faced while integrating technology in their classrooms, how they overcame those challenges, how the PD contributed to their knowledge of teaching, and what they did to disseminate technology integration practices within their schools and communities.

Data Analysis

Qualitative data collected from the open-ended questions in the KWL charts and PD evaluation forms were analyzed to find in what ways the PD impacted science teachers' perceptions of their TPACK development. Teachers' answers to the open-ended questions were analyzed separately and line-by-line to identify emergent themes on their TPACK development before, during, and one year after the PD. The themes, concerning the impact of

PD, were identified (a) before the PD (prior knowledge and expectations), (b) after the PD (impact on CK, TK, PK, TCK, TPK, and TPACK), and (c) one year after the PD (technology use, barriers, solutions, PD contribution, and dissemination of technology integration practices).

Results

Teachers' Reflections About Prior Knowledge, Expectations, and Learning

The analysis of teachers' prior knowledge about technologies according to the KWL charts revealed that teachers had used computers in their classrooms but only a limited number knew how to use animations, simulations, projection devices, and Web 2.0 tools. Teachers noted that they wanted to learn about new technologies, science-based technologies, SMART Boards, and technology-supported material design and development. Participants reported particularly gaining knowledge about using Prezi and video-making software such as Animoto during the PD. They also learned about general technologies such as online puzzles, cloud computing tools, clickers, tablets, and videocasts, plus science-based software such as probeware, simulations, and animations.

Teachers' Reflections After the PD

On the last day, we administered an evaluation form to gather teachers' thoughts about the impact of the PD program on participants' TPACK. All teachers stated that the program positively affected their TK, TCK, and, most of all, TPACK. The main activities that developed their CK were preparing technology-integration materials such as Prezi presentations, simulations, and scientific measurement activities using probeware. When asked what part of the PD contributed to their PK, teachers mentioned preparing technology-integration materials, using puzzle-making software for assessment of student learning, creating lesson plans, and using question-based teaching strategies and the 5E learning model. Teachers particularly emphasized that their PK developed as they interacted with their colleagues and trainers. As for their TK, all teachers stated that the PD helped them develop knowledge about previously unknown technologies, such as Prezi, Animoto, Inspiration, crossword puzzles, student response systems (clickers), SMART Boards, tablets, and Web 2.0 and cloud computing tools. Teachers also indicated that their TCK developed as they interacted with science mobile applications, simulations, and probeware tools. Most teachers also gained knowledge about pedagogical affordances and constraints of technologies used in organizing teaching and learning processes, such as managing classrooms, troubleshooting during lessons, and following the ethical use of technologies for teaching. Finally, all teachers reported that their TPACK developed as they used TK and CK together while teaching a specific science topic with a technological tool. For example, one teacher emphasized, "These three components (PK, CK, and TK) are not enough by themselves, but only effective when considered together." Another teacher explained, "By adding T to PCK, we learned a great deal of things that will contribute to our students' learning."

Teachers' Reflections After One Year

One year after the program, we asked teachers to complete another evaluation form via email to gather their thoughts about the long-term impact of the PD on their teaching. Teachers reported that they had mostly used Prezi, Animoto, and Inspiration in their courses. Creating presentations with Prezi to teach a topic, having students construct concept maps with Inspiration and assessing their learning with these maps, and creating videos with Animoto to gain students' attention at the beginning of a topic or to summarize a unit were some of the technology integration practices they followed. Teachers also noted that they used Dropbox, public service announcements created with Movie Maker, concept and mind maps, simulations (e.g., PhEt, Algodoo, Sterallium), animations, and blogging tools. Teachers emphasized that technologies particularly contributed to gaining student attention, making learning fun, and helping students understand science concepts better. When asked about challenges faced while integrating technologies into their classrooms, teachers described first-order technology integration barriers (Ertmer, 1999), such as inadequate infrastructure, time, and institutional support.

Overall, prior to the PD, teachers expressed limited knowledge about creating materials and science lessons using technologies and feared excessive amounts of time required to prepare such materials. However, after the PD, they could integrate technology even in contexts with no Internet connection and prepare materials quickly with free software introduced during the PD. Their TK was developed, and they realized the importance of TPACK. Teachers also noted that they shared what they learned in the PD with colleagues in their schools and districts, as well as distant teachers via social media. Some of them gave seminars in their schools about the PD activity topics and benefits of using technology in science classrooms.

Conclusion

Our study revealed that the TPACK-based PD with a focus on science education increased teachers' awareness about the integration of domain-specific technologies into science classrooms, such as science simulations and probeware. However, because we have documented a detailed, TPACK-based PD example with participating teachers who were "motivated volunteers" and wanted to learn and use technology in their classrooms, these results may not be generalizable to contexts where teacher attendance and motivation is an issue. Systematic TPACK investigations within science teacher education and the development of domain-specific approaches for science teachers are still in their infancy. More research is needed on the implementation of different PD models and their impact on the development of science teachers' TPACK in different contexts. Linking curriculum goals with the goals of the PD programs, PDs also need to communicate the idea of TPACK to teachers and administrators and illustrate how PDs designed with this unique knowledge may impact teacher practice, student learning, and effective technology use in schools. Developing robust, coherent, and sustainable TPACK-based PD programs that are grounded with evidence-based research on effective teacher learning is crucial to enhancing science teachers' technology integration knowledge and practices.

Recommendations for Future Research

The results of our study and a review of the literature on the integration of TPACK in science teachers' PD programs revealed a number of recommendations for future research.

Conceptualizing Science Teachers' TPACK

Science teachers' TPACK has only been conceptualized in a limited number of research studies (e.g., Graham et al., 2009; Jang, 2010; Jimoyiannis, 2010). The design of TPACK-based PD programs needs to be grounded in science-specific conceptualizations so that proper teacher learning methods are selected and structured. To validate domain-specific science teacher knowledge, further research could observe expert teachers and generate model characteristics (Guzey & Roehrig, 2009). Exemplary TPACK science lessons and cases may also help illustrate these practices.

Tracking Science Teachers' TPACK with Longitudinal Studies

There is a clear need for longitudinal studies that track how science teachers transfer their knowledge gained from the PDs to their authentic teaching contexts and how their TPACK changes over time. Measuring the changes in their knowledge of TK, TCK, TPK, and TPACK is critical to understanding the long-term impact of the PDs (Guzey & Roehrig, 2009). TPACK progressions, therefore, need to be supported and evaluated through long-term initiatives that track teachers' TPACK development over time.

Investigating the Impact of Different PD Models

This research presented a number of methods integrated into science teachers' PD programs. Future research should investigate how different components of PDs (e.g., learning by design, peer coaching) affect teachers' learning of effective technology integration and subsequent student outcomes. More evidence is needed on the connections between PD models, teacher learning, and enhanced student outcomes (Higgins & Spitulnik, 2008).

Recommendations for Practice

Providing Technology Training for Science Education

Teachers who attend PD programs may have limited knowledge about technologies and pedagogies, which may impede their understanding about how technologies afford or limit certain pedagogical practices. Initial training, therefore, needs to develop teachers' technological and pedagogical expertise (Valanides & Angeli, 2008). Hands-on activities that help science teachers explore the affordances and limitations of technologies specific to their domain (e.g., science simulations) would provide them a baseline for making decisions about technology integration in their classrooms.

Designing Authentic Learning Experiences in Real Classroom Contexts

The teachers in our study demanded PD experiences connected to authentic classroom contexts. Research also supports implementing teacher learning opportunities situated in authentic classrooms (Putnam & Borko, 2000). By incorporating TPACK-based PD programs into classroom practice, teacher educators may implement ongoing learning with activities where teachers design technology-enriched materials, implement them in their classrooms, and revise them with mentor and peer feedback after reflecting on the feasibility of their designs (Valanides & Angeli, 2008). These practical and authentic TPACK-based PD programs may also be implemented within science teachers' own schools to strengthen the connection.

Designing PD Programs That Serve Teachers' Needs

If the scope, vision, and format of PD are communicated with teachers, their motivation and participation may increase. The science teachers who participated in our study noted a persistent need for more training and support with regard to preparing science-specific, technology-integrated materials for their classrooms. Teachers need to know how the PD will directly impact classroom practices and serve their needs. Teachers' contextual differences and conditions of technology infrastructure as well as local, administrative, and collegial support mechanisms may inform the selection of best PD approaches.

Building and Sustaining Teacher Learning Communities

Strong professional learning communities also contribute to teachers' instructional improvement (Borko, 2004). While participating in such communities when initiated and sustained through TPACK-based PDs, teachers interact, collaborate, and share. The teachers who participated in our PD continued their conversations through a designated Facebook group throughout the year. Similar technology platforms may help PD trainers and teachers connect, collaborate, and sustain structured or informal conversations online. Science teachers can also share TPACK lessons, reflect on classroom materials and applications, and benefit from peer mentoring and feedback on these social online platforms. Online resource repositories that include science lesson materials and assessment tools may also help teachers access PD content whenever they want. Teachers and teacher educators could create and evaluate the PD content on these platforms together.

Moving from Teacher-Centered to Student-Centered Inquiry-Based Technology Integration

Recent PD programs in science teacher education have mainly focused on the integration of technology into inquiry-based teaching. Teacher learning methods need to emphasize how technologies may transform teacher-centered technology integration to student-centered, inquiry-based models (Graham et al., 2009; Maeng et al., 2013). For example, teacher learning activities may be linked to classroom practices where teachers directly observe how students' use of technologies fosters inquiry processes and then bring their observations back to the PD context, where they can evaluate and refine ideas with colleagues and mentors.

Delivering Long-Term and Sustained Learning Opportunities

PD initiatives need to consider teachers' TPACK development as a continuum. Their learning is enhanced through teaching practice as they try and revise ideas about technology integration. In-service TPACK-based PD programs should be an integral part of a continuous and long-term curriculum implemented to promote and enhance theoretically sound teacher practices in classrooms.

References

Baran, E., & Canbazoglu-Bilici, S. (2015). Teknolojik pedagojik alan bilgisi (TPAB) üzerine alanyazın incelemesi: Türkiye örneği [A review of the research on technological pedagogical content knowledge: The case of Turkey]. *Hacettepe Üniversitesi Eğitim Fakültesi Dergisi [Hacettepe University Journal of Education], 30*(1), 15–32.

Borko, H. (2004). Professional development and teacher learning: Mapping the terrain. *Educational Researcher, 33*(8), 3–15.

Ertmer, P. A. (1999). Addressing first- and second-order barriers to change: Strategies for technology integration. *Educational Technology Research and Development, 47*(4), 47–61.

Graham, C. R., Burgoyne, N., Cantrell, P., Smith, L., St. Clair, L., & Harris, R. (2009). TPACK development in science teaching: Measuring the TPACK confidence of inservice science teachers. *TechTrends, 53*(5), 70–79.

Guzey, S. S., & Roehrig, G. H. (2009). Teaching science with technology: Case studies of science teachers' development of technology, pedagogy, and content knowledge. *Contemporary Issues in Technology and Teacher Education, 9*(1), 25–45.

Higgins, T. E., & Spitulnik, M. W. (2008). Supporting teachers' use of technology in science instruction through professional development: A literature review. *Journal of Science Education and Technology, 17*(5), 511–521.

Jang, S. J. (2010). Integrating the interactive whiteboard and peer coaching to develop the TPACK of secondary science teachers. *Computers & Education, 55*, 1744–1751.

Jang, S. J., & Tsai, M. F. (2012). Exploring the TPACK of Taiwanese elementary mathematics and science teachers with respect to use of interactive whiteboards. *Computers & Education, 59*(2), 327–338.

Jimoyiannis, A. (2010). Designing and implementing an integrated technological pedagogical science knowledge framework for science teachers' professional development. *Computers & Education, 55*, 1259–1269.

Kafyulilo, A., Fisser, P., & Voogt, J. (2014). Teacher design in teams as a professional development arrangement for developing technology integration knowledge and skills of science teachers in Tanzania. *Education and Information Technology*. doi:10.1007/s10639-014-9321-0

Maeng, J. L., Mulvey, B. K., Smetana, L. K., & Bell, R. L. (2013). Preservice teachers' TPACK: Using technology to support inquiry instruction. *Journal of Science Education and Technology, 22*, 838–857.

Putnam, R. T., & Borko, H. (2000). What do new views of knowledge and thinking have to say about research on teacher learning? *Educational Researcher, 29*(1), 4–15.

Richardson, K. W. (2010). TPACK: Game on. *Learning & Leading with Technology, 37*(8), 34–35.

Valanides, N., & Angeli, C. (2008). Professional development for computer-enhanced learning: A case study with science teachers. *Research in Science and Technological Education, 26*(1), 3–12.

Williams, M., Linn, M. C., Ammon, P., & Gearhart, M. (2004). Learning to teach inquiry science in a technology-based environment: A case study. *Journal of Science Education and Technology, 13*(2), 189–206.

Yeh, Y.-F., Hsu, Y. S., Wu, H.-K., Hwang, F. K., & Lin, T. C. (2013). Developing and validating technological pedagogical content knowledge-practical (TPACK-Practical) through the Delphi survey technique. *British Journal of Educational Technology, 45*(4), 707–722.

19

Music TPACK in Higher Education
Educating the Educators

Jordan Mroziak, Judith Bowman

Introduction

Music TPACK brings the TPACK framework into music education. It involves integrating technology into the teaching and learning of music through the major ways that people engage with music—through creating (composing, improvising), performing (singing, playing instruments), and responding (listening to, analyzing, and evaluating). However, these categories play out differently at various educational levels (Bauer, 2013). At the K–12 level, these music activities ordinarily take place within three major categories: classroom or "general" music (varied music experiences that may include creating, performing, and responding to music), instrumental music (band, orchestra), and choral music (choir). At the secondary level some music programs include music technology courses or music theory courses in addition to the instrumental and choral programs (Dammers, 2012). At the higher education level, these types of musical engagement constitute distinct music subdisciplines.

Music in Higher Education

Music instruction at the K–12 level is organized rather simply into instrumental music, choral music, and classroom music. In higher education, however, it is organized within discrete disciplinary frameworks (e.g., performance, music education, musicology, music technology, music theory), each with a distinctive way of thinking, specific subject matter, and signature pedagogy. For example, performance (study of a musical instrument or voice) typically employs a master/apprentice pedagogy. Musicology (study of major style periods, significant composers, and representative compositions) and music theory (study and analysis of musical structures and forms) are sometimes taught separately but instructors may also integrate those content areas for a more comprehensive approach. Most of these subdisciplines also exist as complete degree programs.

Within the music subdisciplines, the integration of technology is likewise more distinctive—for each subdiscipline there are technologies that are more or less appropriate to the subject matter and the specific pedagogy. In music theory courses, students may use computer notation software to notate, listen to, and edit homework assignments, which can be submitted electronically. In an elementary methods course, music education students might design a music WebQuest appropriate for use in a middle school music classroom setting. Within this disciplinary structure, music technology functions concurrently as discipline, degree program, subject matter, and pedagogical tool. The music technology curriculum meets the standards for degree programs in music technology, but it does not typically include pedagogical applications, particularly at the undergraduate level. Its status as specific subject matter within a distinct subdiscipline dominates and, despite its presence in nearly every aspect of daily life, it is often studied as a separate subject and not integrated into other musical/academic content areas (Boehm, 2007; Rees, 2011; Dorfman, 2013).

Music TPACK in Higher Education

The TPACK framework applies to K–12 music instruction in a straightforward way—integrating technology into the creation, performance, and response to music. A solid foundation has been built at that level, including development of specific music learning activity types (Bauer, 2010, 2013; Bauer, Harris, & Hofer, 2012a, 2012b) and design of specific strategies to promote development of TPACK in pre-service music teachers (Bauer, 2014). However, in some music teacher education programs, there is a significant impediment to implementation of these strategies—the music teacher educators themselves. Although technology may be integral to students' everyday experience, it is not necessarily familiar territory for music/music education professors, whose education was most likely grounded in the traditional classical approaches used in colleges, conservatories, and departments of music. In addition, many of today's technologies either did not exist or were not part of these professors' own training. It is not surprising, then, that professors who themselves did not learn with technology are uncomfortable with the idea of teaching with it—TPACK is simply not part of their repertoire. Consequently, pre-service music teachers develop competence with music content and traditional pedagogical approaches, but they do not attain a comparable level of competence in teaching with technology because it is not taught or assessed as are the more traditional competencies (Dorfman, 2013), a phenomenon commonly reported in TPACK research literature (Mishra & Koehler, 2006). This situation highlights the need to help music professors, particularly music education professors, develop their TPACK so they may integrate technology into their own teaching and model its pedagogical use in their courses.

Pedagogical Problems

There are numerous instances of technology integration into K–12 music classrooms (Burns, 2006; Kersten, 2006; Webster, 2011; Dammers, 2012). These examples are often the result of efforts by music educators who have specialized in music technology or who have studied it independently of their formal music teacher education experience, typically by attending music technology workshops that focus on classroom integration of music technology (Reese & Rimmington, 2000; Bauer, Reese, & McAllister, 2003; Rees, 2011; Dammers, 2012). Likewise, some students in pre-service music teacher education programs may have had prior experience with music technology, perhaps gained through high school courses in music technology or through independent efforts, and these students may even have done some peer teaching of technology. However, it is less common for pre-service music educators to experience learning with technology in their methods courses or to receive instruction on teaching with technology (Reese & Rimmington, 2000). Rather, schools and departments of music more often treat technology as a discrete subject, requiring stand-alone introductory music technology courses for all entering undergraduate students (Rees, 2011). These courses typically focus on development of skills in the use of specific music applications and resources such as computer music notation, basic MIDI theory (musical instrument digital interface, a protocol that allows communication between and among computers and various digital musical instruments), sequencing (recording and playback of musical tracks), and computer-assisted instruction in music. Uses of general software applications targeted toward musicians may also be taught in these courses—Internet exploration, electronic database searching—as well as basic functions of common productivity software such as MS Word, PowerPoint, and Excel. However, instruction in how to teach with these technologies is not ordinarily included—the courses are designed to help all students develop knowledge and skills with specific music technologies and with some common software applications for their own use. Students typically learn selected music software applications appropriate to professionals as well as some basic Web design (Dorfman, 2013). Music notation skills learned in these courses may be useful for composition projects in some college music courses, in which students are required to produce music scores for ensemble performances, or for homework assignments in certain courses. Music educators also sometimes use these skills to produce simple scores for student lessons or to arrange musical works for a student ensemble. However, they would likely not use a sophisticated professional-level program for student work in K–12 settings, as simpler, free, cloud-based options are available and appropriate to that level. And, instruction in Web design is usually targeted toward the development of personal or professional websites rather than toward instructional use.

Exacerbating this problem is the nature of the typical music education curriculum, which includes multiple methods courses and little time in which to accommodate additional coursework. Generally speaking, the primary concern of instrumental music education methods instructors (e.g., brass instrument methods, wind instrument methods) is developing student competence with musical instruments and the ability to teach beginning- through intermediate-level students. General music methods instructors are primarily concerned with ensuring competence with the major traditional classroom music methodologies. An optimum solution would be to integrate technology into these music education methods courses, where students could experience the use of technology in context both as learners and as future teachers (Dorfman, 2013). However, music education professors often presume that the stand-alone technology courses will provide music education students with what they need in order to teach with technology—the "leap of faith" described by Mishra and Koehler: "by demonstrating their proficiency with current software and hardware, teachers will be able to successfully incorporate technology into their classrooms" (2006, p. 1031). Unfortunately, this kind of technocentric approach fails to place the learning in context. Consequently, when pre-service music teachers are expected to use available technologies in their early field and student teaching experiences, they find themselves at a disadvantage because of their lack of experience with technology integration into K–12 music instruction.

The need to apply TPACK throughout the pre-service teacher curriculum has been emphasized as a crucial factor in helping these students learn how to integrate technology into their teaching (AACTE Committee, 2008, p. 291). This kind of curriculum integration ordinarily includes instructor modeling and student practice, which might begin with a small-scale use to demonstrate basic proficiency with a technology and a pedagogical application. A next step would involve student design of lessons that integrate technology into the pedagogy of specific subject matter at a particular grade level (AACTE Committee, 2008; Koehler et al., 2011). Integration of technology into the music education program is particularly critical as it directly involves pedagogical applications of technology in the preparation of future music teachers. In an ideal college music curriculum, technology would be integrated into both music education methods courses and other music courses as well (e.g., music history, music theory). Integration across the music curriculum would enhance the development of music TPACK, as it would provide models of technology integration into the teaching and learning of music through the major ways that people engage with music—through creating, performing, and responding to music. It would also extend the issue of educating the educators to include all music professors.

Addressing the Issues: Educating the Educators

The lack of integration of technology into classroom instruction is an ongoing issue in music education. Technology is often treated in isolation, classroom integration is not addressed, and few methods instructors integrate it into their courses for reasons ranging from perceived lack of time to lack of familiarity with appropriate technologies and their pedagogical applications. Music education professors acknowledge the importance of technology in the education of K–12 students. However, if they are unfamiliar with music technology, they will neither integrate it into their methods courses nor provide opportunities for pre-service teachers to design applications appropriate for K–12. The problem persists if professors have gained some familiarity with instructional technologies but have not developed the TPACK that would enable them to model authentic technology integration in a variety of music education courses. This combination of factors results in absence of technology integration into music courses of all types, and again highlights the need to educate the educators.

The interest is there in many cases, but so are obstacles. Most professors' busy schedules leave little time for learning new technology-oriented pedagogies. Additionally, they are unlikely to use that knowledge unless it is consistent with their existing pedagogical beliefs and practices: the further a new practice is from a professor's existing practice, the less likely it is to be implemented (Zhao, Pugh, Sheldon, & Byers, 2002). These two obstacles are usually considered first- and second-order barriers to technology integration. First-order (external) barriers include lack of access to computers and software, insufficient time to plan instruction, and inadequate technical and administrative support. Second-order (internal/personal) barriers include beliefs about teaching, beliefs about computers, established classroom practices, and readiness or unwillingness to change (Ertmer, 1999, 2005). Because first-order barriers are tied to second-order barriers (i.e., we focus on what is important to us, and we make time for what we care about), we need to consider both types of barriers. Addressing first-order barriers involves acquiring technical skills; addressing second-order barriers involves challenging professors' belief systems and established pedagogical practices. Removing second-order barriers presents a greater challenge than simply persuading professors that some new practice is superior to what they are currently doing and expecting them to adopt it. It is more likely that beliefs will change gradually as a result of successful practice involving something important to the person. So the best approach to helping professors learn to teach with technology is discovering what drives their teaching, what they want for their students, what is important to them, and therefore what it is that they care about. Removing these barriers can pave the way for technology integration, but there is still a missing piece—professors still need to design or redesign learning experiences and materials. This missing piece might be considered a third-order barrier (Tsai & Chai, 2012) that deals with practical issues. It goes beyond technology issues and pedagogical beliefs to the art of teaching with technology. TPACK enters in at this stage, with the need to consider how technology, content, and pedagogy interrelate within a specific context.

This situation served as the impetus for us to develop a comprehensive approach that would address needs both within music education courses and across the entire music curriculum. To address these issues we developed an overall strategy: (1) a survey that would simultaneously provide us with information and educate faculty about basic issues and uses of technology in music instruction (Mroziak & Bowman, 2012, November), and (2) professional development in faculty-selected areas of need or interest (Mroziak & Bowman, 2013, October).

Faculty Technology Survey

We used an existing instrument designed as a TPACK assessment survey for pre-service teachers (Schmidt et al., 2009). The initial article includes a comprehensive discussion of the instrument design process with specific attention paid to acquiring an acceptable level of internal consistency based upon factor analysis. After revision, "The internal consistency reliability (coefficient alpha) ranged from .75 to .92 for the seven TPACK subscales. According to George and Mallery (2001), this range is considered to be acceptable to excellent" (Schmidt et al., 2009, p. 131). Music was not among the content areas used for development of this instrument; however, it was relatively easy to adapt it as a music TPACK survey and expand it to inform professors about specific technologies and their potential uses. This is the process that we followed in our institution, a school of music within a university. Based on the existing survey, we developed discipline-specific questions that would yield information about our faculty's TPACK while educating them on how to think about teaching with technology.

- "I know about technologies that I can use for understanding and 'doing' music" (TCK)
- "I am thinking critically about how to use technology in my classroom or studio" (TPK)
- "I can select technologies to use in my classroom or studio that enhance what I teach, how I teach, and what students learn" (TPACK)

It was also important to discover what specific technologies faculty were familiar with, what learning outcomes they considered important, and what their preferences might be for learning more about teaching with technology. Questions unique to our survey addressed those issues.

- Using technology: "Assess the likelihood of your use of particular technologies in your classroom or studio" (recording of applied lessons, PowerPoint presentations, interactive whiteboards, etc.)
- Specific technologies: A technology checklist designed to be educational for faculty as well as to yield information for the survey (GarageBand, iMovie, YouTube/TeacherTube)
- Student needs: "What will your students need to do with technology in order to be successful after graduation?" (create a digital portfolio, create a professional website, educate others about technology)
- Preferred training formats (group or one-on-one focus sessions, 1-day/2-day workshop, week-long course) and time frames for assistance (fall/spring semesters, week after spring commencement, summer)

The Disconnect

The survey was intended to reveal how faculty envision themselves using technology in their classes or lessons, as well as how they perceive the potential use of technology by students. The following bullet points highlight the primary findings within our survey results.

- Faculty felt that their students, upon graduating, will need to:

    Create and maintain a personal/professional website (87%)
    Create a digital portfolio including video/images/audio (74%)
    Create scores for performance/publication/rehearsal + educate others about using technology (tie: 64%)

- Faculty felt that in their classrooms, they were most likely to:

    Record lessons (76%)
    Use PowerPoint (68%)
    Utilize guided Web searches (60%)

The results revealed a striking disparity between faculty use and anticipated student use. Professors envisioned themselves using discrete elements. Anticipated student needs after graduation, however, were projected as contextually relevant (create and maintain a personal or professional website; create a digital portfolio including video, images, and audio; create scores for performance, publication, or rehearsal; and educate others about using technology). In short, the larger picture revealed that students will need to create using technology and educate about technology, but the professors' projections of how they would engage with and implement technology in their classrooms did not appear likely to lead to those outcomes. Unless professors communicate this contextual relevance in some way (e.g., through in-class modeling or direct instruction), there is a gap that cannot be bridged. This disconnect between the classroom experiences and anticipated outcomes highlights the need to reevaluate how to conduct faculty technology development and how to overcome pedagogical barriers.

Closing the Gap: Informal Blended Faculty Development

Informed by the responses to the faculty survey, the next step was follow-up—conversations with individual professors and professional development in faculty-selected areas of need or interest. Although survey responses suggested some interest in short-term group instruction, the initial follow-up revealed an overwhelming desire to work one on one. To accommodate the schedules and needs of individual faculty members, the more plausible solution seemed to be a peer coaching model. We therefore developed an approach that would be easy, convenient, and yield immediately productive results—a just-in-time model using small, targeted, achievable goals. We contacted selected faculty, presented ideas for technology integration based on their own interests, and proposed some easy steps to achieve their goals. The approach was designed to eliminate first-order barriers by focusing on readily accessible technologies that could be used in a number of disciplines, and then to mitigate second-order barriers through informal meetings and open dialogue (Ertmer, 2001). The small and readily achievable tasks smoothed transitions into deeper technological barriers, while opening up previously unseen pathways to student engagement and learning.

Coaching

There is evidence in recent research for the effectiveness of a coaching model, in which colleagues work together to solve problems or instructional challenges: instructors who learn from or with peer coaches develop confidence in the use of technology that enables them to design effective technology-based learning environments (Beglau et al., 2011; International Society for Technology in Education [ISTE], 2011). Its success is due to personalized assessment and support, together with a focus on what the instructor can use immediately, relevance to what the instructor is currently teaching, and ongoing support for the instructor (Beglau et al., 2011, p. 7). We believe this model can be just as effective in higher education as it has been in K–12 settings, because it begins with an informal conversation between colleagues and is tailored specifically to the professor's needs and interests. One of the most valuable aspects of a coaching model is the opportunity to demonstrate how to think about teaching with technology, specifically, using the TPACK framework. Peer coaching may present some challenges with schedule coordination, but it appears to be a useful format for working with higher education faculty. A preliminary meeting with the faculty member to identify needs, interests, and existing technology knowledge can ensure a well-focused, relevant development process. Advance readings can help faculty prepare for a productive coaching session, e.g., a short article on music TPACK (Bauer, 2010) in which they might find useful suggestions for helping their students develop TPACK—notably, integrating technology into their music education methods courses and modeling the use of technology in music instruction. Practice-based articles that describe technology use by classroom music teachers (Burns, 2006; Kersten, 2006) can also be helpful in generating methods-course strategies that would provide similar opportunities for pre-service teachers. We used this peer coaching approach with individual faculty from several departments; an illustration of our work with one professor follows. Our basic process included (1) an initial contact (email); (2) a planning meeting; (3) a learning session; (4) classroom integration; and (5) development of student assignments involving technology.

A music education professor specializing in primary and elementary general music was interested in use of the interactive whiteboard and in ePortfolios. Starting late in the spring semester, she was sent articles on TPACK, interactive whiteboards, and ePortfolios in preparation for the planning meeting, during which she decided to focus on the interactive whiteboard (SMART Board), with the goal of using it in her elementary general music methods course. Based on her choice, the discussion covered strategies for using the SMART Board with emphasis on affordances; guidelines for use and how to think about it (i.e., as one of several options, combining technology and conventional approaches); and a conversation about the articles. At this point, we scheduled a session to try out the SMART Board. This hands-on session included connecting the equipment and becoming acquainted with some basic SMART Board functions, using music tasks appropriate to elementary general methods. In the following fall, this professor integrated use of the SMART Board into the elementary general music methods course, where she demonstrated an Orff-based lesson for the students. With rhythm notation displayed on the SMART Board, she alluded to the affordances of the technology, revealed a rhythm pattern phrase by phrase (a SMART Board function), and dragged solfège letters (the initial letters of syllables used for singing music at sight—do, re, mi, etc.) under the rhythm pattern. She carried out the lesson using full-group activities: techniques included half the class singing and the other half clapping rhythms displayed on the SMART Board. To give students direct experience with integration of technology into music instruction, she developed a project assignment in which they were required to (1) design a lesson that could be used in an actual classroom; (2) use a few specified SMART Board features; (3) include an interactive component where students manipulate something on the board at some point in the lesson; and (4) give a presentation/teaching demonstration in the elementary methods class. This experience seemed to provide the impetus for continued technology integration, as the professor brought additional technologies into the class—clickers for in-class polling and discussion, and an online discussion board for article discussions and elementary classroom repertoire planning.

Plan for the Future

A systematic plan is key to initiating this kind of peer coaching program. The following procedures are recommended to help music teacher educators develop their TPACK.

- Survey the faculty to gain information about their current TPACK, discover what technologies they are familiar with, and identify learning outcomes important to them.
- Arrange an initial planning meeting with individual professors to identify desired learning outcomes, inform them of options they may be unaware of, and plan small, readily achievable steps to achieve their goals.
- Schedule a learning session to experiment with steps agreed upon in the planning meeting.
- Advise on design of learning experiences and materials to support the plan, and target an implementation date.
- Maintain contact, possibly observe a class session, and provide feedback.

Moving forward, it is important to remember that faculty who are new to teaching with technology need ongoing support. Professors can start small and slowly, first "playing" with the technology and discovering what it can do, and then using that one technology in one class—"practicing the practice." Once they have achieved success on a small scale and with encouragement from a knowledgeable colleague, they may be ready to try additional practices, so that, ultimately, teaching music with technology becomes just teaching music.

References

AACTE Committee on Innovation and Technology. (2008). Afterword: TPCK action for teacher education: It's about time! In AACTE Committee on Innovation and Technology (Ed.), *Handbook of technological pedagogical content knowledge (TPCK) for educators* (pp. 289–300). New York: Routledge.

Bauer, W. I. (2010). Technological pedagogical and content knowledge for music teachers. In D. Gibson & B. Dodge (Eds.), *Proceedings of Society for Information Technology & Teacher Education International Conference 2010* (pp. 3977–3980). Chesapeake, VA: AACE.

Bauer, W. I. (2013). The acquisition of musical technological pedagogical and content knowledge. *Journal of Music Teacher Education, 22*(2), 51–64. doi:10.1177/1057083712457881

Bauer, W. I. (2014). *Music learning today: Digital pedagogy for creating, performing, and responding to music.* New York: Oxford University Press.

Bauer, W. I., Harris, J., & Hofer, M. (2012a). Grounded tech integration using K–12 music learning activity types. *Learning & Leading, 40*(3), 30–32.

Bauer, W. I., Harris, J., & Hofer, M. (2012b). Music learning activity types. Retrieved from College of William and Mary, School of Education, Learning Activity Types Wiki: http://activitytypes.wmwikis.net/file/view/MusicLearningATs-June2012.pdf

Bauer, W. I., Reese, S., & McAllister, P. A. (2003). Transforming music teaching via technology: The role of professional development. *Journal of Research in Music Education, 51*(4), 289–301. doi:10.2307/3345656

Beglau, M., Hare, J. C., Foltos, L., Gann, K., James, J., Jobe, H., Knight, J., & Smith, B. (2011). Technology, coaching, and community: Partners for improved professional development in primary and secondary education. International Society for Technology in Education. Retrieved from https://www.iste.org/

Boehm, C. (2007). The discipline that never was: Current developments in music technology in higher education in Britain. *Journal of Music, Technology and Education, 1*(1), 7–21. doi:10.1386/jmte.1.1.7/1

Burns, A. M. (2006). Integrating technology into your elementary music classroom. *General Music Today, 20*(1), 6–10. doi:10.1177/10483713060200010103

Dammers, R. J. (2012). Technology-based music classes in high schools in the United States. *Bulletin of the Council for Research in Music Education, 194*, 73–90. doi:10.5406/bulcouresmusedu.194.0073

Dorfman, J. (2013). *Theory and practice of technology-based music instruction.* New York: Oxford University Press.

Ertmer, P. A. (1999). Addressing first- and second-order barriers to change: Strategies for technology integration. *Educational Technology Research and Development, 47*(4), 47–61.

Ertmer, P. A. (2001). Responsive instructional design: Scaffolding the adoption and change process. *Educational Technology, 41*(6), 33–38.

Ertmer, P. A. (2005). Teacher pedagogical beliefs: The final frontier in our quest for technology integration? *Educational Technology Research and Development, 53*(4), 25–39.

George, D., & Mallery, P. (2001). *SPSS for Windows.* Needham Heights, MA: Allyn & Bacon.

International Society for Technology in Education. (2011). ISTE NETS for technology coaches (NETS• C). Retrieved from https://www.iste.org/

Kersten, F. (2006). Inclusion of technology resources in early childhood music education. *General Music Today, 20*(1), 15–28. doi:10.1177/10483713060200010105

Koehler, M. J., Mishra, P., Bouck, E. C., DeSchryver, M., Kereluik, K., Shin, T. S., & Wolf, L. G. (2011). Deep-play: Developing TPACK for 21st century teachers. *International Journal of Learning Technology, 6*(2), 146–163.

Mishra, P., & Koehler, M. J. (2006). Technological pedagogical content knowledge: A framework for teacher knowledge. *Teachers College Record, 108*(6), 1017–1054.

Mroziak, J., & Bowman, J. (2012, November). Welcome to the future: Educating educators about today's technology. Paper presented at the meeting of the Association for Technology in Music Instruction National Conference, San Diego, CA.

Mroziak, J., & Bowman, J. (2013, October). I want you to want me: Informal blended faculty development. Paper presented at the meeting of the Association for Technology in Music Instruction National Conference, Cambridge, MA.

Rees, F. J. (2011). Redefining music technology in the United States. *Journal of Music, Technology and Education, 4*(2+3), 149–155. doi:10.1386/ jmte.4.2-3.149_1

Reese, S., & Rimmington, J. (2000). Music technology in Illinois public schools. *Update: Applications of Research in Music Education, 18*(2), 27–32. doi:10.1177/875512330001800206

Schmidt, D. A., Baran, E., Thompson, A. D., Mishra, P., Koehler, M. J., & Shin, T. S. (2009). Technological pedagogical content knowledge (TPACK): The development and validation of an assessment instrument for preservice teachers. *Journal of Research on Technology in Education, 42*(2), 123–149.

Tsai, C., & Chai, C. S. (2012). The "third"-order barrier for technology-integration instruction: Implications for teacher education. *Australasian Journal of Educational Technology, 28*(Special issue, 6), 1057–1060.

Webster, P. R. (2011). Key research in music technology and music teaching and learning. *Journal of Music, Technology and Education, 4*(2+3), 115–130. doi:10.1386/jmte.4.2–3.115

Zhao, Y., Pugh, K., Sheldon, S., & Byers, J. L. (2002). Conditions for classroom technology innovations. *Teachers College Record, 104*, 482–515.

20

The Impact of Digital Storytelling on the Development of TPACK Among Student Teachers in Taiwan

Amber Yayin Wang

Introduction

With the importance of TPACK (Technological, Pedagogical, and Content Knowledge) being recognized, TPACK research in general has grown significantly, and has started to explore domain specific nature of TPACK. Computer-assisted language learning (CALL), or technology enhanced language learning (TELL), has become a major trend in the area of English language instruction in recent years (Beach et al., 2010). Thus, the need to develop TPACK among teachers of English is an urgent need (Banas, 2010; CDW-G, 2010; Wang, 2011).

TPACK research in English language learning has covered both conceptual inquiries (e.g., Robin, 2008; van Olphen, 2008) and empirical studies (e.g., Heo, 2009, 2011; Hofer & Swan, 2006; Hughes & Scharber, 2008; Schmidt & Gurbo, 2008; Wang, 2011). A review of the literature on different approaches to developing TPACK in English showed the repeated appearance of digital storytelling. Many researchers (e.g., Heo, 2009, 2011; Hofer & Swan, 2006; Hughes & Scharber, 2008; Robin, 2008; Schmidt & Gurbo, 2008; van Olphen, 2008) have endorsed digital storytelling as an effective means for developing TPACK. For example, Hicks (2006) and Robin (2008) propose theoretical possibilities for digital storytelling to enhance TPACK. Heo (2009, 2011), Hofer and Swan (2006), and Schmidt and Gurbo (2008) provide empirical evidence about how digital storytelling helped develop TPACK among teachers. Additionally, TPACK has also been argued to be a powerful tool for language instruction and fostering creativity (e.g., Ohler, 2008; Mahon & Cherednichenko, 2007).

There are some limitations in the research, however. For instance, Heo (2009, 2011) merely observed the self-efficacy for technological pedagogical knowledge (TPK), rather than the overall TPACK of the pre-service teachers. Although Hofer and Swan (2006) and Schmidt and Gurbo (2008) did record TPACK development, their research focused on case studies of native teachers of English. In fact, most of the research in this area has focused on the role of TPACK in teaching English as a native language (e.g., George, 2011; Parr, Bellis, & Bulfin, 2013; Heo, 2009, 2011; Hofer & Swan, 2006; Hughes & Scharber, 2008; Schmidt & Gurbo, 2008). Studies of TPACK in teaching English as a second, other language (TESOL/ESOL), or foreign language (TEFL/EFL) appear to be scarce.

Some studies in the TESOL or TEFL field simply described the TPACK in ESOL or EFL teachers (e.g., van Olphen, 2008; Wang 2011) without analyzing any development of TPACK. Among the few studies that explored the development of TPACK, Kurt, Mishra and Kocoglu (2013) marked the quantitative TPACK of Turkish teachers in a reflective project and reported the increase of the TPACK scores; Tseng (2011) suggested the self-reported growth of TPACK in a workshop. Still, neither study attempted to analyze the characteristics in the development of TPACK among EFL teachers.

Objectives

With the aim of developing TPACK in English language instruction among EFL teachers, an empirical study was conducted to observe whether digital storytelling influenced the TPACK performance of student teachers in Taiwan. This chapter presents the empirical study, analyzing both quantitative and qualitative TPACK in the domain of English language in the EFL context, and thus investigates whether digital storytelling would have any influence on the development of TPACK. The focus questions were (1) What were the English TPACK profiles of the EFL student teachers at the beginning and at the end of a semester? (2) After the practice of digital storytelling, was there any significant change in the TPACK performance? (3) Was there any significant difference in TPACK between those who had practiced digital storytelling and those who had not?

Method

Given the complexity and ambiguity of TPACK, Archambault and Barnett (2010) suggest that the assessment of TPACK incorporate both quantitative and qualitative data. This study adopted a mixed-method approach, collecting both quantitative (through the TPACK survey) and qualitative (through open-ended survey questions and digital assignment files) data. It cross-examined all sources of data and provided profiles of TPACK performance of EFL student teachers within a semester.

Population

Participants were recruited from an English education course titled Children's English. Students who took the course in the education program were those who had passed an examination to become qualified student teachers. The examination included an aptitude test and ability tests, assessing their educational beliefs and basic academic abilities (mathematics, language arts, and academic performance in their departments). This course provided guiding principles on how children learn English as a foreign language and how teachers help EFL children learning the English language. The course focused more on pedagogical knowledge (PK), content knowledge (CK), and pedagogical content knowledge (PCK) than on any particular TK. Still, TPACK, though not explicitly instructed as a conceptual framework, would be introduced in class whenever technological knowledge (TK), such as digital storytelling (DST), PowerPoint (PPT), or online resources, was introduced.

Two classes of student teachers (N = 58) who took this same course at a university in central Taiwan consented to participate in this study. The two classes included qualified student teachers who took the same required education courses, used the same textbook, and shared the same teaching materials (lesson PPTs), though with two different instructors. One class (the experiment group) was given an assignment to create a DST file for children, whereas the other (the comparison group) was required to create a PPT file for its final teaching assignment. Table 20.1 shows the demographics of the participants. Most (N = 44; 75.9%) of the 58 participants were female; only a few (N = 14; 24.1%) were male. The two classes did not have equal numbers of students: there were 41 students in the DST group and only 17 in the PPT group. The majority (N = 44; 75.9%) were in their sophomore year, age 20 or younger.

Instrument

The instrument for assessing quantitative TPACK was a TPACK survey. It was based on the assessments developed by Koh, Chai, and Tsai (2010) and Sahin (2011). Both measurements were reported to have high validity and credibility (Koh et al., 2010: α=0.96 / Cronbach's α: 0.83–0.96; Sahin, 2011: α=0.92 / Cronbach's α: 0.77–0.86). Because neither of the assessments was domain-specific, the assessments were put together and rephrased to focus specifically on the English language. For example, for the assessment of Koh et al. (2010), the original statement for CK used the term Curriculum Subject 1: "I have various ways and strategies of developing my understanding of Curriculum Subject 1." In the revised survey, only the term "Curriculum Subject 1" was replaced by "English," and the rest of the sentence was kept intact. In the survey of Sahin (2011), the original statements were phrases, such as "Integrating appropriate instructional methods and technologies into my content area." Thus, in the revised survey, each statement was rephrased as a sentence, and the example statement became, "I can integrate appropriate instructional methods and technologies into teaching English." The revised survey was pretested with 38 student teachers in the same school for reliability.

The TPACK survey includes three parts: (1) background information, (2) Likert scale "questions," and (3) and open-ended questions. The Likert scale questions are 42 statements

Table 20.1 Demographics of Participants

		Experiment Group		Comparison Group	
		No.	%	No.	%
Total No. = 58		41		17	
Gender	Male	7	17.1	7	41.2
	Female	34	82.9	10	58.8
Age	20 or less than 20	32	78.0	12	70.6
	21–25	7	17.1	5	29.4
	Above 25	2	4.9	0	0

for the participants to self-evaluate their TK, PK, CK, TPK, technological content knowledge (TCK), PCK, and technological pedagogical content knowledge (TPCK) on a 7-point Likert scale (1 = strongly disagree; 7 = strongly agree). Each knowledge base includes six statements. The average of the scales for the six statements for TK will be its TK scores (1–7). Similar calculations were made for each knowledge base. The overall TPACK score is the sum of the seven subscores (7–42). In the last part, three open-ended questions pertain to opinions about how technology can be integrated into English instruction, what difficulties or challenges there may be, and expectations (feedback) for the course.

Data Analysis

The analysis of TPACK was conducted with both quantitative data (the survey) and qualitative data (the open-ended questions and final lesson plans). For the quantitative data, the TPACK scores were stored and analyzed with SPSS. Descriptive and analytical statistics (t-test) were performed to compare the mean scores. As for the qualitative data, a different framework was employed to analyze their TPACK.

Well-developed TPACK in the English language domain signifies the ability to integrate different knowledge bases to deliver an effective CALL lesson, so being able to demonstrate the characteristics of an optimal CALL lesson may reflect the ability to integrate technology into language learning. Therefore, eight key elements suggested by Egbert and Hanson-Smith (1999) were adopted to analyze their TPACK. According to them, the eight characteristics for a best CALL lesson for ESOL learners are interactivity, meaningfulness, authenticity, creativity, feedback, learning-focused, stress-free, and autonomy. These elements were used as keywords to explore whether their final teaching projects or their answers to the open-ended questions contained the eight characteristics.

Procedure

At the beginning of the semester, both groups of student teachers completed the TPACK survey. Digital storytelling was introduced briefly to the experiment group (DST group) in the first and second weeks of the semester. The student teachers edited their materials with Windows Movie Maker in a laboratory and were reminded in the eighth week to avoid plagiarism or copyright problems. Besides the above instruction, the student teachers in the DST group were totally on their own in the creation of their digital stories and completely free to choose any topic and materials to construct their DST projects. As mentioned earlier, this course explored PK, CK, and PCK, so in class discussion, students were asked to reflect on how to integrate the PK, CK, PCK, or TK they acquired, from the lessons or DST practices, into their English teaching. In the final weeks, student teachers were required to present their digital stories with a brief explanation on how they could be used in their English instruction.

Conversely, the comparison group (PPT group) was introduced briefly to their final PPT project, spent the second week learning how to apply PPT in English instruction, and learned about online resources in the eighth week. The student teachers in the PPT group were also completely on their own for their final PPT project. Again, in class, students discussed and reflected on how to integrate the PK, CK, PCK, or TK they learned during the lessons or PPT exercises into teaching English. In the final weeks, the PPT group demonstrated teaching with their PPT files. At the end of the semester, the two groups of student teachers completed the TPACK survey again. Figure 20.1 is a summary of the procedure.

Results

The results are presented as quantitative and qualitative TPACK in the pretest and posttest. Quantitative TPACK refers to the descriptive and analytical statistics of the TPACK scores. Qualitative TPACK resulted from the analyses done on the open-ended questions in the TPACK survey and on the final lesson plans and digital files. However, not all of the student teachers replied to the open-ended questions; only 53 responses were collected from the pretest (PPT N = 14; DST N = 39) and 39 from the posttest (PPT N = 12; DST N = 27).

Quantitative TPACK

(1) Pretest: No Significant Difference on Overall TPACK

At the beginning of the semester, the TPACK profiles of the two groups were similar. According to the survey results, the two groups did not differ significantly on their overall TPACK performance. The mean of the total TPACK scores of both groups was around 25 (DST = 25.98; PPT = 25.03) on a scale of 42. This means that both groups merely passed the average on a scale of 100 (DST = 61.85%; PPT = 59.61%). The t-test comparing the pretest of the two groups did not show any significant difference (t-test $p > 0.05$). Table 20.2 shows the means and t-test results of the overall TPACK of the two groups in the pretest.

Pretest	Experiment (18 weeks)			Posttest
Week 1	Week 1-2	Week 8	Week 17-18	Week 18
Pretest	Introduction	Laboratory	Final Exam	Posttest
TPACK Survey	DST Project	Movie Maker	DST Demo	TPACK Survey
	PPT Project	The Internet	PPT Demo	

Figure 20.1 Research Procedure

Table 20.2 Overall TPACK Scores of the Two Groups in the Pretest

	Group	Mean*	SD	t-test sig.
TPACK	Experiment (DST)	25.98	4.85	0.385
	Comparison (PPT)	25.03	3.14	

*Scaled scores: TPACK = 7–42.

(2) Pretest: PK Strongest and CK Weakest with Difference on PCK

When the respective component scores were analyzed, the two groups appeared to be similar in most of the areas, except for their PCK. According to the mean scores of each component, PK appeared to be their strongest area (DST: M = 4.68, SD = 0.93; PPT: M = 4.64, SD = 0.53), while CK was the weakest (DST: M = 3.84, SD = 0.87; PPT: M = 3.43, SD = 0.86). However, the PCK scores of the DST group were significantly higher than those of the PPT group (t-test sig= 0.004). Table 20.3 lists the means and t-test results of each component of the two groups in the pretest.

(3) Posttest: Significant TPACK Growth in the DST Group

At the end of the semester, although both groups made progress, the DST group showed amazing growth. The two groups scored higher on the total TPACK in the posttest: when the scores were again converted into a percentage, both groups earned passing scores on a scale of 100 (DST = 74.07%; PPT = 62.07%). Table 20.4 indicates the progress within each group. Compared with their pretests, the PPT group scored significantly higher on CK and PCK in their posttest, but the DST group scored significantly higher in the posttest on almost every aspect of their TPACK (t-test $p < 0.001$), except for their TK (Table 20.4). When comparing the two groups, a low t-test value of 0.001 ($p < 0.05$) was found between the means of their TPACK (Table 20.5). In fact, the two groups not only

Table 20.3 TPACK Component Scores of the Two Groups in the Pretest

Component	Group	Mean*	SD	t-test sig.
TK	Experiment (DST)	4.54	1.00	0.721
	Comparison (PPT)	4.42	1.00	
CK	Experiment (DST)	3.84	0.87	0.112
	Comparison (PPT)	3.43	0.86	
PK	Experiment (DST)	4.68	0.93	0.847
	Comparison (PPT)	4.64	0.53	
PCK	Experiment (DST)	4.39	0.88	0.004**
	Comparison (PPT)	3.80	0.58	
TPK	Experiment (DST)	4.56	1.01	0.931
	Comparison (PPT)	4.54	0.80	
TCK	Experiment (DST)	4.11	1.09	0.181
	Comparison (PPT)	4.41	0.61	
TPCK	Experiment (DST)	4.20	1.13	0.392
	Comparison (PPT)	3.96	0.88	

* Scaled scores: TK, CK, PK, PCK, TPK, TCK = 1–7
** t-test shows significant differences

Table 20.4 Progress Shown on TPACK Pretest and Posttest Scores of Each Group

		PPT Group			DST Group		
		M	SD	t-test sig.	M	SD	t-test sig.
TPACK	Pretest	25.03	3.14	0.458	25.98	4.86	<0.001**
	Posttest	26.07	4.09		31.11	3.88	
TK	Pretest	4.42	1.00	0.943	4.54	1.00	0.071
	Posttest	4.40	0.84		5.02	0.93	
CK	Pretest	3.43	0.86	0.026**	3.84	0.87	<0.001**
	Posttest	4.04	0.55		5.08	0.79	
PK	Pretest	4.64	0.53	0.602	4.68	0.93	<0.001**
	Posttest	4.77	0.77		5.44	0.74	
PCK	Pretest	3.80	0.58	0.015**	4.39	0.88	<0.001**
	Posttest	4.56	0.89		5.18	0.72	
TPK	Pretest	4.54	0.80	0.998	4.56	1.01	<0.001**
	Posttest	4.54	0.75		5.33	0.67	
TCK	Pretest	4.41	0.61	0.288	4.11	1.09	<0.001**
	Posttest	4.08	0.97		5.06	0.68	
TPCK	Pretest	3.96	0.88	0.886	4.20	1.13	<0.001**
	Posttest	4.03	1.08		5.18	0.78	

* Scaled scores: TK, CK, PK, PCK, TPK, TCK =1–7; TPACK = 7–42.
** t-test shows significant differences

Table 20.5 Comparison of TPACK Scores between the Two Groups in the Posttest

Knowledge Base	Group	Mean	SD	t-test sig.
TPACK	Experiment (DST)	31.11	3.88	0.001**
	Comparison (PPT)	26.07	4.09	
TK	Experiment (DST)	5.02	0.93	0.038**
	Comparison (PPT)	4.40	0.84	
CK	Experiment (DST)	5.08	0.79	<0.001**
	Comparison (PPT)	4.04	0.55	
PK	Experiment (DST)	5.44	0.74	0.015**
	Comparison (PPT)	4.77	0.77	
PCK	Experiment (DST)	5.18	0.72	0.038**
	Comparison (PPT)	4.56	0.89	
TPK	Experiment (DST)	5.33	0.67	0.003**
	Comparison (PPT)	4.54	0.75	
TCK	Experiment (DST)	5.06	0.68	0.004**
	Comparison (PPT)	4.08	0.97	
TPCK	Experiment (DST)	5.18	0.78	0.014**
	Comparison (PPT)	4.03	1.42	

* Scaled scores: TK, CK, PK, PCK, TPK, TCK = 1–7; TPACK = 7–42.
** t-test shows significant differences

differed significantly on overall TPACK (t-test $p < 0.001$), but also on every TPACK component (t-test $p < 0.05$).

(4) Posttest: PK Still Strongest With Better Integrative Abilities in the DST Group

As aforementioned, this course focused on PK, CK, and PCK, but not particularly on TK; hence, except for references to online resources (PPT and DST), no specific technological applications were taught during the semester. It is not surprising, therefore, that both groups improved significantly on their CK and PCK (Table 20.4), but not on their TK (both t-test $p > 0.05$). Their PK (DST: M = 5.44, SD = 0.74; PPT: M = 4.77, SD = 0.77) was still the strongest aspect of their TPACK. Their CK was no longer the weakest: the DST group rated TK as the weakest (M = 5.02, SD = 0.93), and the PPT group rated TPCK as the weakest (M = 4.03, SD = 1.42).

As shown in the comparison in Table 20.4, the DST group seemed to acquire better ability on integrating technology than the PPT group did. In the PPT group, the scores related to TK did not improve much (TPACK, TK, TPK, TCK, and TPCK), and some (TK, TPK, and TCK) even dropped slightly. Conversely, although the DST group did not think their TK had improved much, all the other integrative abilities that required TK had significantly improved (TPK, TCK, and TPCK).

Qualitative TPACK

(1) Pretest: Technology Only as Aids for Language Input

Similar to the results of quantitative TPACK, both groups shared similar profiles in the analysis of their pretest qualitative data. In their answers, both groups listed similar possible technology for instruction, such as websites, computer applications, digital books, interactive whiteboards, and audio and video clips. Most of the technological devices they mentioned were mainly for displaying information or providing language input, and most of the answers did not specify how the technological tools could be used to enhance language learning. They seemed to consider technology a powerful aid in providing language input (listening and reading materials), but they did not note much about how technology could be used for assisting language output (speaking and writing opportunities).

Only a few participants referred to technology as aids for language output. In the DST group, three student teachers (N = 3, 7.69%) wrote about using technology to develop "speaking" ability; among them, only two (N = 2, 5.13%) specifically indicated the use of "audio- or video-recording devices to help children practice speaking." In the PPT group, one (N = 1, 7.14%) commented on how technology could provide real-time communicative opportunities: "online chat with native English pupils to practice speaking." A similarly low percentage of the student teachers from the two groups thought of technology as an aid for language output. Most of the student teachers looked at technology in the classroom more as a source of tools for language input than as opportunities for language output or any real communication.

(2) Pretest: Emphasis on the "Interactivity" and "Stress-Free" Characteristics

When analyzing the eight key characteristics of the optimal CALL lesson, at least two elements were repeatedly noted in their statements: "interactivity" and "stress-free." Both groups wrote most frequently about how technology could "motivate," "attract," or "interest" children to learn English (DST = 17/39, 43.92%; PPT = 10/14, 71.43%). They stated that technology could "create vivid and fun environments" and "reduce stress" for children. The "stress-free" component, highly related to children's motivation, appeared to be the element most frequently mentioned. The second element frequently mentioned was "interactivity" (DST = 9/39, 23.08%; PPT = 4/14, 28.57%). Still, a few of them brought up the elements of "authenticity" (DST = 5/39, 12.82%; PPT = 3/14, 17.65%) and "autonomy" (DST = 4/39, 10.26%; PPT = 1/14, 7.14%).

Although it would be difficult to conclude their TPACK with the responses to an open-ended question, the findings shed some light on the initial TPACK. At the very beginning, student teachers focused on giving children a stress-free English class. Using technology to motivate children to learn English and creating a stress-free language class appeared to be the chief concerns of these EFL student teachers.

(3) Posttest: DST Group Using Technology for a Variety of Purposes

In the posttest, the two groups differed in their new ideas about integrating technology in English instruction. The PPT group did not provide many new ideas. Except for one new idea about using technology to "create videos or animations" (N = 1, 8.33%), the responses were very similar to those in their pretest, including using technology to "prepare PPT" (N = 5, 41.67%), "motivate" children (N = 5, 41.67%), "provide language situations" (N = 3, 25.00%), "play music or movie" (N = 2, 16.67%) or "electronic picture books" (N = 1, 8.33%), "review" information (N = 1, 8.33%), and "create stimulations" (N = 1, 8.33%).

Conversely, the DST group provided more concrete examples for integrating technology in instruction than they did in the pretest. Certainly, with their practice in audio- and video-recording in doing digital stories, many (N = 14, 51.85%) wrote about using "Movie Maker" to "create audio" or "video files," "radio plays," or "digital storytelling" to "personalize learning" and "create interactions" with children. Three (N = 3, 11.11%) described how technology could encourage children's creativity in using language: "student creating English works"; "teaching children to use Movie Maker and create [their own] digital picture books or talking books"; using a "tablet" computer to "record creative performance of children in class." It seems that the student teachers in the DST group noticed how to use technology as aids for not only language input, but also for language output, and even for encouraging children to creatively experiment with the new language.

(4) Posttest: DST Group Developing More Integrative Abilities

In their final digital files, both groups of student teachers addressed many aspects of learning: they made an effort to connect learning objectives with "interactive" instruction,

Table 20.6 Overview of Findings

TPACK	Data Source	Analysis	Findings
Quantitative	Survey	TPACK	1. Pretest: No significant difference on overall TPACK 2. Pretest: PK the highest, CK lowest, different on PCK 3. Posttest: Significant TPACK growth in the DST group 4. Posttest: Better integrative abilities in the DST group
Qualitative	Open-ended questions & assignments	CALL	5. Pretest: Technology mainly as aids for language input 6. Pretest: Emphasis on interactivity and stress-free 7. Posttest: DST using technology as more purposes 8. Posttest: DST developing more integrative abilities

"learning-focused" activities, and a "stress-free" assessment. They demonstrated their abilities, though at different levels, to integrate their TK, PK, and CK in designing their lesson plans.

According to the final digital files, the PPT group made much use of PPT to display information (e.g., vocabulary, sentence patterns, and stories), to practice language (e.g., listening and reading), and to give instructions (e.g., how to complete worksheets). The PPT group demonstrated at least four elements of the CALL framework: the stress-free quality, the learning-focused quality, interactivity, and authenticity. With respect to authenticity, the PPT group did use authentic materials, but did not seem to help children in using genuine questions (authentic language) to foster meaning or communicate.

In contrast, the DST group showed more than the above four elements, as they also included meaningfulness and creativity in their statements. Compared with the PPT group, the DST group used relatively fewer mechanical drills and more meaningful language practices. Many of them tried to create opportunities for "meaningful" interactions. Some student teachers in the DST group even demonstrated the element of "creativity," such as helping children create their own questions or mini-books. Clearly, the analysis of both the quantitative and qualitative data show consistent results. Table 20.6 provides a quick overview of the findings.

Conclusion

This chapter begins with questions regarding the influence of digital storytelling on the EFL student teachers and tracking: (1) the TPACK profiles; (2) development of the TPACK; and (3) differences between the groups. From the above findings, the answers seem clear. Both quantitative and qualitative data indicate the same results. With respect to the TPACK profiles, at the beginning of the semester, the two groups shared similar initial TPACK, and at the end, they differed significantly. At the beginning, both groups reported PK as their strongest and CK as their weakest areas, but at the end, although PK was still their strongest, the DST group developed stronger integrative abilities and scored higher than their pretest and the PPT group in all areas that required integrative abilities.

Similarly, analysis of the qualitative data showed that at the beginning, most of them treated technology only as a tool for language input, and focused technology on motivating children and creating a stress-free learning environment. At the end, both groups developed further and added more optimal CALL characteristics to their lessons. However, the greater growth of the DST group on the TPACK dimension was clear. Many of them saw new possibilities for technology helping to create language output, and they made much use of technology to help students in experimenting with the new language in the English classrooms.

The DST group's changes within the semester were prominent, and the differences between the two groups were statistically significant. The nature of digital storytelling may be the cause: it is creative, original, integrative, and complex, with a storyline and whole-language elements. The PPT group was only required to design a lesson in a textbook, which basically presents language as fragments (vocabulary, sentence structures, or dialogues), but the DST group needed to plan a lesson that taught something through their digital story. The DST group became more aware of language as a whole in a real-world setting than as fragments in a textbook. That was probably why the instructional activities they designed did not simply ask children to memorize and understand information; instead, they started to ask deeper cognitive questions that helped children to think and develop their own ideas.

It is obvious that digital storytelling certainly had an important impact on the EFL student teachers. The study reported in this chapter has its limitations due to the sample, the sample size, and some controlling variables. Also, there are some unsolved puzzles, for example, whether the initial difference in PCK at the beginning might influence the later development, and why the scores related to TK of the PPT group dropped slightly. Future research may explore and examine these questions further. Still, the current study serves as empirical evidence of how TPACK in the EFL domain can be developed through digital storytelling.

References

Archambault, L. M., & Barnett, J. H. (2010). Revisiting technological pedagogical content knowledge: Exploring the TPACK framework. *Computers & Education, 55*, 1656–1662.

Banas, J. (2010). Teachers' attitudes toward technology: Considerations for designing preservice and practicing teacher instruction. *Community & Junior College Libraries, 16*(2), 114–127.

Beach, R., Brendler, B., Dillon, D., Dockter, J., Ernst, S., Frederick, A., Galda, L., Helman, L., Kapoor, R., Ngo, B., O'Brien, D., Scharber, C., Jorgensen, K., Liang., L., Braaksma., M., & Janssen, T. (2010). Annotated bibliography of research in the teaching of English. *Research in the Teaching of English, 45*(2), AB1-AB88.

CDW-G. (2010). CDW-G 2010 21st-century classroom report: Preparing students for the future or the past? Vernon Hills, IL: CDW-G. Retrieved from http://www.cdwg.com/21stcenturyclassroomreport

Egbert, J., & Hanson-Smith, E. (Eds.) (1999). *CALL environments: Research, practice, and critical issues.* Alexandria, VA: Teachers of English to Speakers of Other Languages.

George, M. A. (2011). Preparing teachers to teach adolescent literature in the 21st century. *Theory into Practice, 50*, 182–189.

Heo, M. (2009). Digital storytelling: An empirical study of the impact of digital storytelling on pre-service teachers' self-efficacy and dispositions towards educational technology. *Journal of Educational Multimedia and Hypermedia, 18*(4), 405–428.

Heo, M. (2011). Improving technology competency and disposition of beginning pre-service teachers with digital storytelling. *Journal of Educational Multimedia and Hypermedia, 20*(1), 61–81.

Hicks, T. (2006). Expanding the conversation: A commentary toward revision of Swenson, Rozema, Young, McGrail, and Whitin. *Contemporary Issues in Technology and Teacher Education, 6*, 46–55.

Hofer, M., & Swan, K. O. (2006). Technological pedagogical content knowledge in action: A case study of a middle school digital documentary project. *Journal of Research on Technology in Education (JRTE), 41*(2), 179–200.

Hughes, J. E., & Scharber, C. M. (2008). Leveraging the development of English TPCK within the deictic nature of literacy. In AACTE Committee on Innovation and Technology (Ed.), *Handbook of technological pedagogical content knowledge (TPCK) for educators* (pp. 87–106). New York: Routledge.

Koh, J.H.L., Chai, C. S., & Tsai, C. C. (2010). Examining the technological pedagogical content knowledge of Singapore pre-service teachers with a large-scale survey. *Journal of Computer Assisted Learning, 26*, 563–573.

Kurt, G., Mishra, P., & Kocoglu, Z. (2013). Technological pedagogical content knowledge development of Turkish pre-service teachers of English. 2013 Society for Information Technology & Teacher Education (SITE) conference proceedings. Retrieved from http://www.academia.edu/4326347/

Mahon, L., & Cherednichenko, B. (2007). SWIRL (story writing in remote locations): A 12-year IBM/Victoria University community learning partnership in remote indigenous communities. *The Australasian Journal of University Community Engagement, 2*(2), 258–265.

Ohler, J. (2008). *Digital storytelling in the classroom: New media pathways to literacy, learning, and creativity*. Thousand Oaks: Corwin Press.

Parr, G., Bellis, N., & Bulfin, S. (2013). Teaching English teachers for the future: Speaking back to TPACK. *English in Australia, 48*(1), 9–22.

Robin, B. R. (2008). Digital storytelling: A powerful technology tool for the 21st century classroom. *Theory Into Practice, 47*, 220–228.

Sahin, I. (2011). Development of survey of technological pedagogical and content knowledge (TPACK). *The Turkish Online Journal of Educational Technology, 10*(1), 97–105.

Schmidt, D. A., & Gurbo, M. (2008). TPCK in K–6 literacy education: It's not that elementary! In AACTE Committee on Innovation and Technology (Ed.), *Handbook of technological pedagogical content knowledge (TPCK) for educators* (pp. 61–85). New York: Routledge.

Tseng, J. J. 曾俊傑 (2011). 英語老師在以省思為基礎的電腦輔助教學工作坊中之專業成長研究 [A study on English teachers' professional development in a reflection-based computer assisted language learning workshop]. Unpublished doctoral dissertation. Taipei, Taiwan: National Taiwan Normal University.

van Olphen, M. (2008). TPCK: An integrated framework for educating world language teachers. In AACTE Committee on Innovation and Technology (Ed.), *Handbook of technological pedagogical content knowledge (TPCK) for educators* (pp. 107–128). New York: American Association of Colleges of Teacher Education and Routledge.

Wang, A. Y. 王雅茵 (2011). 英語學科教學知能內涵：國小英語教師的形塑表述與自我效能評估 [In search of pedagogical content knowledge in English language: Representation and evaluation of primary teachers of English in Taiwan]. Research Report No. NSC99–2410-H-142–011-. Taipei, Taiwan: Ministry of Science and Technology.

Contributors

Charoula Angeli is an Associate Professor of Instructional Technology at the University of Cyprus in Cyprus. She is one of the principal researchers who conceptualized the framework of Technological Pedagogical Content Knowledge (TPCK) and developed methods for developing and assessing TPCK. She also researches the use of computers as cognitive tools, cognitive style, and its effects of learning with computers, adaptive technology-enhanced learning, and the design of learning environments for the development of critical thinking skills. She has published in more than 40 prestigious referred journals and presented in more than 100 conferences worldwide. She has authored or co-authored three books and edited or co-edited seven books and two special journal issues. She is the recipient of the 2011 and 2012 AERA-TACTL best paper award.

Leanna Archambault, Ph.D., is an Associate Professor of Educational Technology and Innovation in the Mary Lou Fulton Teachers College at Arizona State University. Her research areas include sustainability literacy among pre-service and in-service teachers, teacher preparation for online and blended classrooms, the use of innovative technologies to improve learning outcomes, and the nature of technological pedagogical content knowledge. Archambault was awarded the Online Learning Innovator Award for Important Research from the International Association for K–12 Online Learning in 2010 and 2012 and, in 2013, she was named as the Promising Research Scholar for the Mary Lou Fulton Teachers College. In 2015, Archambault was awarded the President's Award for Sustainability for an interdisciplinary collaboration with the Center for Sustainable Health at ASU.

Evrim Baran, Ph.D., is an Assistant Professor at the Department of Educational Sciences at Middle East Technical University in Turkey. Previously, she worked as a postdoctoral fellow at the University of British Columbia, Canada, and as an instructor and researcher at Iowa State University, USA. Dr. Baran is the recipient of AERA-TACTL special interest group's 2015 early career award. Her research interests center on the integration of emerging technologies into teacher education contexts. She is coordinating several national and international research projects on mobile learning, STEM training, and TPACK supported by the European Commission, the Scientific and Technological Research Council of Turkey, and German Research Foundation (DFG). More information about her research is on her personal website at www.evrimbaran.com and on her research group's website at http://latte.eds.metu.edu.tr/.

Contributors

Beatrice Hope Benton-Borghi, Ph.D. After teaching high school chemistry for a decade, Hope was included in Who's Who of American Women (1980). At CAST (1990, 1995), Hope learned to integrate technology to enable her child with disabilities to succeed in school, and was recognized in 2002 by the Ohio House of Representatives for the first universally designed and accessible digital K–12 library model. In 2006, her doctoral research at OSU resulted in a new Teachers' Sense of Inclusion Efficacy Scale. Hope was an undergraduate and graduate teacher educator at Ohio Dominican University with research interests in UDL, TPACK, technology, and teacher efficacy. Hope retired in 2014 and is writing a general education methods textbook that applies the UDL Infused TPACK model. She served as M.Ed. Coordinator, Secondary Education Coordinator, and Special Education Coordinator during her years at ODU. She can be reached at bentonborghi@me.com.

Judith Bowman is a Professor of Music Education and Music Technology at Duquesne University, where she teaches courses in music research, psychology of music, and digital music pedagogy. She developed online courses for the master's degrees in music education and in music technology and co-developed the B.M. and M.M. degrees in Music Technology. Dr. Bowman is the author of *Online Learning in Music: Foundations, Frameworks, and Practices* (Oxford University Press, 2014). She co-authored *Applications of Research in Music Technology* (MENC, 1994). She has lectured on technology in music education internationally (Tokyo, Helsinki, Prague, London, Amsterdam, Limerick, Quebec) and throughout the United States for The College Music Society, Association for Technology in Music Instruction, International Society for Music Education, National Association for Music Education, Music Teachers National Association, Pennsylvania Music Educators Association, and others. Dr. Bowman is a member of Pi Kappa Lambda Music Honor Society and former Secretary of the Association for Technology in Music Instruction (1991–2003). She is a recipient of a Duquesne University Creative Teaching Award and of the Duquesne University Presidential Scholarship Award. Dr. Bowman earned the Ph.D. and M.M. in Music Education at the Eastman School of Music and a B.S. in Piano Performance at Nazareth College of Rochester.

Sedef Canbazoglu-Bilici, Ph.D., is an Assistant Professor at the Department of Science Education at Aksaray University, Turkey. She worked as a visiting scholar at the University of Minnesota, STEM Education Center in 2011–2012. She received her Ph.D. in Science Education at Gazi University, Turkey in 2012. Her dissertation research focused on pre-service teachers' TPACK and their self-efficacy beliefs toward TPACK. Her research interests include the development of technology-enriched activities for developing science teachers' TPACK and STEM education. Dr. Canbazoglu-Bilici has worked on TPACK and science teachers' competencies as a project coordinator and a researcher in projects supported by European Union and the Scientific and Technological Research Council of Turkey.

Ching Sing Chai is an Associate Professor in the Learning Sciences and Technology Academic Group at National Institute of Education, Nanyang Technological University. His research interests are associated with the use of ICT in classrooms. He has published research work in *Science Education, Instructional Science, Teaching & Teacher Education, Teachers College Record, Computers & Education, Educational Technology & Society*, and other educational journals.

Contributors

Vinesh Chandra is a Senior Lecturer in Education at the Queensland University of Technology in Brisbane, Australia. His teaching areas are in information and communication technology (ICT), design technology, mathematics, and science. His research interests include the investigation of technology-rich learning environments and teacher education. He has worked with teachers in Australia, Fiji, China, and Zambia. Dr. Chandra leads the Share, Engage, and Educate (SEE) Project (theseeproject.org), which has supported a number of schools in Fiji and other developing countries. One of the key objectives of the project is to enhance the quality of education in these countries through ICT.

Andri Christodoulou is a primary school teacher and currently a Ph.D. candidate in Instructional Technology at the University of Cyprus in Cyprus. She is pursuing a doctoral thesis on the topic of e-TPCK, which involves the design of an adaptive e-learning system for the development of teachers' Technological Pedagogical Content Knowledge. Central to her research project is how to embed scaffolds in the instructional design process in order to promote self-regulated learning.

Glenn Finger is a Professor of Education at Griffith University. He was the Dean (Learning and Teaching) of the Arts, Education, and Law Group from 2011–2015, and the Deputy Dean (Learning and Teaching) of the Faculty of Education from 2007 to 2010. He has researched and published extensively on digital technologies and learning and teaching, with more than 150 publications. For his outstanding university teaching, Professor Finger has won various teaching awards and citations and numerous outstanding paper awards at key conferences, and he was the Chair of the Research and Evaluation Working Group of the Teaching Teachers for the Future Project. Prior to his appointment at Griffith University in 1999, Professor Finger had served with Education Queensland for 24 years in a wide variety of schools.

Petra Fisser is a Senior Researcher at the Dutch National Expertise Centre for Curriculum Development. Her current work and research interests focus on the integration of technology in the curriculum of primary and secondary schools. Petra researches the Technological Pedagogical Content Knowledge (TPACK) framework in order to stimulate effective teaching with technology, and she is involved in a national project concerning the integration of 21st-century skills in primary and secondary education.

Karin Forssell directs the Learning, Design & Technology master's program at Stanford University's Graduate School of Education. Her research focuses on teaching and learning using new technologies, primarily in K–12 education. She is interested in the conditions under which teachers choose to use new technologies in classrooms, seeking to understand teachers' reasoning about the work they do with and without digital tools. This research agenda encompasses the knowledge, beliefs, and resources available to teachers on the one hand and the design of digital tools for meaningful learning experiences on the other.

Contributors

Judith B. Harris is a Professor and the Pavey Family Chair in Educational Technology in the School of Education at the College of William & Mary, where she coordinates the Curriculum and Educational Technology doctoral program. Dr. Harris's research and service focus is upon K–12 curriculum-based technology integration and teacher professional development. During the past 35 years of her work in educational computing, she has authored more than 235 research and pedagogical publications on curriculum-based applications of educational technologies. Judi's work is used by teachers, technology specialists, and teacher educators internationally—especially her "activity structures" method for designing curriculum-based learning activities that incorporate the use of online tools and resources. She and colleague Mark Hofer have worked with eight other curriculum specialists to adapt those activity structures to create comprehensive taxonomies of curriculum-based "learning activity types." These taxonomies serve as instructional planning aids that help teachers integrate the full spectrum of digital and nondigital tools and resources into students' learning experiences in ten curriculum areas to date. The taxonomies are available as open educational resources under a Creative Commons license for noncommercial, attributed use by educators at http://activitytypes.wm.edu/.

Mary C. Herring is a Professor and former College of Education Associate Dean, Chair of the Curriculum and Instruction Department, and Coordinator of the Instructional Technology Division at the University of Northern Iowa. Her research and teaching focuses on the effective use of technology to support learning and standards-based curriculum alignment and development. She is a co-primary investigator on UNI's Iowa Teacher Quality Partnership grant. She is the former Chair of the American Association of Colleges of Teacher Education's Innovation and Technology Committee and is a past president of the Association for Educational Communication and Technology (AECT). She has served on the editorial board of the journal *TechTrends* since 2002 and has authored or co-authored in the publishing of multiple books, book chapters, and articles.

Mark Hofer is a Professor of Educational Technology and Associate Dean in the School of Education at the College of William & Mary. He teaches undergraduate, masters, and doctoral courses focusing on curriculum-based technology integration. Dr. Hofer focuses a number of his research and development projects on knowledge development for technology integration (particularly related to TPACK) and strategies to effectively integrate technology in history classrooms. He regularly presents his work at local, national, and international conferences and publishes his work in a variety of scholarly and practitioner journals.

Noortje Janssen is a Ph.D. student at the University of Twente. She holds a bachelor's (honors) and research master's degree in Educational Sciences. Her professional interests include the integration of technology in primary and secondary education. Her current research focuses on supporting pre-service and in-service teachers' lesson planning activities, with a special emphasis on the uptake and effective use of ICT in the classroom.

Yi Jin is a Ph.D. student in curriculum and instructional technology and literacy education in the School of Education at Iowa State University. Her research interests include examining technology integration in 1:1 classrooms, preparing pre-service teachers to integrate technology in classrooms, and investigating online learning and the flipped classroom in higher education.

Matthew J. Koehler is a Professor of Educational Psychology and Educational Technology at the College of Education at Michigan State University. He holds undergraduate degrees in mathematics and computer science, a master's degree in computer science, and a Ph.D. in educational psychology. His work explores the pedagogical affordances (and constraints) of newer technologies for learning, specifically in the context of the professional development of teachers and the design and evaluation of technology-rich and innovated learning. His work with teachers and technology has led to the development (in collaboration with Dr. Punya Mishra) of the Technological Pedagogical Content Knowledge (TPACK) framework. You can learn more about his work by going to http://matt-koehler.com.

Joyce Hwee Ling Koh holds a B.B.A. in business administration from the National University of Singapore. She received her Master of Science and Doctor of Philosophy degrees from Indiana University Bloomington in 2001 and 2008 respectively, majoring in Instructional Systems Technology. She is currently an associate professor at the Learning Sciences and Technologies Academic Group of the National Institute of Education, Nanyang Technological University. She has published numerous studies related to TPACK and teacher ICT education in SSCI-listed journals. Her research interests also include online learning pedagogies and adult learning.

Ard W. Lazonder is an Adjunct Professor of Instructional Technology at the University of Twente. His research revolves around the design and evaluation of technology-enhanced learning environments for inquiry-based science education. The theoretical and practical implications of his work have been published in over 70 journal articles and book chapters.

John K. Lee is a Professor of Social Studies Education at North Carolina State University. His scholarly work focuses on standards and the uses of digital historical resources in teaching and learning, as well as efforts to theorize and develop tools related to new literacies. He is an author of the College, Career, and Civic Life (C3) Framework for Standards in Social Studies and is co-director of the C3 Teachers project (c3teachers.org). He also directs the Digital History and Pedagogy Project (dhpp.org) and co-directs the New Literacies Collaborative (newlit.org). In addition, he is interested in theory and practice related to global learning and democratic education. He is the author of *Visualizing Elementary Social Studies Methods*.

Sohyun Meacham, Ph.D., is an Assistant Professor of Curriculum and Instruction and a research fellow of the Center for Educational Transformation at the University of Northern Iowa. She was formerly an early childhood classroom teacher, a project approach coach, and a reading specialist. Her publications have focused on teachers' language use and its effects on young children's language productivity, the long-term effects of Early

Reading First on dual language learners' language and literacy development, community of learners, and inquiry-based science talk. Her current research interests include STEM integration in language and literacy instruction, early childhood teachers' language use with technology tools, dialogic and democratic use of technology in early childhood classroom, and teachers' TPACK development.

Punya Mishra is Professor of Educational Psychology and Educational Technology at Michigan State University where he directs the Master of Arts in Educational Technology program. He currently chairs the Creativity Special Interest Group at the Society for Information Technology in Teacher Education. He is also a member of the board of education of the Okemos Public School District. He is nationally and internationally recognized for his work in technology integration, teacher creativity, and design. He (in collaboration with Dr. Matthew J. Koehler) developed the Technological Pedagogical Content Knowledge (TPACK) framework. The editors of the journal *Technology & Learning* described him as being "one of the ten most influential people in the field of educational technology." He has received over $7 million in grants, has published over 70 articles and book chapters, and has edited three books. Dr. Mishra is an award-winning instructor who teaches courses in the areas of educational technology, design, and creativity. Dr. Mishra is a gifted, creative, and engaging public speaker, as well as an accomplished visual artist and poet. You can find out more about him by going to http://punyamishra.com/.

Daniel Mourlam is an Assistant Professor of Curriculum and Instruction at the University of South Dakota. He was formerly a K–12 technology director, teacher, and project manager. His research interests are developing educator TPACK, faculty development, and mobile learning. He teaches instructional technology courses and regularly facilitates university faculty and K–12 teacher professional development with a focus on developing instruction that leverages the affordances of digital technologies in ways that support higher order thinking skills.

Chrystalla Mouza is an Associate Professor of Educational Technology and Learning Sciences in the School of Education at the University of Delaware. She earned an Ed.D., M.Ed., and M.A. in Instructional Technology and Media from Teachers College, Columbia University. A first strand of Dr. Mouza's work examines pedagogical strategies that help pre-service teachers enhance their understanding of technology, content, and pedagogy throughout their teacher education program and the ways in which we can assess and measure their learning over time. A second strand of research focuses on the design, implementation, and empirical study of professional development programs for in-service teachers in STEM (Science-Technology-Engineering-Mathematics) fields. Dr. Mouza is the recipient of the Distinguished Research in Teacher Education award by the Association of Teacher Educators.

Jordan Mroziak is an Adjunct Professor of Musicianship at Duquesne University and Coordinator of Student Services in the School of Music. He is currently pursuing an Ed.D. in

Instructional Technology at Duquesne University with an emphasis on popular culture studies. He designed a new course for the university core curriculum, Rock & Roll: An Unruly History, as well as designing and teaching courses in Duquesne's City Music Center Music Technology Program, an iPad-based program for middle and high school students. Graduating magna cum laude from Duquesne University, Jordan attained a master's degree in Digital Music Pedagogy and is a member of Pi Kappa Lambda Music Honor Society. Jordan aids in professional development of faculty involving implementations of technology in their pedagogy. He has presented at the ISTE, ATMI, NMC, and SXSWedu conferences on music technology, creative informal pedagogy, the TPACK model, aesthetic education, and related topics. Other work includes his participation in Arts Educator 2.0, a professional development project that seeks to aid art teachers in the K–12 field with their usage of technology in the classroom. His informal education project, take pART, recently received grant funding in order to work at various locations in the Pittsburgh area educating youth about digital/physical art creation and media literacy.

Margaret (Maggie) L. Niess is Professor Emeritus of Mathematics Education at Oregon State University. Her research emphasizes Technological Pedagogical Content Knowledge as the transformed knowledge teachers rely on for teaching mathematics and science. She has authored multiple peer-reviewed journals and chapters, including multiple teacher preparation books, and co-authored a teacher education textbook titled *Guiding Learning with Technology*. She directed the design, implementation, and evaluation of an online Master of Science degree program for K–12 teachers with an interdisciplinary science, mathematics, and technology emphasis. She has chaired multiple committees for the Association of Mathematics Teacher Educators (AMTE), and most recently served as the Program Chair, Chair, and past Chair for American Educational Research Association's SIG-TACTL (Technology as a Change Agent in Teaching and Learning).

Chandra Hawley Orrill is an Associate Professor and Department Chair of STEM Education and Teacher Development at the University of Massachusetts Dartmouth. Her research focuses on teacher knowledge of mathematics and the ways that teacher knowledge impacts practice. She has a background in designing and implementing a variety of professional development opportunities for elementary and middle school teachers with and without technology. Her research has appeared in *Elementary School Journal*, *Journal of Mathematics Teacher Education*, and *Teaching Children Mathematics*.

Drew Polly is an Associate Professor in the Reading and Elementary Education Program at the University of North Carolina at Charlotte. His research interests focus on examining ways to best support teachers' use of learner-centered pedagogies and educational technologies in elementary school mathematics classrooms. Previously, he edited special issues of the journal *TechTrends: Linking Research and Practice to Improve Learning* on TPACK and has published articles related to TPACK in the *British Journal of*

Educational Technology, the *Journal of Computers in Mathematics and Science Teaching*, and the *International Journal of Technology in Mathematics Education*.

James Ptaszynski is the Senior Fellow for Postsecondary Success at the Bill & Melinda Gates Foundation in Seattle, Washington. In education, the Foundation's mission is to ensure that more low-income and disadvantaged students complete high-quality, affordable postsecondary credentials that lead to sustaining careers. In his role at the Foundation, Jim helps to identify barriers to student success and finds and invests in innovators working on mitigating or eliminating them. He is also involved in the Foundation's work with institutional leaders, faculty and digital learning.

Joshua M. Rosenberg is a Ph.D. student in the Educational Psychology and Educational Technology program at Michigan State University. His research is focused on how teachers use technology to create better opportunities for all students. In particular, his research examines how teachers think about and negotiate aspects of their context—social and motivational and in terms of curricular standards—in their practice. Joshua is the Associate Chair of the Technological Pedagogical Content Knowledge Special Interest Group for the Society for Information Technology and Teacher Education.

Denise A. Schmidt-Crawford is an Associate Professor and Director of the Center for Technology in Learning and Teaching (CTLT) at Iowa State University. Her research focuses on teachers' development of technological pedagogical content knowledge (TPACK), and her teaching interests include using technology as a tool to promote innovation in K–12 schools and teacher education. Denise coordinates the undergraduate learning technologies minor program offered in the School of Education. Keenly interested in K–12 outreach, Denise works extensively with teachers on using technology in innovative ways to facilitate teaching and learning in classrooms.

Cheryl Sim is an Associate Professor at the School of Education and Professional Studies at Griffith University in Australia. She aligns her teaching and research in the area of teachers' professional learning. Her particular research interests relate to the development and influences on teachers' knowledge and the role of experienced teachers as mentors in professional practice settings. She provides leadership in initial teacher education program development and professional practice. Recently, a major outcome of her work is a professional learning site for initial teacher education in the field of assessment of the professional experience, available at teacherevidence.net.

David A. Slykhuis is an Associate Professor of Science Education at James Madison University where he teaches the secondary science methods and educational technology courses. Dr. Slykhuis is also the Director of the Content Teaching Academy at James Madison University and Co-Director of the JMU Center for STEM Education and Outreach. Dr. Slykhuis has recently been elected as the President for the Society of Information Technology and Teacher Education. His research interests lie at the intersection of science, technology, and student learning.

Vicky Smart made the career change into teaching after a technology-using teacher led her to develop an interest into how teachers pedagogically reason with technology. Vicky is currently completing her Ph.D. at Griffith University where she has researched seven technology-using teachers from various schools to understand how they pedagogically reason with technology. She has used various sources of data including video stimulated interview, concept maps, and digital portfolios to understand their pedagogical reasoning with technology. Vicky has presented her work at the SITE and ISTE conferences in the United States and the ACEC and AARE national conferences in Australia. Her thesis will be submitted by the time this book is published.

Shu-Ju Diana Tai is a Professor at the School of International Education and School of Arts and Law at Beijing University of Chemical Technology. Her research focuses on Computer Assisted Language Learning (CALL), Technological Pedagogical Content Knowledge (TPACK), teacher education in CALL, Computer Assisted Language Testing (CALT), English for Specific Purpose (ESP), and International Education.

Jolene Teske is an Ed.D. student in Curriculum and Instruction at the University of Northern Iowa. Her research interests include education doctorate programming, talented and gifted, and TPACK. She was a secondary teacher of high school English and gifted programs. She is the State Director of the Iowa Academic Decathlon.

Jo Tondeur is a Postdoctoral Researcher (Research Foundation Flanders) at the Department of Educational Studies at Ghent University (Belgium). His research interests are in the field of educational innovation and instructional design. Most of his work addresses ICT integration in education. His current research focuses on the interplay between (ICT) innovations and pre- and in-service teacher training. He has published in different journals and books (https://ugent.academia.edu/JoTondeur).

Chin-Chung Tsai is a Chair Professor at the Graduate Institute of Digital Learning and Education, National Taiwan University of Science and Technology, Taipei, Taiwan. Since July 2009, he has been appointed as the Co-Editor of Computers & Education (published by Elsevier, ranked seventh among the educational journals indexed in SSCI by 2012 impact factor values). His research interests deal largely with constructivism, epistemological beliefs, and Internet-based instruction.

Erdem Uygun is a Ph.D. student at the Department of Educational Sciences at Middle East Technical University in Turkey. His master thesis focused on the investigation of the possible pathways in designing TPACK-based lesson plans and instructional practices, and the impact of learning by design activities on the development of TPACK. His major research interests are TPACK development in teacher education, barriers to successful technology integration, and TPACK-based curriculum design and development. He is currently working as an instructional designer at a government institution that aims to improve information technologies in public schools. Uygun is also working as a researcher at projects on mobile learning and TPACK.

Contributors

Nicos Valanides is a Professor of Science Education at Frederick University in Cyprus and the director of the Educational Robotics and Science Organization in Cyprus. His research interests include teacher training, methodology of teaching and curricula for science education, the development of scientific reasoning and epistemological beliefs, science-and-technology literacy, the utilization of ICT in education, blended learning, and the design of educational interventions and learning environments. He is one of the main researchers who advanced the theoretical conceptualization of the concept of Technological Pedagogical Content Knowledge. He authored more than 100 papers in referred journals and proceedings, authored or edited more than 20 books, and presented his work, often as an invited speaker, in more than 150 conferences. During his long career, he received a number of academic awards from various international agencies and associations.

Johan van Braak is a Professor of Curriculum, Innovation and Educational Effectiveness at the Department of Educational Studies at Ghent University. He is mainly involved in studies in the field of information and communication technologies (ICT) in primary education. He is especially interested in the question of how ICT integration in schools and ICT competences of teachers and learners can be assessed.

Joke Voogt is a Professor of ICT and Curriculum at the University of Amsterdam and Professor of Educational Innovation and ICT at Windesheim University of Applied Sciences. Since the 1980s, Voogt has been involved in research in the integration of information and communication technology (ICT) in education, with a particular focus on the role and concerns of teachers. She has been involved in several international studies, is co-editor of the *International Handbook of Information Technology in Primary and Secondary Education*, and founder of the EDUsummIT, the international summit of information technology in education.

Amber Yayin Wang is an Associate Professor and Chair in the Department of English, National Taichung University of Education, Taiwan. She grew up in Taiwan and received her Ph.D. in education at Claremont Graduate University in the United States. Having experienced education in different cultures, she is particularly interested in how English language teaching can help develop multicultural literacy, creative thinking, and critical thinking. Her research explores TPACK in English language arts and the ways in which technology or innovative teaching influences language learning, teaching conceptions, creative thinking, and cultural awareness. Her most recent attempt is to bring the beauty of English poems into elementary education in Taiwan.

Wei Wang is a Doctoral Candidate in Education with an emphasis in Curriculum and Instructional Technology and Human-Computer Interaction in the School of Education at Iowa State University. She is an instructional development specialist in the Center for Excellence in Learning and Teaching (CELT), where she provides faculty development support to enhance online, blended, hybrid, and Web-enhanced teaching and learning through online and multimedia delivery. Her research interests include pre-service teachers' development of Technological Pedagogical Content Knowledge (TPACK), game-based learning in higher education, and instructional design for online teaching.

Chapter Acknowledgments

Chapter 6	This research was supported in part by a grant from Office of Education Research, National Institute of Education (Singapore), project reference number OER 5/13 KHL.
Chapter 8	The writing of this chapter was partially funded by the European Union in the context of the Open Discovery Space project (Grant Agreement no. 297229) under the Digital Content—ICT Policy Support Programme. This document does not represent the opinion of the European Union, and the European Union is not responsible for any use that might be made of its content.
Chapter 15	I am grateful to the principal at Smart High School for his input on this project and publication.
Chapter 17	The projects described in this chapter have been funded by the National Science Foundation, the Georgia Teacher Quality Grant Program, and the North Carolina Mathematics Science Partnership Grant Program.
Chapter 18	The research quoted in this chapter was supported by the Scientific and Technological Research Council of Turkey (project number 113B254).
Chapter 20	The empirical study described in this chapter was supported by the Ministry of Science and Technology, Taiwan (grant number: NSC101-2410-H-142-013-). I am most grateful for this support.

Index

Page numbers in *italics* refer to figures and tables.

AACE *see* Association for the Advancement of Computers in Education (AACE)
AACTE *see* American Association of Colleges for Teacher Education (AACTE)
accreditation standards 210
activity structures 312
activity types 70–2, 196, *199*, 286
affordances 34–7, 72
Algodoo 279
alterity relation 35
American Association of Colleges for Teacher Education (AACTE) 170
American Association of Colleges for Teacher Education Committee on Innovation and Technology (AACTE I&T Committee) 207–8, 210
An, H. 177
analog technologies 251
Anatomy 4D *277*
Angeli, C. 21–4, 179, 202
animations 272, 278–9, 305
Animoto 276, *276*, 278–9
Archambault, L. 213–14
artifact analysis 83
assessment 60; case-based approaches 74–6; case development 76–7; design tasks 72–4; of faculty technology integration 217–18; interviews 78–80; learning activities 70–2; lesson planning 101–2; observation instruments 81; performance-based 67–8, 174–5; of pre-service teachers 169–70, 173–5; qualitative 66–82; quantitative 87–102; survey studies 173–4; technology integration rubric 68–70
Association for the Advancement of Computers in Education (AACE) 67
audio presentations 57, 60
audio recordings 78, 304–5
augmented reality 170
authentic materials 306

background relation 35
Benton-Borghi, B.-H. 19–21, 143–4, 149

biology, technology and 121–5
Blackboard 136
blogging 55, 171, 183, 250, *276*, 279
Blogspot *276*
Bull, G. 226

calculators 78, 263
Calhoun, E. 192
case-based approaches 74–6
case development 76, 180
Chai, C. S. 22, 177
Chang, Y. M. 144, 149
Chen, K. C. 180
classroom observations 107–16
classrooms: technological change in 54–7; virtual 54, 56, 58–60
clickers 36, 274, *276*, 278, 292
cloud computing 274, *276*, 278, 287
coaching 291–3
collaboration 131, 133–4, 191
collaborative instructional design 43–5, 102, 194–5, *198*
collaborative tools 131
college students: perceptions of faculty technology use 97; technology use 170–1, 184
Common Core Standards of Mathematical Practice 261
communication 131, 133–4
community knowledge 74
community of learners 135
competencies: lesson design 97–9; online instruction 216; technology integration and 174, 213, 227, 271, 286; TPACK and 14–15, 179, 213; web-based 174
complex systems 248
complicated systems 248
computer-adaptive technology development 195–6
computer-assisted language learning (CALL) 297, 300, 305–7
computer science, technology integration in 22–3
concept maps 272, 274, *276*, 279
concrete artifacts 34
constructivist-based professional development 79
content analysis 74–5, 99–100, 102

Index

Content Development for Investigations (CoDe-I) project 263–4, 266
content knowledge (CK) 15–*16*, 57, 89–90, *145*, 149, 172, 178, 277, 298
content-specific strategies 73–4
context: domain-general knowledge 22–3; domain-specific knowledge 22–3; technology integration and 4, 236, 250; types of 18–20
context knowledge 16–18, 25–6
Correlation Coefficient (ICC) 69
co-teaching 214–15
Council for the Accreditation of Educator Preparation 171
course design: distance education 217; online learning environments 133–4, 140–1; technology integration competencies 97–9
Cox, S. 24
cross validation 102–3
Crosswordlabs *277*
culture: school 19, 209, 237, 239; technology and 250
curriculum: ICT-infused 18; learning activities in 71; pre-service teachers 177, 182–3, 288; standards-based 264, 286; teacher education 42; technology affordances 19, 72; technology-enhanced 40, 80, 132, 174, 196
curriculum alignment 121, 266

Data Analysis Spiral 107, 111
deep-play 45
Delphi technique 18
demographics 95–6
design *see* technology design
designers *see* technology designers
design rationale 102
"design talk" 72–3
design tasks 72–4
Devlin-Scherer, R. 214–15
digital cameras 254
digital fabrication technology 186
digital images 272
digital microscopes 272
digital natives 170–1
digital portfolios 60, 181, 290–2
digital storytelling 297–307
digital tools *see* educational technology
digital video 92, 240
disabilities 145, 149
discussion forums 93
distance education 217
diversity 145
Doering, A. 22
domain-general knowledge 22–3, 25
domain-specific knowledge 22–3, 25
Dropbox *276*, 279

early childhood teachers 89, 101, 179
eBooks 57

educational technology: authentic classroom experiences 281; case development 180; communication tools 131; conceptual frameworks 65; design of 247–54; field experience 181; history of 1; instructional design 179–80; integration of 14–16; interactive whiteboards 92; language outputs and 304; learning communities 281; meaningful advances in 254–5; outcomes 184–5; reflection 180–1; researching 2–3, 11; stand-alone courses 175–8; tools for 161; usefulness of 247–8 *see also* technological pedagogical content knowledge (TPACK)
Elbow, P. 4
elementary school teachers: lesson planning 39, 42; mathematics instruction 196, 259–67; music education 286, 292; pedagogical beliefs 38; science instruction 272, 274; technology integration and 40, 77, 89–90, 93, 96, 99, 101, 108, 148, 175, 177, 179, 185
Elements, The (Gray) *274*
email 54–5, 58, 171
embodiment relation 35
emerging technologies 131, 170–1, 186
English as a foreign language (TEFL/EFL) 297–8
English as a second/other language (TESOL/ESOL) 297–8, 300
English language instruction: digital storytelling 297–307; language outputs and 304; research on 297–8; TPACK frameworks and 297–307
e-portfolios 60, 181, 290–2
Ertmer, P. A. 38

Facebook 251
faculty development 211; learner-centered pedagogy 215; Learning Technology by Design approach 212–13; mentoring approach 212; online learning environments 216–17; peer coaching model 291–3; sustainable development of TPACK *218*; technology integration and 214–20, 226–33; workshop approach 212–13 *see also* professional development (PD)
field experience 181
Fiji: computer use in 242; technology integration in 235–43
5 E's inquiry instructional model 134–5
Foulger, T. S. 176
frameworks, value of 3–4
fully integrated technology and mathematics professional development 260–1

game-based technological pedagogical content knowledge 91
game knowledge (GK) 91
game pedagogical content knowledge (GPCK) 91
game pedagogical knowledge (GPK) 91

gaming technologies 170, 184, 186
Gawande, A. 254
geographical technological pedagogical content knowledge (G-TPCK) 22
geography 22
Geometer 261
geospatial technologies 22
GeoThentic 195–6
Gess-Newsome, J. 21
Gibson, J. J. 34
Glogster 230
Google Docs 131, 134, *276*
Google Drive *276*
Google Sites 93
Graham, C. R. 23–4, 179
Grandgenett, N. 174, 182–3
Grant, G. 57
graphing calculators 78, 263
Gray, T. *274*
Greeno, J. G. 37
Grossman, P. L. 14
Guerrero, S. 22

Habowski, T. 178
Handbook of Technological Pedagogical Content Knowledge for Educators (AACTE) 170, 207
Harris, J. 68–71, 174–5, 196, 229
Hashweh, M. 201
hermeneutic relation 35
higher education: faculty development 211–20, 291–3; faculty technology surveys 289–91; leadership in 210, 219; learner-centered pedagogy 215; lecturing-centered instruction 215–16; music education in 285–93; technology-oriented investment 215–16; TPACK-aligned programs 191, 207–12, 220–1, 226
high school teachers *see* secondary school teachers
Hofer, M. 70–1, 174, 182–3, 196
human-centered approach to technology 248

ICT-infused curriculum 18
ICT-related PCK framework *14, 19,* 21–2
information and communication technologies (ICT) 14
inquiry-based teaching 281
inquiry model 131, 133–6
inquiry tools 131
in-service teachers: pedagogical content knowledge 121; students with disabilities and 145; support for 119, 123–4, 126–7; survey studies 96; technological pedagogical content knowledge 192–7, 200–2; technology and 43; technology integration 81, 83 *see also* teachers
Inspiration 278–9
instant messaging 171
instruction *see* teaching
instructional design 11, 74, 174, 178–80, 191, 194–6, *198*, 217, 229–33, 262

instructional planning technology development 196
instructional strategies 73, 75, 132, *134*–7, 173–5, 179, 181, 184
instructional technology courses 108
integrated support 122–6
integrative view 21, 25, 172
interactive whiteboards (IWB) 92, 161, 263–4, 272, 274, *276*, 278, 292
InterMath 261, 265–6
Internet 58, 170, 176, 184, 186, 250, 287
Internet-based activities 262, 264
interviews 78–80, 110, 112, 175
Ioannou, I. 22–3
iPad applications 264
iPods 161

Jang, S.-J. 180
Jimoyiannis, A. 23
Jing 131, 134, 139
Joyce, B. 192

Karchmer-Klein, R. 180
Kennedy, A. 192
Kim, B. 40
Kincheloe, J. L. 236
kindergarten teachers 42–3
Kinuthia, W. 74–5
knowledge-based economy 169
knowledge base of teachers 13–15, 21–2, 26, 33, 38, 41–3, 45–6, 53, 57–9, 61, 126, 169, 172, 176–7, 179–80, 183, 300
knowledge building 71
knowledge expression 71
Knowledge Growth in a Profession project 54, 60
Koehler, M. J. 2, 4, 15–16, 21, 33, 36, 39, 45, 65–7, 71–2, 89, 126, 143, 173, 175, 186, 213–14, 225, 229
Koh, J.H.L. 42
Kopcha, T. J. 181

Lamb, A. 215
language arts instruction: assessment instruments 175; digital fabrication technology 186; taxonomies 71; technology integration in 7, 22
language outputs 304
languages, taxonomies 71
laptop computers 54–6, 58, 60, 161, 240, 242
Laurillard, D. 33
Leadership Theory of Action *209*
learner-centered pedagogy 38, 215
learner-centered professional development (LCPD) 259–60, 266; fully integrated technology and mathematics 260–1; technology-integration focused 261–4
learners, knowledge of 58
learning activities 70–2, 196, *199*, 286
learning activity types (LATs) 196
learning-by-design experiences 225

Index

learning communities 281
learning environments: cyclical nature of 44; technology-enhanced 43–6, 96–7; technology integration and 236
learning management systems 54–60, 251
Learning Technology by Design approach 73, 212–13
learning trajectory: explain and evaluate 138–9; learning processes 138; technology and 139–40; tools for learning 137
lecturing-centered instruction 215–16
lesson planning: assessment of 101–2; content analysis 102; cross validation 102–3; design competencies 97–9; design rationale 102; support for 124–7; technology and 121–2, 181; technology integration competencies 97–9
Likert scale 149
literacy instruction: content knowledge 89; mobile technologies and 186; pedagogical content knowledge 58, 91; taxonomies 71; technology integration in 39, 42–4, 59
literacy skills 58
LS-TPACK process 76

macro context 18–19
mathematics instruction: assessment instruments 175; content knowledge (CK) 89; learner-centered professional development (LCPD) 259–63; standards-based pedagogy 263; systems pedagogical approach 133–4; taxonomies 71; technology integration in 22, 182, 259–64, 266
Mathematics Science Partnership (MSP) 263
Mathematics Teacher TPACK Development Model 22
Meagher, M. 181
Meaningful Learning 92–4, 96
meaningful reflection 135
Meijer, P. C. 37
methods courses: content-specific 26, 74, 179, 182, 184; educational technology and 179–85, 267; music technology 286–8, 292; technology integration 177–8; UDL infused TPACK 145–8, 153–9
Meyer, A. 143
Meyer, K. A. 217
mezzo context 18–19
micro context 18–19
Microsoft 208, 226–7
Microsoft Excel 177
Microsoft Higher Education Advisory Board 226
Microworlds 261
middle school teachers 90, 96, 175, 183, 186, 216, 261, 286
Miller, C. 22
mind-mapping tools 272, 279
Mindmaps 93
Mishra, P. 2, 4, 15–16, 21, 33, 36, 39, 65–7, 71–2, 89, 126, 143, 212–13, 225, 229
mobile apps 274, *277*, 278
mobile devices 100, 170, 184, 186, 264

mobile phones 171
Model of Pedagogical Reasoning and Action 60
Mouza, C. 178, 180, 183
Movement of Enhancing Opportunities and Improving Technology project 274
Movie Maker *277*, 279, 300–*1*, 305
Murrell, V. S. 217
music education: barriers to technology integration 288–9; curriculum for 287–8; faculty technology surveys 289–91; in higher education 285–93; K-12 286–8; subdisciplines 285–6; taxonomies 71; TPACK frameworks and 285–9, 292–3
music technology 286–7

National Council of Teachers of Mathematics (NCTM) 264
National Science Foundation (NSF) 261
National Technology Leadership Coalition (NTLC) 208, 221, 226
National Technology Leadership Summit 229
NCTM *see* National Council of Teachers of Mathematics
Niess, M. L. 22, 40, 182–3
novel technologies 186

observation instruments 77, 80–1
observations 56, 67, 77–9, 107–11, 112, 115, 173, 175, 272, 282
online learning environments 119; competencies in 216, 220; designing 45; explain and evaluate 138–9; faculty development 216–17; learning processes 138; learning trajectory 132–40; teaching heuristics and 39; tools for learning 137
online puzzles *277*–8
open-ended questionnaires 175
Opfer, V. D. 200
Oxford, R. L. 214

Pajares, M. F. 38
Partners in Learning Higher Education Teacher Education Initiative 208
PCK *see* pedagogical content knowledge (PCK)
pedagogical beliefs 96
pedagogical content knowledge (PCK) 3, 13, 15, 58, 60, 65, 75, 201, 253; ICT-related 14; operationalization of 89; pre-service teachers and 121; in-service teachers and 121; transition to technological pedagogical content knowledge (TPACK) 193–4
pedagogical knowledge (PK) 15, 57, 172, 251, 277, 298
pedagogical knowledge for meaningful learning (PKML) 174
pedagogical reasoning 59–60
pedagogical systems approach 133
pedagogical technology integration content knowledge (PTICK) 74–5
pedagogy: content and 13; survey studies 92–4
Pedder, D. 200

peer coaching 291–3
performance-based assessments 67–8, 80; pre-service teacher knowledge 174–5; of teachers 77, 80
phenomenological strand 45
PhEt 279
physical education, taxonomies 71
Porras-Hernández, L. H. 18–19, 236
Potter, W. J. 3
PowerPoint 134–5, 139, 230
pre-service teachers: case-based approaches 74–5; case development 76–7; design tasks 73–4; emerging technologies and 170–1, 186; field experience 181; instructional decision-making 73–4; interviews 78–9; lesson design competencies 97–9; novel technologies 186; pedagogical content knowledge 121; performance-based assessments 174–5; reflection 180–1; self-regulated learning 96; sense of efficacy 155–8; students with disabilities and 145; support for 123–6; survey studies 89–90, 95–6, 173–4; technological pedagogical content knowledge (TPACK) 181; technology and 39–40, 43; technology integration 81, 83; technology preparation 169–86, 226–7, 266–7; UDL infused technological pedagogical content knowledge (TPACK) 146–59; Web 2.0 technologies 171, 174 *see also* teacher education
Prezi *276*, 278–9
principal component analysis (PCA) 150–1
principals *see* school principals
probeware technology 131, 272, 274, *276*, 278
problem-based technology development 195
productivity tools 184, 186, 287
professional development (PD) 191; content-focused 265–6; learner-centered 259–65; mathematics-specific technologies 259–64; science-specific technologies 272–3; strategies for 192, 194–200; teacher learning methods *273*; technology challenges in 265–6; TPACK-based program outline *276–7*; TPACK frameworks and 264–5, 274–82 *see also* faculty development
professional reasoning 37–8, 41
Ptaszynski, J. 226
PTICK *see* pedagogical technology integration content knowledge (PTICK)
public service announcements (PSAs) *277*, 279
Puzzle-Maker 277

qualitative assessment methods 66, 84; case-based approaches 74–6; case development 76–7; challenges of 81–3; design tasks 72–4; development of instruments 82–3; interviews 78–80; learning activities 70–2; observation instruments 81; performance-based assessments 67–8; technology integration rubric 68–70
quantitative assessment measurements 87–8; content analysis 99–100; content-specific 94–5; cross validation of 102–3; demographics 95–6; learning environments 97; lesson design competencies 97–9; lesson planning assessment 101–2; pedagogical beliefs 96; pedagogy-specific 92–4; survey studies 88–101; technology-specific 91–2

realist strand 46
reflection 180–1
reflective knowledge 74–5
reflective/reflexive technology development 195
Remote Network School project 44
restorying 54
Rose, D. H. 143

Salinas-Amescua, B. 18–19, 236
Sardone, N. B. 214–15
Scharber, C. 22
school culture 19, 209, 237, 239
school principals: leadership of 237, 242–3; role in technology integration 235–44; as role models 243–4
schools: complex systems of 248; leadership of 236–43
science instruction: 5 E's inquiry instructional model 134–5; assessment instruments 175; content knowledge (CK) 89; content-specific quantitative measures 94–5; student engagement and 271; systems pedagogical approach 133–5; taxonomies 71; teacher learning methods *273*; technology integration in 23, 44, 178, 182, 271–82; technology training 280
Scratch 186
screen time 250
secondary school teachers 101, 175; computer science 22–3; music education 285; science instruction 95, 121, 178; technology integration and 75, 90, 94, 121, 145–9, 153–5, 157, 182, 185
SEE Project 237, 240
separate support 122–5
Share, Engage, and Educate (SEE) Project 237, 240
Shin, T. S. 67
Shulman, L. 3, 13–15, 21, 53–4, 57, 59, 61, 65, 207, 252
simulations 272, 274, *276*, 278–9, 305
situated cognition 33, 37–8, 43
Sketchpad 261
Skype 136
SMARTboards *see* interactive whiteboards (IWB)
So, H. J. 40
social constructivist learning 131–3
social networking 17, 79, 170–1, 231–2
social studies instruction: assessment instruments 175; content knowledge (CK) 89; learning activity types (LATs) 71; taxonomies 71; technology integration 22; technology integration in 71, 114
Society for Information Technology & Teacher Education (SITE) 67, 208, 226–7
Spacecraft 277
special education: technology-mediated instruction 19–21, 143–4; Universal Design for Learning (UDL) and 144–5

Index

spreadsheets 177, 272, 274, *276*
SPSS software 150
SRI International 228
standards: accreditation 210; Common Core 261; content 68, 181; curricular 179, 264, 272, 286; national 70; teacher education 171, 179; technology 68, 171, 196, 262; TPACK 22
standards-based pedagogy 262–5
standards-based professional development 192
Sterallium 279
Structural Equation Modeling (SEM) 92–4
student engagement: science and 271; technology and 56, 58, 60, 254
student response systems (clickers) 278
students: disabilities and 145, 149; knowledge-building 71; knowledge-expression 71; outcomes 254
student teachers *see* pre-service teachers
support: effectiveness of 124–7; integrated 119, 123–6; for lesson planning 124–7; research on 120; separate 119, 123–5; technology integration and 119–27
Survey of Pre-Service Teachers Knowledge of Teaching and Technology, 173, 177–8, 181, 183
survey studies 88; development of 100–1; general 89–91; lesson design competencies 97–9; pre-service teacher knowledge 173–4; pre-service teachers 95–7; for specific content 94–5; for specific pedagogy 92–4; for specific technology 91–2; student perspectives 97
systems pedagogical approach 131, 133, 135

tablets 56, 186, 264, *274*, 278
Taiwan, English language instruction 298–307
taxonomies 71
teacher agency 44
teacher-directed pedagogy 38, 57
teacher education: case development 180; curriculum for 176–8, 182–5; educational technology and 3, 13, 25–6; faculty development 211–15; field experience 181; inquiry-based teaching 281; instructional design 179–80; leadership modules 208–9; mathematical TPCK 22; music 285–9; online 132; reflection 180–1; science 178; in-service teachers 43; standards for 171, 179; student-centered 281–2; subject matter courses 40; technology and 39, 43, 81; technology assessment 169–70; technology preparation 170–2, 175–86, 208–9, 226–33, 287–9; technology standards 171; TPACK-aligned programs 207–12, 219–20 *see also* pre-service teachers
Teacher Education Initiative 226–34
teacher efficacy 143–59, 165–6
teacher knowledge 37–41, 45–6, 53–4, 57–61
teacher performance 144
teachers: authentic classroom experiences 281; classroom observations 107–16; collaborative design 43–5, 191; competencies 14–15; conditions for technology use 247–8; content knowledge 15, 57; design knowledge 45–6; formal knowledge 38, 40–2; instructional technology courses and 108; interviews 112; knowledge base 13–15, 21–2, 26, 33, 38, 41–3, 45–6, 53, 57–9, 61, 126, 169, 172, 176–7, 179–80, 183, 300; knowledge of learners 58; learning communities 281; mathematics-specific technologies 259–64; online teaching 39; pedagogical beliefs 38, 96; pedagogical content knowledge 58, 60; pedagogical knowledge 15, 57; pedagogical reasoning 59–61; practical knowledge 42; professional development 191–7, 200; professional knowledge 54; professional reasoning 37–8, 41; role of 34; science-specific technologies 271–82; standards for 196; support for 119–27; tacit knowledge 38; technological knowledge 36–7, 41, 53; technological mediation 34; technological pedagogical content knowledge 191–202; technology design and 249–55; technology integration 11, 13–22, 25–6, 41–2, 70–2, 119–26, 131, 240–2; technology-using 107–12, 114–16 *see also* elementary school teachers; in-service teachers; kindergarten teachers; pre-service teachers
Teachers' Sense of Diversity Efficacy Scale (D-TSES) 146, 149, 152
Teachers' Sense of Efficacy Scale (TSES) 149, 151, 158–9
Teachers' Sense of Inclusion Efficacy Scale (I-TSES) 146, 149, 152
teaching: assessment 60; collaboration 131, 133–4; communication 131, 133–4; context knowledge 18, 37, 39; as a design science 33–4, 43–6; heuristics and 39; inquiry 131, 134–6; online learning environments 132–40; restorying 54; social dimensions of 37–9, 41; systems pedagogical approach 133–4
technical strand 45
technological content knowledge (TCK) 15, 69, 75, 82, 265; operationalization of 89
technological knowledge 36–7, 41, 53–7, 73
technological mediation 34
technological pedagogical content knowledge (TPACK) 15; adoption of 1–2, 7, 33, 37, 41; artifact analysis 83; assessment rubric 68–70; case-based approaches 74–6; case development 76–7; classroom observations 107–16; collaborative design 102; competencies and 14–15; conceptualization of 15; content analysis 99–100; context knowledge and 39; context of 236–44; design tasks 72–4; development of 23–5, 65–6, 108, 191–202, 207–15, 225–6, 249; digital video 92; domain-general knowledge 22–3, 25; domain-specific knowledge 22–3, 25; faculty surveys 289–91; framework model *16*; functions of 4; game-based 91; higher education and 207–15; integrative view of 21, 25, 172; interviews 78–80, 110; knowledge base and 58–61; learning activities 70–2; learning trajectory 133–40; lesson study 76;

326

models of 16, *16*–20; observation instruments 77, 80–1; online learning environments 131–40; outcomes 184–5; performance-based assessments 67–8, 80; pre-service teacher assessment 172–5; pre-service teacher preparation for 169–86; qualitative assessment methods 66–84; quantitative measurements 87–103; reasons for using 41–2; research on 11–25, *31–2*, 101, 200–2, 220–1; in-service teachers 192–7; special education and 19–21; student engagement and 56, 58, 60; support for 119–27; survey studies 88–101, 299–300; teacher efficacy 143–4, 146; as teacher knowledge 38; teacher use of 107–16; theoretical aspects of 12, 24–5, 33–4, 46; transformative view of 21, 25, 172; Universal Design for Learning and 144; web-based learning 91

technological pedagogical knowledge (TPK) 15, 69, 73, 82, 194–5

Technological Pedagogical Science Knowledge (TPASK) 23

technology: adoption of 247–8; affordances 34–7, 72; alterity relation 35; background relation 35; collaborative design 43–5; defined 34; development processes of 192; embodiment relation 35; hermeneutic relation 35; human-centered approach 248; integration of 11; mediation of 34–8; shared knowledge base about 42–3; standards for 171 *see also* educational technology

Technology, Pedagogy, and Content Knowledge (TPACK) special interest group (SIG) 208

technology adoption model (TAM) 247

technology design: content and 252; context of 250; meaningful advances in 254–5; pedagogical content knowledge and 253–4; pedagogy and 251–2; phenomenological strand 45; rationale for 102; realist strand 46; for schools 248–9; teacher technology knowledge 250–1; technical strand 45; TPACK frameworks and 249–55

technology designers 247–55

technology development, processes of 193–5, *198–9*

technology enhanced language learning (TELL) 297

technology-enhanced learning (TEL) 249

technology enriched instruction 226–31

technology integration 75; barriers to 236, 288–9; classroom-based support for 266; context of 236–44; curriculum alignment 266; peer coaching model 291–2; pre-service teachers 81, 83; in-service teachers 81, 83; student-centered 281; support for 119–27; systems pedagogical approach 131; teachers and 11, 13–22, 25–6, 41–2, 70–2, 119–26, 131, 240–2

Technology Integration Assessment Instrument (TIAI) 68–70

Technology Integration Assessment Rubric 68–9, 76–7, 80–1, 83

Technology Integration in Mathematics (TIM) 262–3, 265–6

Technology Integration Observation Instrument 80–1

technology knowledge (TK) 13, 15

technology mapping (TM) 98, 179, 194–5

technology-mediated instruction 20

technology standards 171

Teclehaimanot, B. 215

TEFL/EFL *see* English as a foreign language (TEFL/EFL)

TESOL/ESOL *see* English as a second/other language (TESOL/ESOL)

Thompson, A. 16

TK *see* technology knowledge (TK)

tools for learning 137

TPACK *see* technological pedagogical content knowledge (TPACK)

TPACK frameworks *see* technological pedagogical content knowledge (TPACK)

TPACK game 229–31

TPACK Leadership Theory of Action 208–9

TPACK Newsletter 192–3

TPACK-Practical 17–18

TPCK *see* TPACK

transformative view 21, 25, 172

transparent technologies 170

Turkey: English language instruction 298; science-specific technologies 274–8

21st Century Learning Design (21CLD) framework 228–34

Twenty-First Century Teachers' Sense of Efficacy Scale (T-TSES) 146, 149, 152, 165–6

Ubuntu operating system 240–1

UDL *see* Universal Design for Learning (UDL)

UDL infused technological pedagogical content knowledge (TPACK) 144–62

Universal Design for Learning (UDL) 20, 143; curriculum development and 19; resistance to 144–5

user authentication systems 250

Valanides, N. 21–2, 24, 179, 202

Van Driel, J. H. 37

Veletsianos, G. 22

Verloop, N. 37, 42

videocasts *276*, 278

video clips 37, 41, 54–5, 58, 74, 134, 304

videoconferencing 229

video editing 92, 176

video-making software 92, 278–9, 305

video presentations 57, 59–60

video-recorded lessons 78, 80–1, 135, 139, 148, 175, 181, 194, 254, 276

virtual classrooms 54, 56, 58–60

virtual manipulatives 263–4

virtual worlds 171

Index

visual arts, taxonomies 71
Voicethread *276*
Voogt J. 22, 41, 44

Web 2.0 technologies 79, 92, 135, *166*, 170–1, 174, 184, 213, 274, 278
Web 3.0 technologies *166*
web-based competencies 174
web-based learning 91
WebQuest 286
Webspiration 93
Wetzel, K. 176
whiteboards *see* interactive whiteboards (IWB)
"wicked problem" of technology 248

wikis 71, 93, 114, 171, 176
Williams, M. K. 176
Windows 300
wireless technologies 250
workplace learning technology development 196–7

Yahya, K. 72, 213
Yammer 230–1
Yeh, Y.-F. 18, 24
Yilmazel-Sahin, Y. 214
Young, J. R. 185
YouTube 92

zone of proximal development 126–7